ME AND
A GUY NAMED ELVIS

· · ·

ME AND
A GUY NAMED
ELVIS

MY LIFELONG FRIENDSHIP
WITH ELVIS PRESLEY

. . .

JERRY SCHILLING

WITH

CHUCK CRISAFULLI

GOTHAM BOOKS

GOTHAM BOOKS
Published by Penguin Group (USA) Inc.
375 Hudson Street, New York, New York 10014, U.S.A.
Penguin Group (Canada), 90 Eglinton Avenue East, Suite 700, Toronto, Ontario M4P 2Y3, Canada
(a division of Pearson Penguin Canada Inc.); Penguin Books Ltd, 80 Strand, London
WC2R 0RL, England; Penguin Ireland, 25 St Stephen's Green, Dublin 2, Ireland
(a division of Penguin Books Ltd); Penguin Group (Australia), 250 Camberwell Road,
Camberwell, Victoria 3124, Australia (a division of Pearson Australia Group Pty Ltd);
Penguin Books India Pvt Ltd, 11 Community Centre, Panchsheel Park,
New Delhi – 110 017, India; Penguin Group (NZ), cnr Airborne and Rosedale Roads,
Albany, Auckland 1310, New Zealand (a division of Pearson New Zealand Ltd);
Penguin Books (South Africa) (Pty) Ltd,
24 Sturdee Avenue, Rosebank, Johannesburg 2196, South Africa

Penguin Books Ltd, Registered Offices: 80 Strand, London WC2R 0RL, England

Published by Gotham Books, a member of Penguin Group (USA) Inc.

First printing, August 2006
3   5   7   9   10   8   6   4

Gotham Books and the skyscraper logo are trademarks of Penguin Group (USA) Inc.

LIBRARY OF CONGRESS CATALOGING-IN-PUBLICATION DATA
Schilling, Jerry.
Me and a guy named Elvis : my lifelong friendship with Elvis Presley / by Jerry Schilling with
Chuck Crisafulli. —1st ed.
p.   cm.
ISBN 1-592-40231-3 (hardcover)
1. Presley, Elvis, 1935–1977.   2. Schilling, Jerry.   3. Rock musicians—United States—
Biography.   I. Crisafulli, Chuck.   II. Title.
ML420.P96S33 2006
782.42166092—dc22
[B]   2006014507

Printed in the United States of America
Set in Janson Text • Designed by Elke Sigal

Photo credits appear on page 352.

While the author has made every effort to provide accurate telephone numbers and Internet
addresses at the time of publication, neither the publisher nor the author assumes any responsibility for errors, or for changes that occur after publication. Further, the publisher does not have
any control over and does not assume any responsibility for author or third-party Web sites or
their content.

Dedicated to the one I love . . . Cindy

CONTENTS

. . .

FOREWORD

. . .

BY

PETER GURALNICK

I don't have any trouble recalling my impressions of Jerry Schilling when we first met in 1989. He was hard at work on the set of the thirteen-episode *Young Elvis* television series that he was coproducing for ABC. This particular set was located at the Vapors, a club out by the Memphis airport, and I was interviewing Jerry for the first time for the biography of Elvis on which I had recently embarked. It turned out to be unlike any interview I had ever done—or any interview I have done since. Here we were in a room needing very little in the way of transformation to approximate the setting for one of Elvis's earliest public appearances. And here was Jerry, with a roomful of people (actors, camera operators, writers, researchers, technicians) hanging on his every word—unquestionably giving them his full attention but at the same time doing all he could to turn some of that attention to the importunate interviewer. He thought long and hard about every question I asked, his answers were complex, coherent, the furthest thing from glib, but as often as not they were in-terrupted by the need to excuse himself politely. "I'm sorry, Peter," he would say, "can you hold on a second," as he went off to attend to a problem on the set. It might be a matter of historic verisimilitude, it could be a question of dramatic motivation or the eruption of some mi-nor conflict that needed to be addressed. Whatever it was, Jerry was de-termined to deal with it on the spot, to do all in his power to get it right. And when he returned to our perch at the edge of the action—the time elapsed might have been anywhere from five minutes to half an hour—he always picked up his answer just where he had left off.

That's the picture of Jerry that remains indelibly imprinted on my memory. As long as I've now known him, that's how I continue to see him: thoughtful, gracious, quietly in charge; a born diplomat, but one who takes his mission far too seriously to be thought of as, simply, the most relaxed person in the room.

Maybe that's why it worried me a little when Jerry told me he was finally planning to write his own book. Not because I doubted that Jerry would work hard to tell his story, or because there was any question in my mind that he had a story to tell. From the friendship that had grown out of our initial interviews, I had come to know Jerry as a man with his own carefully thought-out insights and perspectives on everything from film, music, politics, and the music business to the vagaries of memory, history, and wishful historical thinking. No, what worried me about Jerry writing a book on a subject he knew so well, and one about which he had thought so long and so hard, was not that he wouldn't take it seriously enough but that he would take it *too* seriously, that it might place too much of a burden on him to confront hard truths not so much about others as about himself.

I shouldn't have worried. What Jerry has written in *Me and a Guy Named Elvis* is an account of one man's experience, a personal memoir that, while it places its narrator squarely in the midst of historic events, never claims credit for those events in the way that so many self-serving memoirs are inclined to do. It is a balanced treatment of a complex subject, the story of a lonely boy who struggles with the contradictions in his own life and the society in which he grows up. It's a Memphis story, a book about race and rock and roll told, to begin with, through the eyes of a child. Most of all, though, it's a story of friendship and growth, one that focuses on the demands and rewards of love, and, ultimately, the necessity of forging an independent identity of one's own.

At the center of it, of course, is the figure of Elvis Presley, whom Jerry met at twelve when the nineteen-year-old singer, with one record on the radio, welcomed him into a Sunday-afternoon touch-football game. There are any number of surprising behind-the-scenes glimpses of this Elvis, the off-stage Elvis whom Jerry would come to know over the next twenty-three years, an Elvis whom readers will certainly recognize from the celebrated public image but will rarely have seen in such relaxed and unposed settings. It is a nuanced portrait, sharply drawn, closely observed, but never presented with anything less than heartfelt feeling. There are illuminating insights into such frequently misunderstood figures as Vernon Presley and Colonel Parker, and telling individual portraits of each of the guys around Elvis, so often lumped together as a cartoon collective. What I think distinguishes the book most of all, though, is its emotional honesty, the generosity of spirit with which Jerry seeks to emulate his friend and mentor. Things are rarely all one way or another in Jerry's account, but at its heart is the simple declaration, "I think of Elvis every day." After reading this book, there can be no doubt of the truth of that statement.

AUTHOR'S NOTE

I wouldn't want to speak for Elvis Presley and tell you that I was his best friend. But I can tell you this: He was *my* best friend.

I met Elvis when I was just a boy and he was a teenager. I met him on one of the last weekends before he became "Elvis," when he was simply a truck driver who did some singing on the side.

I knew him for twenty-three years, and in those years I grew up with him, lived with him, worked for him, learned from him, laughed with him, and shared one amazing experience after another with him.

Elvis was the first rock-and-roll superstar. And he became one of the world's biggest movie stars. But I didn't know him as a star; I knew him as a friend. In writing this book my hope has been to present Elvis not as the larger-than-life figure known around the globe, but as, simply, a very real and quite remarkable human. That's important to me because as Elvis has become an icon and a figure of legend, I think an appreciation of his humanity has been lost. Viewing Elvis as some kind of rock-and-roll superhero doesn't do justice to his very human struggle, his talent, his life, or his legacy.

He was my friend, and this book is, above all, a story of friendship. The book is also a personal history, and, as such, it's a work of memory. Sifting through six decades' worth of memories has been no easy task, but wherever possible, efforts have been made to ensure that the "history" part of the personal history is accurate. My life's history is very much interwoven with Elvis's, and much of his life has been extensively documented. So, if it was possible to look up or double-check a who, what, when, or where, I've done it.

Documents don't often capture the more personal moments of life, though, and that's where memories must be sorted out. In thinking back on my life and experiences, I've tried to balance the way I remember things now with the way I might have experienced them at the time. I've tried to be as honest as possible about how and why things happened, and have tried to resist the temptation to describe a past I might wish for rather than the one I experienced.

The places, people, and events of the book are real—as I remember them. No scenes have been invented, no characters made up, and the timeline of events reflects a real chronology. The dialogue people speak in these pages may not be a verbatim transcription, but always reflects the words I remember hearing. In just a couple of cases, when it wasn't possible to contact someone from my past, I've changed a name in deference to the sensitivity of the situation described.

People have been making up all kinds of stories about Elvis since his first record came out, and in the years since his death the stories have become so big that my friend's very real life has often been obscured, or ignored. In putting this book together, I've discovered again and again that, with Elvis, the truth is the best story of all.

ME AND
A GUY NAMED ELVIS

. . .

1

. . .

IF I CAN DREAM

July 11, 1954 began as a hot, lazy Sunday, just another sticky summer day in North Memphis. And I was a scrawny twelve-year-old kid, living at the little brick duplex my father rented on Breedlove Street, looking for some way to fight off the boredom of one more stretch of sweltering afternoon.

My father worked long shifts at the Firestone factory, and that Sunday, his day off, he was sleeping in. My closest friend—the kid next door, Wayne Martin—was off somewhere on an outing with his family. It looked like I was going to be on my own for the day, so I decided to kill some time by wandering over to Guthrie Park.

The park was maybe a half-mile from my daddy's place, down Chelsea Avenue, an open field of scraggly grass and dusty patches laid out in front of an elementary school and a community center. Close to the street was a kiddie wading pool, and a little farther back was a playground, some basketball hoops, and a horseshoe pitch—where I'd learned to enjoy the satisfying clang of a shoe hitting the iron post.

As I arrived at the park, the heat of the day was broken by just a hint of breeze drifting over from the Mississippi River. There were a few moms watching their splashing toddlers at the wading pool, and a bunch of older kids out on the grass. I figured I'd walk around to the community center to see if anything half-interesting was going on inside. The sky was a hazy, summer gray, and I guess I was lost in a bit of haze of my own. It took me a moment to realize that my name was being called out from across the park.

"Jerry! Hey, Jerry. C'mere!"

It was one of the older kids out on the grass. I recognized him as a local boy named Red West, one of the toughest guys I knew of in North Memphis. Red had been a ferocious All-Memphis football player at Humes High School, and he and his family lived over in a low-income housing project that had the very fitting name Hurt Village. Just knowing a guy was from Hurt gave him a kind of battlefield credibility around North Memphis. Kids in my neighborhood whispered stories about the rough gangs that lurked around Hurt, and how you'd be lucky to get out of there alive if you were ever foolish enough to walk through the projects alone at night.

I wasn't sure how Red knew my name, but I figured he might know my older brother, Billy Ray, who'd been a pretty strong football player at the private high school he'd attended across town. Maybe Red had heard that I was turning out to be a decent wide receiver on the team from my Catholic grade school, Holy Names. Football was the one thing I felt good at. My grades were lousy, I didn't have a lot of friends, but on the Holy Names football field I was having my first taste of personal success. It didn't really matter how Red knew me, though—I wasn't going to ignore the call. I started over to the group of older boys, trying to throw just a touch of Brando from *The Wild One* into my walk.

"Hi, Red," I said when I got to them, immediately hating the fact that my voice sounded so little, so young. So not Brando.

I didn't know the other guys, and I didn't pay too much attention to them. I assumed they were either from Hurt or Humes.

Red looked me over hard for a moment.

"Jerry, we're a player short of a six-man game here. You want to play ball?"

Of all the things I thought Red might ask me, I hadn't seen this one coming. A chance to play football with Red West and some older kids? Of course I was in.

"Sure, Red. I'll play."

"All right, then," he growled. "We got a game. Full blocking. Two-hand touch. Let's mark out a field."

Red and a couple of the guys walked off to figure out the out-of-bounds and goal lines. The other two players started warming up by throwing long passes to each other. I kept my eyes on Red, who wasn't a real big guy but a commanding figure anyway. I had a feeling that with him, even a touch football game was going to be played hard and rough.

With the field set, the guys regrouped.

"Our ball," said Red. "We'll take Jerry. The rest of y'all get back on some defense."

Three of the guys broke away and took positions down the field. I followed Red and another boy and we leaned together in a tight huddle behind our starting line of scrimmage. Red handed the ball to the other boy.

"What's the play, man?" Red asked him.

I looked to this guy who Red had just made our quarterback—really looked at him for the first time—and felt a jolt.

It was him.

There wasn't any one thing about this other guy that hit you right away. He was wearing plain work pants and a white T-shirt. He had blotches of acne on his face and neck. He was kind of on the skinny side. He certainly didn't look any tougher than Red West.

But he had a cool I'd never seen before in person. His hair was greased and swept up and back into some very impressive ducktails, the kind of look I wanted as soon as I could get away from the disapproving nuns at Holy Names. You had to put some work into hair like that, and you had to know that it marked you as a probable juvenile delinquent in the eyes of grown-up North Memphis.

There was something about the way this guy stood and leaned into the huddle—nonchalant, but no-nonsense. Something a little loose, but cocky, too. It looked like he was pulling off the Brando thing without even trying.

It had to be him.

A couple of nights before I'd heard a brand-new song on the radio— so new the record wasn't even out yet—and had been amazed to learn that the singer was a boy from Humes High in North Memphis. This had seemed astonishing to me—how could a guy from my neighborhood have a song on the radio? And a great song at that—a song that really stood out among all the hot R & B records I'd heard on the show that night. For the last two days I'd been wondering—what guy in North Memphis could make a record like that and get it on the radio? This guy across from me in the huddle looked like he could.

"All right, now—what's your name? Jerry?" asked the quarterback.

"Yeah."

"You can catch a football?"

"Yeah."

"You know how to run a slant?"

"Sure."

He held his hand out, palm up, and sketched out a play. "You run down the sidelines about ten yards—run it easy, not full speed. Red, you go up the middle and buttonhook. Jerry, when you see Red make his turn, you hit the gas, man, and run your slant. If you get past whoever's covering you, the ball's coming to you."

"Yes, sir."

The quarterback's serious expression shifted a bit. He looked at me dead-on. He had ice-blue eyes, and when he looked straight at you, you felt it. A little twist of half-smile showed up on his face.

" 'Sir?' Hey, Red, I like this kid's attitude," said the quarterback.

"He's all right," said Red, giving me a clap on the back that just about knocked the breath out of me.

Red didn't introduce us. I didn't hear his name spoken by any of the other guys. But I didn't have to hear it. I knew who he was.

This was the boy from Humes High named Elvis Presley.

My mother, Dorothy Schilling, died when I was a little over a year old. She contracted rheumatic fever shortly after I was born, and spent most of a year in bed, wasting away. The disease was close to a death sentence back then, but it wasn't always quick. From what I was told later by my grandmother and my aunts, my mother held me as much as she could for as long as she could. But eventually her skin was so sensitive that even the weight of the sheets was painful, and I can only imagine the heartache she must have felt not being able to hold her new baby to her.

My mother's dying request to her mother, my Mamaw Gilkey, was to secure a promise that my brother and I would be loved and taken care of when she was gone. Mamaw delivered wonderfully on that sad promise. I grew up with a fair amount of confusion about how exactly I fit into my family, but I never doubted for a moment that my Mamaw loved me with all of her heart.

From bits of conversations—little hushed pieces of grown-up talk I'd occasionally catch as a kid, I got the impression that my mom had been happy, pretty, and the kind of person who took care of everybody else first. The peacemaker and pep-talker who made everybody around her feel special. She was one of seven children and my father was one of four children, and growing up I heard plenty of grumbling and complaining from and about each side of the family. But I never heard anybody say anything mean about my mother. And I don't think that was just because she was gone—I think it was because she was considered a truly special person by everyone who knew her.

My father, Bill, grew up in Memphis, and from what I know of my dad's early years he didn't have much of a childhood at all. He was the oldest son, and when his father abandoned the family, he had to drop out of middle school and start working to help put food on the table. He started at a grocery store and, as soon as he could drive, moved on to a better-paying job as a truck driver. Before he got married, he'd landed his job over at the Firestone factory.

I think my dad may have spotted my mother on a dance floor at some local Memphis event. Both of them loved to dance, and both of them got into contests when they could, so it makes sense that that's where they crossed paths. I do know that my mother and father got married when he was twenty-one and she was nineteen. Within a year they had a baby boy—my older brother, Billy Ray. My mom had me when she was twenty-six, and at twenty-seven she was gone.

My dad had been living a humble workingman's dream—a steady job with a few benefits, a beautiful wife, and a couple of baby boys. Suddenly that dream was smashed to pieces. I think that the only thing he could think to do was to keep working as hard as he could to provide for his kids. That meant taking extra shifts at the factory, which meant he couldn't raise us on his own. My brother got sent off to a boarding school a couple hours away in Searcy, Arkansas—maybe my father figured it would be easier for him to be away from everything that might remind him of our mother. I was moved into my Mamaw and Papaw's house on Leath Street in North Memphis, a neat little white clapboard home in a poor but well-kept neighborhood. For quite a while as a kid, I assumed I was an only child. I remember telling Mamaw that I wished I had a brother and she said, "Why, Jerry—you do. Billy Ray." I hadn't realized that the older kid who showed up for a week at Christmas was actually related to me.

Mamaw and Papaw, who made his living as a housepainter, opened up their home to me as warmly and as lovingly as they knew how. Sometimes they barely had enough money to put any dinner on the table—white bread and sorghum molasses wasn't an uncommon supper. But they let me, their little grandson, feast on all the donuts and sugared-up cinnamon toast my belly could hold.

The people around us in the neighborhood were just as poor, and some of the homes weren't much more than the classic Southern shotgun shack. But everybody seemed to take pride in the little bit that they did have. Pride in holding a job. Pride in having made it through to the other side of a depression and a war. Lawns were well tended, cars were washed and gleaming—nobody let their little house go too long without a fresh coat of paint. People on Leath Street didn't have much, and knew they probably weren't ever going to get much, but they tried to carry themselves with some dignity.

I don't ever remember thinking that I was particularly poor when I was little. I just felt out of place. Other kids lived with a mom and dad. I didn't. I learned to make do with that feeling, though, because it just so happened that every single day, I had a looming vision of just how much worse things could be. At the end of Leath, just a stone's throw from my Mamaw's house, was the chain-link fence that marked off the grounds of the Porter-Leath orphanage. Across a wide field on the other side of that fence, I could see the big old, Southern Gothic orphanage building itself—looking like the kind of place Dr. Frankenstein might use to hide his laboratory. Way off in the distance you could see a bit of playground that the orphans used, and once in a while you might see a few of them out there. But in all the years I lived on Leath I never saw those kids playing out on the open field. An uncle would occasionally tease me, "Better behave yourself, Jerry, or we'll send you over to Porter-Leath." Other kids might have known that wasn't a real possibility, but I always felt way too close to the edge of those grounds. I walked a couple blocks out of my way to get to Holy Names—avoiding Porter-Leath completely—so as not to take any chances.

Mamaw and Papaw's place on Leath Street was the closest I had to a steady home, but I also spent a lot of time bouncing around the homes of all my aunts and uncles—from little houses scattered through North Memphis, to an apartment over a bar and grill near downtown Memphis, to Aunt Jinky and Uncle Bernard's place on Jackson Avenue, the busy thoroughfare that marked the beginning of the North Memphis neighborhoods.

Attached to Jinky and Bernard's house was one of my favorite places in the world—John's Little Kitchen. John was Uncle John Gilkey, my mom's brother, and his place was the finest hamburger joint in North Memphis, popular as an after-school hangout for the kids from Humes. The Little Kitchen was a tiny structure, with just a few tables and a counter inside. It had twinkling lights and a great jukebox, and always smelled of a heady mix of sizzling grease, the sour tang of empty beer glasses, and the whiff of Clorox off the well-scrubbed floor. John himself had tattoos up and down his arms and a great sense of humor, and when he had time out of the little kitchen area, he'd sit me on his lap by one of the few tables, sometimes drawing a tattoo or two on my arm with one of his pens. He'd also sneak me an occasional sip of beer along with my burger.

John's Kitchen was a place where I felt comfortable, even special. But there was one thing about the place that puzzled me: All his customers seemed to enjoy the hamburgers just as much, but the white ones got to come inside through the front door and eat at a counter or at tables, while the darker customers had to come through a side door labeled COLORED and could only eat standing up at their own little bit of counter. And for some reason, my fun-loving, good-natured Uncle John just always sounded impatient and irritated when he had to deal with those "colored" customers.

The Gilkeys had a great sense of family, and a lot of the aunts and uncles would often get together at the end of the workweek to enjoy a dinner of Uncle John's burgers and then watch the Friday-night fights on Bernard and Jinky's TV. I spent less time with my dad's side of the family, and was a little less comfortable in those homes. Looking back, I realize that both sides of the family lived within a couple miles of each other, and everybody was working hard to make ends meet. But the Schillings had made it up to solid little brick houses with the fancy three-pillar porches, while the Gilkeys lived in little wood houses with cement slab porches. To my eyes, that seemed like the difference between mansions and shacks.

I was generally treated well throughout my childhood, but I think I also knew that all that shuffling from home to home wasn't quite right, and I could sense that I didn't really belong in any one place. I was always sharing someone else's room and someone else's toys. I remember one night, as I was falling asleep at Mamaw's house, I heard her out in the kitchen talking to one of my aunts.

"I love Jerry like he was one of my own," she said.

I felt a shiver go through me, and I curled up a little tighter in the blankets. I'd thought I *was* one of her own.

My insecurities weren't helped by the fact that I was a sickly little kid. Maybe it was all those donuts and cinnamon toast, but I just never seemed to be healthy for any decent stretch of time. I had headaches, earaches, and stomachaches so bad that there were weeks when I just didn't get out of bed. My dad had signed me up to start first grade at Holy Names after I turned five (there wasn't any kindergarten back then). But I was so sick and missed so much school that first year that I ended up having to do the grade again. I was little, but not so little that I didn't understand that I had flunked first grade. My first experience with academics was an experience of failure, and that didn't do anything to boost my low levels of self-confidence.

So, on Leath Street, I spent a lot of time by myself, listening to Mamaw's great big Zenith floor-model radio. I couldn't get enough of *The Lone Ranger*. But unlike a lot of kids who listened, I didn't imagine myself to be the one with the silver bullets. When the show was over, I'd go out in Mamaw's backyard, draped in ceremonial battle washrags, pretending to be Tonto. I'd climb up in the big apple tree there and sit for hours, staring out at North Memphis and wondering which direction the Lone Ranger was going to ride in from.

Throughout my childhood, I sometimes stayed with my father on weekends and through the summers, but in that summer of 1954, I moved in with him for good. It wasn't an easy transition. At my grandparents' and aunts and uncles' houses I'd been allowed to do as I pleased, but Daddy had rules he expected me to follow. Chores had to get done and vegetables had to be eaten. My father wanted to do everything in his power to get me strong enough and smart enough to make something of myself but, at the time, I didn't appreciate that kind of concern at all. I was angry that my dad was the sort of guy who would waste my Saturday morning to take me to the dentist. Years later it dawned on me that, in a part of town where there were plenty of crooked, toothless smiles, he was the sort of guy who would give up his own day off to get his kid's teeth taken care of.

My father worked at the nearby Firestone factory, a place with smokestacks that towered over that part of town. He worked a lot of double shifts, but off the factory clock and on his own time, he was a sharp dresser and a great dancer, and being able to get out on the town on Fridays and Saturdays was a big deal for him. On weekends, he and his younger brother, my Uncle Joe, headed out to the local nightclubs, where they might find some pretty girls to dance away their worries with for a while. So, when I'd stayed at my father's house in the past, I'd often ended up with the house to myself. Back then, in that part of town, hiring a babysitter for a boy my age would have been an unthinkable waste of money—the kind of thing rich people did. After I turned nine, my father had considered me old enough to be left alone while he went out. I liked being given that responsibility, but the truth was that, at nine, it didn't take much to put me in a state of fear.

There'd be strange creaks in the floorboards, loud knocks from the pipes, and shadows in the hallway, all of which could get the worst parts of my imagination working. Even the breeze rustling the bushes and trees outside could start to sound a little spooky. With a few rumbles from the occasional thunderhead rolling up the Mississippi River, and a flash of lightning or two, I would end up just plain terrified. Deep down, I always knew that if there were any kind of real emergency, help was close by. Wayne Martin, his mother, and his Aunt Bea lived right next door, and I had relatives a few blocks away in almost every direction. And no matter how loud the floor creaked, and how hard the pipes knocked, I always eventually fell asleep and lived through the night.

At age twelve, living at my daddy's house full-time, I wasn't so easy to scare anymore, and I'd discovered something that made my nights alone in that little house something I looked forward to. In my bedroom, on the dusty chest of drawers, right by the side of the heavy wooden bed, was the one thing in that plain little room that really sparkled—the only thing that hinted at a world of excitement outside: my bright white, plastic, battery-powered Silvertone radio.

It was a beauty, with a molded grille over its speaker, two great big knobs for the tuning and the volume, and a giant slash of a red needle to tune in your station. Sometimes, in the afternoons and evenings, I moved the needle around to pull in broadcasts of *The Shadow*, *The Lone Ranger*, or *The Fibber McGee and Molly Show*. But six nights a week, from nine to midnight, that needle was locked into place at the far left side of the dial at 560, WHBQ. Dewey's station.

Dewey Phillips was a half-crazed, speed-talking wildman of a disc jockey who had become the hottest thing on late-night radio in Memphis. His show *Red, Hot & Blue*, played an inspired mix of R & B records, country boogie, hard-core blues, pure gospel, and a few love songs from the silkiest of harmony groups. For good measure, he might toss in a lesser-known tune from a big pop act of the day. Spend a night with Dewey and you might hear Ruth Brown's "Mama He Treats Your Daughter Mean," a new cut by the Clovers, then Johnny Ace singing "Pledging My Love," followed by Hank Ballard and the Midnighters knocking out "Work with Me Annie." You might even get a Dean Martin B-side followed by Sister Rosetta Tharpe's "Strange Things Happening Every Day."

"Heeeee gaw!" Dewey would holler. "You just roll a wheelbarrow full of—full of—full of mad dogs, just wheel it right up through the big front doors over there; you get down on the floor and kick your legs up in the air—AND TELL 'EM PHILLIPS SENT YA!! You hearin' me out there? Ahh—I know you are. Just ain't no three ways about it—ain't that right, Myrtle?"

Myrtle, an imaginary cow who served as Dewey's sometime sidekick, would respond with a low, forlorn "Mooo."

Wayne next door had tipped me off about Dewey's show, but when I first started listening to him I could barely understand a thing he was saying—unlike other radio guys, he didn't seem to be trying at all to smooth out his backwoods Tennessee twang. But when he played the Dominoes' "Sixty Minute Man," I was hooked. Neither Wayne or I knew precisely what the man of the title was doing for sixty minutes, but the song had such a feel of crazy fun and happy secrets, and the way the guy with the low voice sang "Fifteen minutes of blowing my top" was such a kick, that I couldn't wait to hear it again.

By that summer of 1954, whenever I had the house on Breedlove to myself, I was listening to *Red, Hot & Blue*. Slowly, I got a little better at figuring out what Dewey was talking about. And man, did he talk. He talked right through some of the songs, fumbled his way through ad-libbed advertisements, shouted out updates on local concerts, and dispensed a constant stream of cracked, countrified wisdom ("Hey, good people—Saturday's just around the corner and don't you forget now—that's payday AND bath day!"). On the regular popular music radio shows, the DJs sounded so smooth, so calm, so dull. Dewey got all worked up and banged his equipment—you could almost hear him breaking a sweat. He was a grown-up, but he was just barely under control. Dewey, and his music, seemed fun and dangerous at the same time. And if a kid wanted to hear something other than the unexciting flow of hits like those on the *Your Hit Parade* TV show—if you wanted to hear LaVern Baker, the Drifters, Big Joe Turner, Howlin' Wolf, and laugh all the way through, Dewey's show was the show you tuned in to. That is, it was the show you tuned in to if you were a white kid.

Memphis was also home to WDIA, the first station in the whole country to have a black on-air staff (though the station itself was white-owned). You could also hear some of the same songs Dewey played on some of WDIA's shows, which were jockeyed by the likes of a very young guitar player named B. B. King, and bluesman Rufus Thomas. But that was a black station meant for black listeners, and for a white kid—for any white person—to turn that radio needle to 1070 would be doing the unthinkable. In the unquestioningly segregated South, you were never, ever supposed to step over the very clear lines of color. And I knew color was serious business. As a little kid, I'd been spanked for drinking from COLOREDS ONLY water fountains, and had been punished for making the mistake of shooting marbles with some black kids during an outing to Moon Lake.

That didn't stop me from listening to WDIA—a lot of the songs were just as great as what was on *Red, Hot & Blue*, and you could hear them in the afternoon, well before Dewey was on. But even as a kid I could sense there was something very different around the music—a language I didn't quite understand describing a world I didn't quite recognize. It was, I know now, simply black voices talking about black Memphis—discussing church events, employment opportunities, or putting out "calls for action" that helped people in trouble find the groups or agencies that could help them. You might even hear a DJ like the Reverend "Gatemouth" Moore talk about how crazy it was that the local ambulance companies were separated by race: He'd seen a white lady die because the black-run ambulance that got to her first wasn't allowed to handle her. Listening to WDIA, I didn't understand the logic behind the color lines in my town any better, but I couldn't help but be aware of them.

Dewey didn't seem to care about black music or white music—he liked music that was honest and energetic; unpolished stuff that grabbed and shook you in some indefinable way. And he wasn't sending that music out to white people or black people—he was always calling us "good people." Dewey didn't make a listener think about the world this music was pulled from—a hard, tense world of separate drinking fountains and lunch counters, streets that couldn't be crossed, and a whole tangled mix of official laws and accepted habits that kept people fearful and apart. Listening to Dewey, you didn't hear black and white. You just heard excitement. Good music for us good people.

That music was intoxicating stuff to a kid like me. All the other grown-ups around town seemed so steadily in control. People went to work. Kids went to school. Families went to church. The days moved along at the same slow, predictable rhythm. A holiday or a community event might break things up a little, but, to me anyway, there was always something a little sad even about the supposed good times.

At twelve, I didn't have any real overview of the world beyond my few blocks of North Memphis, just a vague, achy feeling that sometimes the grown-up world didn't make a lot of sense, and I wasn't sure how I was ever going to fit into it. And while I didn't know it that summer, I wasn't the only kid starting to sense that joyless sameness around us, and, as it turned out, there were more than a few of us who desperately wanted to believe that there was something else out there—something that moved a little faster and wilder. When we found Dewey, we felt like we'd found somebody who understood what we were after. Some of us even took the bolder step of walking down to Home of the Blues, a record store on Beale Street—downtown Memphis's historic strip of neon-lit shops, jazz joints, and nightclubs for an all-black clientele—to buy the music we heard Dewey play. Or we'd head over to Poplar Tunes, a record shop at the edge of the white part of North Memphis, to get the songs we wanted. I didn't even have a record player, but I'd gone out and bought a few 78s, feeling like a secret agent on an extremely perilous mission. I was earning pocket change that summer delivering circulars for a little market down the street from my dad's house, and just about every cent I earned eventually got spent at Home of the Blues or Poplar Tunes.

Shortly after I started listening to Dewey Phillips, and right after I'd bought my own first few records, I learned that the music he played could have a very frightening effect on people. I'd become friendly with a couple of boys on the Holy Names football team, a pair of brothers named Doolittle, and was impressed to hear that they had their own record player. Their mother was a nice lady who was very involved with the school's PTA, and who was always willing to carpool us football players around between games and practices. One day, after a practice, the Doolittle boys asked me if I'd like to spend a weekend at their house. The way I lived, I was excited about spending a weekend with anybody outside of the family loop. I said a quick yes, and went home to pack up. There wasn't much to pack, but, thinking about a weekend of unlimited access to the Doolittle boys' turntable, I made sure to bring my stack of four or five precious 78s.

Mrs. Doolittle came by to pick me up, and before long I was settling in over at the Doolittle home. In the boys' bedroom, I showed them my records and asked if they wanted to hear some music. They did. I think I may have had the McGuire Sisters' "Sincerely" and maybe "Till I Waltz Again with You" by Teresa Brewer—both acts were pre-Dewey favorites of mine. But I also had a couple of things I'd bought down on Beale Street: songs by LaVern Baker and Ruth Brown, and, most prized of all, my copy of "Sixty Minute Man."

If we'd stuck with the McGuire Sisters, things might have turned out differently, but I put "Sixty Minute Man" on the record player and turned it up about as loud as it would go (which on the players back then was not all that loud). The Doolittle boys started smiling and nodding along, and I was feeling pretty big—those trips to Beale Street had paid off.

I'll rock'em, roll'em all night long, I'm a sixty minute man.

This time, though, the sixty-minute man lasted only about thirty seconds. Mrs. Doolittle stormed into the room, went straight for the record player, dragged the needle off the disc and picked the record up.

She wheeled around and I saw a fury in this lady's eyes unlike anything

I'd ever seen before. The nice, sweet, carpooling PTA mom was re-placed by a woman almost trembling with rage. In a voice harder and harsher than anything I'd ever heard come out of Mrs. Doolittle, she said, "You're not going to play that nigger music in my house."

Then, with a bit of effort, she cracked the record she was holding in half, and proceeded to pick up the rest of the collection and break those, too. Even the McGuire Sisters.

"Pack your things back up," said Mrs. Doolittle.

Within minutes, I was sitting back at home, with no more special weekend plans, no chance for a pair of new friends, and no more record collection. From then on, I realized that music had a great, deep, and sometimes unpredictable power. And I realized that the R & B records I was beginning to love so much weren't just songs—they were some-thing bigger. They were statements. Statements of what, I wasn't quite sure yet. But as soon as I could save up enough money—mowing lawns, delivering circulars for the local market—I was heading down to Beale Street to buy more records.

I never did get invited back to the Doolittle house.

In that summer of 1954, I'd been living at my father's place for about a month or so when, one weeknight in early July, Daddy headed out with Uncle Joe, and I had the house to myself again. The thunder rumbled outside a couple of times—I couldn't tell if it was getting closer or not. A little after nine I folded myself up on the big bed and clicked on the Silvertone's volume knob. I put my head back on my pillow and listened as Roy "Good Rockin' " Brown's "Hurry Hurry Baby" came to an end.

"Ahh, that's a good old one—take it from your Daddy-O Dewey," said the DJ. There were some sounds of fumbling and crashing, like Dewey had banged into his microphone. "Shoo—somebody give me a hand with this pea-pickin' thing."

My mind started to drift a bit, and I was vaguely aware of Dewey doing one of his improvised ads for Champagne Velvet Beer and then playing a couple more songs. I may have been thinking about how I was going to fill the long stretch of summer days ahead of me. Then, some-thing caught my ear.

"Look out, good people," Dewey said. "I got something here that's so good, when I heard this one I almost swallowed my gold tooth. We got a new record here that ain't even dry yet, and this little number is sung by a fine young man who just one year ago received his dee-ploma from Humes High School right up there in North Memphis . . . how 'bout that?"

My head shot up off the pillow. Humes High School was just blocks away from my Mamaw and Papaw's house. From the back of the Holy Names elementary school playground you could look right through a vacant lot to the grounds of Humes. My mother and my Aunt Jinky had gone to Humes. My cousin Teddy had just finished his freshman year there. I had it in my head that one day I'd be one of those grown-up-looking kids over at Humes.

Before that moment, to me, the music you heard on the radio didn't seem connected to the real world around us—it existed only as stuff that came out of your radio speaker or that you could buy in the record stores. Once in a while Dewey might mention that a particular musician was from Memphis, but Memphis was a huge place in my mind. I guess I had some idea that there were musicians in Memphis, but I really had no idea where those people lived and less idea how they wrote their songs, made their records, and got them to people like Dewey. It was a mystery I really hadn't had much reason to ponder. You simply turned a radio on and you heard music.

But now Dewey was saying that a boy who had to live just blocks away from me had actually made his own record. Dewey intro'd the song, saying he himself had heard it for the first time just the day before, courtesy of Mr. Sam Phillips—no relation, I'd learn—over at Memphis Recording Service. It was a cover of an old Arthur "Big Boy" Crudup tune. I didn't catch the name of the boy from Humes at first; it was something kind of old-fashioned.

The record started playing, and the boy from Humes High started singing. He sounded great. The music was simple, just a couple guitars and a plunking bass, but it sounded unlike anything else I'd ever heard. The rhythm was easygoing and driving at the same time—not quite blues, not quite country. The boy from Humes High had a voice that was strong but gentle, too. Right away, he was soaring up to sweet high notes, sounding like it didn't take him any effort at all to get there.

That's all right now Mama, anyway you do . . .

He sounded tough at times, and sang with unbelievable confidence, but there was also a little tremble in his voice that kind of pulled you in. The way he sang, you could feel both a little smile and an ache. Whatever secret world of excitement was out there beneath the boring surface of grown-up, day-to-day life, it sounded like this guy from Humes High had found it.

The song was over too fast, and the voice was gone. The voice of a boy from Humes High.

Elvis Presley. That's what Dewey said the singer's name was. I was wide awake now. And I wanted to hear that song again. Dewey must have known there would be some other listeners feeling the way I did, because after a station break Dewey played the song again. And again. And again. Dewey did that sometimes when he really liked a record, and he clearly liked this one. I think I got to hear that brand-new song six or seven times. And it sounded just as fine every time Dewey played it.

That's all right, that's all right . . .

Already, I liked it even better than "Sixty Minute Man."

But the new record turned out to be only half the thrill of that night's show. After some more fumbling with the mikes, Dewey let us know that the boy from Humes High was sitting right there next to him, "right here in the magazine level of the beeeyooootiful Chisca Hotel" (for some reason "mezzanine" was always "magazine" to Dewey). The boy's song was getting such an enthusiastic response from around town that Dewey had called to get him down to the studio. His mom and dad had gone out looking for him, had finally found him hunched down in a seat in the back of the Suzore #2 movie theater, and had brought him straight over to the Chisca to go live on the air with Dewey.

I'd be lying if I said I remembered exactly what was said that night by this new singer. But I do remember that hearing Elvis Presley talk had me just as excited as hearing him sing. His speaking voice was kind of high and soft, like his singing voice, but, in conversation, he wasn't so smooth—you could hear that he was nervous. He was perfectly polite with Dewey, calling him "Sir," and thanking him for playing the record. He sounded like a nice guy, even a little shy maybe, but always cool. He even sounded good when he stuttered and stammered his way through most of his answers. Kind of made me want to stammer, too.

Dewey thanked him for being there, played "That's All Right" one more time, and then worked his way toward his sign-off. I finally clicked off the Silvertone and lay back down. Maybe Dewey would play the song again tomorrow night. I hoped so, because I wanted to hear it again. And I wanted to hear Elvis Presley talk some more.

Most of all, I wanted to meet this boy from Humes High.

I'd had the importance of prayer pretty well drummed into me in my years at Holy Names, but as far as I could tell, it hadn't done me any good. At first I figured maybe I was just praying wrong, then I figured maybe I wasn't important enough to have my prayers heard. Finally, somewhere around third or fourth grade, I began to have the sneaking suspicion that the whole system was just another thing the grown-ups said was good for you that didn't really have any discernible upside. Like eating your vegetables.

This night, though, I decided to give it another shot. I didn't kneel by the bed. I didn't fold my hands or squinch up my eyes. I just lay in bed and stared up at the ceiling. I thought about that boy from Humes High. As much as I'd heard the song that night, I couldn't quite hum the melody he'd sung—it was already slipping away. But the feeling that song gave me didn't go away. It took me a while to figure out what that feeling was, because it was a feeling I wasn't used to.

It was hope.

So I threw together a bit of improvised prayer, just for the heck of it. Staring up at the ceiling, hands at my side, I prayed: *Look, the neighborhood's not that big. Just let me meet this guy. Please.*

I already knew that hope was a dangerous thing in North Memphis—it usually just led to more disappointment than if you went through life without it. And I didn't expect that my prayer now—simple as it was—had any better chance of being answered than any previous prayer. But on this sticky summer night, when the sound of the pipes and the floorboards and the thunder had been drowned out by one strong voice from Humes High, it didn't seem like a little hope and a little prayer could hurt.

The breeze had died off in Guthrie Park, and the afternoon air started to feel a little hotter and heavier. We broke from the huddle and got set for the play. As I toed up to the line of scrimmage, I felt pumped and couldn't wait for that ball to come my way. Maybe I should have been nervous playing with older kids, but I knew what I was doing playing football. If I'd come across these guys singing or playing guitars and been asked to join in, I wouldn't have been able to step up. But running a slant and catching a pass—I felt like all those long, hard practices in full pads at Holy Names had prepared me for this particular moment.

"Hike!" shouted Elvis Presley.

I took off down the sideline, a little above half-speed, and when I saw Red begin to turn I ran as hard as I could up and across the field. Elvis pumped the ball to Red, and when the guys in the backfield stepped toward him, I flew right past them. The quarterback broke to his right and threw.

He had an awkward kind of sidearm style, but the ball came my way hard and fast—a spiraled bullet aimed just ahead of where I was running. I got my hands up and out and reeled it in, feeling like there was nothing more natural in the world than to receive a perfect pass from a quarterback who'd had his record played on the radio. There wasn't a chance the defenders could catch me, but I kept up the run full speed to the end zone.

When I got back to my teammates, I felt the urge to smile—but smiling seemed like something a little kid would do. I kept my game face on.

"Nice hands, little man," said Red. He gave me a congratulatory shove.

"He's got something," said the quarterback. "We got a game going."

I caught a lot more passes on the Guthrie field that Sunday. Made a couple of interceptions, too. And got knocked on my ass at least a dozen times. I don't know how long we played, but I would have kept going all night.

I didn't have to ask Red—and I didn't hear anybody else say his name, but I knew that in some unfigurable way, my little North Memphis radio prayer had been answered. I'd met the guy from Humes High. I wasn't sure if I should thank God or Dewey Phillips, but here I was in Guthrie Park with Elvis Presley.

Outside of listeners to *Red, Hot & Blue*, that name wouldn't have meant anything to anybody in North Memphis on this particular Sunday. Elvis Presley, on that day, was still a nineteen-year-old truck driver for the Crown Electric Company—a year out of high school and less than a week into a recording career that carried no guarantee of turning into steady work. There wasn't anything about him you could point to that day that really made him look like a star. His hair, though impressively combed, was an average-looking sandy brown—not the dyed, jet black that would become so familiar later on. In most ways he was just another poor North Memphis kid from the government projects over at Lauderdale Courts.

But even as he scrapped and blocked and fell and played just as hard as the rest of us, there was something else there. He didn't so much stand out as stand apart. He wasn't just another older kid, not just another tough guy. And not your typical full-of-himself quarterback. It was like he was already the star of his own movie, but he wasn't playing it up.

There was only one way in which Elvis's cool looked a little more like comedy. He had grit and determination, and could throw a ball, but he was not a natural athlete—not the way Red was. This became very clear whenever Elvis broke into an open-field run. Those loose legs of his seemed to shoot out in every direction at once, like Crazy Legs Hirsch, and it seemed to take him an extra effort just to keep himself moving forward.

It occurred to me toward the end of the game that Red and Elvis and the three other older guys didn't really talk to each other like they were any kind of familiar, best buddies—they were just getting to know each other that day, too. I don't think anybody said anything about Elvis having been on the radio, but I'd guess that was the icebreaker that had pulled these guys together. I'd later learn that Elvis had been something of a misfit and an outsider during his high school days, and now, with the cachet of a song that had been played on Dewey Phillips's show, he'd finally found some guys to hang out with. Elvis's musical talents would eventually bring him just about everything he wanted in his life, but on that weekend all he wanted was to play football with a bunch of guys, and having his first record out helped make that happen. In fact, I happened to show up at Guthrie Park on probably the last weekend of Elvis Presley's life in which he would have any trouble finding a sixth man for a three-on-three football game.

At some point the gray skies got dark enough that the guys just stopped playing. A couple of them gave me a nod, and a "Good game." Elvis and Red started to shuffle toward the community center.

I was wondering whether I should seize the moment and blurt out "I like your song," when Elvis turned back to the rest of us and said, "We'll meet again here next Sunday."

The guys nodded and mumbled, "Yes." I nodded, too.

A couple of days ago I'd been a lonely kid without much more than a radio to get me through the summer. Now I was standing here in Guthrie Park, feeling like I'd become part of something exciting. There'd be another game next Sunday, and there wasn't any question that I would be there.

I'd be ready to play football on Elvis Presley's team.

2

. . .

I WAS THE ONE

Music has always had a magic for me. One of my very earliest memories is of the sound of the radio broadcasts of the Grand Ole Opry, coming over the set at Mamaw's house. When I was probably just three or four, it occurred to me that in between the talking parts of the show, the people on the radio were doing something very unusual with their voices. When I asked Mamaw what it was, she told me, "That's singing, Jerry—the people are singing." From my small perspective, the talking didn't make much sense, but that singing stuff was clear and powerful.

I saw that music had a certain power over the adults around me, too. Before I was staying alone at my dad's house, he'd sometimes just take me with him when he went out at night, a deal that saved him the hassle of finding another place to drop me off, and gave me a peek at that secret world of grown-ups having fun. One of my dad's favorite spots was up at the top of the Peabody Hotel, where there was a large ballroom with panoramic views of Memphis and the Mississippi River. The bands up there played the kind of swinging, jitterbug dance music my dad loved, and occasionally a top national act like Harry James or Tommy Dorsey would have an engagement there. The walls of the ballroom were black, with tiny lights set up in the ceiling, so you could almost believe you were at a party up in the stars somewhere. I remember sitting happily under tables in that ballroom, sipping away at endless sodas and watching the adults shimmy and shake around the room's sunken dance floor with a kind of smile and a kind of twinkle in their eyes that you just didn't see anywhere else.

I loved the sense of peace and calm I got from the music that played during the daily Mass at Holy Names. Of course, I was only Catholic until the the last school bell rang—when I went home to Mamaw, I was part of a Baptist home (I spent three years at a Catholic school being the non-Catholic kid, and I couldn't wait until I finally took enough catechism classes to take first communion with my classmates). As far as my Baptist upbringing went, there wasn't a lot of churchgoing, but Mamaw and some of the other people on my mom's side of the family would sometimes take me to weekend revivals—many of them under a pitched tent on the same field in Guthrie Park where I would eventually play horseshoes and football. At a time before television was widespread, and when there were nowhere near the kind of leisure-time activities available today, a revival wasn't just more church—it was grand spectacle and high-energy entertainment. I remember how the soul-stirring music that played under those tents could get a crowd of adults up off its feet, clapping and shouting together, and sometimes that crowd would get so worked up that the smiles and twinkles in the eyes you'd see around you under the tent weren't really all that different from the ones you'd see at the top of the Peabody.

Of course, over at the Doolittles' house, I'd learned that there was some music that elicited a much different reaction, hardly smiles and twinkles. I think the Doolittle episode must have been in the back of my mind when I first heard Elvis's record, because by then I knew that if you found something good, you were better off keeping it a secret.

So, I didn't tell anybody about the record I'd heard by a guy from Humes High, or that I'd met the guy himself over at Guthrie Park. Not my dad, not Uncle John, not even Wayne Martin. Keeping it all to myself seemed like the best way to keep it special. I figured I'd managed to get lucky with one little prayer—I didn't want to do anything or say anything that might jinx my chances of playing ball again with Red West and Elvis Presley. Also, Elvis himself hadn't made a big deal out of his record—in fact he hadn't said a word about it. If he was going to keep cool and quiet about it, I'd do the same. I'd only spent half of one afternoon catching his passes, but I guess I already felt some sense of loyalty to this new quarterback of mine.

I kept listening, though. Dewey Phillips played "That's All Right," at least once every night on *Red, Hot & Blue*, and the more I heard the song, the more I kept running through the last few moments on that football field: Elvis himself had said he wanted to play again, hadn't he? He meant there at Guthrie, same time, next Sunday—wasn't that right? And—the biggest question of all—he meant for me to be part of the game again, didn't he?

By the Saturday after that first game, I guess I was worked up enough that, despite my desire not to jinx anything, I had to tell somebody. I needed a witness. And somewhere that day I crossed paths with Frankie Grisanti, a kid from the Holy Names football team who was a year behind me in school. Frankie was a short, stocky kid, but he was fast and tough as a player, and the few times we talked I'd found him easy enough to get along with. I was more interested in hanging out with older kids than younger ones, but Frankie had a special connection— his brother, Ronnie, a few years older than me, was Holy Names's dependable brick wall of a center.

I didn't tell Frankie about hearing the song and didn't go into much about meeting Elvis. I just told him that I'd had the chance to play football with older kids from Humes and had had a great time. The older guys had said they were going to play again tomorrow at Guthrie, and if Frankie came along with me, maybe he could play, too. It sounded good to Frankie. He said he'd come by my house and we'd go to the park together.

Frankie showed up right on time early Sunday afternoon and we headed down Decatur Street toward Guthrie. When we got to the park I saw a couple of the older kids from the week before on the field (after all these years, I'm still not sure exactly who was at those first games—I knew Red, but after seeing Elvis, I didn't care who else was there). I walked up toward them and got a couple of nods, relieved to see that at least these guys remembered me. We stood around for a while until we heard some laughs coming from across the field, over by the community center. I turned, and, sure enough, there he was, walking next to Red, looking just as cool as the last time. I was going to have to use a lot more Brylcreem to get ducktails like that.

It was when I took a closer look behind Elvis and Red that my spirits sank. There were maybe six or seven older guys ready to play this time. All the guys they needed to play an evenly matched game. Damn. I was going to be knocked off this guy's team after just one game.

Red was starting to explain some Guthrie ground rules to the newer guys when Elvis noticed Frankie and me standing there. He took a couple of lazy steps in our direction, checking his grip on the ball he was holding. He pointed the ball at Frankie.

"Hey, Penrod, go out for a pass."

Frankie took off like a spooked bulldog, pumping his hams faster than I'd ever seen, and Elvis reared back and threw one of his bullets. I hoped that Frankie would do the Holy Names squad proud and hang on to it. Sure enough, he did—though the force of the ball seemed to actually pick him up in the air and move him a little farther down the field.

"That a way, Penrod," called Elvis. He started to turn away. I figured I better speak to him before the older guys gathered around again and I lost the chance.

"Why'd you call him Penrod?" I asked.

"Aww—just a name I saw in this book I'm reading," he said.

He was a year out of school and still reading books, which seemed strange to me. In North Memphis, reading anything other than postcards and the Bible was maybe even more radical than listening to Dewey Phillips. Not only was the guy cool—he was a reader.

"You going to run those nice posts again?" Elvis was looking down the field, but he was talking to me.

"Sure. I'll run anything you want me to," I said.

Maybe I was hoping for a slap on the back. But he just turned to walk away, calling out to one of the older guys across the field.

I could see that Elvis Presley wasn't the kind of guy you got to know real well real fast. I wasn't either. But I had plenty of time.

We ended up playing six-on-six, with both Frankie and me in the game. I'm sure that most of the older guys would have been just as happy not to have younger kids in the game. But somehow Elvis, without ever making much of an issue out of it, kept us included. He was going to be quarterback again, he wanted me to be one of his receivers, and that meant the other team got Frankie to line up against me. He kind of acted like that was just the way it was supposed to be, and nobody else there seemed to have any interest in disagreeing with him. I know that Elvis could just as easily have told us to get lost, but it seemed clear that, even though he looked and moved like a rebel, and even though he kept himself just a little apart, a little distant—he didn't have the kind of mean streak I'd seen in other older kids, especially older kids from the projects.

From what I knew of Red West, he would have had no problem telling us to get lost, and quick. But Elvis wanted us around. So we were in.

Again, it was a great game. Elvis was a little more serious than he had been the week before, running the huddles like a military man. But whenever we pulled off one of his plays, he lit up with a big smile. And those smiles meant a lot, because you didn't see too many of them. There were a few other occasions when he'd let his serious game face slip; if anybody took a particularly awkward fall, got knocked on their ass with a brutal block, or otherwise ended up sprawled in some embarrassing position on the field, Elvis just about doubled over with a rush of laughter. It felt great to laugh along with him.

We played that second game at Guthrie, and then a third the next Sunday, and it seemed that the games on that field were going to be a regular part of every weekend. And it seemed that Elvis Presley was going to be a regular part of radio programming. "That's All Right" kept getting played on Dewey's show, and other shows started picking it up, too. It was even being played on WDIA. Pretty soon the record itself was out as a single, and the flip side, a revved-up cover of Bill Monroe's "Blue Moon of Kentucky," started getting radio play, too. Up in Poplar Tunes there was a great big hand-painted sign proudly advertising the fact that they had in stock plenty of records by the new local sensation, Elvis "The Cat" Presley ("available in 45 or 78").

It was also pretty clear that I wasn't the only one excited about the sound and the person of Elvis Presley—at each game that summer, there were a few more guys showing up to play, and increasingly there were groups of people just showing up to watch.

I was hearing Elvis's songs on the radio, but he and his band—guitarist Scotty Moore and bassist Bill Black—were starting to make a name for themselves as a live act, too. On July 30, 1954, Elvis played his first major concert in Memphis at the Overton Park bandshell, being added as a featured attraction to a lineup of country artists that was headlined by Slim Whitman. By the end of the summer the trio had a regular Friday-night gig at a little dance club called the Eagle's Nest. In the fall, Elvis,

Scotty, and Bill were stepping up to some big-deal gigs like the Grand Ole Opry and the Louisiana Hayride, and by the end of the year they were playing shows as far away as Texas. The trio also stayed busy working with Sam Phillips over at Memphis Recording Service on Union Street, and the records that followed their debut—"Good Rockin' Tonight," "Milkcow Blues Boogie"—proved that the excitement of "That's All Right" was no fluke.

His career was starting to take off, but if Elvis was in North Memphis on a Sunday, he'd pull together another football game. And a Sunday didn't go by that summer that I wasn't hanging around the park, waiting to see if he would show up. I kept thinking the games were getting big enough that they wouldn't want a kid out there, but I always made the cut. Elvis would see me hanging around and maybe toss me the ball while he was warming up, or somehow make it clear that he wanted me to play—though, again, not much was ever said.

Into the fall of 1954 we were usually playing six-on-six, and though the teams were generally set, sometimes the rosters got mixed up just to keep things interesting. I remember it felt a little awkward the first time I was on a team playing against Elvis. And since I was well acquainted with his play-calling style, I found myself in the odd position of intercepting Elvis Presley. It felt wrong—but really, really good.

At one of those fall games, I received the first open acknowledgment that I was officially a part of Elvis's team. The games were attracting big enough crowds that Elvis thought it would be a good idea for the players to wear jerseys. I showed up at the park one day to find one of the older guys handing out some green, sleeveless pullovers—the kind you might wear over a T-shirt in gym class. I thought this might be the moment I'd be pushed out—nobody would have to say anything, I just wouldn't get a jersey.

Elvis made sure I got one. Didn't say "Welcome to the team," or "Here's for all your great catches." Just tossed a jersey at me and said, "It's a large—try not to trip over it."

I'd heard that he lived with his mom and dad over on Alabama Street by the Lauderdale Courts, but to me he had a presence that didn't quite fit the streets I was used to. I couldn't imagine Elvis having a job, or taking out the trash, or answering to a mom and dad. It seemed to me that he stepped right out of the radio and into Guthrie Park. But he was a real North Memphis guy, and one day in early 1955 I spotted him on my very block of Breedlove Street.

Across the street from my daddy's house and a couple of houses over, there was a girl a couple years older than me named Meredith Glass. She listened to Dewey, too, and had a record player, and a couple of times Wayne Martin and I had gone over there to listen to music with her (I remember being very impressed that she had her own copy of "Sixty Minute Man"). Meredith went to Humes High, and somewhere along the way had become Red West's girlfriend.

I was sitting in the front room at Breedlove not doing much of anything, when I happened to notice a beat-up, black, forties-model car pull up to Meredith's house—a car I immediately recognized as the one Elvis and Red West came to the games in. Sure enough, both of them got out of that car and headed right into Meredith's house. I wanted nothing more than to bolt out the door, dash across the street, and be a part of whatever the older kids were doing over there. But there was no way I was going to make that bold a move. On the field, I could prove myself as a player. Knocking on Meredith's door, I'd just be the little kid from down the street. I waited in the front room and, after a while, Red and Elvis came back out—it looked like they had borrowed a stack of records from Meredith. They drove off, and Breedlove went back to being the same boring old street.

But it was nice to know that Elvis really was out there, living his life in my part of the city. Maybe nobody else on the block cared but me and Meredith, but Elvis was a part of our neighborhood. That was pretty cool.

With "That's All Right" climbing up the charts, and all sorts of press surrounding his live appearances, Elvis Presley was on the rise. But it would be a mistake to think that everybody that heard him or saw him in those early days liked him.

Mrs. Doolittle wasn't the only person in Memphis concerned with the mixing of the races or the threat of the growing black population— one of the meanest nuns at Holy Names used to try to scare us by saying that because so many whites had embraced the immorality of birth control, the blacks would take over the earth (though they hadn't yet managed to infiltrate Holy Names's all-white student body). Those kinds of feelings were prevalent, and to a lot of people Elvis Presley was nothing more than white trash playing black music.

Some of the early press reports treated Elvis with interest and enthusiasm, or at least treated him as a phenomenon worth taking note of, but the general feeling of conservative old-school Memphis was that the city should be more embarrassed by Elvis than proud of him. From the early concert clips we see these days, it might be assumed that even if old-school Memphis didn't get Elvis, the kids did. But that's not quite true, either. Memphis kids were not automatically Elvis fans. He was a poor white boy, and that was something that a lot of people in Memphis were used to looking down on (the thinking being that blacks were poor because that was just their nature, but whites who were as poor as blacks were truly despicable). A lot of the kids who'd been used to looking down at somebody like Elvis weren't going to suddenly change their minds because he had a popular record out. If anything, they disliked him more now because they had something to be jealous about.

These were the early days of what would soon be called "the youth culture." And for all the kids who got excited about the first sounds of rock and roll, there were at least twice as many who thought it sounded just plain horrible. Those of us excited about Elvis were part of an underground that a lot of our generation still didn't want anything to do with.

The reaction of my brother, Billy Ray, to Elvis was probably pretty typical of the time. When he found out about my ongoing participation in the Guthrie Park games, Billy Ray—a serious, clean-living, hard-working athlete—could not disguise his utter contempt when he asked, "Why are you always hanging around THAT guy?"

As Elvis started to get bigger and bigger, I had a few up-close views of the split feelings toward him. I saw the positive side in a significant way on February 6, 1955—the day I became an official teenager and the day of Elvis's first big show at the premier concert venue in Memphis, Ellis Auditorium. My birthday treat to myself was to spend some of my hard-earned paper-delivery money on a pair of tickets to both the 3:00 P.M. and 8:00 P.M. shows at Ellis. It was my first chance to see Elvis Presley as a performer on stage.

Because of his success at the Louisiana Hayride shows, Elvis was finding himself booked on some bills with top country artists, as he was at these shows. The flyers around town listed Faron Young, Martha Carson, and Ferlin Husky as the headlining acts and had "Memphis's Own Elvis Presley" down at the bottom of the bill. Those other acts didn't mean anything to me—I was there for Elvis. Most people inside the auditorium seemed to feel the same way, too—there was a buzz and an energy, not to mention a fair amount of female squealing, that couldn't be mistaken for anything but Elvis-generated excitement. I don't remember much about the Faron Young or Ferlin Husky performances except that the crowd was as attentive as could be expected and clapped where it was supposed to.

It was when Elvis took the stage that the place just about exploded. I'd never heard such a human-made roar as Elvis, in loose slacks and a fancy tailored jacket, strapped on his guitar and took his place in front of a mike, flanked by Scotty with his guitar and Bill with his bass. But as soon as they started playing—and as soon as Elvis started moving— the energy that came off that stage was even bigger than anything the crowd was throwing back at it. For a guy who hadn't been on that many big stages yet, and for a guy with so much wild energy to burn, he handled the show like a real pro, moving around and working the crowd masterfully, making sure that everybody got plenty of what they'd come for. This guy wasn't just a kid with some records out: He was an entertainer.

I'd heard Elvis sing on record and on the radio, and I'd seen him move on a football field, but the musicality and physicality I saw come together on that stage was something else. I was already impressed by the way the guy walked and the way he threw a football. And I liked his records. But it was a shock to see the way he threw himself so completely into the music as a stage performer. Those crazy legs shook and trembled, his arms pinwheeled, he tossed his body around like he was nothing more than a rag doll with a great head of ducktails. And he treated his mike stand like it was the object of a passionate seduction— sometimes holding it close with tenderness, sometimes just dragging it across the stage like a worked-up wild man dragging his mate off to the nearest cave. His moves were more outrageous than anything I'd ever seen or heard of, but they were also perfectly timed and executed. It had an effect on me—I hadn't felt this much adrenaline pumping through me since I'd seen Rocky Marciano knock out Joe Louis on the *Friday Night Fights* over at Aunt Jinky's.

People had been calling Elvis "The Hillbilly Cat." What I saw up on stage was a hungry tiger.

The Ellis crowd loved every minute of it. Everything the records had promised, the show delivered. We even had the thrill of seeing good old Dewey Phillips share the mike with Elvis for a while. Maybe there were some people around me who had just come to see Ferlin Huskey, but I don't remember seeing a face that wasn't smiling at the end of Elvis's four- or five-song set. It felt like the first great meeting of a secret club. Being an Elvis fan at this point was a little unusual. But all of us "unusual" people had come together in downtown Memphis and felt the first life-changing rumble of rock and roll's big bang. We walked out of that auditorium absolutely knowing that we'd been witnesses to the start of something new and explosive. Elvis wasn't going to just be a voice on the radio or records anymore—he was out in the real world, and, to those of us who welcomed him, that world began to look and sound like a much more exciting place.

The "usual" reactions to Elvis weren't as positive. A crowd of supporters was regularly coming to watch Elvis play ball at the park, but almost every Sunday there'd also be cars full of guys driving by the park just for the chance to heckle him, with something along the lines of "pretty boy" being the insult of choice. I'd also heard that a couple of times guys had blindsided Elvis, pretending to come up to him for an autograph and then taking a swing at him when they got close enough. Or calling him over to a car for an autograph, throwing a punch, and then driving away. Occasionally carloads of young sailors from the Millington Naval Base north of Memphis would make the trip to Guthrie just to drive past and yell, "Hey, sideburns!" at the degenerate rock and roller they'd heard about. Incidents like that led Elvis to rely more and more on guys like Red West to stick around him and play some real-life defense for him.

At one of our bigger games in the spring of 1955, we'd been playing for a while when a couple of very large men showed up and asked if they could get in the game. They explained that they were semipro players, had heard about the Elvis games, and wanted to be a part of it. The rest of us were not so eager to play with these big guys, but as far as Elvis was concerned, these players were stepping onto his turf and he wasn't going to stand down. He wanted them in. We worked out the teams again to include them and got set to play. On one of the first offensive drives, Elvis was taking a break from quarterbacking duties and was on the line blocking. When the ball was snapped, this 200-pound-plus semipro hit Elvis hard and ran right over him. Elvis took his time getting up—he was obviously a little shaken.

Now, we played tough at these games, with all-out effort, and we regularly knocked the hell out of each other. But the point was that everybody got knocked around—nobody ever specifically targeted Elvis. You wouldn't think twice about hitting him if that's the way the play went, but nobody was ever going out of their way to try to hurt him. From the look of that semipro player's first hit, it seemed that maybe these guys weren't so interested in playing ball for fun—they were going to teach "Pretty Boy" Presley a lesson.

As we got back into a huddle, it was clear that Red West was furious. "I'll take that son of a bitch out," he said.

"No, Red," said Elvis sharply. "Damn it, no. Just play the game."

We ran a few more plays, and it was the same thing each time—Elvis got a tremendous hit from this charging rhino. But Elvis made a point of hopping up a little faster each time and just shaking it off. It got to a point where the day just didn't feel like fun anymore. All the regular players were furious, and we were all telling Elvis that the game couldn't go on like this, but he wouldn't hear it. He wanted to play through. I found myself lined up next to Elvis, with the same big guy ready to charge at him again.

"Hit me from the left side," said Elvis.

"What?" asked the rhino.

"Hit me from the left side."

"Why?"

"I got a few bones over there that ain't broke yet," said Elvis.

The big guy started laughing, and by the time the ball was snapped he was laughing hard enough that he didn't have the strength to steamroll Elvis. After the play, we took a break and the guy went over to his fellow rhino. In a few minutes they walked back toward Elvis. Now the big guys were all smiles.

"Excuse me, Elvis," said the one who'd been knocking him down. "We sure did enjoy the game. Hope there aren't any hard feelings."

Red was still ready to lunge at them, but Elvis just shrugged.

"No hard feelings," said Elvis. "Just bruises. Good luck with your season."

Their big faces lit up like they'd just been blessed by the Pope. They started to walk away, when the guy who'd been knocking Elvis down turned around and came back.

"Uh, just one more thing, Elvis? Our wives are over there—can we bring them over to meet you?"

"Sure," says Elvis. "Bring 'em over."

As Elvis signed autographs for their wives, it all came together for me; if he had let Red and the rest of us go after these guys, then he would have ended up with some more enemies. Instead, he took a little punishment and ended up with four new fans. There were a lot of people in Memphis that wanted to knock Elvis down, figuratively and literally, but what I saw happen on that field with the semipro guys was something I'd witness over and over again: A lot of people thought they had something against Elvis, but I never saw anybody who spent any time with him walk away not liking him.

As my eighth-grade year started in the fall of 1955, I felt a bit like I was living in two worlds—there was school, home, and everything in the ordinary world. Then there were Sundays at Guthrie Park.

One day, early in the school year, the worlds collided. I was out on the playground behind the school during lunchtime, not doing much of anything (I'd become more careful about playground ballgames since one of my football passes had knocked the headwear off a very startled nun). When I heard the roar of a motor coming down Woodlawn Street, I looked toward the street and saw a vehicle that would have turned heads anywhere but certainly stood out around Holy Names—a big, beautiful, pink Cadillac. In the driver's seat was Elvis, steering with one arm on top of the steering wheel. I was surprised, and very happy, to see him pull a quick left on Looney Avenue—the street that bordered the Holy Names playground—and pull up to the curb.

"Hey, man," Elvis called out.

Didn't seem like there was any other Holy Names grade schooler he could possibly be calling to. I took a couple of steps toward him. He'd gotten out of the car and was leaning against it, drumming his fingers on the hood and peering past me at the school. I could sense that the playground behind me had become a little quieter.

"Hey, Elvis. What are you doing over here?"

"Just came from Humes. Seeing how the place is holding up." Elvis smiled past me and waved at somebody. I heard giggles.

I was standing just yards away from first-graders and hopscotch grids, racking my brain for something to say that would make me sound solid, older—just a little bit cool.

"I heard your shows are going great."

Elvis let loose a laugh. "Yeah, well—we're just having some fun."

We stood there a few more moments, not talking about much of anything. He kept smiling past me. And I kept hearing those giggles. He slapped at the car hard and spun away.

"Gotta go. See you later, Chief," said Elvis.

"See ya. At the next game," I said.

He went back around the car, flung open the driver's door, and, just before climbing in, gave a casual wave to the playground. I heard more giggles behind me.

Elvis came by Holy Names a few more times that fall, and I was always proud of the fact that I was the kid Elvis came over to talk to. Years later, it occurred to me that while, from my perspective, those playground visits were about me and Elvis, from his perspective the visits served another purpose. Holy Names was a boys and girls grade school, but an all-girls high school. For those of us too young to go out to the likes of the Eagle's Nest, the coolest music you could hear was at the Holy Names High School dances on Saturday nights. Elvis's first girlfriend had been from Holy Names, and during his time at Humes, he went to plenty of those Holy Names dances. The grade school and the high school were in two separate brick buildings on the same lot, but they shared the same playground. The point is, when Elvis pulled up to that curb, he wasn't thinking about talking to me. He was thinking about checking out a playground full of Catholic high school girls.

Just across Thomas Avenue from the perilous Hurt Village was a little shotgun shack that had been turned into a hamburger joint and candy store called the Stand. It was just a couple of blocks away from Holy Names, but it felt like a tougher part of town, and I liked the feel of walking over there to get my lunch. On a chilly March afternoon in 1956, I was in the Stand, about to pull the cap off a bottle of Coke with the built-in opener on the big metal pop machine in there, when a new song started playing on the jukebox. The voice was unmistakable. Rich. Confident. Soft and strong at the same time. It was Elvis, singing a new song called "I Was the One."

She lived, she loved, she laughed, she cried . . .

I was used to hearing Elvis rock, but here was an Elvis song that grabbed me in a whole different way. It went straight for the emotions, and hit like a fist to the gut. I'd recently been dumped by my first "girlfriend"—Loretta Cuccia, a real looker from Holy Names's rival school Little Flower—and here was Elvis singing out all those tangled feelings that I hadn't been able to put into words.

Who learned the lesson when she broke my heart—I was the one.

That was exactly what I wanted to tell Harvey Vaughan, the tough Golden Gloves champ my girl had moved on to. I stood frozen at the Coke machine until the song was over. A beautiful tune, packed full of truth, sung from the heart. I took a swig of my Coke and went back to my burger over at the counter. It occurred to me that Elvis Presley wasn't just getting by on cool. This guy could really sing.

A few days later at the Stand I heard the A-side of the "I Was the One" single—a song called "Heartbreak Hotel." If the B-side had grabbed me, the A-side just blew me away. With "Heartbreak Hotel," Elvis seemed to be inventing his own kind of music from scratch—that song didn't sound like anything else on the jukebox. It rocked, but it was haunting, too. When Elvis sang "feel so lonely" in that odd, hiccupy way, it cut right through you. And I wasn't the only one blown away by the song—within a few weeks it was at the top of the pop charts, giving Elvis his first number-one hit.

I wasn't following record-label politics back in 1956, but the release of "Heartbreak Hotel" marked Elvis's debut as an RCA recording artist, having moved on from Sun Records and producer Sam Phillips. The usual line on Sam is that he "discovered Elvis," but that doesn't quite give Sam credit for the care and guidance he applied to the young singer. Elvis showed up at Sun Studio wanting to croon ballads—the first thing he recorded there was the sweet, non-rocking "My Happiness." Elvis thought that was the kind of tune serious singers were supposed to sing. Sam's ear picked up on the potential in Elvis's voice, and he encouraged the young singer to break away from the standard pop approach. When you go back and listen to "Good Rockin' Tonight" or "Mystery Train," there's both an excitement and a mystique to the sound that still holds up after decades of listens. The music Sam encouraged and captured in the humble, no-frills storefront of Sun Records still sounds extraordinary.

Sam is supposed to have said, "If I could find a white boy who could sing like a black man, I could make a million dollars." The quote has sometimes been referred to as if it were some kind of devious strategy on Sam's part. But if he did say anything close to that, it was simply a statement of fact about race and music in 1950s Memphis. Sam knew that there was a huge audience of white kids hungry for the excitement they heard on the black R & B records, and he also knew that, given the deep-seated anger and fear that white society had when it came to matters of race, it was going to take a white voice with a black feel for the music to ever fully "cross over."

But I think people forget how much Sam loved R & B, and what a fearless pioneer he was in putting all his energies into making great records for artists like Rufus Thomas, Howlin' Wolf, Ike Turner, and B. B. King. Today those artists are seen as brilliant talents, and Sun Records has achieved respected, iconic status. But back when Sam Phillips was spending long nights in that little storefront studio with groups of black musicians, he was doing something that made him a target for the most vicious kinds of personal attacks. Sam didn't spend the roughest years of his life recording all those great black artists wishing they were white. His passion for exciting music was stronger than any regard for color lines or a "sensible" career path, and his dedication to that music and those artists made him a despised outcast to much of the Memphis business community. It's hard for anyone looking at the music world today to imagine what he went through—but to stand up and do what he did makes him, at least to me, rock and roll's ultimate hero.

I had a chance to see Elvis perform again over at the Chisca Hotel in March of 1956, after I heard about a special show Dewey Phillips was putting on in the hotel's basement lounge, the Chickasaw Ballroom. Elvis was performing as a special guest with the Sy Rose Band. I dragged my old witness Frankie Grisanti along with me to see Elvis in action, promising him that—after what I'd seen at Ellis Auditorium—it would be worth the trip downtown. But when we got to the Chisca, we ran straight into a major obstacle: Alcohol was going to be served in the Ballroom, and tickets were not being sold to minors.

I'd spent enough time crawling through the sewer pipes of North Memphis for Saturday kicks to know that there was usually more than one way to get where you wanted to get. So Frankie and I backed away from the main entrance to the Chickasaw and casually slipped into a service hallway. We snuck around past laundry chutes and water heaters until we got to a little area around the other side of the ballroom—a hallway with a big soda machine and a door that led right to the stage.

We watched as much of the first show as we could through the crack in that door, but the biggest thrill came after Elvis finished his first show, when he headed offstage right toward us. We scattered from the door just as he came through.

He was sweating something fierce and a little out of breath—looking like he'd gotten a more intense workout than he did at any of the football games. I don't know if he nodded at us or if he was just getting his hair back in place, but he acted like it was the most natural thing in the world for Frankie and me to be in that basement hallway. There wasn't a place to sit, so he just leaned up against one of the big basement pillars.

"Get me a Pepsi, would you?"

"Sure, Elvis."

I brought him the cold bottle, and he tipped his head back and chugged away. The sweat was just pouring off of him. And I remember noticing that, as sharp as he looked in his black pants and red jacket, he still had a bad patch of acne on his neck. He was human.

Elvis didn't say much to Frankie and me, but he seemed perfectly comfortable to have us around. We hung around for the whole break between shows, and after a while there were other people around who wanted to talk to Elvis. He talked to them, but if he wanted another Pepsi, he got it from me or Frankie. The moment seemed special because it wasn't special—just him and us, standing around drinking soda.

He'd just walked away from a screaming audience to stand out here in the hallway, Frankie and I were in the hallway, and it was no big deal.

But it was. At the Ellis Auditorium, I'd gotten the sense that something really big and exciting was happening around Elvis. Now, standing close to the guy, working the soda machine in the Chisca Hotel basement, I started feeling that, in some small way, I was a part of what was happening.

Down South, when I was growing up, the most common summer vacation was to get the family piled in a car and drive down to Florida. My dad was a big advocate for Florida vacations—he felt that if he could get down there for a couple of weeks and spend as much time as possible in the salt water, it would keep him healthy throughout the year. An August trip to Miami became his annual vacation, and, come to think of it, I don't actually remember him getting sick very often.

In August of 1956, we loaded up his Pontiac for the trip to Miami, leaving room for four passengers—he was also bringing along his girlfriend, Lula, who would eventually become my stepmother, and one of their mutual friends, a lady named Helen. I wasn't especially thrilled to be a part of this quartet, but I did look forward to the adventure of a trip out of town.

On our way into Miami, we drove past a Lincoln dealership, and I spotted something that made the trip suddenly much more worthwhile. As Elvis's fortunes had risen, he'd quickly bumped up from his pink Caddy to a yellow Cadillac convertible with a continental kit, and then to his latest ride, a brand-new, purple, white-top Lincoln Premiere. And passing that dealership, I spotted Elvis's purple Lincoln sitting in the showroom window, sporting an unusual detailing job: The car was covered with love messages and phone numbers written in lipstick. Elvis was in town.

In Miami, we checked into a not-too-pricey hotel that was within walking distance of the fancier Fontainbleau, where my dad and his female companions would hit the nightly dances. The three of them had plans for how they were going to spend their days and nights, and my dad didn't pressure me to be a part of that group—I was trusted to take in Miami on my own. On the first day there, while the others were out getting some sun, I stayed next to the radio until I got the information I was after: Elvis was going to be performing in Miami at the Olympia Theatre over the next couple of days.

I'd seen him that July 4th playing his biggest concert in Memphis to date, packing 7,000 fans into the Russwood Park ball field, but hadn't seen him around much after that. I knew he was taking his own summer Florida trip, doing a string of theater dates during which he'd perform three or four times a day. And when this Florida tour was over he was heading out to Hollywood to start work on his first feature film. I can't remember if I had to twist my dad's arm much to get me a ticket to one of the Olympia shows, or if he just figured we should do at least one special father-son thing while we were away, but he and I ended up with a pair of tickets to a Saturday afternoon Elvis performance.

I'd felt a little lost in the crowd at the Russwood show, so it was great to see Elvis perform in a small theater this time. Even on a little stage for a smaller audience, he didn't hold anything back. Even before a note of music was played, he had the crowd going wild. He took the stage almost casually, walking out like that tiger again—knowing he could take his time before going in for the kill. He strolled right up to the corner edge of the stage, grabbed the curtain, and leaned out right over the audience. The girls went wild. He pulled himself back, walked over to his spot behind the mike, and then snapped into action as the band kicked in. When the crowd went even wilder, he feigned a moment of surprise—like he couldn't understand what all the fuss was about. Then a little devilish smile flashed across his face—almost as though he were smiling at himself.

Elvis certainly wasn't a Memphis secret anymore at this point. He'd been seen by a national television audience on Tommy and Jimmy Dorsey's *Stage Show*, *The Milton Berle Show*, and *The Steve Allen Show*, and his first album, *Elvis Presley*—the one with his name in pink and green letters—had shot to number one on the pop charts. But with all his success, Elvis was also starting to get a lot of negative attention from the national press: the New York *Daily News* had decried Elvis's "Grunt and groin antics," the *New York Times* announced that he had "no discernible singing ability," and the Catholic weekly *America* called him "downright obscene." With all that coming down on him, however, he wasn't going to change a thing about his show. On that little Miami theater stage he was as unhinged and exciting as he'd been at Ellis, putting everything he had into his performance and again grabbing and dragging that mike around in a way that the Holy Names nuns would certainly not approve of. I'm not sure what my father, a big-band fan, made of it all, but I think I got him to at least concede that the music had a solid, danceable beat.

Elvis got a huge reaction out of two of his newest songs, "Don't Be Cruel" and his big closer, "Hound Dog" (both would be number-one hits through the rest of the summer). It was a heck of a jump for popular music to go from "(How Much Is) That Doggie in the Window" to "Hound Dog" in just a few years, but Elvis led us there fearlessly, and at this performance left us begging for more. But at these kinds of shows, Elvis did only about a half hour of material, and the theater management wanted to turn the crowd over pretty fast. When Elvis finished and the curtains closed and the screams started to die down, my father got up to go. Before we headed out, I spotted Red West over by the side of the stage. I went over to say hello, and Red told me what hotel they were staying at, and that they were leaving late that night to head for more shows in Tampa. He also explained that Elvis had driven into town in the purple Lincoln, but as soon as it was discovered outside his hotel by fans, it was thoroughly and lovingly defaced in the lipsticked manner we'd seen. Elvis had traded it in at the dealership we saw for a brand-new, white Lincoln Continental Mark II.

That night, my dad and the ladies went out for another night of dancing at the Fontainbleau. And a couple hours later I headed out on the town with a different musical incentive. I wandered awhile before I came around a corner and knew instantly that I was in the right place. There was a small throng of excited girls clustering around something in front of a big building, and the closer I got, the more I could just about make out the outline of a shiny white Lincoln beyond the girls. I started milling around the edge of the crowd, feeling almost overcome by the smell of so many competing perfumes. The girls were desperately trying to edge each other out, but somehow they let little me slip through—and pretty soon I was close enough to see Elvis leaning against the Lincoln, apparently trying to sign as many autographs as he could before he left town.

I always felt a little pang of insecurity when I hadn't seen Elvis for a while—would our friendship pick up wherever it had left off, or had he just gotten too big? Too busy? I was starting to feel that pang now, when suddenly a few girls in front of me moved to the side and there I was, standing just a few feet away from Elvis. He had autograph albums and pictures being shoved in front of him, and dozens of very attractive girls bobbing all around him, and there's no reason a fourteen-year-old boy should have caught his attention. But he saw me, and stopped signing whatever he was signing. He squinted for a moment like he wanted to make sure he was seeing what he thought he was seeing.

Then he said, "Jerry! What in the hell are you doing here?"

I didn't have a chance to tell him much before the girls closed in again, but it didn't matter. In the middle of all these crazy strangers, I was a guy he knew by name.

3

. . .

MIDNIGHT RAMBLES

After September 9, 1956, it was hard to believe that there was anyone left in the United States who wasn't aware of Elvis Presley. That was the night he appeared on the season premiere of *The Ed Sullivan Show*. Sullivan was recuperating from injuries suffered in a recent car accident, so Elvis's debut performance on the show was introduced by a surprising guest host, actor Charles Laughton. Laughton was hosting the show in New York City, but Elvis's segments were broadcast from the CBS studios in Los Angeles, where he was working on his first movie. Elvis sang "Don't Be Cruel," "Ready Teddy," "Hound Dog," and a song from the new film called "Love Me Tender." In the days after the broadcast, newspapers were saying that eighty percent of American TV viewers had watched Elvis that night. And a huge national audience watched again when he returned to the show at the end of October (Sullivan was back hosting by that time).

I watched those Sullivan shows with a great deal of excitement—it was almost unbelievable that a guy who had started as a local talent was now on the biggest TV show in America. And it was made a little more exciting by the fact that Sullivan had at one point said that he wouldn't ever have Elvis on the show—Elvis was just too controversial. After Elvis appeared on *The Steve Allen Show* and trounced Sullivan in the ratings, Sullivan changed his mind and welcomed Elvis.

Even at the time, Elvis's *Sullivan* performances felt historic. You had to admit that the world was a different place after Elvis shook hands with Ed Sullivan at the end of that second show. But for me, his most memorable television moment had come back in January, when Elvis made his first appearance on the Dorsey Brothers' *Stage Show*. On that program, Elvis delivered a wild, untamed performance of "Shake, Rattle, and Roll," but almost as powerful as the performance itself was just the way he walked out on stage when he was introduced. If you just saw that walk and turned the TV off before a note of music was played, you'd still get the message: This guy was sex, danger, and good times all rolled into one. I guess that message was clear to the Sullivan producers—during Elvis's first appearance, they had the cameras cut away from him when he began to dance during "Ready Teddy."

As big as Elvis had become, when he was back in Memphis he still liked to play football. So, on a crisp, beautiful fall November day, we football regulars had our green jerseys on, and a crowd of spectators was fanned around the edges of the field at Guthrie Park. Elvis, quarterbacking as usual, seemed to be in a particularly good mood. There was just one problem: For the first time ever at a Guthrie game, I was having a hard time following what he was saying, and having an even harder time keeping my eyes on him as he sketched out our plays and pass patterns. As much as I'd been looking forward to this game while Elvis was away, now that I was here in the middle of a huddle, I was thoroughly distracted.

Natalie Wood was standing on the sidelines.

I'd seen *Rebel Without a Cause* the year before and, just like a few million other adolescent boys, had developed a mad crush on the lovely brown-eyed girl who jeopardizes her "respectable" standing by falling in love with the brooding James Dean. Elvis had met her while he'd been out in Hollywood shooting his own movie. Word was that Elvis and Natalie had dated a few times, and when Elvis asked her and his newfound Hollywood actor pal Nick Adams to come with him for a few days of Memphis fun, they'd accepted the invitation.

A bunch of the players and I had stood around the park for about half an hour after what had been the agreed-upon start time of the game that day, which was a little unusual, because even though Elvis had his own schedule for just about everything else, he was always on time for football. Looking back, I think this was a day that he wanted to make an especially big entrance, which is exactly what he did, roaring up to the park in great rebel style on a huge, brand-new Harley-Davidson motorcycle. And it made perfect sense that on the back of that motorcycle, clinging tightly to the driver, was a female passenger. It was only after that passenger dismounted and shook her hair out that I realized who I was looking at, and right away I felt my stomach twisting up and my knees getting shaky.

I suppose that after hanging around Elvis so much, I should have known how to handle being in the presence of a celebrity. But with Elvis, I'd had the chance to know him as a regular guy before he'd gone on to be a local phenomenon and then a full-fledged star. I'd had some time to process the strange way in which a flesh-and-blood human becomes a famous face.

But Natalie Wood seemed to have stepped right out of the movies and onto that field, and I had no idea how to make sense of that. She seemed at once incredibly petite and also too big to be standing under a North Memphis sky. Either way, she was absolutely stunning, and I couldn't keep my eyes off of her. Catching an Elvis pass was one thing, but Natalie Wood on the back of Elvis's motorcycle—that was pretty exciting stuff for a day in the park.

"Come on, Jerry, look alive. Don't let 'em get past you on a plain old slant."

Elvis was not happy with our defense—the guys lining up against us kept having success with the long ball, and since I was playing back in the secondary, that was my responsibility. Of course, I didn't tell Elvis I was distracted by his imported cheerleader. I also didn't tell him that I was having some trouble getting any kind of support from my partner in the secondary—Nick Adams. Adams had also been in *Rebel Without a Cause* and was getting steady work in features like *Picnic* and *Our Miss Brooks*. He was a little guy who looked like he could probably move with some speed when he wanted to, and Elvis had insisted that the actor side up with our team, but it was clear that Nick did not approach competitive athletics with anything near the kind of intensity that Elvis did. Not only did he never break a sweat, he's the only guy I've ever seen reading a newspaper while playing cornerback.

I eventually got my head in the game enough to bat down a few passes on defense and make a few catches on offense, but I never quite forgot that a Hollywood beauty was just a few yards away at the side of the field. At the end of the game, Elvis and Natalie stood together, and a few of the guys went up and said hello to her. I didn't go anywhere near them. I loved Natalie within the safe, dark confines of the Rialto movie theater, but the idea of actually talking to her was a little too much.

The crowd of spectators that the Guthrie games drew sometimes made it difficult for Elvis to make as quick an exit as he liked, and this was a day when he used one of his rather ingenious escape maneuvers. Standing with Natalie, he casually pulled a comb from his pocket and began to work it through his hair. Then, in equally casual manner, he tossed the comb out on the field. When a cluster of the most avid fans surged out on the grass to try and grab up the souvenir, Elvis and Natalie darted the other way, toward the waiting Harley, and sped off down Chelsea Avenue.

Hollywood had come to North Memphis, and a few weeks later I got to witness North Memphis returning the favor. On November 21, I was at the Loews State Theater as part of one of the first paying audiences to get a look at Elvis Presley's debut feature film, *Love Me Tender.* The screams of the girls around me made it just about impossible to follow the story—this was the first time I'd ever seen an audience treat a film like it was a live concert, loudly responding to every move made and word uttered by their favorite star. I concentrated as best I could on watching the movie.

I'd sat in that same theater just a month before on a school field trip to see *The Ten Commandments.* That epic film had a tremendous, enduring impact on me—I didn't see how anything on screen could be bigger or better. But I'd never played football with Charlton Heston. Watching *Love Me Tender*, I saw Elvis, someone I knew pretty well, holding his own up on the same big screen where Moses had worked miracles. I was watching Elvis play a character, but at the same time I could recognize a whole lot of the guy I'd played football with. Between seeing Natalie Wood off the screen and Elvis up on it, I felt I was starting to understand some of the mystery of the movies—the people up on screen were real people doing a job. And, at the Loews, Elvis was doing his job pretty darn well.

As Elvis began his film career, he was taking a step closer to mainstream American entertainment, but he was still seen by many as a dangerous element in American society. That split was made very clear during

Elvis's third and final appearance on *The Ed Sullivan Show* in January of 1957. Elvis had become an even more controversial figure after his first two appearances, but Sullivan didn't flinch from having him back. However, a concession was made to the moral outrage that Elvis had stirred up—when he performed this time, he was only filmed from the waist up (as with most acts of censorship, this only made its target even more exciting). But in a way, Elvis was already way ahead of the cameras. On TV now, he was not the wild, untamed performer I'd seen on the Dorsey Brothers' show—he was having fun, but he was also clearly determined. As much as the camera tried to contain him, he'd already figured out how to look right through that lens and reach a TV audience with the smallest of gestures.

Here was a performer so "dangerous" that we couldn't see his whole body, and yet, at the end of the show, Ed Sullivan did something very surprising, announcing to his huge American TV audience, "I just wanted to say to Elvis Presley and the country that this is a real decent, fine boy," and going on to say that he'd never had a more pleasant experience dealing with a big-name guest. The way Elvis looked out at us at that moment, I thought I could see a mix of hurt over the attacks he'd been subjected to in the press, and a deep pride in who he was and what he was doing.

In some ways, "rebel" is the perfect word for Elvis—just by being who he was and making the music he wanted to make, he was taking on the musical and social conventions of the day. But "rebel" doesn't get all of it—the word can feel too negative, and you have to be against something to stage a rebellion. On a personal level, Elvis was not fired up with anger and negativity—he wasn't raging against the world he saw around him. He was fired up with a passion for great music—music that happened to come from both black and white experiences—and he simply wasn't going to let the world around him get in the way. As far as those early days go, I think "pioneer," and "trailblazer" fit Elvis as much as "rebel" does.

While Elvis was still a teenager, he was being told that he was a "corrupter of youth" and a "traitor to his race." But rather than answering with any kind of "screw you," he handled it all with dignity and humility—a manner that could come only from an inner strength. As his career started to pick up—when he really started to get to the point where he had something to lose—he had the strength of purpose to casually step over the color lines in Memphis, turning up, for example, as a respectful white face in an all-black audience at WDIA's annual "Goodwill Revue" gala concert. (When he was brought out on stage by Rufus Thomas to say hello to the crowd, he received a warm and enthusiastic ovation. Despite lingering notions to the contrary, the black population of Memphis got what Elvis was doing and knew what he was up against, and he deeply appreciated their support.)

The way Elvis handled his fame in the early years tells you a lot about his character. By early 1957, Elvis was successful enough that he could have said good-bye to Memphis forever and become a permanent resident of a Beverly Hills mansion. He'd moved on from his role in *Love Me Tender* to a starring role in *Loving You*. In the spring he had another number-one hit with "All Shook Up," and then he was back out to Los Angeles to star in his third film, *Jailhouse Rock*. But Memphis was home, and home meant everything to Elvis. So he was very excited when he found a beautiful place just south of downtown that he felt might make a perfect Memphis home for him, his mom and dad, and his grandmother. A place called Graceland.

I stood in front of a custom-built gate decorated with an iron guitar and music notes, peering up the gentle sloping hill of oak trees to the grandest structure I'd ever laid eyes on. The impressive stone facade, the huge colonial pillars, the welcoming portico—this was a long way from Lauderdale Courts, and I was a long way from Leath Street.

After finishing eighth grade at Holy Names, I'd ended up at Catholic High School out in Midtown Memphis, not too far from Overton Park. There had been a brief detour at Christian Brothers College—the school my brother had attended—but I felt miserable and out of place there. Billy Ray, again stepping up to his big-brother duties, suggested to my father that I'd be a lot happier and better off at Catholic High. I did have a good first year there, and I also got used to exploring a wider circle of Memphis, riding the bus, hitchhiking, or, when I could get it, driving Dad's Pontiac.

So, on a fine summer day, I had decided to head down Highway 51 to check out Graceland. The gates I stood at had clearly gone up for a reason—there was a group of fans, mostly girls, clustered around the entrance, chatting away and showing off pictures and autographs to each other. Elvis and his family had been in the house for only a few months, but already these fans seemed like they were very comfortable just spending a day at the edge of the property, hoping they might catch sight of Elvis coming or going. They were inspired by Elvis and wanted some way to get closer to him. I could certainly understand that. At this point Elvis was out of town more than he was in Memphis, but these fans were on top of the Elvis schedule enough to know when he was up at the house.

Through Red West and some of the other football guys, I'd become friendly with George Klein. George was a Humes classmate of Elvis's, and though the two had not been close while in high school, their paths had continued to cross as Elvis's music career took off and George headed off on a radio career (he had learned the business hanging around Dewey Phillips, and went on to become a top DJ in his own right—also one of the very first to play Elvis's records). George was a strong, early, enthusiastic supporter of Elvis, and out of their professional contact, a real friendship grew.

As a rock-and-roll DJ back then, George had a cool and a toughness all his own—he was a sharp, solid guy who had an almost superhuman knowledge of everything going on in popular music. His family had actually lived on Leath Street for a while, and my mother had babysat for him when he was small. He was an Elvis inner-circle guy that I considered very approachable. I don't remember him playing much football, but he came to a lot of the Guthrie games, and our own friendship began to develop. Through George, I heard that Elvis was starting to have people up to the house. That's what had brought me to the gate.

Just behind the brick columns on the right side of the gate was a small guardhouse, which was being manned by an older guy with the strong chin and great hair of the Presley clan: This, I would learn, was Uncle Vester, brother of Elvis's father, Vernon Presley, who had already been assigned the gatekeeper position that he would hold for many years. I gathered up my courage and signaled to him. I cleared my throat and hoped that I could keep my voice low without having it crack the way it had been doing lately.

"My name is Jerry Schilling. I was wondering if I could go up to the house. If . . . if it's all right."

Vester eyed me for a moment.

"Jerry, is it?" he asked.

"Yes, sir. Jerry Schilling."

Vester ambled over to the guardhouse and picked up a phone. I couldn't hear what was said, but a minute later the gate started to swing open. The crowd of fans began to buzz with excitement, but they knew the drill well enough not to try to swarm through the open gate. I think I remember a few startled breaths when the group realized that I was the one who was being granted access—and to be honest, I was a little startled myself. Vester waved me up the long driveway, and I headed up the hill.

I was excited and a little anxious to be on Elvis's property, headed for his home. But as soon as I stepped into the dappled shadows of those oak trees, I was hit with a feeling that was quite unusual for me: peacefulness. There was a calm and tranquillity that seemed to be part of the air around Graceland, and I couldn't help but relax, breathe a little deeper, and walk a little easier.

About halfway up the drive I realized that there was a figure coming toward me. There was the Presley chin and the hair again, but this time it was Vernon. I was struck by the fact that Vernon had an easy walk that looked very familiar to me—he seemed to have adopted Elvis's unique loping, shoulder-rolling manner of strolling, even keeping one arm at his belt just the way Elvis did. (Later I would mention to Billy Ray how strange it was that the dad would copy his son's walk. Billy Ray asked if I had considered that maybe Elvis had gotten the walk from his dad. Frankly, I hadn't considered that. It seemed to me that everything in the world keyed on Elvis. But Billy Ray was right, and Vernon deserves credit for the distinctive Presley walk.)

"Vester let you up?" Vernon asked. The voice was a little rougher around the edges, but had the same warm lilt as his son's.

"Yes, sir."

"Go ahead, then. Elvis is down. All the boys are downstairs." (I'd soon learn that at Graceland, Elvis was either upstairs, seeking privacy in the bedroom and office that took up most of the second floor of the house, or he was "down," ready and willing to spend time with visitors.)

I walked past a pair of cement lions guarding the walkway to the house and stepped past the magnificent columns to the front door. It'd be great to say that Elvis was right there at the door, welcoming me in, but it would be a lie. I'm not sure who walked me into Graceland on that first visit—all I know is that in taking that first step into that incredible home, I felt like I was stepping into a place better than anything I could have dreamed up. To me, a really nice house was one that had fairly fresh paint and a bedroom for each kid living there. I had no idea that a house could be a thing of overwhelming beauty, but that's what I took in as soon as I was over the Graceland threshold. There was a blue ceiling that gave the illusion of an indoor sky, impossibly white carpets, a stairway trimmed in gold, mirrors everywhere, and furnishings that looked fit for a palace.

I followed the sounds of voices and music down a mirrored stairway to a pair of rooms that, even at first glance, struck me as just about any boy's vision of the ultimate secret clubhouse. To the left was a hangout room with low-slung sofas, a TV and record player set into the far wall, and what looked like a fully stocked soda fountain (the room became known as "the TV room"). A room to the right was dominated by a full-size, ornate pool table. Framed gold 45s created a one-of-a-kind molding at the top of the walls.

The rooms weren't immense, but were big enough to comfortably hold the dozen or so people partying down there. I recognized a few faces right away. George Klein was there, and so was Billy Smith, one of Elvis's cousins who was about my age and who'd become a speedy, wide-receiving regular at the football games. Alan Fortas was a friend of George's who'd recently started showing up at games—he was a sturdy, good-humored guy from Central High on the east side of town (Elvis liked him enough to give him a nickname derived from his short haircut and prominent appendages: "Hog Ears"). A few girls were sitting in the TV room, including Elvis's girlfriend Anita Wood—a pretty, upbeat blonde who was often at our football games. She'd caught Elvis's eye as the cohost of a local TV show called *Dance Party with Wink Martindale*, and the two now seemed to be a pretty serious couple. There was also Patsy Presley, Elvis's double first cousin (their fathers were brothers, their mothers were sisters). She was also about my age, a quiet, centered girl who proved that the Presley good looks translated very well to the female form.

Maybe I got a hello or a nod from some of the other guests, but I know nobody made any big fuss about my arrival. Remember, even though we were in one of the biggest houses in Memphis, in the presence of the biggest star in the world, this was still essentially just a bunch of kids getting together. Our host was only twenty-two. And, like any bunch of young people hanging out, everything was informal and casual. Nobody made a big deal out of anything; the big deal was that we were all there.

I spotted Elvis in the pool room—he was just lining up his next shot. He was smoking a cigarette, which he never did at the football games, and he had a great way of holding the cigarette in his teeth as he leaned over the table. As cool as he looked, he missed sinking a striped ball in a corner pocket. It didn't look like it fazed him, but with the bottom of his cue he gave a sharp poke to the guy standing behind him—his cousin Gene Smith.

"Ow! Wuzzat for, cuz?" howled Gene.

Elvis kept his eyes on the table, looking like he had no idea what Gene was fussing about. As he watched the other players take their shots, the intensity on his face never waned. He was home, relaxing with friends, but he still clearly played to win.

Gene had served as Elvis's man Friday since the first records had taken off. Elvis and Gene were very close and had a great relationship—sometimes it seemed that they spoke their own private language together. The funny thing about Gene was that, even though Elvis understood him, it was hard for anybody else to make sense of what he said. And early on, when Elvis started to get a sense of how precious his own time was and how many people wanted a piece of it, he put Gene in charge of access: If you wanted to talk business with Elvis, you had to talk to Gene first. And if you could handle Gene-time, then Elvis knew you might be worth some of his own time. Gene rose to the challenge of his position with Elvis by adopting a more businesslike appearance—he began to carry a briefcase. But the contents of the briefcase weren't often very business-oriented—it was more likely that Gene would be carrying around a doorknob, a pair of pliers, and a sandwich than any kind of Elvis-related paperwork.

I recognized some of the other pool sharks. One was a very big fellow named Lamar Fike, who'd met Elvis through George Klein. Lamar had spent time with Elvis out in Los Angeles while Elvis was working on *Jailhouse Rock*, and had quickly become a part of his inner circle.

Lamar's natural facial expression was a scowl, but he had a dark, dry sense of humor that became more evident as you got to know him. Gene and Lamar were characters, but the fact was that just about everyone around Elvis was a character of some sort. You had to do something a little out of the ordinary to get his attention and make it worth his while to let you into his world. Elvis was a very young guy suddenly caught up in the big business of the entertainment world, and the last thing he wanted was to spend time with business types. He was looking for people he could trust and people he could have fun with. I didn't want to disappoint him on either count.

"Who's the wise guy that put that goddamn music on?" It was Elvis, calling loudly from the pool room to the TV room. He kind of sounded like he was joking, but his voice had an angry edge to it—an edge I hadn't heard ever before. "All Shook Up" was playing on the built-in record player in the corner of the TV room.

"Get that crap off," yelled Elvis, coming through the doorway. There was no doubt that he was really angry. It was a Graceland lesson I wouldn't forget: Elvis didn't like hearing his records played at his own parties. He was proud of his work, but it was just that—his work. He lived with his music outside of the house—he didn't need to hear it while he was trying to relax in his own basement.

Both rooms went silent and somebody scrambled over to the machine to put on another record. Apologies were mumbled. Elvis didn't yell again, but his mood remained darkened. And I quickly learned that when Elvis was in a dark mood, it put a chill in the room that everyone felt. He went back to the pool room and stood staring down hard at the table. Voices in the TV room remained subdued, and there was no more of the easy laughter that had been tumbling around between conversations. Elvis looked like he was caught between the urge to chew somebody out and the desire to calm himself down. After a few minutes, he tossed his cue hard against the wall and headed toward the doorway.

I was feeling a little disappointed that even though I'd made it into his house, I hadn't spoken a word to him. But as he passed me on the way to the stairs he said, in a quiet, almost somber voice: "Come up again some time, Jerry."

That's all I needed. I'd be back.

. . .

I started turning up at the Graceland gates whenever I knew Elvis was in town. Sometimes I was waved through by Uncle Vester just the way I had been the first time. Other times word came down that Elvis wasn't seeing anybody. Sometimes there was a lot of waiting at the gate before word either way came down. At least one time I was waved up to the house (it was always "the house"—nobody in the know ever said "Graceland") and ended up spending forty minutes at the front door, in the winter cold, waiting for somebody to remember to let me in. I know there were probably a lot of fans across the country who would have given anything just to be able to stand right outside that Graceland gate to catch a glimpse of the owner, even if they never got in. (Many times the folks at the gate got more than a glimpse—if Elvis was in the right mood, he was happy to stop his car at the gate and roll down the window and sign a few autographs.)

For the people gathered at the gate, the big distinction was obviously between those who were allowed through and those who weren't. Occasionally a new face would get the OK to go up to the house, though those faces were almost always female—I think Vester kept Elvis apprised when there were pretty young ladies down the drive, and, when Elvis was having people up, he didn't mind including some new, unfamiliar girls. I had the chance to get to know some of these fan-friends pretty well—there was Sherry and Frances from Memphis and Darlene and Eileen who came all the way from Chicago (I even took Darlene out on a couple of dates).

It was extremely rare that an unfamiliar guy would make it through the gate—Elvis had been put down or actually attacked enough times by strangers that he wasn't going to take any chances in his own home. I'd also seen an offhand, stupid comment from some guy at the football games suck the fun out of those days for Elvis. It was already becoming hard for Elvis to find time to relax, and he wasn't going to take a chance that a guy he couldn't trust would spoil his fun.

Times up at the house in that period really did feel like a little stretch of paradise. Sometimes we hung around outside, at a beautiful gazebo area off the side of the house (where the trophy room is today). There was a bar out there that served up cold sodas, and a carefully stocked jukebox that played the hits of the day (I'm not sure who loaded the records—maybe someone from the jukebox company—but the problem was that the hits of the day always included a fair amount of Elvis tunes—"Teddy Bear," "Jailhouse Rock," and "Don't" were all number-one songs in late '57 and early '58, and the *Loving You* and *Christmas* albums were at the top of charts. We became very careful about what song buttons we pressed).

Graceland had, and still has, a look of luxury. But I can't stress enough the low-key, easy, good-natured feel of those early days there. There was cold Pepsi, play-to-win eight-ball games, a little dancing, a little teasing, and a lot of joking around. Of course, we didn't feel like we were being "wholesome"—this was life on the edge back then. We were staying up later than anybody else in town (in my case certainly later than anybody else at Catholic High) and hanging out at the "in" place in Memphis. Elvis was still considered dangerous, and we were all willing to have a little of that danger rub off on us.

The Graceland gatherings might be described as "parties," but they never had the feeling of events. It was just a natural get-together of the people Elvis considered friends, and I think in a lot of ways those days at Graceland were his way to catch up and enjoy the kind of good times and friendships that he hadn't had in high school, and that were extremely difficult to come by now that the world saw him as a star.

In that regard, I don't think my youth ever counted against me in getting through those Graceland gates. I was fifteen, and Billy Smith and Patsy Presley were right around that age, too, and I think Elvis liked having some young, innocent energy around him. Away from Graceland, he'd been catapulted into a grown-up world of burdens and responsibilities that he hadn't ever imagined when he first sang "That's All Right" in Sam Phillips's storefront studio, and I think that the chance to spend time with people like us who didn't want anything from him but his friendship was the real luxury that Graceland offered.

I fit in pretty well with that crowd, but I made one significant misstep at one of the first parties I went to. I was standing with George Klein ("GK") in the TV room when Elvis came over. He mentioned to George that he liked the way I played football. Swelling with pride, I said, "Well, my cousin is David Lawrence."

Cousin David had been a star football player at Humes High, and I thought dropping the name might work in my favor. Elvis looked away—his expression blank. Not angry, just blank. Then he nodded and walked across the room to talk to somebody else. George had a stricken look on his face. He leaned in toward me and whispered, "David Lawrence, and the guys like David Lawrence, were the ones who gave Elvis a real hard time back in high school."

I don't think I mentioned any branch of my family tree up there again. And it meant an awful lot when, later that day, Elvis waved me over with his cue stick to play a game of pool with him.

Elvis was an incredibly active, physical guy, and sometimes the fun had to move off the estate property. Elvis was a big amusement park fan, but his profile had become so high that just stepping into a place like that would lead to an unmanageable mob scene. So he'd gotten in the habit of renting out the nearby Memphis Fairgrounds after hours, hiring a park attendant or two to keep the place running, and bringing along groups of trusted companions for wild nights of rides on the Pippin—a huge, wooden-track roller coaster—collisions in the Dodgem cars, and unlimited Pronto Pups (basically an irresistible corn-dog-on-a-stick). The saying goes that youth is wasted on the young, but I think that even back then I had a sense that I was a part of something magical. Not only were we friends with Elvis, we were getting to live out a kind of fantasy life along with him—it was like having that carnival in *East of Eden* all to ourselves.

Occasionally that living fantasy could toss up some frights. The very first time I went to the Fairgrounds, I found myself lined up with the group to take a ride on the Pippin, which even in the fifties seemed old and rickety enough to add a little actual terror to every ride. Elvis got in the first car, and had Anita Wood snuggle up close to him. Patsy Presley, Gene and Billy Smith, and a few others got in the cars behind them. Those of us new to the Fairground experience stood on the platform as the ride began and the cars started their slow climb over the first hill. Then, just as the cars were out of sight, the ride roared into action. We could see the shadows of the cars zigging and zagging and shooting around turns, and making their seven-story climbs. We could hear continual yells of fear and excitement. But when the car finally came back around to the starting platform, we saw a heart-stopping sight: Anita Wood sat in the first car alone.

Elvis had been thrown from the Pippin. Some of the girls around me screamed. The rest of us stood frozen in shock. And then, just before the horror of what had happened really grabbed ahold of us, we heard a tremendous laugh coming up the stairs behind us. We turned to see Elvis, grinning like a happy, misbehaving little kid. It was a trick I saw him pull almost every time he brought new people to the Fairgrounds—he'd figured out a spot at the top of the first hill where he could jump out just before the ride took off at top speed. Then he'd scale down and sneak around back. And every time, he got a tremendous kick out of the looks of panic on everybody else's faces.

Other nights were spent out at the Rainbow Roller Rink, which Elvis would also rent for after-hour private get-togethers. The Rainbow was a pretty typical roller rink, with a mirrored ball over the center of the floor, mirrors up on the walls, flashing lights, and an organ providing a stream of skatable pop tunes. But again, there was something special and dream-come-true about having a place like that all to ourselves. And again, Elvis would let loose his daredevil streak and turn an activity that I'd always seen as kind of dull into something thrilling, if not outright scary. I can picture him in his leather jacket and rider's cap, organizing us into giant whips, which would spin around and pick up speed until the person at the end lost control and rocketed off. We might put on some knee pads and elbow pads—never helmets—and work up our own roller-derby games. There was a "last man standing" type of thing where you'd try to take somebody down by skating into them. People took some pretty good shots at Elvis—and he took hard shots at everybody else—but more than likely he'd be the one still on wheels at the end of the game (actually, I think he and Billy had some secret agreement worked out—more than once I saw somebody just about to take Elvis down, when little Billy would come zooming out of nowhere and knock the threat right down on its ass).

This was still good clean fun—I don't remember anybody drinking anything stronger than root beer. But it was fun that left you sore the next morning. Over the years the Rainbow was home to quite a few contusions, several chipped teeth, and even a couple of concussions.

When the weather was nice enough through the fall and winter of '57 into '58, we'd still get a football game together. Though now we moved on from Guthrie Park to the lighted field at Whitehaven High

School that Elvis rented for us to play night games. I can't say that Elvis and I actually got closer during these times, but I did start to feel that I was accepted, that he actually liked having me around. There was a smile he'd throw my way when I was the one on my ass at the Rainbow—or a way he'd bark out "Jerry, c'mere," to show me something at the Fairgrounds—that just felt friendly and familiar. At the Fairgrounds and the rink and the football games I started to get a sense of the incredible energy and love of life he had. He could get crazy, silly, and unpredictable, too—an amazing blend of an amiable cockiness and an openhearted sensitivity. The cockiness was clearly backed up by talent, but the sensitivity was the real surprise, and if you got to see even the slightest bit of it, you felt further drawn to the guy.

Some of those late nights at the Fairgrounds or the Rainbow seemed to go on forever, but actually that period of easy good times shot by very quickly. I got used to going a month or two or three without seeing Elvis as he kept up his frenetic work schedule (in addition to his film and recording work, there were concert tours of the West Coast and Hawaii). At the beginning of 1958, word quickly spread that Graceland would be without its host for a much longer period: Elvis had been drafted.

Elvis was not thrilled about becoming a GI, and yet, whatever strings he might have been able to pull back then, he wasn't going to refuse to go. He felt he was no different from anybody else in that regard. The army did allow Elvis a few months' deferment so that he could finish making *King Creole* (taking over a lead role that had first been developed for the late James Dean). Then, without much fanfare, Elvis shipped off to basic training in Texas.

Did the government target Elvis specifically to try to shut down rock and roll? We won't ever know for sure. This much is certain: From 1954 to 1958, Elvis wasn't making speeches, but he was making a statement. And following his lead, young people were starting to have a voice—a voice with a melody and a rhythm to it—and that was heard as a powerful and frightening threat to the status quo. I know that when Elvis got his military haircut and headed off to boot camp, a lot of parents in Memphis and the rest of the country heaved a sigh of relief and hoped that maybe now that boy and his music would just fade away.

. . .

There were significant changes in Elvis's life and in my life while he was off in the army. For him, the biggest change was a tragic one—his mother, Gladys, died of liver failure while he was in basic training (he was somewhat begrudgingly allowed time off to be with her in her final days). I never had the chance to meet Mrs. Presley, but it had always been clear just how much she meant to Elvis.

For me, the changes were both highly positive and a little surprising. Suddenly, I wasn't just keeping up academically—I was excelling. And now, I was a good enough football player to be a varsity starter and co-captain of the team, with a shot at a college scholarship. Football had brought me and Elvis together in the first place, and I think it was the combination of success on the field and my friendship with Elvis that thoroughly transformed me from that lost little Tonto in Mamaw's apple tree to a guy popular enough to be elected class president in my freshman, sophomore, and junior years, and vice president in my senior year.

The friendship with Elvis gave me confidence, but it wasn't something I played on for popularity. Just as I'd held tight to my first Elvis-Guthrie Park experiences, I kept my Elvis association very quiet all through high school. I think all of us who had been accepted into the inner circles around Elvis considered it a real honor, and all of us understood that what went on at Graceland or at the other outings wasn't something you used to boost your own status away from the house. We realized that the time we spent with Elvis was a good portion of the only private time he ever got, and we all felt a stake in protecting that privacy for him. I would never have considered saying to any classmates, "Oh, yeah—I was up at Graceland last night . . ." and I really don't think most of them ever realized that I was one of the lucky few who was riding the Pippin at two in the morning with Elvis Presley.

Life was very different with Elvis away in the army. Even though I was becoming a fairly big man on the Catholic High campus, I missed hanging out at Graceland, and the football field, and the Rainbow. I missed hanging out with Elvis and the guys. I went and saw *King Creole* a half dozen times and was again impressed with Elvis's talents, but having him twenty feet tall on a movie screen was just never as satisfying as getting hit by his Dodgem car at the Fairgrounds.

I also spent a lot of time listening to Elvis's records. I'd always enjoyed his music for the way it made me feel. But now I started listening harder to the feelings that Elvis had been putting into his songs. I went back again and again to that great first album, with his name in pink and green letters on the black-and-white cover, and really listened to what Elvis was doing. I'd always been grabbed hardest by Elvis's rockers, but now I was caught in the spell of some of the quieter tunes: "I'll Never Let You Go (Little Darlin')" and "One-Sided Love Affair." I'd recognized the range and the power of Elvis's voice on "I Was the One," but now I really thought about the feelings that had to be inside Elvis in order for him to use his voice the way he did. I listened countless times to his eerie cover of "Blue Moon," thinking that nobody could sing that song that way unless they truly knew what loneliness felt like. I figured that, somewhere along the line, he too must have been dumped by a young love like Loretta Cuccia.

True romance came my way during senior year. "One-Sided Love Affair" had pretty much summed up my love life until then, and I'd gotten used to falling for girls who were somehow unattainable. But at a local dance my senior year I spotted a beautiful girl with auburn hair who was the wildest dancer out on the dance floor. I summoned my newfound confidence and walked up and introduced myself. Instead of a brush-off, I got an invitation to dance along. Her name was Carol Cook, she went to Central High, and she lived out in the well-to-do neighborhoods of East Memphis. She was also Jewish, and there were probably a good number of my Catholic High classmates who would have recoiled at that religious difference. But this was a case where my mixed-up, semirootless childhood came in handy: It never occurred to me to let somebody else's prejudice get in the way of my dancing with a pretty girl.

The night wasn't all budding romance. There was a guy from Central High who felt he had a stronger claim to be Carol's dance partner, and the situation could not be resolved without some punches being thrown. The intruder ended up with a bloody nose, and I ended up with his blood all over my white dress shirt. I also ended up with Carol Cook, who took me back to her house and tenderly attempted to clean me up. She was obviously impressed with my heroic stand on the dance floor, and the more she dabbed at my shirt, the more hooked I felt. Suddenly that Elvis song "I'll Never Let You Go (Little Darlin')" was making sense to me in a whole new way.

. . .

It felt both strange and familiar to be standing at those Graceland gates again on a chilly March evening in 1960. Strange in that I wasn't the same little kid anymore, and I was sure Elvis had been through some changes of his own. But familiar in that I was just as excited to get through those gates as I'd ever been. After two years overseas, Elvis was home.

It felt great to walk through that front door again—almost as if I were the one coming home. I immediately encountered a cluster of people off to the right in the living room. There were plenty of familiar faces around, and I met each smile with a smile, but my eyes went to the figure standing at the end of the room in a kind of fighting stance: Elvis, looking serious and formidable in a white karate *gi* and a black belt. He was in the process of putting on a martial-arts demonstration. I'd soon learn that karate was a new passion that he had developed over in Germany. He'd met a German karate expert who'd given him intensive personal training in the physical and spiritual aspects of the discipline. Karate was still something entirely exotic and odd to most of us in Memphis, but Elvis had become a fiercely devoted student.

Big Lamar Fike and a somewhat fidgety Gene Smith were standing a few paces in front of Elvis, and both were holding up a cushion from the white living-room sofa. He checked their grips on the cushions, and positioned their hands so that the cushions were right in front of their faces. He stepped back and got into a sort of fighting crouch, with his arms out and his hands extended in front of him. Some of the spectators were still smiling, but Elvis stayed intently focused.

He took two quick steps forward, shouted something, and leapt into the air, simultaneously kicking a foot into each cushion. The kicks were full force, but he had enough control to make contact with the cushions without hurting the faces behind them. That distinctively loose-limbed manner of his that turned up on the football field disappeared—his karate moves were executed precisely and emphatically. There was applause, and Elvis, still looking intense and focused, nodded our way. He spotted me.

"Jerry, c'mere," he said, motioning me over. "Help me with something."

That little moment felt huge. There was no slap on the back. No "Hello" or "How you been?" Just a "Jerry, c'mere." And with one gesture to join him on the snow-white carpet of the Graceland living room, I was right back in.

He squared me off opposite him and began to slowly demonstrate how his kicks and punches would work against an opponent. He coached me a little on how to defend against a move, then would show a countermove that would cut through the defense. I got the hang of a couple of blocking moves and we gradually picked up speed and got closer to full-force strikes. We were going at it pretty good, and I started to feel proud that I was keeping up, blocking his punches and counterpunches. I was learning fast, but not quite fast enough—my wrestler's stance left me vulnerable to kick attacks, and Elvis faked a punch, spun, and then landed his leather boot in my groin, just barely making contact with my most delicate region. Thank God he'd studied hard enough to have the control he had, because if he'd kicked any harder I would have been writhing on the floor, hitting soprano notes. And as I stepped back to join the small living-room crowd, I realized that, coming from Elvis, a kick in the groin was a lot more personal and heartfelt than a slap on the back.

Almost as soon as Elvis got back to Memphis, he resumed the hectic pace of his film career (*GI Blues* was up first) and began traveling back and forth to Los Angeles. When he was in town, he still had people up to Graceland, but the get-togethers didn't have the easy spirit of pre-army times. I'm sure part of this was due to the fact that Elvis's mother was gone, and it just wasn't easy for him to have the same carefree feeling around the house. But there was a different kind of shift in the atmosphere, too. There was still the basic excitement of being at Elvis's house, but there was a new intensity, too. Instead of just leading a pool game, Elvis might read to us from some of the books he'd read about karate, impressing upon us the fact that it was a mental and spiritual pursuit as well as a system of self-defense. And instead of the sounds of a jukebox, it became more common to hear the sounds of practice boards snapping with the impact of karate kicks and punches. It almost felt like the discipline of Elvis's army training was carrying over to Graceland.

But there were still wild nights at the Fairgrounds or the Rainbow and a lot of movie nights at the Memphian, and on those nights I got familiar with a few new faces that had been welcomed into the circle.

There was one fellow from Chicago named Joe Esposito, a close army buddy whom Elvis had convinced to come back with him to Memphis. And there were some new Memphis guys—Richard Davis and Jimmy Kingsley and Ray "Chief" Sitton. And Red West's cousin Sonny West had become a part of things, too. Some of these guys traveled with Elvis when he made his trips to L.A., and most had developed a mix of friendship and working relationship with Elvis. When Elvis took these guys to Las Vegas for a weekend break during the making of *GI Blues*, the group strutted around town in dark suits and dark shades, looking like Graceland's answer to the Rat Pack. The local press dubbed Elvis's entourage "The Memphis Mafia." The name stuck. As far as I could tell, there weren't any official jobs or duties for the Memphis Mafia guys, they just knew what had to be taken care of, though it did become clear pretty quickly that Joe Esposito was going to be in the role of right-hand man.

There was one more new face that actually did manage to bring back some moments of carefree fun to Graceland—Scatter, a pet chimpanzee that Elvis had brought into the house. Scatter lived in style in an air-conditioned, converted laundry room downstairs at Graceland, and he and Elvis would play around together like they were best buddies. But what I remember most about Scatter is his forward manner with women. When there were mixed parties at Graceland now, most of us guys were on our best behavior. But Scatter thought nothing of darting around the room and looking up girls' skirts.

Surrounded by old and new friends, Elvis could still be the same exciting, mischievous, unpredictable, and fun-loving (though moody) guy to hang around with. But there was something different about Elvis, too. He wasn't so much a young rebel anymore, but very much a man. He was still only twenty-five, but you could now sense a maturity quite a bit beyond his years. And that maturity translated into the way he presented himself as a performer. When he came back the first thing he did was the Frank Sinatra TV show, and watching Elvis come out in a tux and sing with Sinatra, you couldn't help but notice that this wasn't quite the same guy who had gotten the pundits and preachers upset by shaking his hips on Ed Sullivan's show.

Over the course of his first year back, attitudes toward him seemed to shift as well. Even the diehard Elvis detractors seemed to accept the fact that this supposedly antisocial force had gone into the army without a complaint and happily served his country (maybe "proudly" is a better word than "happily"—I happen to know that Elvis hated being away, and would have much preferred two years of performing onstage to two years of sitting in a jeep). I witnessed the changes in Elvis and his fans firsthand at a big charity show he did in Memphis at the good old Ellis auditorium in early 1961—his first big post-army concert. This show didn't have the feel of any gathering of underground rock and rollers or squealing teenyboppers. This was a packed house of respectable, middle-America Memphians. In fact, the Tennessee governor and Memphis mayor had declared Saturday "Elvis Presley Day"—a pretty big endorsement for a guy who had once been considered the worst possible influence on America's youth.

The show was great and Elvis was still a phenomenal talent to watch in action, but what I remember most from that show is the moment he first walked out on stage. This was a very different walk from the one I'd seen on the Dorsey Brothers' TV show. There was a little less slouch and a little more strut. Before the army, Elvis was the loose, shoulder-rolling James Dean kind of guy. Now, he took the stage more like John Wayne.

By the end of high school, I'd felt ready and eager to move toward some of my own goals. While I always enjoyed the time I got to spend around Elvis, it also seemed pretty obvious to me that he was going to keep living his amazing life on his own terms, and I had to think about living a life of my own.

Kids from North Memphis weren't naturally expected to go to college, but my daddy—a guy who'd never gotten past the eighth grade—was very encouraging about my getting a higher education. And though my brother and I didn't always have the easiest relationship, Billy Ray also gave me a push and made sure I got out applications on time and pursued football scholarships through the proper channels. (To be honest, I think Billy Ray was more than a little surprised at how well Little Brother had ended up doing in high school, and didn't want to see him go from class president and All-Memphis wide receiver to gas-pumping grease monkey at the Texaco station on Breedlove.)

With Billy Ray's help, I managed to line up a couple of scholarships

to play ball at either Southwestern University or Arkansas State College, and, after a bit of a false start at Southwestern, I ended up at the
AS campus in Jonesboro, Arkansas—a dry little college town about seventy miles outside of Memphis. I was redshirted my first year and had a
good season working out with the team as a wide receiver, really learning the subtleties of the game from my sharp-eyed backfield coach,
Larry Lacewell. When the football season was over, I headed back to
Memphis just about every weekend, but I spent very little time at
home—I was either hanging out with Elvis if he was around, or spending time at Carol Cook's house (she and I hadn't done much more than
dance, hold hands, and neck a bit, but we considered ours to be a very
serious relationship). Though Memphis was only seventy miles away,
the trip in my '49 Dodge sometimes took most of a day—I had to stop
four or five times to add oil to the engine, and I started driving around
with a case of oil in the trunk at all times.

Early on in my freshman year, I began to aim toward a major in history and a minor in education, and I did as well in the college classes as
I had done toward the end of high school. Not being around on the
weekends, I didn't make too many close friends on campus, but through
football I did strike up a friendship with a guy from Philadelphia named
Rick Husky. Rick was a big sports fan and was always around at football
practices, which is where we met. We hit it off pretty quickly, and I soon
discovered that Rick was a big music fan, too. On the weekends that I
didn't go back to Memphis, Rick and I would go out searching for some
cool music to listen to (I can distinctly remember driving to Truman,
Arkansas, to see Charlie Rich play in a club so small and informal that
Charlie was using a Coca-Cola crate for a piano bench). Rick also happened to be president of the Tau Kappa Epsilon fraternity on campus,
and before long he had me pledged into the frat as his "little brother." A
lot of the stuff that went on at the frat house struck me as pretty silly—
after years of hanging out with Elvis, scavenger hunts and chug-a-lugs
didn't seem all that exciting. But Rick's room was this big dark space at
the back of the house that he had decorated with large, colorful neon
bar signs for Schlitz and Pabst Blue Ribbon beer. When those neon
lights were the only light in the room, and the right record was on in
there, it felt a little more like what I had been used to in the TV room at
Graceland.

As it turned out, in becoming Rick's brother I was becoming Elvis's brother, too. At the beginning of the school year, Rick had sent a letter to Elvis asking him to become an honorary brother in TKE. To everyone's surprise, Elvis accepted (I would come to learn that one of Elvis's great regrets was his lack of higher education, and he was sincerely touched by the frat's offer). Elvis even invited Rick and some TKE brothers to Graceland so that he could receive a ceremonial plaque from them. Later on we three brothers—Rick, Elvis, and I—would spend a lot more time together in Los Angeles.

My football dreams ended in my sophomore year, when, after running too many buttonhook patterns and taking too many direct hits from oversize linebackers, my back started to give out. After having to crawl off the field during one practice and barely making it to the locker room, I realized I just wasn't going to make it through the season. The trouble was, if I wasn't going to play ball, the school wanted to cut my scholarship in half. That didn't strike me as fair—I'd played as hard as I could and had been willing to offer up my spine in the name of school spirit. So I quit Arkansas State, moved back to Memphis, transferred my units to Memphis State, and got a job at the Midtown Sears (my Aunt Dot worked there, and I think she put in the good word for me). I'd get my education, stay closer to Carol Cook, and be able to hang out more with Elvis and the guys.

I was increasingly convinced that Carol Cook and I had a future together. But a couple of times it seemed like having both Elvis and Carol in my life was going to be a problem.

By 1962, Elvis was having some larger parties up at Graceland again, and I was very happy to show up at one with Carol on my arm. I figured that bringing a sweet, smart, beautiful girl up to the house was a good move. This was one of the gazebo nights, when people were hanging outside and playing a lot of music. Carol thought the place and the people were just as special as I did, and that made me love her even more. We were both in a great mood and started dancing together.

Carol was a wild dancer, and I don't think there was a guy there who didn't notice the way this lovely girl was moving to the music. And as her proud date, I'm sure I was probably looking very pleased with myself. Around the dance floor we saw nothing but smiles shining out at us. What we didn't see was Elvis. Elvis was a star, but he was a flesh-and-blood male who had a jealous streak and suffered bouts of insecurity just like any other guy. This was his party, and if there was going to be a girl there that was going to get the attention, it had better be Elvis's girl. Not Jerry Schilling's. The sight of my knockout date as the center of attention at his party—that didn't make Elvis happy.

When Carol and I took a break and I noticed that Elvis wasn't around, I approached Alan Fortas. He told me Elvis was inside the house, and when I asked if I could bring Carol in to say hello, Alan shook his head.

"I don't think that's a good idea, Jerry."

"Why not?"

"Well, there was something he said before he left."

"What, Alan?"

"Uh—he said, 'Who the hell does Jerry Schilling think he is, bringing that chick up here?' "

Suddenly I didn't feel like dancing much anymore. I didn't see Elvis the rest of the night, and for a tense week or so I didn't call the house or show up at the Graceland gates again. Then I got a call from Alan. Elvis wanted to get a football game together, and he wanted me to be there. I was still in. Though apparently Elvis preferred to see me in cleats rather than dancing shoes.

There was one other interesting Elvis/Carol Cook incident when we were invited as a couple to Elvis's private New Year's Eve party at the end of 1962, to be held at the Manhattan Club, a small, out-of-the-way nightspot down on Highway 51 near Graceland. Elvis wanted some great music for everybody to enjoy, so he lined up Carla Thomas (Rufus's daughter), who'd had a big hit with "Gee Whiz (Look At His Eyes)." Also on the bill was Sir Isaac and the Doo-dads, led by a muscular keyboard player named Isaac Hayes.

All the familiar faces were there, including Elvis's serious new love interest, a striking young girl named Priscilla Beaulieu.

Priscilla was the daughter of an Air Force officer, and Elvis had met her when he was stationed over in Germany. They'd stayed in touch over the next couple of years, and that summer of 1962 Elvis had flown her from Germany for a two-week visit in Los Angeles, where he'd just finished filming *Girls! Girls! Girls!* Back in Memphis, Elvis hadn't talked much about Priscilla to us guys, but his feelings about her must have been pretty clear to some—by the end of the summer, Anita Wood, who'd been living at Graceland, moved out and announced to the local press that she and Elvis had broken up.

Now, Priscilla had come to Memphis for the first time, and she'd been a presence at some of the usual gatherings in the week around Christmas. She'd watched us knock each other off our skates at the Rainbow, and she was right there beside Elvis when we got together for a private movie screening at the Memphian or Malco theaters. She was only sixteen, but there was a seriousness about her that made her seem older. Watching the way Elvis treated her, it was clear that he was in love, and one of the great images I have of that night is the sight of Elvis and Priscilla dancing—it was one of the few times I ever saw Elvis dance when not on a stage.

But the image that had the more powerful effect on me that night was the sight of Carol dancing—with other guys. Now it was my turn to be jealous. And my jealous streak, helped along by one of my first-ever nights of excessive alcohol consumption, got the better of me. Carol and I had a blowout argument, and I got worked up enough that I stormed to the back of the club and hit one of the side walls with all the charging linebacker force I could muster. Then I went home to my daddy's house and celebrated the New Year by suffering through my first-ever hangover.

The phone rang the evening of New Year's Day. I was hoping it might be Carol Cook begging forgiveness. Instead, it was Alan Fortas.

"Hey, Jerry, how you doing?"

"OK. Why?"

"I just wanted to let you know—that wall you hit last night . . . ?"

"Oh, yeah. Sorry about that. I lost control of myself. Why?"

"Well, it's just that there's a liquor store on the other side of that wall. When you hit it, a whole shelf of bottles fell over. Elvis paid for the lost liquor, but he wanted me to check up on you."

I felt young and stupid and about as embarrassed as I'd ever been. But as I fought my way through the fog of that hangover, I was comforted by one thought: Who else but a real friend would cover for you when you broke a wall's worth of liquor bottles?

. . .

I was making money for tuition working in the order-filling department at Sears, a job in which I prowled about the top floors of the store, receiving customers' order slips from the floors below through a system of pneumatic tubes. Once the order was fired up to me, I ran around to find the requested item, which I would then slide down to the appropriate department by way of a system of chutes (for a low-tech system it was pretty darned cool). There was one other guy manning the tubes, chutes, and inventory with me—a very interesting fellow named George Gill. George was a small, wiry, highly intense guy with a head of bright red hair.

Maybe having gotten used to all the characters around Elvis, I approached George with more of an open mind than he probably expected from an ex-jock, and we became fast friends. George was using his Sears paychecks to support a budding career as an artist and painter, and hearing the way he talked about painting got me excited about it, too. When George got word that he was actually going to have some of his work shown at a gallery up in New York City, he asked me to take a road trip up there with him. I said yes.

It wasn't just George and art that made up my mind, though. Carol and I had made up after the New Year's Eve incident and had gotten serious enough again to start talking about getting married. Her parents, who had always been welcoming and loving toward me, drew the line there. The combination of my not being Jewish and my working-class background made me less than ideal son-in-law material. Carol was shipped up to New Rochelle, New York, to live with an older sister, whose husband had a seat on the New York Stock Exchange.

With visions of the big city in my head, Carol in my heart, George at my side, and a couple of hundred dollars in my pocket, I boarded a New York–bound train in early 1964. The dollars didn't last long—when we got to the D.C. station and had a couple of hours before our transfer, I fell asleep on a bench and was promptly pickpocketed. But George and I did make it up there, and I consider the six months I spent in New York—the time when I was technically a "college dropout"—to be one of the most important periods of my education.

George and I got a just barely livable one-room apartment on West 75th Street, and I got a job whistling for cabs as a doorman at the Carlyle

Hotel and, later, as a reservations agent for Eastern Airlines. Just about every spare dollar I earned was spent on New York's public transportation system—specifically, the trains to New Rochelle. Carol's sister, Connie, was not supposed to find out that I had followed Carol up north, so protocol was that I'd take the train up, walk to Connie's house, sneak around back, crawl through a basement window, and wait for Carol to sneak down to join me. We'd whisper and neck a bit, until it was time for me to crawl out the window again and get back down to the city in time for work. More than once while I sat in that New Rochelle basement, Carol went out with some other guy—a decoy date—to keep her sister from suspecting anything. (The fact that this plan made perfect sense to me at the time tells you how head over heels I was for this girl.)

A couple of times, Carol and I did manage to get out on the city together, and I was always impressed with her adventurous streak. One night, she insisted that we check out a Harlem nightclub she'd heard about called Smalls Paradise. We got uptown and found the place, and maybe the door staff was a little surprised to see a young white couple up there, but we were welcomed right in. The place had an incredible vibe to it—a swinging, upscale hangout for what looked like the wealthiest and most beautiful of NYC's black elite. This wasn't like any Beale Street joint I'd been around—more like a black version of the nightclub at the top of the Peabody Hotel. More Quincy Jones than Rufus Thomas.

I guess we didn't know enough to feel as out of place as we might have—we settled into a booth and got comfortable pretty quickly. We weren't drinking anything stronger than sodas, and when Carol asked for some extra cherries, she was presented with a beautiful dish of them that looked like something from a floral shop. She was surprised and excited to spot some models she recognized from the cover of *Ebony* magazine. I was surprised to hear that Carol read *Ebony*, but, then again, one of things that I loved about her was that I was always learning or experiencing something new when I was with her.

We had a few great outings like that, and some nice times in the New Rochelle basement, but eventually, despite all our careful sneaking around, our forbidden love affair was discovered. Carol was immediately sent back to Memphis, and I stayed down on 75th Street. At first I was consumed with heartache, but without any more commuter trains to catch, I really started to take in the city around me and open myself up to its pleasures: concerts at Carnegie Hall, museums full of the works I'd seen in my freshman art class books, old-style steakhouses, and neighborhood coffee shops. Just walking the streets and riding the subway, I began to feel more alive, more present, and I dedicated myself to exploring what the city had to offer. I toured the UN building, sat in Central Park reading James Baldwin novels, and hung out in Washington Square Park, marveling at the beautiful children of the mixed-race couples strolling by. I picked up discount theater tickets to catch Richard Burton's performance as Hamlet. My spirits soared in Manhattan— around me I saw opportunities for adventure and new ways to expand my perspective.

The move to New York was a permanent one for George Gill, and I think it might have been for me except for one factor that I couldn't quite dismiss: phone calls from Carol Cook. It took only a few of them, with her getting teary and both of us professing our love all over again, before New York—for all its wonders—just didn't feel right.

Being in love wasn't quite the thrill it had started out as—I didn't want to climb through any more basement windows. But great theater and affordable steak were no match for a beautiful girl crying over a long-distance connection. Pretty soon I had a ticket back to Memphis.

4

. . .

WELCOME TO MY WORLD

In the fall of 1964, the Beatles were revolutionizing rock and roll and starring in their own film, *A Hard Day's Night*. The American military had begun to drop bombs on some place called Vietnam. Cassius Clay had renamed himself Muhammad Ali and was riding high as the new heavyweight boxing champ. The first Ford Mustangs were burning rubber on roads all over the United States, and *Dr. Strangelove* was teaching moviegoers how to love the bomb and have a good laugh at the very idea of nuclear annihilation. Elvis was now a full-time movie star, and he had just had one of his biggest hits with *Viva Las Vegas*.

Back home in Memphis, I was just about ready to embark on a future that seemed clear, straight, and utterly respectable. In between stints of shift work at a trucking company, a cotton gin, a chemical plant, and the new airport, I had taken as many classes as I could at Memphis State, and was now just a semester of student-teaching away from launching myself into adult life as a qualified history teacher, potential football coach, and generally upstanding citizen. It was a good, solid plan for a good, solid future. And it was about to be tossed right out the window.

When I got back to Memphis after my New York adventure, I moved into my daddy's house—he now had a place in Frazier, a part of town north of North Memphis. Because of my Eastern Airlines experience up north, it was easy to score a job with Eastern as a reservation agent at the brand-new Memphis International Airport. On one of my first days on the job there, I served up a ticket to George Klein, who was heading to L.A. to meet up with Elvis on the set of his next film, *Girl Happy*. I distinctly remember saying to GK, "Man, you've got the life. I wish I was going with you."

Carol Cook and I saw a bit of each other, but things never really got back on track. Her calls had tipped the scales in my decision to come back to Memphis, but I'd grown a little tired of being the love-struck guy trailing after the girl—even a girl as exciting and attractive as Carol. I think we both began to realize that as much as we'd tried to convince ourselves that we were soul mates, we'd reached the end of our relationship.

I started taking regular classes at the university and putting in graveyard shifts loading trucks. I also tried to find some of the excite-ment (and decent coffee) that I had experienced in New York, and I began to spend a fair amount of time at a brand-new combination coffeehouse/art gallery in midtown called the Bitter Lemon. The place was owned and managed by a wild-eyed, shaggy-haired artist named John McIntire, who reigned as the central figure of bohemian life in Memphis. I liked going to the Bitter Lemon, and while I don't think there was ever much chance that I was going to go entirely beatnik, I was thrilled to learn that there was a vibrant, underground culture blos-soming in my hometown. The place was a stronghold of the budding folk scene, and I started to hear a new kind of music there from artists such as Odetta; Peter, Paul, and Mary; Pete Seeger; and Phil Ochs. This was stuff in which the beat didn't matter as much as the message of up-lift, hope, and togetherness. Hearing some of those aching voices and strummed guitars, I realized that some of the simplest music could be the most honest, and the most powerful.

Between classes, coffee, and work shifts, my only long stretches of free time were either late night or late-late night. Elvis hours. I'd check in with Alan Fortas or GK periodically, and when everybody was back in town there might be get-togethers at the house. There were still some Fairgrounds and Rainbow nights, but if Elvis wasn't having peo-ple up at the house, it was more than likely he'd be at the Memphian Theater.

One of Elvis's earliest supporters from the Memphis business com-munity was a man named Mr. Schaeffer, who owned the Memphian and ran the Mid-South Film Exchange (out of that Southern-bred respect for elders, even Elvis always called him "Mr. Schaeffer"). The 35 mm film prints for all the theaters in the Mid-Southern states came through that exchange, and Mr. Schaeffer was always happy to lend any of them out to Elvis. He'd make sure that Elvis got the weekly catalogue of everything that was coming through, and he even let Elvis have his own keys to the Exchange, which was actually a huge warehouse in downtown Memphis.

I'd been at the Memphian when Elvis had screened some of his own films, and I used to love watching him watch himself. Elvis, Red, Alan and the rest of the guys would talk right through the picture, as if they were all sitting in a living room. The interesting thing was that they wouldn't talk about the story of the film, but would instead point out strange little details of the set or the face of somebody in the background: "Hey, there's what's-his-face the stuntman!" or "Hey, there's that girl Red was after!" They'd all been together through the making of the film, and what I saw as a piece of entertainment, they saw as a strange kind of home movie. I thought that if I could ever be a part of those kinds of conversations, I would have made it to the innermost circle.

On a typical movie night, Elvis would send a couple of his guys with the keys to the Exchange, and they'd go in, call him up, and read titles off the giant film cans that were stacked up there in rows and rows. Elvis would look up the titles in the catalogue, check the casts and plot summaries, and would eventually pick five or six films he wanted the guys to bring to the Memphian (he wouldn't watch that many in a night, but if something didn't grab him, he'd switch reels and start another). He'd watch anything and everything, as long as it was quality work. He had a great and broad curiosity about films, and could be just as happy with a crazy comedy as a heavyweight drama. By 1964, Elvis was already frustrated with the quality of his own films, and when I think back on some of the choices Elvis made for those Memphian nights, it's almost heartbreaking to think how sophisticated his tastes were. He was completely taken with the artistry of *Lawrence of Arabia*, and was moved by *To Kill a Mockingbird*. He really loved Rod Steiger's powerful and wrenching performance in *The Pawnbroker*, and was also impressed with that film's cutting-edge jazz score by Quincy Jones.

There was one stretch during which Elvis had us watch *Dr. Strangelove* at least a dozen times. Me and the boys were probably not the most astute judges of political satire, but, hearing Elvis bust up laughing, we'd start to see the film through his eyes and end up laughing just as hard. Even better on some of those nights was the impromptu after-show that Elvis would put on. He knew how to use that remarkable voice of his not just as a singer but as an expert mimic, and he'd do drop-dead impersonations of every part in the film—George C. Scott's General Buck Turgidson, Sterling Hayden's General Jack D. Ripper, and of course Peter Sellers's good Dr. Strangelove (Elvis was a huge Peter Sellers fan). He had every word and mannerism down, and it was always amazing to watch him. As a matter of fact, he did a masterful impression of Dr. Strangelove being choked by his own misbehaving prosthetic hand, an impression that he startled us with countless times over the years.

I remember that Elvis used to impress me with what seemed like a bit of movie-insider magic. We'd be sitting there watching a film and he'd lean back and whisper, "Reel change, Jerry." Sure enough, seconds later, there'd be a little jump in a scene or that telltale shift of sound and color that marked a reel change. I thought maybe from his experiences in Hollywood he'd somehow become an expert at timing the projectionists, until one night he laughingly explained that there was a little blip in the corner of the screen that was a signal to the projectionist. I started seeing those blips on every film I watched in the theater. And even though Elvis had let me in on his secret, every so often he'd lean back and say, in an ultraserious voice, "Reel change, Jerry."

On a late September night in that fall of '64, I was finishing up work at the trucking company, forklifting pallets of cargo onto tractor-trailers. By punch-out time, I was dead tired, but I got a jolt of energy as I drove past the Memphian. The theater was on my route to and from work, and since Elvis had been out of town for a couple of months, I'd gotten used to driving past the theater's empty parking lot late at night. But now the lot had some cars in it—chief among them Elvis's newest big, dark Cadillac.

I parked and went around to knock on the front glass. Somebody came and let me in and when I walked into the theater it looked like a movie had just ended. Elvis was down by one of the side entrances near the screen, talking to a group of people and apparently signing autographs for a friend of a friend of somebody. He looked as tired as I was feeling, so I figured I'd just slip back out, get my sleep, and try to hook up with him the next day. As I turned to go, I just about bumped into Richard Davis, one of the guys who had started hanging around with the Memphis crowd after Elvis got out of the army, and who was now working for Elvis.

"Hey, Jerry," said Richard. "I've got to take the films back to the exchange. You want to take the ride with me to take them back, and we can go out and get some breakfast?"

I hadn't even had time to change out of my dirty work clothes. "I'd like to, Richard, but I'm a mess. Let's do it tomorrow."

"Can't do it tomorrow, Jerry," said Richard.

"Why not?"

"We're going to California tomorrow."

Richard wasn't Elvis, but he was very likable, fun to be around, and a good guy to have as a friend. You never saw Elvis standing at the gates of Graceland, or at the entrance to the Memphian, or the turnstiles to the Fairgrounds—it was guys like Richard who checked with Elvis about who got in and who didn't, just like the guys guarding the velvet rope in front of some VIP nightclub. Suddenly I wasn't so tired anymore.

"OK," I told Richard. "Let's get some breakfast."

We had just finished getting the films back on the right shelves at the Exchange, when the phone rang in the office over there. Richard answered. He talked a moment, then hung up and turned to me. "Elvis just called and told me he couldn't find Jerry Schilling. I told him you were here, and he said he wanted me to ask you if you'd come to the house."

I liked hearing that Elvis himself had made a call to track me down. Of course I'd come to the house.

I'd been to Graceland so many times before that morning, but I distinctly remember driving through those grand gates and thinking that this was the first time I'd actually been personally summoned there. I quickly learned, though, that even an urgent summoning didn't mean there'd be an immediate meeting—I waited in the living room for a long, long time, watching the dawn start to break outside and wondering if perhaps Elvis had forgotten about calling for me.

Richard had wandered off to tend to the cars and head off to bed, and I was just beginning to think that maybe I should head back home, when Elvis and his father, Vernon, appeared at the top of the stairs and started slowly descending a step at a time, arm-in-arm. Elvis was twenty-nine years old at the time, and I knew him as a guy in absolute peak physical shape, so what I saw when I looked closely at him shocked me—he had an oxygen mask over his face and was taking deep hits from a small tank that trailed behind him. He seemed a little bit out of it—not just tired from a long night out but truly, deeply exhausted—and it was the first time I'd ever seen him looking less than perfect, a sign of just how early there was trouble stemming from Elvis-the-man's attempts to live up to the demands of Elvis, the superstar.

When Elvis saw me from the stairs, and took in the surprised expression on my face, he casually tugged the mask off, pocketed it, and said, "You know, Jerry—this California smog will get to you." As stunned as I was to see him looking worn-down, I was equally surprised to see how he could snap himself out of it—how he could physically will the sparkle back into his eyes even when he didn't feel it inside.

He asked me to wait for him out on the front porch. So I stepped back outside and sat in one of the wrought-iron chairs there. I looked out at the gentle, sloping hill of the property and watched the first few smudges of sunshine break through the gray sky of a Memphis morning. A few minutes later, Elvis came out the front door—now looking perfectly put together—and took a seat next to me. He ran a hand through his hair and kind of squinted at the sky over Graceland. "Might be a nice day coming."

"Yeah. Might be, Elvis." I knew he didn't call me here to talk about the weather.

He looked a little lost in his thoughts for a moment. Then he leaned in, and focused on me with a look that was about as serious as any I'd ever seen on him.

"Jerry—I need you to come work for me."

I was dumbfounded for a moment. Ever since I was a scrawny, lonely twelve-year-old kid, this guy had been the epitome of everything I wanted to be. I'd wanted nothing more than to get closer to him, and I'd only dreamed that someday he might really need me for something. But after ten years of those dreams, I'd stopped thinking there was any chance of them becoming a reality.

"Work for you, Elvis?" I stammered a bit.

"Yeah. Things aren't working out with Jimmy and Joe right now. They're not going to be around here anymore. I need somebody. Should be you, Jerry."

"Well, uh—when, Elvis? When would you want me to start?"

"We're leaving for California today—driving the bus back to Los Angeles. You ought to be with us."

"Today?"

"That's right, Jerry." A little bit of a smile crept across his face. "I need you on board, man."

For maybe one full second I thought about how silly it would be to turn my life upside down on the basis of a quick, early-morning, Graceland front-porch conversation; how ridiculous it was to scuttle all the plans for my future that I'd put together so carefully; how absolutely crazy it seemed to forget about everything else in my life and simply jump on a bus with Elvis Presley. Maybe a second. Then I heard myself say, "OK, Elvis. Do I have time to pack a bag?"

I was in a daze by the time I got back home, but I think I managed to throw a couple of pairs of pants and a few shirts in a suitcase. I know I did make calls to my employers to tell them I wouldn't be coming in; I called my student counselor at the university to apologize for the unscheduled break in my studies; and I had a short but heartfelt talk with my father. He'd been deeply proud of my decision to put myself through college, and had been tremendously concerned about my academic career when I'd taken the time off to go to New York—he worried that I was throwing all my education away without getting a degree. I insisted to him that whatever happened, wherever I ended up, I'd get back to school somehow and try to finish my studies (I didn't think too hard about where or when that might be—my main concern was getting back to Graceland before Elvis changed his mind about inviting me along). My dad still didn't warm up much to the idea of my hitting the road with Elvis, but he told me that he had confidence in me and just wanted to know that whatever I was doing was what I really wanted to be doing. He knew that my friendship with Elvis was real and that what was being offered to me was a very solid opportunity of sorts.

He was concerned, but, as always, basically supportive of what I wanted to do.

I headed back to Graceland, was waved through the gates by Uncle Vester, who didn't even stop to call up to the house first. I don't know if he spotted the grin on my face, but I'd been waiting for years to be waved in like that. I drove up the hill and parked my car in the most out-of-the-way spot I could find around the side of the house. I'd worked my way up from the '49 Dodge to a little MG sports car, but it still didn't quite fit the ambience Elvis was shooting for around Graceland. I went in through the screened-in porch in the back of the house (years later this room was converted into the Jungle Room). The house was absolutely quiet, and again it was hard to believe that the conversation with Elvis just a couple hours before had taken place. I didn't want to walk around the house and disturb anybody who was trying to sleep, so I settled into one of the more comfortable wicker chairs on the porch and, though I felt charged up with energy and excitement, might have eventually dozed off for a while.

A few hours later, the house was an entirely different place, buzzing and humming with activity. Richard Davis was running around with suitcases, taking care of Elvis's wardrobe. Billy Smith was moving almost as fast as he did on skates as he packed up audio and video equipment. Alan "Hog Ears" Fortas was running back and forth like the friendliest of linebackers, stocking up the forty-foot Dodge mobile home parked in front of the house. Marty Lacker, an acquaintance of George Klein's who also had a background in radio, had become the new right-hand man for Elvis, and was very carefully going through a pile of papers. Mike Keaton, a guy who had been hired on by Elvis just a couple of weeks before, was carrying boxes around with a dead serious expression on his face. Mike was a friendly, dependable guy, but that serious expression was about the only one you'd ever see on his face—the rest of the guys kidded around a lot but a smile out of Mike was a rarity. Red West had been working steadily for Elvis, but was also getting film work on his own and was already out in L.A.

The guys had varied personalities and temperaments, but each could generally be described as a "Memphis boy." I'd recently met one member of the inner circle who definitely did not fit that description—

Larry Geller, a hairstylist from Jay Sebring's upscale Los Angeles salon who had recenty begun cutting Elvis's hair. Larry wasn't a football-and-roller-skates kind of guy—his main outside interest was in reading all he could on theories of spirituality. Apparently, his discussions with Elvis during haircuts had gotten deep, and the two had bonded quickly. Larry had been out in Memphis for a while over the summer, but he and his family had just flown back to L.A. a few days before.

The Memphis boys seemed pleased to see me in the house, and whether or not they knew I was now part of the team, they took it in stride. I was trying to figure out how to pitch in and help somebody when I heard that familiar voice right behind me.

"Jerry. You ready for California?"

With all his clout and all his stardom, Elvis still insisted on driving every mile of these Memphis-to-L.A. trips, and he had dressed up for this bon voyage in full trucker's regalia: leather gloves, leather jacket, *Wild One*–style motorcycle cap, and the kind of thin white scarf you saw on all the guys at the truck stop. He was almost certainly the coolest-looking long-haul driver in all of Memphis that morning.

"I'm ready, Elvis."

"Yeah. Just wait until you live with these guys. That'll get your nerves in the dirt."

There were a few laughs from the guys as they went about their work. I'd learn soon enough that one of the ways Elvis welcomed you into his inner circle was by needling and teasing. The teasing could sometimes have a mean edge to it, but it was also a guy's-guy way of injecting some real camaraderie into what was a complicated living and working relationship between all of us.

Near midnight, after hours of "last-minute" preparations, we were ready to pull out through the Graceland gates and hit the road. Elvis, myself, Mike Keaton, Billy Smith, and Marty Lacker were going to be riding in the Dodge mobile home. Richard Davis and Alan Fortas would follow in two cars, each pulling a trailer full of stuff Elvis wanted to bring to the house in California. With everything loaded up and engines revved, there was one final delay—Elvis took about another half an hour to say special, private good-byes to both Priscilla and Grandma (Vernon's mother).

When those farewells were taken care of, our hard-truckin' leader bounded onto the bus, took his place behind the wheel, and put that road-monster into gear. We slowly pulled out, with the guys waving to the friends and family that had come to see them off. There was a crowd of fans outside the Graceland gates waving good-bye as well. I felt a rush of excitement as we passed those fans—they were waving to Elvis and here I was sitting right behind him on his California-bound mobile home. That excitement settled into a deeper sense of satisfaction just a couple of miles later, as Elvis helmed the vehicle over the Memphis-Arkansas Bridge—across the Mississippi River. Crossing that first state line, I took a deep breath and thought about what was happening: Elvis's big ride was making its way toward L.A. And I was on it.

"Jerry, listen to this."

We weren't too many miles into Arkansas when Elvis started playing a reel-to-reel tape player he'd had Billy Smith rig up at the front of the bus. He fiddled with the volume knob and out of the small speakers boomed the unmistakable voice of Roy Orbison. For all of his long drives, Elvis would have one of the guys put together some tapes of his favorite music, and on this trip, Elvis wanted to listen to Roy over and over again.

"Damn—you hear that?" Elvis's features softened as he listened. He looked unconcerned by anything else in the world but the music he was soaking up. "Damn." He shook his head gently to the music.

After all those years of tuning into Dewey Phillips's broadcasts, I could tell you what I liked based on how a particular piece of music made me feel. But I'd never really thought about what it was in the music itself that would create those feelings. I heard a basic beat, a catchy tune, and words that stuck in your head, but I didn't have much idea at all about the craft and artistry that could be packed into a two-and-a-half-minute record. On this first night of the California trip, I was about to receive a musical education at the hands of Maestro Presley.

"The voice, man, the voice. You hear what he's doing?"

"He's singing great," I offered.

Elvis nodded. "Yeah, man. He's singing great. But listen here . . ." He turned the volume up a little higher. "Listen to those high notes. Nobody else can do that. Most guys go up high like that, they back off the note, take it on softly. Or they growl it out—blues it up and cheat it a little. Roy takes it high and sings it stronger than he does in his natural voice. And keeps it clear. Clear as a bell. Nobody else does that. Amazing."

I'd always liked Roy Orbison's music, without being a particularly avid fan. Now, through Elvis, I felt like I was hearing him for the first time. As the tape kept rolling, Elvis delighted in pointing out all the nuances of this music that he loved—the expert storytelling of Roy's lyrics, the fine, understated support of the backing band, the emotion behind every vocal delivery. And after a while we were talking not just about Roy, but music in general, girls, family, sports, Memphis—anything two guys might talk about.

This was the first time I'd ever had a chance to speak like this with Elvis. As our conversation started to kick into high gear, however, it occurred to me that maybe I was making a bad impression with the other guys, monopolizing Elvis's time this way. But as I looked around the bus at Billy, Marty, and Mike, I didn't sense any resentment. In fact, I got the impression that these guys were sort of relieved. Billy and Marty had made this trip many times already and may well have felt all talked out. They actually seemed glad to have a new guy aboard who could go head-to-head with Elvis in conversation—not ever a task to be taken lightly—and keep the driver-in-chief happy. When Elvis was "on," he was on all the way, and you had to give him full attention and keep up with him. I was eager and willing to do that, while Billy and Marty were just as happy to play cards, and Mike—the other "new guy"—seemed perfectly content to smoke cigarettes and quietly read his Bible.

After about 200 miles on good old Route 66, Elvis pulled off at a truck stop. He parked a good distance from the gas pumps, where the truck-stop lights shined out over an expanse of dusty gravel beyond the parking lot. He told Alan Fortas and a couple of the other guys to fill up the bus, check the oil, and buy coffee and donuts for anybody that needed them. Then he reached behind his seat for a football, and nodded my way.

"We got some business to take care of."

We walked out by the lights, and he suddenly smacked at the ball and said, "Go long, man."

I started out on the gravel at a tentative jog, apparently not running the pattern that my quarterback wanted.

"Come on—run it out, Jack," Elvis shouted.

I went into my full, All-Memphis open-field run, and when I was about forty yards out into the middle of nowhere, Elvis reared back and fired one of his perfectly arced spiral bombs. I threw on the afterburners, adjusted my slant, and managed to get to the ball in time for an unpretty but successful completion.

"That's what I'm talking about, Jack," said Elvis.

I sent the ball back his way, and he reeled it in for a catch. Then he called me back to our truck-stop line of scrimmage and gave me another pattern to run. And another. And another. Pretty soon, he called Billy Smith over to run some defensive coverage. Forty-five minutes later, my legs were about to give, my elbows were scraped from a couple of tumbles, I was huffing like a freight train and sweating like a pig. After one final long ball, Elvis gave us the all-aboard signal to get back on the road.

Making time to L.A. was clearly not a top priority for Elvis, though, because we drove less than an hour before he spotted one of his favorite mom-and-pop burger joints and pulled off again so that we could have a meal. Alan and Marty headed inside to buy food for the group, while Elvis and I wandered down a small brushy trail off the side of the road.

"You believe in coincidence, Jerry?"

"I guess so, Elvis."

"I don't think there's any such thing. What we call coincidence is just life coming together. Takes us by surprise sometimes."

"Yeah. I suppose that's true. What makes you think about that?"

"Well, if I'm not mistaken, you caught the first pass I threw you back in Guthrie Park. If you hadn't, maybe we wouldn't have played so much ball together. And if you hadn't caught the first pass I threw you just now, I might've sent you home. But it all worked out, didn't it?"

It felt OK to laugh—I was catching on to Elvis's slightly wicked sense of humor. "We haven't gone too far yet, Elvis. You want to send me home, I'll walk it."

He let loose a laugh this time. "You a long way from home already, Jack. Ain't no walkin' back now."

Our walks, talks, burger stops, and ball-playing set the leisurely pace for the whole trip. From the first night, this slow approach to cross-country travel was allowing me more one-on-one time with Elvis than I'd thought possible. For the other guys, this mode of travel was clearly a source of frustration and annoyance. For them, the excitement wasn't in the drive, but in the destination, where girls, sunshine, and movie sets awaited. They would have preferred to make the Memphis-to-L.A. drive a three- or four-day trip. But for Elvis, road time was the only time now that he was completely free of demands and distractions, and he was never in a hurry. On this trip, he found enough reasons to stop that it was over a week before we reached Los Angeles.

Occasionally we'd hear on a local radio station that there was an "Elvis Watch"—fans knew he was headed west to make another movie and knew he'd be on Route 66. But we managed to keep things very quiet and under the radar—eating on the bus, getting Elvis in and out of his motel rooms without any interactions he wasn't looking for. If the owners of the motels or burger stands or truck stops ever knew that Elvis Presley was sitting in a Dodge mobile home on their property, they were also smart enough to keep it quiet—they didn't want to lose the nice chunk of money that came their way several times a year with Presley caravan visits.

We drove through the nights, with Elvis pulling over almost every time he spotted a truck stop that seemed a good spot for more work on our passing game. Then, no matter how many or how few miles we'd covered, just before each dawn, Elvis and Alan and Marty would decide on a suitable motel for us to crash in. Rooms would be selected and paid for in advance, and, with Elvis still on the bus, we'd all work to set up his room just the way he wanted it. Elvis had learned early on in his travels that the blinds and shades on motel windows often didn't do a very good job of blocking out morning sun, so he'd come up with the idea of covering the windows with tin foil to darken the room and allow him some uninterrupted sleep. We had an extensive supply of the stuff to cover up all the windows on the way to L.A., and that was always the first thing taken care of in Elvis's room. Then we'd cart in just about all his clothes, so that he'd have a full selection of wardrobe to pick from for the next night's drive.

We'd also frequently set up some of his state-of-the-art videotape equipment. Even though the first "home video" players were just becoming available in 1964, Elvis had gotten a prototype machine through

RCA, and he'd put together a just barely portable reel-to-reel videotape deck system that he could hook up in his motel room. He'd had the system put together at Graceland, where he had already accumulated a private library of favorite TV shows and a few films transferred to tape. At first it seemed like a lot of trouble to cart this stuff around, just so Elvis could watch something when we checked into a place after the regular TV stations had signed off. But I soon learned that within his small collection of tapes he had a few very special ones that one or two girlfriends had made for him. These weren't talked about openly, and nobody else in the group ever saw who or what was on these tapes, but at least we understood why this back-straining gear was an Elvis-room priority.

The odd schedule and off-hour sleeping arrangements were hard for me to get adjusted to at first, and it was just a day or two into the trip that one of the guys let me in on the secret of staying up all night—prescription dexedrine tablets. Elvis was using those to stay up and stay attentive behind the wheel, and would then often use prescription sleeping pills so that he could get his rest. Now, up until those first dexedrine tablets, I hadn't had any experiences with drugs. My nickname around Graceland had been "Mr. Milk," because I was seen as the clean-living jock who rarely took a drink of alcohol (and, in fact, the couple of times that I'd overindulged in booze, I hated the temper and the foggy head that it gave me). But Elvis was a smart guy, and was in great physical shape. Why wouldn't I take the same pills he was taking?

I got into the same "better living through chemistry" rhythm, and pretty soon those football-tossing stops weren't just a fun way to stretch the legs—they were a required method for burning off all that amphetamine energy. And by the time we finally got to motel rooms in the morning, a sleeping pill started to feel entirely appropriate. Although it's quite clear to me now that the cycle of pills eventually took a toll on all of us, I still say I was playing the best football of my life on that trip, racing, diving, and rolling around those truck stops, fiercely proud of every scrape, cut, and bruise I got on the way to another end-zone reception.

The first indication that a sleep-cycle induced by pills could have a harsh downside for me came during our stop in Albuquerque, New Mexico, when we happened to check into a motel with a circular layout.

After we all got Elvis checked in and taken care of, I was handed a key with a number on it, but no matter how hard I tried to concentrate and how many circles I walked, I could not find my room. I think I was about to just lie down in a hallway when Alan Fortas spotted me and walked me to the right one. I remember lying on that motel-room bed, frightened by the fact that I seemed to have lost control of myself. But I must have eventually slumbered deeply enough to ease those fears away, because when I woke up later that day and peered out the window, the vista I took in looked amazing to me. Spread out in the distance, like some unbelievable postcard picture, were these huge, majestic New Mexico mountains. I'd never seen a more imposing or beautiful sight, and if heart-to-heart talks with Elvis Presley hadn't made it clear enough, these mountains slammed it home: I was truly living in another world now.

I think Elvis was making a somewhat special effort on that trip to make me feel comfortable—he really did appreciate the fact that I was leaving work, school, home, and essentially everything I knew to become part of his crew. And on the home stretch of our drive, the talks with Elvis got both deeper and more relaxed. Elvis seemed to enjoy stretching the mental muscles as much as he enjoyed working out his throwing arm. I'd spent a lot of time around guys who thought the best way a book could be used was to prop up a wobbly table. But Elvis was a voracious reader, always thrilled to talk about whatever book he was in the middle of and always eager to get started on the next one. Hearing him talk, hearing him work over topics from the most mundane questions of sports and girls to the meaning-of-life explorations of spirituality and philosophy, I felt I was getting the chance to give my own mental muscles a workout. It was fun to run a pass pattern for the guy, but it was even more satisfying to go head-to-head in a discussion or debate.

At one of our last stops, somewhere out by Barstow, we'd gotten Elvis into his room and the rest of the guys had gone off to find some breakfast. Elvis wasn't eating much—he was just days away from having to be on the film set and was already trying to diet off any extra pounds he'd picked up from Memphis home cooking. And I wasn't eating anything—the dexedrine and sleeping pills had virtually erased my appetite (Elvis would be at his trim "fighting weight" on the first day of shooting, but I ended up dropping twenty pounds off a frame that was pretty spare to start with: Elvis would keep looking at me, laughing, and asking "What happened to that big guy I hired?"). We usually left Elvis alone as soon as his room was set up—that was the way he wanted it. But this night, after the others had left, he flicked on the TV and told me to sit down with him. In that little motel room, with dawn not far off, Elvis and I just kept talking, like we'd been doing on the bus.

We talked a lot about karate—he was still an eager and enthusiastic student of the sport, which at the time still seemed a highly unusual and mysterious discipline. I remember that as we stretched out in that little room, Elvis started telling me about his admiration for the mix of spiritual philosophies and practical concepts behind karate—the significance of inner strength, the preciousness of the *chi* life force, the power of restraint, the secrets of using your opponent's force against him. He talked about the power of stillness and concentration, and how he was able to apply that to his acting and his recording work. It was a serious talk for a while, but eventually things got looser, as they usually did. The talk of concentration got us talking about hunting, and pretty soon Elvis was sharing some of his field-tested secrets for snake hunting ("You just let the snake slither right into the bullet"). And before long, he was sharing what he saw as some of the crucial differences between California girls and Memphis girls.

I think we'd finally worked our way through to some laughing reminiscences of nights at the Rainbow Roller Rink in Memphis, when Elvis suddenly sat up on his bed and stared at the TV with a strange, intent expression. I looked over at the screen to see an image of a group of jet fighters climbing into the sky. It didn't look like a scene from a movie, and I guessed from the late hour that it might be the station's way of signing off. This was a little unusual—I'd stayed up late enough to see plenty of sign-offs in Memphis, and they generally consisted of footage of the flag and a playing of the national anthem. But there was no anthem now. Instead, the images of the soaring planes and sunlit skies were accompanied by a poem that I'd never heard before. But Elvis— after so many nights in so many motels—knew these strange words by heart, and he intoned them dramatically along with the voice from the TV:

Oh! I have slipped the surly bonds of Earth
And danced the skies on laughter-silvered wings;
Sunward I've climbed and joined the tumbling mirth
of sun-split clouds,—and done a hundred things . . .

I thought at first he was doing this for another laugh, but as he went on I could tell that these words meant something to him. Through Elvis, I really focused in on the words coming from the screen, and, though I was hardly a poetry expert, I too began to pick up on their power. Elvis, exhibiting the very stillness and concentration he'd just told me about, brought his voice down to a whisper as he got to the final lines of the poem.

. . . And, while with silent lifting mind I've trod
The high, untrespassed sanctity of space,
Put out my hand, and touched the face of God.

The image on the TV switched over to the classic Indian-head logo and a test-tone began to come through the speaker. Elvis had his eyes closed and stayed quiet and still for a moment more. Then he looked over at me with a tired smile.

"That's a pretty good way to call it a night."

I had to agree.

And I think it was as I left his room that night that I had my first Elvis epiphany: What I loved about him so much was no longer an image, but the real guy behind the image. The more I got to know him, the more he was turning out to be exactly the person I had hoped he would be. As an insecure twelve-year-old, I suppose I'd created my own sort of fantasy about the Elvis I was friends with. But now, as a slightly more discerning twenty-one-year-old, I was discovering that the real Elvis was an even better friend.

525 Perugia Way, Bel Air. Even the addresses in California seemed beautiful—so much more exotic and promising than any address I'd ever been around. And as we stood in front of the gorgeous, modern, white-walled home in the hills above Beverly Hills—crickets chirping, the scent of lemon in the air—you could have told me that I'd traveled

not just across country but to some better planet and I wouldn't have put up an argument. The house seemed to be a small, single-level structure from the street, but once you got in, the space opened and flowed down the hill. It was decorated in a style that was spare and elegant— like nothing I'd ever seen before. Graceland had the dignified, comfortable look of the Old South. This place couldn't be mistaken for anything but West Coast. To me, it looked like a whole new life. It looked like freedom.

It was probably two A.M. on a mid-October morning. We'd made it to L.A., and the guys, desperately tired after all those miles on the road, quickly worked through all their arrival tasks before heading off to various sleeping quarters. I think it was Marty who told me that I'd be sharing a room with Billy Smith, and for the first time since leaving Memphis, I felt a touch of disappointment. I didn't know Billy all that well, but I hadn't been all that fond of some of the cousins I had met back in Memphis, and I would have much preferred to room with a guy I knew I could get along with, like Richard Davis. (As it turned out, Billy was quiet, friendly, and accommodating, and, even sharing close quarters, we never had a single cross word between us.) I didn't feel the need to make friendly with a roommate that night, however. In fact, I didn't actually feel the need for a room at all. Everyone else seemed ready to crash hard in a familiar bed, but the house, the hills, and the air seemed so unfamiliar and intoxicating that even though the dexedrine had worn off, I was far too buzzed with sheer adrenaline to even consider lying down.

I walked the grounds several times, marveling at the beautiful swimming pool that seemed designed for Greek gods to splash in. I looked up at the stars over Bel Air, which, in that crisp night air, seemed to twinkle with the same sense of excitement that I was feeling. Eventually I settled down on a couch in a small TV room off the house's huge central circular den. The room was full of soft indirect lighting, subtle shades of green and red, and just sitting on the couch in there I felt like I was already living inside a movie.

Nobody had explicitly gone over any particular security measures for the Bel Air house with me, but I knew that keeping Elvis safe was a part of my unofficial job. Which is why I immediately tensed up when I heard the click of a key in the front door. The door creaked open and shut again, and I didn't hear any familiar voices. In fact, I heard nothing. Somebody, it seemed, was trying to be very quiet about coming in. I was about to get up and investigate, when a shadowy figure crept right past the alcove my couch was set in, past the room's big TV, and over to the far wall. In the darkness I could just about make out some long hair down this stranger's back, and I knew that Elvis had occasionally had trouble with fans—especially females—finding their way to his homes and acting crazy.

Sure enough, this girl began knocking on the wall, looking for Elvis's bedroom. This was my moment to take action.

"Miss—" I called out in a firm, sharp voice.

The woman spun around and let loose a bloodcurdling scream.

And at that very moment, the wall behind her opened up to reveal Elvis. He flicked on the lights in the room. There was a huge smile on his face. The girl being there didn't seem to bother him at all. In fact, he seemed to know her.

My eyes adjusted to the light. Now I recognized the girl, too. It was Ann-Margret.

Elvis put an arm around her and grinned in my direction. "It's OK, Jerry. It's just Ammo. She's not gonna hurt anybody."

Ann calmed down, collected herself, and giggled. Elvis and she stepped back into Elvis's bedroom, and the secret sliding-wall entrance closed up again. When the shock wore off enough that I could move, I headed back outside to take another look at that pool, and those stars. I'd just met my first woman in California, and it was Ann-Margret.

Yeah, I'm a long way from home.

Just a few hours later, after some minimal sleep, I began my first proper day in Los Angeles. Alan Fortas, who took care of all of Elvis's cars and motorcycles, wanted to tune up the massive Harley-Davidson Elvis kept in the Perugia Way garage. It hadn't been ridden for months, and might sit for several more, but Alan wanted it to be ready whenever Elvis decided to go for a ride. Alan told me he was going to take it out himself for a long test ride, and wanted to know if I wanted to come along. I did.

I hopped on the back of the bike and we zoomed down the Bel Air hills out onto the Sunset Strip. And maybe it's just the haze of a romanticized memory, but I think it was on that first Harley ride that I fell in love with Los Angeles. The sunlight seemed brighter than any place I'd ever been to. The colors crisper. The people more attractive. And as much as I felt part of a vibrant and sophisticated city, I was also thrilled at the natural beauty of the place—the hills and canyons and ocean breezes.

Alan and I toured for hours, eventually working our way down the PCH to the Santa Monica Civic Auditorium, where some kind of large-scale musical event was taking place. Alan had been invited down there by a friend of his, a tour manager, to check out something called the Teenage Music International show, or TAMI, a massive, multi-artist concert that was being filmed as a theatrical feature. The bill was made up of a mix of R & B acts and British and American pop and rock acts, including the Beach Boys, James Brown, Leslie Gore, Jan & Dean, Bo Diddley, the Supremes, Gerry and the Pacemakers, and many others.

Alan and I didn't have much desire to go inside the auditorium, though—we were just checking out the scene before heading back to Perugia Way. After drifting around for a while, we found Alan's tour-manager friend standing in front of a beat-up, rickety-looking bus—I remember it as a kind of converted school bus, quite a few comfort-and-style notches down from the Elvis Dodge mobile home. We had just made introductions all around and had started to chat, when a scraggly group of odd-looking guys ran out the back of the auditorium and onto the bus. I offered a general hello as they passed, but didn't get a response from any of them—not even a nod. As I learned a few moments later, that was my not-so-chummy introduction to the Rolling Stones.

We were back in Bel Air by sunset, and when I wandered into the small den where I'd sat the night before, I found Elvis and Ann-Margret on the same couch, joking around with a couple of the guys. I took the only remaining spot on the couch, on the other side of Ann. Right away, Elvis busted out laughing again. "Careful, now, Jerry. We've got a dangerous intruder here."

I laughed along with everybody else. I suppose I could have been embarrassed about the whole thing, but I was actually too nervous about sitting next to Ann-Margret to think of anything else. Hanging around with Elvis had come to feel completely natural, but being so close to this gorgeous redheaded actress threw me. I didn't see how it was humanly possible, but she was even more beautiful in person than she was in the movies. I poured myself a glass of water and proceeded to spill it all over myself every time I tried to take a sip—my hands were shaking so badly.

Within a few days, I would understand the situation with Elvis and Ann. They'd met on set while making *Viva Las Vegas* the year before, and had hit it off as kindred spirits almost immediately. Elvis called her "Ammo"—for Ann-Margret Olsson—and had been having her up at the house as much as their schedules would allow. You didn't have to be around them long to see that they brought out an energetic, fun-loving side of each other.

Elvis started telling the story of "the intruder" all over again, teasing me about how panicked I looked. He began laughing, and the more he laughed, the more she laughed. The more they both laughed, the more comfortable I started to feel sitting on that couch in Bel Air.

Eventually, I started to laugh, too.

In the past twenty-four hours of my life, I'd scared the hell out of Ann-Margret, I'd been ignored by the Rolling Stones, and I'd made Elvis Presley laugh. Not bad for a Memphis kid's first day in California.

5

. . .

TALES OF TWO CITIES

I kept waking up to startlingly sunny California mornings, and I continued to feel like I was living in a dream. First of all, it was a little strange to be around Elvis and actually see mornings—or at least see them at the start of a day. Back in Memphis, Elvis was on his own distinctive, nocturnal schedule, but in Los Angeles he was strictly disciplined about his duties in the moviemaking process, and he was rarely even a minute late for the early call times we got during the week.

"Six-seven for eight," Marty Lacker or Alan Fortas would shout through the Perugia house at the end of a night—meaning a 6:00 A.M. wake-up time to leave the house by seven so that Elvis could be in makeup by eight. Elvis Presley was never at his best when you woke him up at six in the morning, but the rest of us were pretty grouchy, too. Still, there was something exciting about all of us shuffling about at that unlikely early hour, getting ready for a day on a movie set on the Paramount lot.

Elvis was beginning work on his eighteenth film (in nine years!), a production called *Tickle Me*. And as we arrived for our first day of work, I remember thinking that I probably couldn't feel happier rolling through the gates of Heaven than I did rolling through the famed Paramount archway in a limo with Elvis Presley. While Heaven might have had more angels, Paramount seemed pretty close—*Tickle Me* was set on a female dude ranch, and as I stepped on to my first soundstage and got a look at the extras for the first day's shoot, I very quickly became aware of the fact that I had never seen so many drop-dead beautiful women collected in one place.

I guess I felt a little like a wide-eyed kid from North Memphis, awed by my step into movieland. But in a strange way, despite the speed with which I'd thrown myself into this wild new world, I felt ready for anything. I was still on the shy side, willing to defer to those who were older or smarter than me. But I wasn't the kid at Guthrie Park anymore, feeling like my happiness depended entirely on the whims of some bigger boys. I'd been a class president. I'd taken my share of hits on a college football field. I'd thrown myself at New York City and ended up not only surviving but thriving. I'd picked up some battle scars from falling in and out of love. And I'd just spent a cross-country ride with Elvis. Everything around me was new, but if all my bouncing around as a kid, all my attempts to find my way in life, and all my Elvis adventures had taught me one thing, it was this: I could take care of myself. True, I couldn't sit on a couch next to Ann-Margret without spilling water on myself, but that didn't trouble me much—or at least not enough to give up my spot on the couch. Or in the limo.

Elvis was already extremely frustrated with the quality of his movies, and on top of that frustration, he was never in a good mood at the beginning of a film, when he had to spend a lot of time standing around for wardrobe fittings and publicity stills. For most of the other Elvis guys, movies had just become business as usual, and when they weren't carrying out specific duties for Elvis they spent most of the time on set away from the action, playing cards. But I couldn't help approaching the world of moviemaking with some fresh eyes and fresh energy, and I think Elvis appreciated having that around—it helped him laugh his way through some of the more tedious responsibilities of a leading man. I know Elvis seemed pleased when I was very impressed the first time I stepped into the dressing room that Paramount always had ready for him—a huge, well-appointed space with its own bar, makeup room and dressing area, designed for Jerry Lewis when he and Dean Martin were the hottest of Paramount stars. I would have been happy to have it as an apartment.

Elvis gave a grand wave around the room. "All this for little old me," he said with a shake of the head.

"I guess they like you out here, Elvis," I answered.

"Yeah, well—don't breathe too much of the air. They bring it in special for me from the mountains."

I was just about ready to start holding my breath when he laughed.

"Man, they'll tell you anything out here, Jerry."

Elvis could tease me as much as he did the other guys, but it didn't escape my attention that in the weeks that followed, no matter how frustrated he got or how foul a mood might have been brewing, Elvis often went out of his way to give me a nod or a comment that would put me at ease in the new surroundings.

Working as one of Elvis's guys, I got my first look into the inner workings of his career.

On one of the first shoot days on the lot, I was walking down a darkened corridor that ran between the scenery flats and the exterior wall of one of the huge soundstage buildings, when I became aware of a strange thumping ahead of me. I stopped in my tracks, squinted into the dim light before me, and realized that whatever was making the noise was coming straight toward me, and fast. As I stared down the corridor, I saw a small head-high dot of glowing orange appear and disappear, appear and disappear. The thumping continued, getting louder, and I began to hear a fair amount of shuffling along with the low chatter of subdued voices. A few more thumps, a few more orange glows, and I could just about make out the sizable shadow of a massive man, holding a cane, puffing a cigar, and moving toward me at alarming speed.

I didn't have to hear the name. Just like that first day at Guthrie, when I knew Elvis was Elvis without having to be told, I knew exactly who was doing the thumping and the puffing. The Colonel was on the set.

I found a place to step through the flats out of the corridor, and watched as the imposing figure thundered by, followed by a bunch of younger, smaller guys, desperately trying to both keep up and satisfactorily answer the Colonel's gruff queries.

Colonel Tom Parker had been booking and then managing Elvis's career since the Louisiana Hayride days back in 1955. To me, he had always been something of a mysterious figure—I occasionally heard his name, but he was certainly never around at football games or at Graceland. The Colonel had a strange business background that included work as a carnival barker, a dog catcher, a pet-cemetery owner, and a booker and promoter on the Southern country-music circuit. His rank was apparently the result of self-promotion rather than military promotion. But since he'd taken Elvis on as a sole client, his deal-making had become legendary. The Colonel was behind the early TV appearances that had given Elvis a national profile, the top-dollar deals with the RCA record label, and the movie deals that had made Elvis one of the highest-paid performers in Hollywood. To the Colonel, it didn't matter much what ended up on screen—the challenge, and the triumph, was in wrangling the most lucrative contract he could for his star. I didn't know any of these business details at the time, but just watching him walk I could see this much: The Colonel radiated power.

Those who weren't aware of the Colonel's reputation might, for a moment, take him as some kind of clownish figure, with his tweed cap, out-of-style jackets and string ties, and trousers pulled high over his ample belly. But that moment had better not last long. As I would witness many times over the years, those who underestimated the Colonel always made a terrible mistake. What I saw on the lot was that, whether this guy was a real colonel or not, he was a powerful, commanding presence, and he had a pronounced effect on the dynamic of any situation he walked into. People have often called him a P. T. Barnum, but the character he always reminded me of was one from the world of drama: Big Daddy from *Cat on a Hot Tin Roof*. If the Colonel was in the room, everybody knew it.

Of course, the same was true of Elvis, and watching him and the Colonel together was like watching a couple of forces of nature accommodate each other. Throughout Elvis's career, you never heard about him sitting down with accountants and teams of lawyers and business managers—between the Colonel, Vernon, and the guys, everything got taken care of. Elvis deeply appreciated what the Colonel could do for him on a business level, but he didn't want the Colonel involved in his personal affairs at all (the idea of the Colonel as some kind of Southern Rasputin, moving his "boy" around like a chess piece, is a grossly inaccurate cartoon of their relationship).

When Elvis and the Colonel were together that first day on the *Tickle Me* set, there was no hugging or backslapping, and no loose, happy chitchat between them. The Colonel stopped his barreling around and carefully picked his moment to approach Elvis. There was a wary friendliness between them—some smiles, a bit of joking around, but, for all the work they'd done together and as closely aligned as they were, neither one seemed to let his guard down entirely. As I'd see again and again, Elvis and the Colonel entertained each other just enough to take care of whatever business was at hand. They were like a pair of high-tension lines—incredibly powerful when working together, but you hated to think what would happen if the lines crossed and started sparking.

I assumed that, as part of Elvis's team, and knowing how important the Colonel was, it was my duty to introduce myself to the man. On one of those first days, I walked straight up to him and said, "Hello, Colonel."

His teeth might have clenched a little tighter on the cigar, but other than that I got no response whatsoever. He just stared right through me with the coldest eyes I'd ever encountered. Then he simply moved away to talk to whomever it was he deemed worthy of speaking to. I tried a few more times throughout the shoot to make my introduction, but my attempts at friendliness were always met with the same cold, piercingly empty stare. I gave up, and, without any personal contact with the guy, started working up a pretty strong dislike for him. I'd spot him barreling off somewhere in that improbably fast manner of his, and a choice string of profanities would come to mind. Then one day, I came around a corner and found the Colonel barreling toward me. Before I even had time to think ill of him, the Colonel's face lit up with a knowing smile and he shouted out, "Good morning, Jerry."

I stammered a hello back, and was surprised to find how happy I was to be recognized by someone I thought I was on my way to hating. Lesson number one from the Colonel: Keep everybody around you off balance, and you stay in charge.

You couldn't help but have a love/hate relationship with the Colonel. And you had to admit he was brilliant. I figured out quickly that it was very wise to understand that if you were stepping into Elvis's world, you were stepping into the Colonel's as well.

I think probably anybody visiting a film set for the first time is struck by two things: how much waiting around there is, and how much hands-on labor is involved in every shot of a film. While the "talent" spends a lot of time in dressing rooms or trailers, the crew always has work to do. I found myself fascinated with the hands-on elements of filmmaking and spent a lot of time watching the way lights got set up, the way camera moves were worked out, the way sound was handled, the way sets went up or came down. The craft that had to go into a film, regardless of that film's artistic merits, was very interesting to me, and I started to become a student of the process.

I also quickly discovered that if you were one of Elvis's guys, everybody took time to talk to you—cast, crew, cameramen, assistant directors. Elvis didn't have to demand that we be allowed on set—the "Memphis Mafia" were simply part of the deal, and I never sensed any resentment or distrust from others around us. In fact, I discovered that as one of Elvis's guys, there was a reputation to live up to—we needed to be sharp and responsible, and needed to get things done for Elvis before they were asked for. The crew appreciated the fact that we did everything we could to ensure that Elvis was always where he was supposed to be and ready to work. The Hollywood higher-ups may have been a little suspicious of our rough-around-the-edges Memphis ways, but the folks we dealt with day-to-day came to consider us important allies.

I suppose we guys were simply following the cues from Elvis. He may have been disheartened over the way his film career was going, but he was always calm and professional on the set. He might let his temper flare in the privacy of the dressing room, but he never let cast, crew, or director see he was mad (I became pretty good at detecting a burn in his gaze that let us know he was very unhappy with something). These films were built entirely around Elvis, but he never acted like a spoiled, demanding superstar on the set. That's one of the reasons why the crews loved him so much, although many of them were equally enamored of the personal interest he took in them. It took Elvis only a few days on a set before he knew everybody's names, their hobbies, what was going on with their families. I think he always had a great connection with the crew on his sets because, in some ways, he never really stopped thinking of himself as a simple, working man. He was always more comfortable kidding around with a grip or a carpenter than trying to make small talk with a studio lawyer.

Throughout my years with Elvis, every time I saw him tap his creative abilities to take on some new kind of artistic challenge, I came away amazed again at the breadth of his talent. And standing around on that first movie set, it happened again. I'd seen him looking good on screen, but it was a revelation to see him do the work that got him up on screen. He was just such a natural, making it look like it was the easiest thing in the world to be at the center of a film. Even to my untrained eye, it was pretty clear that a film like *Tickle Me* wasn't giving Elvis the chance to do all he could—the script didn't give him much to work with, and the shooting schedule was pretty clearly set to favor cost containment over artistic excellence. But once in a while there'd be a scene here or there where Elvis did some great stuff—little stuff like a perfectly timed comic expression, or a fitting throwaway line.

And sometimes, despite the weakness of the script, he'd still be able to pull some real drama or nuanced emotion out of his lines. In his first few films, he comes across as a fine, developing Method actor learning his craft, and while publicly he shied away from comparisons to James Dean, I know he would have relished the chance to prove himself worthy of those comparisons. We can't know what he was truly capable of, but certainly the guy had some solid acting ability, and the material rarely gave his talents a chance to shine. If the films had been as good as Elvis, they'd be remembered a lot differently these days.

A week or so into the *Tickle Me* shooting schedule, I had a strange sort of Guthrie Park flashback when Red West turned up on the lot to stage a fight scene with Elvis (Red's uncredited role in the film was, aptly enough, "Bully in the Saloon"). I thought about some of the well-executed football plays the three of us had run as I watched Red and Elvis carefully choreograph the big brawl. It had never occurred to me that movie fights had to be worked out as precisely as dance numbers, and I was intrigued watching the two of them work. Red and Elvis had a great physical chemistry together—they knew how to read each other and how to move together and trusted each other enough to cut loose with confidence.

Between takes I noticed that Elvis, as a result of the all-out physical exertion, was flushed and sweaty. He drank a lot of water whenever he worked, and while he may not have had mountain air piped into his dressing room, he did insist on a ready supply of his favorite brand of bottled water: Mountain Valley Spring Water, from Hot Springs National Park in Arkansas. I took it upon myself to make sure that between scenes he always had a fresh, cool bottle of water ready. Not only did that keep the star from getting thirsty, but it gave me a chance to talk some more with him. These on-set talks weren't quite as deep as some we'd had on the ride out—most often we compared notes on which of the female dude ranchers were looking the prettiest that day. (In Elvis's films, there was a strange, inverse ratio between the quality of the scripts and the number of girls on the set—I guess the studio figured that if it wasn't paying for decent writing, the least it could do was fill the scenes with attractive extras.)

If Elvis had asked me to come to California to be his water boy, I would have turned him down. My experience with and without Elvis had given me confidence and pride, and as much as I loved the guy, I had no interest in a future as a servant. But he hadn't asked that. He had just asked me to come with him, and to be a part of his team. I understood that my job vaguely had something to do with security—I was, after all, the ex–Golden Glover who, after Red, was probably the physically strongest of the bunch. But Elvis hadn't even been that explicit about my role. Working for Elvis meant that you were becoming not only a part of his support system but a part of his circle of trusted friends. For better or worse, we were everything for him: his staff, his pals, and, in a personal guy-to-guy way, his peers. In that spirit, I had no trouble bringing the star his water. I didn't feel like the kid in the basement outside the Chickasaw Ballroom, mooning over the chance to bring Elvis a Pepsi. I was a friend, doing what I could for an overheated buddy.

After one of the fight scenes, somebody in the crew commented that they liked a fight move Elvis had made, and he responded that it was based on a karate move. When they asked how much Elvis knew about karate, his eyes lit up. He squinted out at those of us standing on the other side of the lights and called to me.

"Jerry—c'mere. Let's show these people something."

We squared off and started going through some karate demonstrations, just like in the living room at Graceland—though by now I was quick enough to avoid any crotch-kicks. We worked out hard, building up speed and force, until Elvis backed away and stood in a relaxed stance.

"I taught him everything he knows, folks," he said to our small audience. "But not everything I know."

He wheeled around, made a sudden lunge, and tried to clip me with an open hand, but I managed to block him away.

"Ahh . . . the old North Memphis knife-hand block," laughed Elvis. "He's learning."

• • •

My new Los Angeles career included one responsibility that I didn't enjoy at all—grocery shopping with Marty Lacker. As foreman, Marty had
decided that the Perugia Way housekeeper was spending too much on
food, and figured Elvis could save a hundred bucks a week if we kept the
pantry stocked ourselves. I highly doubted that Elvis cared much about
getting a good deal on eggs and butter. But on some shoot days I'd get
the signal from Marty and would soon find myself at a market, pushing
a grocery cart down aisle after aisle. Back on the lot, the other guys
were with Elvis, surrounded by attractive women in Western-wear. I
was in front of frozen foods, watching Marty Lacker hunt for a good
price on bulk chicken legs.

I managed not to hold a grocery-grudge, though. When work was
done on the lot, Elvis and all of us guys headed home to Perugia Way,
where we became the unified membership of the world's most exclusive
fraternity. The guys—Billy Smith, Alan Fortas, Richard Davis, Mike
Keaton, Marty, Red, and sometimes a visiting George Klein or Lamar
Fike—would all have a late, family-style dinner around the big dining-
room table, with Elvis sitting at the head.

I think at those dinnertimes everybody there felt privileged to have
a seat at the table, including Elvis. The vibe was a mix of rock-and-roll
backstage, football locker room, and White House situation room, and
you couldn't help but feel that by pulling up a chair, you were part of
something amazing. Some of the details of our responsibilities and
arrangements got hashed out over dinner, but it was pretty rare for a
meal to go by without a good laugh over something. And the best laugh
was usually at the expense of one of us. Elvis loved to tease—the voice
that could expertly mimic Peter Sellers in *Dr. Strangelove* could also
perfectly imitate anybody around him, and he had a way of finding the
one inflection or mannerism in your speech you didn't want anyone to
focus on and turn it into a whole routine. Of course, we enjoyed going
right back at him. Everything was fair game for a well-delivered gibe:
Elvis's neck (he thought it was too long), Lamar's weight, Alan's ears,
my romantic "inexperience," or the way Marty looked in the Fred Segal
black stretch pants that he insisted on squeezing into. There was a brutal honesty among us that was a real key to the relationship.

And there were some plain old brutal backhands that figured in, too—Elvis loved to smack somebody when they least expected it, and he always expected that he'd get smacked right back. This was some highly charged male bonding, and you couldn't have gotten away with being a slow-on-the-uptake country bumpkin. These guys were fast with the cutting one-liners, and if you couldn't keep up, you probably didn't belong there. Lamar was so fast with his deadpan put-downs that sometimes it took even Elvis a minute to realize he'd been put down— and then he'd crack up. Billy Smith became an expert at timing his lines with a dash from the table (he was usually sitting within Elvis's smacking range). I tried to hold my own when I had to (reminding the guys of Elvis's running style always worked), and otherwise kept out of the way as much as possible.

Around the house we loved talking in movie lingo ("All right—one hour lunch, forty-five for crew, thirty for stand-ins"). But away from the Paramount lot we weren't really living what most would consider a Hollywood social life and didn't go out on the town much. As at Graceland, Elvis and the guys had a small circle of female friends who they were comfortable hanging out with, and they'd come up to the house from time to time. There was Pat Parry, an L.A. teenager with a great sense of humor who was accepted as one of the guys. And there were Bonnie, Sherry, and Alan's friend Sandy Hovey, all local girls who were equally comfortable being a part of things at the house. Living in Los Angeles might have been more of a culture shock if I'd come out on my own, but I really didn't have to get used to L.A. because we lived in our own little world around Elvis.

For all our locker-room-style bonding, Elvis ran a tight organization and wanted everything around him—house, cars, guys—to make a good appearance. We probably spent as much time keeping the place clean and washing the cars as we did "partying." In fact, there was very little alcohol around Elvis, and the only drugs were the ones we still considered medicine—the stimulants and sleeping pills that helped keep everybody running on schedule. Maybe it sounds self-serving or naive, but in the days before rehab was an accepted part of a career path, we really didn't see how using drugs prescribed to us could hurt us.

The film moved along very quickly. And while *Tickle Me* may not stand tall as a significant event in Elvis's life, I must admit that it brought about a significant change in mine. One of the beautiful women filling out the cast of the film was an actress named Paula Tyden, a spirited, gorgeous redhead who drove around town in a Cadillac convertible. Red West pointed her out to me on the set as an example of the kind of girl you just didn't see back in Memphis. I had to agree, and I was more than a little flustered when I found myself talking to Paula one day and realized that we had just made a date to get together. I would readily admit that Paula Tyden was out of my league, but if she wanted to see me, I wasn't going to fight it.

She picked me up in her Caddy on a Saturday night and took me out for dinner in Malibu. I was hoping for a stroll on the beach after dessert, but we skipped the stroll (we may have even skipped dessert) and ended up checked into a motel right on the beach. There, to the sound of crashing surf, I finally became "experienced," and I have to say that it was every bit as pleasurable as I'd been warned by the nuns at Holy Names. I didn't have much time for any afterglow, however. When I got dropped off back at the Perugia house, Alan Fortas greeted me by saying, "Man, you really screwed up."

"What are you talking about, Alan?"

"You don't mess with Elvis's girl," he said.

"I was out with Paula. From the movie."

"Who do you think he went out with last movie? That's big trouble, man."

Alan was an easygoing guy who didn't get unnecessarily upset about anything, so to see him worked up got me extremely worried. I knew from all those Graceland parties that Elvis did not take kindly to anybody flirting with his girlfriends, and could only imagine how he'd feel about a guy who'd slept with one. I started to think that maybe I'd managed to lose my old virginity and my new job in the same night.

I found Elvis sitting by himself, reading in the den. I approached slowly, a little sheepishly.

"Elvis?"

He looked up, his expression cold, hard, dead serious. I knew right away that he knew where I'd been. I started talking away—"I had no idea who she was; she didn't say anything; I would have never if I'd known . . ."

When I finished, Elvis furrowed his brow slightly but kept his stare focused hard on me.

"You're talking about Paula Tyden?"

"Yeah, Elvis. Paula. I didn't know."

Elvis took a deep breath, let it out, and looked back down at his book. "That's all over, Jerry. Don't worry about it. She's a nice girl."

He wasn't happy. No guy likes hearing about another guy fooling around with an old girlfriend, and in those matters, Elvis was very much like any other guy. But he knew I wasn't trying to sneak around him— there I was coming to confess to him with my head hung down after the fact. He was going to let things slide this time.

A wave of conflicted feelings came over me. Chief among them was relief. As intense and wonderful as the night with Paula had been, I certainly didn't want that sort of thing to mess up my friendship with Elvis. He stayed focused on his book, and after a moment I left the room quietly, realizing for the first time just how complicated the mix of professional and personal lives could be around Elvis. I did see Paula Tyden a few more times, though—enough times to know that I really was in over my head with her. We parted as friends.

By the end of November the film was done and we were getting ready to drive back to Memphis. On one of the days just before we left, a strange delivery was made to the Perugia Way house—a crumpled, twisted motorcycle. Some of the guys quickly recognized it as Sonny West's. Sonny and Elvis had had a blow-out argument on one of the last films, and Sonny had left the group, moving in with a girlfriend in L.A. Looking at the wreck of a motorcycle, we were all worried about what might have happened to Sonny. Alan Fortas made some calls and found out that Sonny was alive but very banged up, and recuperating over at the girlfriend's house.

Whatever their disagreement had been, Elvis decided to put it behind them, and he sent Alan over to Sonny's place with money to help Sonny with any medical bills. The next day Sonny turned up at Perugia Way, hobbling along on crutches, to thank Elvis personally. We had just finished loading up the Dodge mobile home and were about ready to hit the road, when Elvis told Sonny to get in the Dodge and make the trip with us. Sonny looked very surprised, and pointed out that he hadn't packed up any of his things. All he had with him was his clothes and his crutches.

"We'll get you what you need along the way," said Elvis. Sonny climbed aboard.

Back in Memphis that fall, I moved into a new home: Graceland. As with most things around Elvis, this change—a huge, amazing one for me—came with little fanfare. There was no heart-to-heart talk about making me a part of the family, no grand invitation into his home. As I recall, somewhere during the trip back I mentioned to Alan Fortas that I'd be doing a lot of driving between my dad's house and Graceland. Alan shrugged and said "I think Elvis wants you to stay at the house." Sure enough, at one of our last meal stops before crossing the Mississippi River, Elvis was talking to Marty Lacker, who had been living at Graceland in a converted garage always referred to as "the annex." And at some point, he turned to me and said, "Jerry—you'll get the room downstairs." That was it. I was living in the house.

There are some bedrooms at Graceland that are off-limits to visitors nowadays—including Elvis's and mine, though for very different reasons. Elvis's upstairs bedroom is not part of any tour because it was a place he turned to for privacy, and it feels wrong even now to violate that. My room downstairs isn't part of any tour because, frankly, it just ain't much to look at, and it wasn't much to look at back then, either. Down in the basement, off the TV room, and directly across from the bar, a door leads to what was really designed as a storage room, and what was sort of half-converted to a bedroom when I moved in. There was, and still is, a white linoleum floor, walls that are white brick on one side and wood paneled on the other, and a drop ceiling that can't quite hide some of the pipes running through the room. The flashiest bit of decor down there remains the tattered silver insulation that hangs from some of the heating ducts.

I did get my own bathroom and a walk-in closet, which my few bits of wardrobe shared with the Graceland Christmas decorations. I soon discovered that when it snowed or rained, water found its way into my quarters, and stepping into my room often meant stepping over a sizable puddle of seepage. My first act of personalizing the place was to leave a plank by the door, so that I could get over those puddles with reasonably dry feet.

Just outside my door were gold records, stylishly mod sofas, and state-of-the-art TV and stereo equipment. Lying on my small twin bed, I stared up at water stains and a bare-bulb light fixture. But the state of my furnishings didn't bother me a bit. I was living at Graceland, and, for the first time in my life, I really felt like I wasn't just "staying" somewhere. I felt like I was home.

Up until I moved in, Graceland had always been a place of excitement for me—a fun place where something was always happening. But living there, I realized that the peacefulness I'd felt out on the grounds was really a part of the home, too. I've never felt safer in my life than I did living at Graceland in that damp, bare-bulbed basement room. I felt like I was within a kind of loving fortress, and it was impossible to be worried too much about life in general now that I was inside the Graceland gates (still manned by Uncle Vester).

Actually, you didn't see much of life in general when living at Graceland. Things stayed as tightly organized around Elvis as they had out in Los Angeles—it wasn't like everybody went back to some kind of "normal" Memphis life. Marty and his family and I were in Graceland itself, but nobody else was too far away. Some guys had nearby houses, some stayed in the Graceland Apartments just across the street, some in rooms at the Howard Johnson's just down Highway 51. The big difference was that in Los Angeles, making movies, the guys in the group all had a sense of what the day's working schedule would be. In Memphis, the workday centered entirely on Elvis, which meant that a couple of days might go by without anything happening at all and then, just when you might be considering sneaking off for a ride or a visit somewhere, Elvis would need things done and the whole house would snap into action. I don't think I even saw my daddy, brother, or any family when I first got back to town—Graceland was where I was supposed to be, where I wanted to be, and it was far enough away from my old neighborhoods that I didn't cross paths with many familiar faces. We also went back to keeping Elvis hours in Memphis, and that made it very unlikely that we'd cross paths with anyone outside the circle. We generally slept through the day and were up and around when the rest of the city was asleep.

Elvis didn't run his house like a tyrant, and he didn't lord over us like he was master of the house. On a day-to-day basis we treated the house as our own. There might be a bad day when Elvis was in a dark mood and everybody walked on eggshells, but that wasn't the norm. He wanted us to treat Graceland as a home—you had to respect the place, but you could also be entirely comfortable there. It was understood that he was the one doing the work that made life at Graceland possible, and what he asked for in return for all that he shared with us was that we help and support him. If you thought of being with Elvis simply as a job, then maybe there were things to gripe about. But I thought of being with Elvis as simply being with Elvis—I couldn't have been happier, and it seemed like pure gravy that I got a paycheck, too (I've still got the stubs—$75 dollars a week, $69 after taxes).

My internal clock didn't always synch with Elvis time, so I was usually up before him or any of the other guys, and spent a lot of late-morning hours just walking around the calm, beautiful grounds. I got in the habit of turning up in the kitchen around noon, where I'd sit at the little counter there and have my breakfast while Vernon's mother, Minnie, at the other end of counter near the red phone that called up to Elvis's room, tucked into her lunch. Grandma Presley was warm and welcoming to me from the start—in fact, I always addressed her as Grandma and she always called me "son." Gradually, our talks moved from idle talk to something deeper and more special, and our meal together became an opportunity for shared confidences and commentary about all the goings-on in the house. I'd come to Graceland as a friend of Elvis, but it meant a great deal to me that Grandma considered me a part of the family. (Not all of the Presley family members were quite as easy to get along with: A few years later, Graceland also became home for Elvis's Aunt Delta, Vernon's sister, after her husband died. I don't think anybody who knew Delta would describe her as "warm and welcoming"; in fact, she was fairly nasty, and after a hit from her "secret" whiskey stash, she'd start cursing out anybody she laid eyes on—except Elvis, of course. Luckily, for some reason, she liked me, too, and I didn't get cursed at nearly as much as some of the other guys.)

For all the luxurious trappings of Graceland, that little kitchen counter served as an important social hub of the house. Not only was that the spot for breakfast with Grandma, it was also where Elvis and the rest of us would gather at the very end of the night when we got back from the movies or the roller rink. We'd sit on the kitchen stools, and Elvis would put his feet up on the counter. There'd be some quiet talk, going over the events of the day, and if we needed a final snack or a cool drink we were tended to by Graceland's night-shift maid, Pauline, one of the dearest and most beloved members of the Graceland staff (Pauline was black, but I heard Elvis say several times that he thought she looked a lot like his mother). At four or five in the morning, we'd call it a night and head from the humble counter back to our beds, while Pauline would continue cooking and cleaning for the coming day, always taking time to send us off with one of the sweetest smiles in Memphis.

Just before Christmas of 1964, Elvis asked me to come with him and Marty for a ride across town. We drove to a small home in a working-class neighborhood in Midtown. This was the home of Gary Pepper, one of Elvis's earliest fans, who had become his first fan-club president. When Elvis stepped off the train in Memphis after returning from Germany, the first person to greet him was Gary.

Gary suffered from cerebral palsy, and had a hard time communicating and getting around without a wheelchair. But he was a very bright guy, and for all the special care he required, in some ways he was taking care of his not-very-well-off family. Marty had let Elvis know that Gary needed a new wheelchair, and this trip was made to deliver the chair as a Christmas present. We knocked on the front door but got no answer. Elvis peeked through a window, and then quickly walked into the home. The scene that greeted us when we stepped in behind Elvis was, to my eyes, nightmarish. Gary was crawling across the floor of the small living room. His father wasn't around, but his mother was, and she seemed to be completely out of it—in a trancelike state. Elvis immediately went right for Gary, got his arms around him, and helped get him up and comfortable. Gary was terribly embarrassed to be seen this way, but Elvis talked to him quietly and let him know it was OK—he was there to help him in any way he could. Once we had the new chair inside, Elvis lifted Gary into it and made sure it was adjusted correctly.

I remember feeling weak. This scene was so awful, and I felt I wouldn't have known how to go about helping this poor disabled young man. But Elvis didn't hesitate to put his hands on him and comfort him.

To him, this was simply a friend who needed his help. Elvis was a Holly-wood star and a rock-and-roll legend, but nothing seemed more impor-tant to him right then than lifting Gary Pepper into a new wheelchair.

Christmas was a big deal at Graceland, and the guys were always concerned with finding a great gift for Elvis. That first holiday, we presented him with a fancy leather-bound Bible that had a sketch of the tree of life on its front page—Elvis's name was on the trunk of the tree and each of the guys got their own branch. Written below the tree in English, Latin, and Hebrew was one of Elvis's favorite quotations: "And ye shall know the truth, and the truth shall set you free." In return, Elvis gave each of us a $1,000 bonus and a fancy jeweled wristwatch that had been made by Harry Levitch, a favorite Memphis jeweler who'd been a very early supporter of Elvis's career. Mr. Levitch was also happy to do special work for Elvis, and these watches had an unusual face that could go black and then reveal either a cross or the Star of David. When I asked Elvis what it meant, he said, "To make you think."

A couple of weeks later, the guys presented Elvis with a collective gift for his thirtieth birthday—a gold tree-of-life pendant (which be-came one of his most-worn pieces of jewelry). I spent most of my Christmas bonus to purchase my first, personal gift to Elvis—an intri-cately detailed collector's gun with a very unusual curved handle (at the time, it didn't strike me as strange to follow up a Bible and a Tree of Life with a firearm—now I think it probably says a lot about the dy-namics of the Memphis Mafia). Elvis didn't say much about the gun at first—it was always easier for him to be a gift-giver than a gift-receiver. But I was happy to see that on movie nights at the Memphian, he car-ried my present around in its leather case.

In addition to my new watch, I had a connection to Elvis right in my wallet—an Elvis A. Presley American Express credit card and an Elvis A. Presley Shell service-station credit card (I was authorized to sign for both). If things looked like they were going to stay quiet, I often spent some time taking care of Elvis's small fleet of luxury cars. I'd get behind the wheel of a Rolls-Royce or a Lincoln Continental or a new Cadillac and take the car out to get washed and gassed up. There was a car wash just down the street from Graceland where the vehicles always got special treatment, and I loved just cruising down there, watching heads turn. Handling a Rolls was a much finer experience than piloting my old '49 Dodge, and I certainly didn't have to keep a case of oil ready in the trunk of the Caddies. In fact, I now had a much finer ride to call my own—for personal trips I was using the same white '56 Lincoln Continental that I'd seen Elvis leaning up against in Miami.

Most of the other guys would turn up at the house around five or six P.M., and if things got busy it was usually to work out the logistics for one of our usual activities: a football game, or a night at the Rainbow, the Memphian, or the Fairgrounds. All those outings still held a thrill for me, but the nicest part of living at Graceland was the chance it offered to spend time with Elvis. In those days at the house, I think one of my greatest pleasures was simply the fact that moments with him didn't have to feel like special events anymore. We were close, we were friends, and it was the most normal thing in the world to spend time together. Yes, he was my boss, but I never called him that, and he didn't expect me to. I was proud to work for him, but the friendship was always more important than the business relationship.

One day when I was down in my basement room, Elvis came through the door—a fairly rare occurrence—carefully stepped over my puddle and, in a low, quiet voice, said, "Let's go for a ride."

A few minutes later Elvis was at the wheel of the latest Lincoln and we were driving north on Highway 51. I'd assumed Elvis wanted my company for some conversation, but he was quiet and intense—clearly not in a talking mood. A few miles down the road we pulled off into the Forest Hill Cemetery, and Elvis expertly navigated the twists in the road to get to a spot he was familiar with—his mother's grave site. He didn't say anything, and I stayed in the car for a moment while he got out and walked up the grassy, sloping hill to the massive monument marking the grave. It was maybe eight feet high—a Christ with his arms outstretched standing before a cross and flanked by angels, all atop a large, multitiered pedestal. Seeing him before that monument, it came to me that, perhaps for the very first time, I could see my friend as a small, fragile human—just like any other. Despite everything else in his life, he was a guy who had lost his mother and missed her terribly.

Elvis stood there for a while, and then, slowly, carefully, with his bare hands, he began to clean the grave—dusting the stone, brushing away some spiderwebs, clearing away some weeds at the base. His hands moved deliberately, with care and tenderness, and I found myself moved with sympathy for him. But I really had no way of understanding what he was feeling—I'd been so young when I lost my mother that I had no idea of what exactly I'd lost. I had no memory of her, and only a single locket photograph. Watching Elvis act as a humble, loving son, I found myself wondering what that kind of love felt like.

He got back in the car, and we rode back quietly to Graceland. Nothing was said, and nothing needed to be said.

I went on a few of those rides to Forest Hill through the years, and I was with Elvis the day he went to the monument maker across from the cemetery to sketch out his own design that he wanted added to the stone—a design that included a Star of David, a crucifix, and the Bible quote, "Not my will, but thine, be done." In all the years I knew Elvis, these trips were the only times I witnessed him openly demonstrating his feelings for his mother. As on that first trip, he never said a word about her. And perhaps he wanted me with him because I had lost a mother, too, but we never talked about that, either.

Elvis's readings had taken a decidedly spiritual turn—a turn very much encouraged by the well-read and spiritually minded Larry Geller. Larry was still officially working as Elvis's hairstylist, but it was clear that Elvis valued the esoteric discussions he could have with Larry even more than he valued the haircuts. And while Larry still sometimes had some trouble mixing in with the Memphis guys, I found him a very interesting and likable personality.

Elvis devoured the books Larry suggested to him, and then expanded his reading list to include works he discovered on his own. It wasn't unusual to sit up late at night with Elvis and hear him discuss the intricacies of books like *Autobiography of a Yogi*, Khalil Gibran's *The Prophet*, *The Impersonal Life*, by Joseph Benner, or *Cheiro's Book of Numbers*. Elvis hasn't ever gotten much credit as a thinker, but it was striking to me back then how much he struggled to make sense of the life he was blessed with and how hungry he was for a sense of meaning and purpose. He hadn't had the opportunity for a formal education, so he'd sometimes head down a path that would turn out to be unsatisfactory or just too far out, but eventually he'd sense that happening, and with a little more education I think he might have understood better what he was looking for and how to look for it.

Elvis was always a little embarrassed about his lack of formal education, and he was well aware that he was seen by many as a poor, dumb, Southern country boy who had gotten lucky. But I have to say that I learned more from him in our late-night conversations than I ever learned from anybody else, and if I could get any moment back with him I'd ask for one of those nights: he and I staying up late, chugging Mountain Valley water and seeking out the meaning of life.

Living at Graceland, it wasn't only Elvis that I got closer to. I also began to develop a much closer relationship with his father, Vernon, and with the young woman he'd chosen to share his home and life with, Priscilla Beaulieu.

A lot of the guys did not have warm feelings toward Vernon, primarily because of his perceived role as tight-fisted money-handler and bearer of bad news (Elvis never wanted to be the bad guy—if someone was going to be fired, Vernon conveyed the message). There was also some resentment toward Vernon because of the perception that he didn't have the skills to match the supervisory position he was in around Elvis. But I don't think Vernon gets enough credit for rising to the occasion the way he did. He was a dirt-poor working man who suddenly found himself managing the personal affairs and finances of the world's biggest superstar, and he did a pretty good job of it (given the spending habits of that superstar, I don't think a team of expert accountants could have done any better).

Some of the guys joked that Vernon was just plain cheap, because if Elvis wanted something special for Graceland, Vernon's idea of going upscale was to shop at Sears. True, but understanding how he and his family had lived for so long with nothing and how hard they had worked, it made sense that he knew the value of a dollar. And it definitely helped to have Vernon watching the checkbook when Elvis went on a buying spree. Compared to some of the folks I'd known in North Memphis, Vernon struck me as being fairly sophisticated—always looking like a kind of poor man's Clark Gable. He wasn't really "one of the guys," and never tried to be. But I always enjoyed talking with him in his office out behind Graceland—he had both a sense of calm and a dry, offbeat sense of humor. And I can picture him shuffling in from the office and coming through the kitchen, stopping over every pot to take a little taste—pinching up some greens here, some chicken there—and giving a little grunt that meant the meal was going to turn out all right.

Priscilla Presley is one of my dearest friends today, but in the early days at Graceland our relationship was a distant one. It had to be, because Elvis didn't really want the guys to be close friends with Priscilla, especially not a younger, single guy like me. He didn't want her to be considered one of the guys—she was to be respected as lady of the house. So even though I lived in the same house, I was a friend of Elvis's and knew Priscilla only as his girlfriend. As Priscilla has said, she and I were growing up together at Graceland. But at first, there wasn't supposed to be much of a direct friendship between us.

This was fine by me—after the Paula Tyden incident I had no desire to test Elvis's jealous streak again. But I know the general situation was hard for Priscilla. In early 1963 she'd left her family in Germany and come to Memphis to finish high school and to gradually become a full-time Graceland resident. Priscilla was shy, quiet, stunningly beautiful, and it was apparent that she and Elvis were deeply in love. But I know it wasn't easy for her to step into what had been essentially a bachelor's world. She was with the man she loved, in a house she could only have dreamed of, but I don't think her dreams would have ever included Jerry Schilling in the basement, Marty Lacker in the annex, and a football squad of strange guys coming and going at all hours of the day and night. Priscilla didn't fall in love with us—she fell in love with Elvis and wanted a life with him. On the guys' side—we had been used to Elvis's having girlfriends who had very little impact on the way things worked around him. But Priscilla was someone on a much different level, and it took some adjusting to on all sides.

The delicacy of the situation became clear to Priscilla and me one night after an encounter in the Graceland kitchen. I was pouring myself a glass of milk when Priscilla walked in, and it was the first time I saw her not looking great. She looked like maybe she had the flu—eyes red and watery and face flushed.

"Are you feeling OK, Priscilla?" I asked.

"Yeah," she said weakly.

"Are you sure?"

"Yeah. I'm just tired."

She went back upstairs, and I went out to the back room of the house. It seemed like that was that. Except that now I became aware of some very loud voices upstairs.

Priscilla did not have the flu. What I hadn't known in the kitchen was that Elvis and Priscilla were in the middle of a hellacious argument. They were both furious with each other over something, and Priscilla, after bursting into tears, had come downstairs just to take a breather. When she went back upstairs the fight started all over again, and one of the first things she said to Elvis was "At least Jerry Schilling cares about how I feel." This was not a good thing to say to an already angry Elvis.

I took a seat in the back room of the house, joining a couple of the other guys there. The noises continued upstairs, but I became more focused on the football game the guys were watching on TV.

All of a sudden Elvis stormed into the room, so agitated he couldn't quite stand still. He stared down at the floor and announced to the group of us, "Goddamn it—I don't need anybody else taking care of Priscilla and checking how she is. Is that goddamn clear?"

The other guys nodded, though they weren't quite sure what Elvis was talking about. But I knew exactly what he was talking about and who he was talking to. He didn't wait for any answer from anyone, and just stormed back out of the room and up the stairs.

No, I hadn't done anything wrong. But I didn't need to see Elvis that worked up again on my account. It was almost a full year before I had another conversation with Priscilla.

Elvis plays to the crowd at one of his legendary performances on
The Ed Sullivan Show in 1956.

Above: The Holy Names football team. I'm #25 in the first row.

Right: Me in high school, about the time I started hanging out at Graceland.

Above: Elvis and me on the set of *Paradise, Hawaiian Style*.

Below: Elvis with Hawaiian dancers on the set. Sandy is to his right.

Above: Elvis, Priscilla, me, and Sandy in the Graceland Meditation Garden.

Right: Elvis, Alan Fortas, Billy Smith, and me eating ice cream made from snow outside Graceland.

Below: Elvis posing in his best motorcycle outfit in Beverly Hills.

Above: Elvis and me preparing to cruise the PCH. I'm on a Triumph Bonneville, which Elvis bought for me.

Right: The Tree of Life pendant the Memphis Mafia gave Elvis on his thirtieth birthday.

Below: Elvis's wedding, 1967. I'm second from the left.

Left: Elvis riding a fake bull on the set of *Stay Away, Joe* as I look on.

Below: Elvis punching Red West in *Paradise, Hawaiian Style.* I'm in the background in the Hawaiian shirt, and Richard Davis is to my left.

Below: Elvis and me in *Frankie and Johnny.*

Above: Elvis as the real Charro.

Right: Me posing as Elvis's photo double in *Charro!*

Above: Elvis and Priscilla leaving the hospital with a newborn Lisa Marie. I'm on the far left.

Right: Elvis riding down the Graceland lawn to greet fans at the gate.

Below: Helping Elvis with a necklace.

6

. . .

PARADISE FOUND

In March of 1965, Elvis and us guys were back out in L.A., where he went to work making three films almost back-to-back (*Harum Scarum*, *Frankie and Johnny*, and *Paradise, Hawaiian Style*). The days on the lot and the nights at the Perugia house were similar to what I'd experienced during the *Tickle Me* shoot, but there was one significant roster change for us. Returning to the group, and serving as a co-foreman with Marty, was Joe Esposito. Joe was an army buddy who had begun working for Elvis almost as soon as they were both back from Germany, and whatever disagreement had caused them to part ways for a while seemed to be completely forgotten once Joe was back with Elvis and the guys.

It quickly became apparent to me that Joe was a great asset to the group. He wasn't a Southern boy, but he fit right in with his mix of Chicago street smarts and an easygoing sense of humor. More importantly, Joe had a great knack for projecting calm while handling all the organizational tasks always swirling around Elvis and the group. And he had a very natural way of delegating responsibilities that left a minimum of ruffled feathers. Joe dependably took care of things, and almost made it look easy. I could also see that, as different as he and I were in background and temperament, Joe too shared a special, devoted friendship with Elvis.

A few weeks into this L.A. trip, I met for the first time another long-running member of the inner circle. It was a quiet Saturday evening at the Perugia house, and I happened to be in the main den when I heard a loud knock at the door. It wasn't too often that a knock at that door was unexpected—we usually knew who was coming by and when.

So this knock immediately put me into security mode. I opened the door, ready to turn away any overeager fan or unwanted visitor.

"Who is it?" I asked the small, intense-looking figure before me.

"Charlie Hodge!" he answered, obviously a little upset that I didn't know him by sight.

"Hang on, I'll check with Elvis."

I'd heard the name, and I knew Elvis and Charlie were close, but given Elvis's shifting moods and aversion to surprise guests, I was going to make sure Elvis was feeling up for a visitor. But as I turned to go find Elvis, Charlie shot right past me into the house—and obviously knew his way around well enough to dart around the corner into the little den where Elvis usually hung out. I was stunned, wondering what the security protocol was for a situation like this—but a second after the alleged Charlie Hodge disappeared I heard Elvis call out in a happy voice, "Hey, Charlie!"

That was my introduction to Mr. Hodge, an army buddy of Elvis's who also became a well-traveled member of the inner circle. Charlie was also deeply devoted to Elvis, and, as I soon learned, functioned a bit like the court jester of the Memphis Mafia—quick with a gag and always a steady source of laughter. Through the years he was also a key figure in supporting and encouraging Elvis's musical development.

Not all Saturday evenings were quiet for the group—but more often than not the L.A. house operated much in the manner of a Graceland West, with Elvis and the rest of us living in the same self-contained, self-reliant manner we did back East. We didn't mix with the neighbors, who included Dean Martin, Alfred Hitchcock, Jerry Lewis, and Howard Hughes (a future employer of mine, Brian Wilson, lived two blocks away on Bellagio). And there were very few Hollywood celebrities who were welcomed in—Bing's son Gary Crosby hung out with us a few times, and Ricky Nelson participated in some football games, but that was about it. But aside from the basic courtesy meetings, Elvis hardly spent any time with power players from the studios.

It might seem strange that a star like Elvis would not become a toast of the town in L.A., but for all his success, and the steady, profitable film work he was engaged in, Elvis always had a curious relationship with Hollywood. He was still "Elvis" out there, but I think he knew that he was "Elvis" based on what he'd done in the past, not what he was doing now. His movies weren't automatic hits anymore, and his years of hit records seemed farther away than ever. He was treated like royalty at every movie lot and recording studio, but it had to be agonizing for him that though he was potentially at the peak of his powers, he couldn't find a way to really flex his creative muscles. At thirty, he sometimes felt he was being looked at more as a quaint bit of pop history than as a vital talent. He was given all due respect for past glories, but what had he done lately? "Harem Holiday" was no "Heartbreak Hotel." He knew that as well as anyone.

One thing that was true about Elvis throughout his life—he wasn't going to walk himself into any situation where he'd feel uncomfortable. And most of the Hollywood social scene made him uncomfortable. So he didn't go out on the town much, and didn't make any attempt to crack into Hollywood social circles. This aspect of Elvis's life has earned him the reputation as a recluse, and living with Elvis there were certainly times when it felt like he was acting a bit like our neighbor Mr. Hughes. But Elvis was a guy who had been dealing with uncomfortable situations since he was nineteen—putting up with authorities that denounced him, a huge segment of the public that despised him, and adoring crowds that wanted to lovingly rip him to pieces. I don't think his wanting to stay in was crazy. Given how much time he spent living his life in public, his desire for privacy was one of the most "normal" things about him.

Throughout this time at the Perugia house, I could see that for all the fine trappings of the luxurious lifestyle Elvis had earned, there were pressures, burdens, and doubts that wore on him heavily. His success had given him a great life, but it was an extremely complicated one. He'd started out as a kid who wanted to sing, and had turned into an industry. On one of the quiet days, he and I were in that little den off the side of the house by ourselves, just watching TV. At one point he turned to me and said, "Jerry—you know the hardest thing you're ever going to have to learn?"

"No, Elvis—what's that?"

"How to not do anything."

It took me years before I really understood that, but it's turned out to be one of the smartest things anybody's ever said to me. In my personal life and in my career, I've learned again and again that having nothing to do can be a lot harder than having something to do, and that living a dream isn't always as satisfying as having a dream.

On the nights we stayed in at the Perugia house, we spent a lot of time around the pool table in the big round den with the open fireplace, and even more time hanging out in that little den. Elvis had become infatuated with playing a Fender electric bass guitar, and a lot of nights he'd plug in, sit in front of a TV with the sound turned down, and play along at extremely high volume with a stack of records.

Elvis had learned very early on in his career that if he tried to plan any personal outings in advance, word would get out, he'd be mobbed, and what was supposed to be personal time would become a public appearance. So he got in the habit of making last-minute decisions to do whatever it was he wanted to do (a habit that fit very well with his temperament). Occasionally, a buzz would ripple through the house, and we'd all snap into action like the White House staff and the Secret Service getting ready for a presidential excursion: We were going out.

Elvis's club of choice in Los Angeles was the Red Velvet on Sunset Boulevard. The TV rock-and-roll show *Shindig*, which had recently debuted and was an instant hit, was taped nearby on Monday afternoons. Monday nights, guys from the house band, the Shindogs, and some of the artists that appeared on the show would head to the Red Velvet afterward (one of those Shindogs was a twangy guitar player named James Burton, later a member of Elvis's band). The Red Velvet had the feel of a hipster lounge: big red-leather booths, low lights, a small stage, and a cool clientele. Elvis had become friendly with the owner of the club, Tony Ferra, who was always happy to rope off a few booths and get the place ready for an Elvis entrance when he got the word from a couple of us guys working as an advance team.

The very first time I was part of a Red Velvet expedition, I was understandably excited and wanted to make the best impression possible. The guys had started making Saturday shopping trips to the Fred Segal store to pick up clothes for ourselves and Elvis, and I put on what I thought was my best Segal-bought stuff to go out. As I left my room to head toward the door I passed Elvis, who was looking killer sharp in his black pants and tailored jacket with the collar up. He just glanced at me and said, "You better get ready, Jerry, we're going out."

Obviously I had not passed muster. I went back to my room, put on a different set of still pretty-nice slacks and shirt, and headed out again. This time, I met Elvis and some of the other guys by the front door. Elvis eyed me up and down.

"Jerry—you're gonna wear that? We're going to a club."

Now I broke out in a nervous sweat. I couldn't figure out what I was doing wrong. I'd already picked up on some of Elvis's wardrobe tricks, like cutting out the pockets of pants to get a smoother, tighter fit. But apparently something about my fashion sense wasn't working. I ran back to the room, threw on my last possible going-out outfit, and ran back to the group. Now Elvis actually looked angry.

"Would you stop messin' around? You're gonna wear that? C'mon man, it's a club. A Hollywood club."

I must have looked red-faced and desperate enough that before I could ask what wardrobe mistake I was making, the whole group of guys cracked up. I'd just been given a traditional Memphis Mafia hazing. Elvis came over to shoot an elbow at my ribs. My red face might have clashed with whatever I had on, but it didn't matter. I'd be riding with Elvis for a night on the town.

At the Red Velvet, we mixed with members of acts like the Buffalo Springfield, the Righteous Brothers, and a Memphis trio called the Guilloteens, who'd scored both a *Shindig* appearance and a Phil Spector recording session. It's surprising how low-key it felt to be hanging out with some of the hottest names on the L.A. music scene at the time. I suppose I felt I was already with the biggest star in the room—everybody else was just a nice guy to have a drink with. And I wasn't that interested in drinks with the guys—I'd started taking out a very cute extra from *Harum Scarum* named Vicki, and she, along with some of the other guys' dates, would often come with us to the club.

It seemed like a lot of the other musicians still considered Elvis to be the biggest star in the room. One time we were watching singer P. J. Proby perform his big hit, a cover of "Somewhere" from *West Side Story*. Elvis sent up a note to the stage asking him if he'd sing the song again. Proby, a polished professional, read the note, stopped dead, and sat down on the stage. After a moment, he said to the crowd, "I've just received the biggest honor I could ever hope for—a personal request from Elvis Presley."

. . .

Around our work and home schedules, I started making some outings of my own. Elvis was still passionately interested in explorations of spirituality and was constantly poring over his collection of books, marking them up, and occasionally reading out sections to some of us. I got the feeling that some of the other guys saw this as the "weird" side of Elvis—something that just had to be put up with (their attitude toward Elvis's books was no doubt colored by their strong antipathy toward Larry Geller—who was always much more of a California dude than a Memphis fella). But I was fascinated by the fact that Elvis was still curious and hungry for education, and that sharpened my own hunger for knowledge.

So in the spring of 1965, I worked for Elvis by day and started taking classes at UCLA at night. Back in my high school football days, I had always nursed a dream of playing for USC. But working for Elvis, we drove through the UCLA campus in Westwood almost every day to get to our regular market, or pharmacy, or pizza place. I fell in love with that sprawling, stately campus and realized how much I actually missed being a student. So I signed up for some anthropology and history classes there to pick up my last credits toward a degree. While I didn't hear anything directly from the guys about my new nighttime activity, I'm sure they took it as evidence that I too was getting weird: Why would anybody in their right mind choose to go back to school?

As it turned out, some nights I might have learned more by staying home. In one class we were going to discuss something about the "dynamics of social structure" and the power of popular culture. I opened up my textbook—and there was a picture of Elvis. I had a brief temptation to shout out, "Hey—I just walked down the hill from this guy's house," but I kept quiet. I just couldn't believe I'd gone to the trouble of enrolling in a night class to study the guy I was spending all day with. It was one of the better discussions that semester, though.

I think my long walks from Bel Air to UCLA influenced another independent decision I made—to become a motorcycle owner. I'd always wanted to have my own bike, to see if I couldn't pull off a bit of that Brando-in-*The Wild One* mystique. A motorcycle seemed just the thing to make my California dream perfect and complete. So, despite my resistance to the idea of taking on debt, I went down one day to the

Robertson Triumph Motorcycle dealership, where Alan Fortas had developed a relationship with the owner, put down as much as I could, signed up for years of payments, and became the owner of a brand-new Triumph Bonneville 750.

A few days after I got the Triumph, Elvis took note of it and asked me if he could take it for a ride. He had always been a Harley-Davidson rider and wanted to compare the feel of the rides. He rode around the circle in front of the Perugia house and into Bel Air a little bit, then came back and casually told Alan Fortas that he wanted everybody in the group to have a Triumph Bonneville. And he wanted his guys to have the bikes that night. Alan soon discovered that there were only three Bonnevilles at the Robertson lot, and those were in crates, not fully assembled. Alan must have called every Triumph dealer in Southern California, and by midnight we had nine Bonnevilles being uncrated and assembled in the Perugia front yard. Three hours later, we had all of them roaring away through the streets of Bel Air. (When George Klein came out for a vacation visit and guest deejayed at KFWB, the number-one rock station in town at the time, he'd send out mysterious dedications to the "Bel Air Bonnevilles" and then play an Elvis record.) The Bel Air Homeowners' Society was a little less impressed with us, and threatened to have Elvis kicked out of the neighborhood if there was any more late-night rumbling. Elvis's response was to buy a truck and trailer so that all the bikes could be hauled in and out of Bel Air with minimum noise.

It occurred to me that I'd spent all I had and put myself into hock to get my bike, and then, because Elvis liked it, everybody else got a free one. But within days the unfairness of the situation must have occurred to Elvis, too. I got a call from the Robertson lot letting me know that Elvis had paid off my motorcycle.

Motorcyle-riding became a big part of our L.A. experience—maybe standing in as the West Coast version of our Rainbow skating nights. Almost every Sunday, Elvis and a group of eight to fifteen of us would go riding up the Pacific Coast Highway and through the spectacular, winding canyon roads of the Santa Monica Mountains. Despite the noise, these were very relaxing rides for everybody, which often ended at a little log cabin market at the top of Topanga Canyon where we'd stop and drink some Pepsis.

But of course, you put Elvis on a motorcycle and his competitive spirit is going to come out somehow. He also liked to lead us on these late-night charges up the PCH when the sea air had gotten chilly and the fog was starting to roll in. We had the speedy Triumphs, but he was on a big, rock-steady Harley Electra-Glide. He'd get the group up to 105, when our front wheels would be shaking enough to scare the hell out of us, and he'd still pass us, nice and easy and all smiles. And no—none of us were ever wearing helmets.

It was on one of those Sunday rides that I saw how easily Elvis could shift from daredevil to seeker. Seven or eight of us, including Priscilla on the back of Elvis's Harley, were thundering back up Sunset Boulevard off of the PCH. Elvis was in the lead, and it seemed like some estate or building caught his eye—he pulled off Sunset through the open gates of an entryway, and we all followed. We pulled up alongside him, read a few of the posted signs around us, and realized we were on the grounds of the Self-Realization Fellowship.

Elvis had intently studied *Autobiography of a Yogi*, the principal work of the movement's founder, Paramahansa Yogananda. From what I had learned from Elvis in many of our late-night conversations, part of Yogananda's focus was to understand that there was something miraculous in the simplest of natural everyday occurrences, and he encouraged those simple joys to be meditated upon. Some of the SRF teachings were on the proper way to breathe, the proper state of mind with which to go to sleep, the proper way to wake up and start the day. The notion of being deeply connected with your inner self—of simply being comfortable in your own skin, and of being able to live in the moment—had tremendous appeal to Elvis. It might seem strange that a guy who would insist that a dozen new motorcycles be delivered to his house at midnight was in search of a simpler life, but I think that's the point— Elvis knew better than anybody that the money and the expensive toys were not going to lead him to any sense of deeper purpose.

We got off our bikes that day and began to stroll through the grounds of the Fellowship—a beautiful spread of winding paths, ponds, gardens, waterfalls, and meditation chapels. Maybe some of the guys were more skeptical about the benefits of the Self-Realization philosophy, but I don't think anybody failed to feel what I felt that day—the place had a magic. You couldn't walk through there without feeling yourself calm down and open up.

I could see the subtle change the place had on Elvis as we strolled along. He seemed to let himself relax and let his defenses drop. At the same time, he did not exactly slip into meditation mode. After a while, I could see a kind of antsy energy get the better of him. If a taste of tranquility was this good, then Elvis wanted access to the Fellowship's deepest secrets of the soul as quickly as possible. He had a long talk with Brother Adolph, one of the Fellowship members on the grounds (and a guy who seemed to take in remarkably casual stride the fact that Elvis Presley had dropped in). Elvis learned that the leader of the movement was now a woman named Daya Mata, who had been personally tutored for the position by Yogananda. Daya Mata stayed at a separate, private retreat up on Mt. Washington, east of Hollywood.

In the weeks that followed, Elvis got permission to visit Daya Mata, and many times I accompanied him up to her home—a place that had the feel of a wealthy estate, religious shrine, and working farm all at once. Again, whatever quibbles one might have had with the SRF philosophy, the Daya Mata was prime evidence that the practices worked. She was so calm and centered, so at peace with herself, that she absolutely radiated a feeling of maternal goodwill and gentle understanding. She was wise enough to know that Elvis couldn't just jump into the Fellowship the way he wanted to—the secrets of the soul couldn't be delivered in crates like so many motorcycles. But she was wonderfully gracious to him and truly appreciative of his search for something of substance. They developed a great friendship, and every time we drove away from that Mt. Washington retreat, usually with baskets of homegrown fruits on our laps, I could sense that Elvis had gotten some small piece of the peace he was after.

In late spring of 1965, Elvis began work on the film *Frankie and Johnny*, and I found myself with a new Elvis-related job: on-screen talent. Elvis liked to include his friends in the films—Red or Sonny West turned up regularly in fight scenes, Joe had some speaking parts from time to time, and you could usually spot Alan, Richard, and Billy in the the background of crowd scenes. I'd started to do some stand-in and photo-double work for Elvis, and on this film I got my first nonspeaking bit part in front of the cameras.

It was customary for me to ride to the studio with Elvis, but on one particular day my scene was going to shoot before his, so I took off early for the Samuel Goldwyn Studios on my Bonneville. It was a wet, misty morning, and I couldn't wait to get to the coffee station on the sound-stage. Coming through a bend in Sunset, I had the right of way, but apparently a woman in a car coming toward me didn't see me—she started a left turn that cut me off. I tried to lay the bike down but I hit the side of her car, flipped over it, flew through the air, and landed on my back. As usual, I wasn't wearing a helmet, so I'm lucky that collision wasn't the end of me. I felt paralyzed for a moment, then started crawling down the street in a daze. Some other bikers just happened to see the accident happen and got me off the road, wrapped me in a blanket, and called for an ambulance.

I spent a couple of weeks in the hospital, and though nothing was broken I had extensive internal injuries—my back and chest were so sore that every breath was painful. (A top gossip columnist in one of the papers managed to be inaccurate and insensitive at the same time, writing that "One of Elvis's buddies had a motorcycle accident and broke his pelvis. Good thing it wasn't Elvis." I saved the clip for years because it was the first time he and I were mentioned together in a newspaper.) Joe Esposito and Billy Smith and Richard Davis came to visit me, and I even got a surprise visit from Elvis's *Frankie and Johnny* costar, Donna Douglas (a fellow Self-Realization advocate, best-known as "Elly Mae" from *The Beverly Hillbillies*). She cried when she saw the shape I was in and sat with me quietly for a long time, holding my hand. She left me with a reading light as a gift.

One strange benefit of my hospital stay was that it may have kept me out of Vietnam. I'd gotten my draft notice a month earlier and had taken a physical in which it was decided that my football-injured back required a follow-up physical. The date for that follow-up fell during the time I was laid up recovering from the accident, and after the draft board was informed of what had happened to me and the extent of my injuries, I didn't receive any further notices. If I had, I would have gone. Not happily, but I don't think I would have felt I had any choice but to serve.

When I finally did get back to the Perugia house, all I wanted was to be left alone. I had healed up enough to get around, but I was in a tremendous amount of pain, and wasn't really sure if I'd ever be completely able-bodied again. I think most people hit some point in their early adulthood where they suddenly realize that maybe they're not indestructible. This was that point for me. The constant pain had me frustrated, and the frustration led to depression. As I hobbled into the house, I was perspiring and wincing in pain, and despite the fact that I could tell that Elvis was glad to see me, I was hurting enough that I had no desire to talk to him. I just hobbled to my room and lay down on my bed, gritting my teeth and waiting for the throbbing in my back to subside.

A little while later, there was a soft knock at the door, and Elvis stepped into the room.

"The boys were worried about you, Jerry. They told me how banged up you were."

"Yeah. I still don't feel so hot," I said, hoping he wasn't planning on a long talk.

"You know, I've been reading something on the power of touch," he said. "Healing power of the hands. Get over on your stomach for a minute."

I have to admit it flashed through my mind—"Please, Elvis, let's not get into some crazy philosophy thing right now." But, at the same time, I was desperate for relief, and it was nice to have him in the room.

I rolled over and got as comfortable I could. Elvis lowered his voice and talked, calmly and slowly, about the idea that each human body had an energy, and through touch those energies could connect. "Sounds a little half-mad," he said, "but you use touch just the right way, maybe you can pull away somebody else's pain."

As he spoke, he put his hands on my back and applied a bit of pressure. I hadn't read the stuff he was talking about, and he didn't really make a big deal out of it. There was nothing mystical about the moment, and he wasn't trying to be some kind of shaman. But dammit if by the time he lifted his hands from my back, the pain was gone. I did notice that he shook his hands out—as if he were shaking off whatever pain he had managed to soak up.

"Get better, man. Let me know what you need," he said quietly, then left.

I lay there, surprised to find myself relaxed and comfortable for the first time in weeks.

I don't think Elvis was harnessing any supernatural powers to take my pain away. I think what really took away the pain was the kind of comfort that only a loving friend can provide. It's lonely and scary to be that hurt, and having Elvis care enough to do whatever he could to make me feel better—to relax me and let me know I'd be looked after— meant everything to me. I think what made my back feel better wasn't any more mystical than the concern of a good friend.

That summer, my father came out for a visit, traveling in his usual vacation custom with two women—my stepmom, Lula, and Helen, the same friend of theirs that had been with us in Miami almost a decade before. We spent some time at the Perugia house, where my father finally met Elvis. Elvis was extremely gracious and courteous, and said some very nice things about me to my father. I could see that little twinkle in my dad's eye—he liked knowing that I was doing OK for myself. I showed the visitors all around Los Angeles, and since the Fourth of July fell during their trip, we decided we'd do something special that day. We'd take a ferry out to Catalina Island for lunch and be back in time for a homey backyard Fourth party that Joanie Esposito and some of the other wives were organizing. It was a great day, with Dad and the two ladies duly impressed by everything they saw. But after we got up to Perugia, Mike Keaton pulled me aside.

"Listen, I thought you should know. Marty was real upset about you taking off today. I don't know what he might have told Elvis."

Mike was one of the most solid and down-to-earth of the guys and also one of the quietest. When he did speak up about something, it was worth paying attention to. I thanked him for the heads-up.

The party was a pleasant, family-style backyard barbecue. And just as it was starting to get dark, Elvis made his entrance (even at his own parties, he could make a hell of an entrance). He said his hellos and after a while came over to where I was standing with my father and the ladies.

"Did you take your daddy out to Catalina today?" he asked.

"Yeah, Elvis. We had a nice time out there."

He smiled and nodded. "Well, I'm proud of you. That's a real nice thing to do."

Whatever the guys had been worried about, it wasn't bothering Elvis at all. He did have his black moods, and he had a temper, and sometimes he could be unreasonable. But a lot of times, it was the personal politics around him that created more worry and fuss than anything he did. The temper and the moodiness were part of his makeup, but most of the time Elvis chose not to let them affect the way he treated other people. Looking back on all our time together, what's remarkable to me is not the handful of times that he did let a crazy temper get the better of him—what's remarkable is that, with all that went on in his life, most of the time he chose to be a nice guy.

By the end of that summer I was healed up enough from my bike accident to be back as a full-strength member of the Elvis team, and as preparations were made for the filming of *Paradise, Hawaiian Style*, my job profile came to include an interesting duty. Because the film would include a couple weeks of location shooting in Oahu, Colonel Parker was going to get to the island first and make sure everything was properly organized for Elvis. On such trips, the Colonel would travel with his chief "lieutenant," Tom Diskin, and would also bring along one of Elvis's guys to take care of personal and security arrangements at the hotel we were using (this also meant that the Colonel, in his inimitable way, could keep tabs on the information flowing in and out of Elvis's inner circle). For this particular trip, he was also bringing along his wife and his teenage step-granddaughter, Sharon. I was the Elvis guy picked to travel with them.

My security duties included making sure that access to the floor Elvis would be on could be controlled, and making sure that the hotel was going to allow us use of back doors and staff elevators. The primary concern was making sure that Elvis could be kept safe at the hotel and on the set, but I also made sure he could be comfortable, arranging for a piano to be brought to his room and making sure that room service would have some of his favorite foods available at the hours he was most likely to want them.

I took my responsibilities very seriously, but it was an education to witness the Colonel in action. He always maintained his outsized presence and bluff demeanor, but he backed it up with masterful organizational skills. From finalizing contacts, to working out police escorts, to overseeing special conditions on the set, there wasn't a single detail that the Colonel was not on top of, and not a single deal in which he didn't get the special treatment he was after for his client. In addition, he expertly worked press and publicity angles—creating an interest and excitement in the film that otherwise would not have existed. The Colonel may not have had a clue as to how to address Elvis's creative frustrations or spiritual questions, but he demanded that Elvis be treated as the biggest star in the world, and in his ability to have those demands met, he was astounding.

My time in Hawaii started off in almost surreal fashion. On my first afternoon there, while the Colonel was off for a nap, I wandered down to the pool at the Ilikai Hotel, found a seat at a table near the poolside bar, and decided to order up the first mai tai of my life. I noticed a large table of guys who were talking and laughing it up together, and I was just a few sips into my drink when one of them started waving me over. I got up to approach, and quickly realized that the guy doing the waving was actor Richard Harris, the great "angry young man" of British film, who'd sometimes been described as England's Brando. I'd thought he was great as a particularly angry rugby player in *This Sporting Life*, and I was also quite sure that he had no idea who I was. But that didn't seem to matter. He had me pull up a chair and join him and the members of his film crew from the epic production *Hawaii*. And before long, he was talking to me like his new best drinking buddy—telling me all sorts of stories about his adventurous career. We proceeded to drink the afternoon away. Richard put down cocktail after cocktail, while I took my time with the one mai tai—which was strong enough to knock me back to my room for a nap later on.

By the next day on the island I realized that brushes with celebrity were nothing compared to the sheer natural beauty of the place I found myself in. Spectacular beaches, gorgeous mountain vistas, lush greenery, that sweet, balmy air that made every breeze feel like a kiss—I couldn't imagine any paradise better than the Hawaiian-style one all around me. And as we began filming at the Polynesian Cultural Center in Oahu, I saw that the beauty of the place was not just in the land but in the Hawaiian people, too. The Center had been founded by the

Mormon church just a couple years before we got there, as a means of preserving the traditions of many of the South Pacific islands—Hawaii, Samoa, Fiji, Tahiti, and others—as well as offering a chance for some higher education to young islanders. Students could take classes at the nearby Brigham Young University Hawaii campus during the day, and in the evening they displayed crafts and artwork and performed traditional music and dance for the public. Filming at the center meant that many of these students were a part of our production, and on one of the first days that we shot a big production number, my eyes were drawn to one of the dancers—the most beautiful girl I'd ever seen.

All the dancers had a glowing beauty about them, but the way I felt my heart flip when I saw this one slight dancer—I knew it wasn't just the thrill of an infatuation with physical beauty. Watching her dance felt almost like a religious experience. And the more I watched, the more I felt drawn to her.

In the days that followed, I couldn't take my eyes off this girl when she was around the set, and I couldn't stop thinking about her when I was back at the Ilikai. Finally I approached her, feeling a lot more shy than I had around any L.A. girls. Her name was Sandy Kawelo (pronounced "kavelo"), and it took only a few moments of conversation to sense that she was as sweet as she looked—a woman whose inner beauty matched her physical charms. I was hooked, and I felt like there was a connection between us. But I couldn't figure out how any relationship would be possible once the shoot was over.

Others took note of Sandy's exceptional beauty—producer Hal Wallis set up a screen test for her in the middle of work on the film—a very big deal. I was pained at the thought of this pure, graceful creature being subjected to the whims of a studio (that was hard enough on Elvis!) and was relieved when Sandy—though appearing just as beautiful on screen as she did in sunlight and moonlight—showed no interest in a Hollywood career.

The *Paradise* shoot went smoothly, and our time on the island included one very moving side trip—to the recently completed memorial built over the sunken USS *Arizona*. The battleship was a casualty of the attack on Pearl Harbor, and Elvis and the Colonel had been very involved in raising money to get the memorial built, staging a hugely successful benefit concert for the *Arizona* in March of 1961, just before

Elvis began work on *Blue Hawaii*. It had meant a great deal to Elvis to be able to give something back to his country that way, and for all the Colonel's usual attention to the bottom line, this had been a situation where he, too, wanted to be as charitable as possible. Elvis, the Colonel, Vernon, and the guys were given a special tour of the memorial by an admiral, using his private boat. I could see how moved both Elvis and the Colonel were by the powerful tribute to fallen servicemen that their efforts had made possible. I remember standing next to Elvis at a rail that looked over the submerged ship, and we were shocked to see that oil from the engines was still bubbling up to the surface of the water. "Those guys are still down there," he said very softly.

We had a few afternoons off during the course of the shoot, and on one of those days a group of the guys—Joe, Marty, Billy, Charlie Hodge, and myself—were with Elvis up in his hotel suite. Red West was with us, too—he had a part in the film as "Rusty," a character who, in typical Red fashion, picks a fight with Elvis. Elvis could sometimes go long stretches without making any music outside of what was required for his soundtrack work, but in Hawaii, the relaxed pace of life, the warm breezes, and the sweet smell of the island's flowers must have put him in a more musical mood. The Ilikai had obliged my request for a piano by putting a baby grand in the room, and this day, Elvis sat down at the keyboard and without hesitation began rolling out the chords of a favorite song of his that fit the tropical locale, "Beyond the Reef."

When Elvis sang a song like this, one that he'd sung hundreds of times, it was almost as if the music just flowed right out of him. But as soon as the music began to fill the room, it wasn't just about Elvis anymore. The sound of that piano pulled us all together, and it took only a few bars before Red and Charlie joined in strong on harmony. The rest of us joined in, too, although those of us who knew we might contribute a sour note if we pushed too hard kept things a little on the quiet side.

We started singing through song after song—"Red Sails in the Sunset," "I'll Remember You," "Cool, Cool Water,"—with Elvis sometimes picking the tune and sometimes following the suggestions of one of the guys. Elvis could be just as happy singing as a backup voice, adding Irish tenor harmony when Red or Charlie sang a strong lead on a tune. Just as our football games were a mix of serious sports and good times, the singing was a mix of some great music and a lot of kidding around. There was teasing and joking before and after almost every song, and a moment of sweet group harmony would lead to unrestrained laughter when somebody made a funny or risqué alteration to some lyrics—Elvis himself was fond of changing "Red Sails in the Sunset" to "Pat Sails in the Sunset"—Pat was Red West's wife.

Yes it was Elvis's piano, and his hotel suite, and his movie that had brought us all there. But what you could feel in that room was the easy camaraderie of a great group of guys, enjoying the simple pleasure of singing together before a Hawaiian sunset.

After the last day of filming, the people of the Polynesian Cultural Center threw a farewell party for us at the Queen's hut—a sign of great respect. It was a private affair, with students performing special dances just for us. Sandy performed a hula that had my heart in my throat—she was so pure and so radiant. All the wonderful performances started having an emotional impact on me that night. In some ways we were simply in the middle of business as usual—putting together another Elvis film. But his connection to Hawaii and the Hawaiian people was deeply felt, and the openhearted affection, respect, and appreciation they poured back at us was overwhelming.

I wasn't the only one who responded to the emotions of the night. I rode back to the hotel sitting next to Elvis, and in the quiet hum of the drive, I turned to look at him. There were tears running down his face. It's one of the few times I ever saw him moved enough to cry.

My emotions got worked up all over again as we headed for the flight that would take us back to Los Angeles. Just as I was starting to reconcile myself to the fact that I'd never see Sandy again, she appeared with a special, intricate flower lei for me that she'd made herself—her way of letting me know that our brief time together meant something to her as well. I've never been much of a letter writer, but I spent just about the entire flight back to the mainland composing a love letter to Sandy, and I sent it off to her as soon as I got hold of an envelope and a stamp.

Just a week after we got back from Hawaii, a historic event took place at the Perugia house: Elvis met the Beatles. The group's second film,

Help!, had just come out, and they were in L.A. for concerts at the Hollywood Bowl. Despite the way Elvis felt about his career, the Beatles still considered him an idol, and pushed their manager, Brian Epstein, to work with Colonel Parker to set up a meeting. Elvis consented, and invited them to come by the Perugia house.

After all sorts of elaborate security measures were put in place, the Beatles dropped by the house around ten o'clock one August night. Careerwise, the Beatles were at the top of their game—putting out number-one records, garnering enthusiastic critical praise for their films, and creating pandemonium at all their sold-out concert appearances. But they seemed truly delighted to be meeting Elvis and were willing to defer to him to set the tone for the evening. Elvis wanted the evening to feel natural.

Maybe it would be better history if this meeting of great talents had turned into some phenomenal jam session or an outrageous, headline-making party, but in fact it had the quiet, easygoing feel of most get-togethers at the house. Well—as quiet and easygoing as is possible when you've got Elvis, the Beatles, Colonel Parker, Brian Epstein, and some Colonel-provided roulette wheels together in the same room.

It's been reported that Elvis cold-shouldered the Beatles that night, or that he wasn't happy to have them in his house. But what I saw was Elvis welcoming them into his home the way he would anyone else—as Elvis. The guy was never a phony, and I never saw him change the way he acted to try to make any particular impression on the people he met. He wasn't going to suddenly become the sparkling host or the bubbly jokester for the sake of making a better impression. If he wanted to cold-shoulder you, you never got the invitation to come over. But if you were invited, you got Elvis.

Things were a little awkward at first as introductions were made, and there was a lull when everyone first sat down together. But Elvis broke the ice by saying to the Beatles, "If you're just going to sit around and stare at me, I'm going to bed." Elvis and the guys began to laugh, and once the Beatles realized they were dealing with someone who shared their skewed sense of humor, everybody got along great. At some point, Elvis pulled out his Fender bass and began to play along with records, impressing Paul McCartney (one of Elvis's favorite tunes at the time was Charlie Rich's "Mohair Sam," and he could really nail the bass line). Elvis also clearly got a kick out of some of the freewheeling banter of John Lennon, and they talked about their shared love of the films of Peter Sellers. I think for a good deal of the evening George was out back smoking something or other and kicking philosophical ideas around with Larry Geller. I hooked up with Ringo at the pool table, and we took on a team of Billy Smith and Mal Evans, the Beatles' tour manager (we won).

Throughout the night I kept finding myself bumping into John Lennon, and in our bits of joking conversation we seemed to connect pretty quickly. From what I'd read and heard of him, I suppose I expected him to have more of an edge. But he was actually a bit on the shy side, extremely polite and good-natured, and of course funny as hell. He came up to me as the Beatles were finally getting ready to head back to the house they were staying at up in Benedict Canyon (a house that Elvis had considered renting for himself).

"Jerry, I know Elvis can't get out, but if you want to come over to our place over the next three days, feel free."

I thanked John, but I knew I wouldn't take him up on the offer. I was a Beatles fan, and thought John was a tremendous guy, but I wasn't quite so independent a spirit as to start hanging out with the Beatles on my own.

The next day I was up before anyone else at the house and decided to go for a motorcycle ride (after my accident, my Triumph had been beautifully rebuilt, customized, and repainted shades of metallic blue at no charge by the Robertson garage). There had been a multitude of fans trying to make their way past the police to Elvis's house all night, and as I prepared to speed off, I noticed one straggler who had made it up to Perugia—a beautiful blonde girl. I could appreciate how good-looking this girl was, but the sight of her just reminded me of how much I missed Sandy Kawelo. I was ready to drive on by when the blonde held up a hand to stop me.

"Can I get a ride down to Sunset?" she asked.

It seemed a little extreme to say "No, I love a girl in Hawaii," so I indicated that she could hop on. I didn't say a word to her as we drove down to Sunset and began heading east.

Finally, she broke the silence. "You know, the Beatles are in town," she shouted over the noise of the revving engine.

I'm not sure what came over me. After all those years of being so se-cretive about my Elvis connection, all the situations where I could have dropped names or used my Elvis status to impress but didn't—I found myself wanting to show off a bit.

"You want to meet them?" I shouted back.

She laughed in my ear—as though she assumed I was kidding but wasn't quite sure.

With perfect movie timing, I turned just before the Beverly Hills Hotel, gunned the bike up Benedict Canyon, and headed to the Beatles' pad. There was the predictable throng of fans outside the entrance to the hillside home the group was staying in, along with a large detail of policemen and sheriffs. I got my bike up to the gate of the driveway, but it seemed like it was going to be impossible to explain who I was and get past the security guards. I was about to motor away when I realized that someone was calling out my name. It was Mal Evans, my pool-table opponent.

"Jerry—come on in."

I was in.

As I found a place to park the Triumph, Mal must have let John know that I'd come by, because when the girl and I got up to the door of the house, John was there to welcome us in. And again, I was struck by what a warm and friendly guy he was—not at all the edgy cutup he played in films and press conferences. He wasn't quite groomed into Fab form yet—he had a towel wrapped turban-style around his just-washed hair. I don't remember how exactly I introduced my passenger, but I know that she quickly joined in with the informal party of Beatles people that drifted through a few of the bigger rooms, and I didn't see her again. I, on the other hand, was escorted out to a patio overlooking the spectacular canyon, to hang out with the Beatles themselves. George and Paul were sitting around a table on the patio, with their heads wrapped in towels, too. John sat down and indicated that I should take the fourth chair. John, Paul, George, and Jerry.

I was sitting facing the canyon, and as the four of us talked, I saw a rather remarkable sight. A couple of girls had scaled their way up the al-most perpendicular canyon wall to reach the fence around the edge of the patio. Just as they got there, ready to squeal, a couple of obviously well-practiced security guys scooped them up and carted them away.

John, Paul, and George didn't even notice. I guess crazy fans being whisked away had become quite routine for them. I'd seen a lot of crazy things happen around Elvis, but no one had been scaling canyon walls to get to him lately.

We talked some more, and then John leaned in toward me.

"Jerry, would you do me a favor?"

"Sure, John."

"I couldn't say this to Elvis last night, but you see these sideburns? I almost got kicked out of high school trying to be like Elvis. Tell Elvis that if it hadn't been for him, I would have been nothing."

"I'll tell him, John."

Before I left that day John made a point of getting a group picture signed for me. He and Paul and George signed it at the table, then John handed it to me. "Ringo's on the phone with his wife—go get him to sign it."

"I couldn't do that, John—I don't want to interrupt him."

"Oh, all right," said Lennon with mock exasperation, "Come on, then."

He led me through to the bedroom where Ringo was on the phone. Maybe our pool table triumph made the difference, but Ringo gave me a big smile and didn't seem to mind being interrupted to sign a picture. John took the picture back and added, "To Jerry Schilling, from the Beatles." It's still one of my most prized possessions.

Back at Perugia, when the time was right and I was alone with Elvis, I passed along John's message. He smiled warmly and nodded. I could see he didn't want to talk much about it, but I could see the glimmer of pride in his eyes. He would have preferred to be competition rather than inspiration as far as the Beatles were concerned, but I know that the esteem they held him in meant a great deal to him.

I went back to the Beatles' place the next day, this time with Billy Smith and Marty Lacker instead of a blonde. This was the afternoon of the first night of a two-night stand at the Hollywood Bowl, and there was a bit more of a charged buzz inside. Paul was on a couch, strumming some chords on a guitar, and I went over to listen. John stood next to me. What Paul was playing reminded me of something I'd heard back in my time sipping coffee at the Bitter Lemon, and I decided to go out on a limb and talk music with Mr. McCartney.

"You know, that sounds a lot like a Joan Baez song."

"That's exactly what it is," said Paul.

"You want to meet her?" asked John.

Before I could answer, he sprinted away, and moments later came back towing Joan Baez by the arm. And a couple of hours later I was with her and John in one of five separate limos bringing the group to the Bowl (a car each for John, Paul, George, Ringo, and Brian Epstein). At some point, John had asked Billy and Marty and me if we wanted to come to the show. Billy and Marty declined and headed back to the Perugia house, but I was swept up in the moment and had stuck alongside John.

It was like a presidential motorcade pulling through town, with a police escort moving traffic out of the Beatles path. I was impressed, but the ride gave me some time to rethink my decision to attend the concert. Elvis was happy to know the Beatles thought highly of him, but he might not be so happy to know that one of his guys had wandered off to a Beatles concert rather than stick by him. And while Marty hadn't managed to stir up any ill will around my Catalina excursion, this was the kind of odd test of loyalty that really might get Elvis upset. By the time we pulled through the artist's entrance under the Bowl, I felt like I'd made a real mistake, and couldn't get out of there fast enough. As the Beatles were ushered off to their dressing rooms, I commandeered somebody's car and driver and got myself back to Perugia Way.

Elvis never said anything about it—and I have the strange distinction of being possibly the only Beatles fan ever to run away from a Beatles concert.

As excited as I was to have the Beatles come to town, I was even more excited when I got word that I'd get the chance to see my favorite part of Hawaii again: Sandy was coming to Los Angeles for a visit. Through an intensive series of letters and then phone calls, I'd discovered that she wanted to see some more of me, too, and I'd put in motion plans to get her to L.A. Of course, her parents weren't about to send their young daughter to the mainland simply to be wooed by a friend of Elvis. The deal was that she would stay with the family of Jack Rigas, the choreographer who had worked closely with the dancers of the Polynesian Cultural Center both in designing the long-running show at PCC and in putting together the production numbers for *Paradise, Hawaiian Style*. Jack had lived in Hawaii and had become close with Sandy's family, and it was acceptable that she would come over to visit Hollywood under his watch.

I was with Elvis, finishing up the film on the Paramount lot, but Sandy and I spent as much time as we could together, and went on a few chaste dates. One of those dates took us to the home of the Osmond family—Jack had also begun working with the Osmonds, who happened to live just down the street from him. There we spent the night learning some of the sign language the family used to communicate with a couple of older, nonperforming siblings who were deaf.

After a couple of weeks, it was time for Sandy to head back to her family. But as we went through another round of very emotional good-byes, the nature of our relationship was inescapably clear: We were in love.

By mid-October, after another cross-country drive with Elvis at the wheel, I was back at Graceland. Elvis had done three movies in seven months and had certainly earned himself a break. There were football games, nights at the Memphian, and hours spent with one of Elvis's latest favorite toys—low-slung, high-powered go-karts. I still considered myself lucky to be one of the few people in the world who went "home" to Graceland. But I also found myself growing increasingly preoccupied and unable to concentrate on much of anything.

One day, I was sitting by myself out behind the house, just staring out at the grounds. Suddenly there was a hand on my shoulder. I looked up to see Elvis. He waited a moment, and then spoke.

"Jerry, you're just no use to me anymore."

I'd heard that Vernon usually did the firing. At least I was getting the personal send-off. But I wanted to know why.

"What do you mean, Elvis?"

He handed me a thick, folded-up envelope. I opened it up, and was quite surprised to find that I was staring at an open-ended, round-trip ticket to Hawaii. I looked back at Elvis, unable to speak.

"Go get her, man," he laughed. "Bring her back. Then maybe I'll be able to get some work out of you."

Soon I was back in Oahu, living in the Polynesian Motel near the Cultural Center and waiting for Sandy to have some free time between her classes and her dance performances. She brought me fresh fruit every morning for breakfast on her way to the campus, and every time she left I was overcome with loneliness, counting the minutes until I'd see her again. In some ways, my romantic circumstances hadn't changed too much from all those times in New York that I waited for Carol Cook, but it was a lot nicer to be stuck on a Hawaiian beach than in a New Rochelle basement.

I started spending a lot of time with Sandy's extended family, who lived in traditional Polynesian style in a collection of humble homes overlooking a bay on the west side of the island. It wasn't always easy to understand each other—most of her family spoke a mix of Polynesian and pidgin English. But they were incredibly welcoming and friendly, and they accepted me and made me feel at home. I was a part of family luaus, and even developed a taste for the dried octopus the women prepared on the family clotheslines. The only trouble I had fitting in was when Sandy's brothers took me out fishing—the smell of captured sea turtles mixing with the fumes from the small outboard engine and the nonstop rocking of the boat reduced me to a violently seasick *haoli* (visiting white guy).

By the end of my visit, Sandy and I were more in love than ever, and I'd earned enough trust with her parents that they agreed to a rather unusual plan for their daughter: When she finished her studies for the term, she could come visit me in Memphis.

That Christmas season was probably the happiest I'd ever had. I was living at Graceland, back to staying up late for deep conversations with Elvis, and waiting for the beautiful girl I loved to come be a part of my life. Only one thing bothered me—getting a motorcycle from Elvis was one thing, but it seemed like my own pursuit of true love should have been paid for by me. I made a plan with Vernon that a few dollars would be subtracted from my paycheck each week until my ticket was paid off. I think Vernon was a little shocked that one of the guys was actually trying to give money back to Elvis, but he agreed to the plan. When Elvis eventually found out what I'd done he was surprised, too, and appreciative. The price of one plane ticket didn't mean anything to him, but I know he understood the feeling behind my settling of the debt.

Graceland at Christmastime was always beautiful. The trees in front of the house were lit from beneath with soft-colored lights, decorations were everywhere, and there was a life-size nativity scene on the hill outside the front door. The place became a social hub, with all sorts of people coming by to pay their regards. This was also a time when Elvis was at his most generous. A few days before Christmas, he'd sit in the living room with his father and go through a list of fifty local Memphis charities he'd asked the city to provide for him. He'd go through the list and ask Vernon questions about the groups. Vernon would have done his research, and could tell Elvis exactly what each of the wide-ranging charities did and who they were helping. Every year, each of the charities on the list got a thousand-dollar check from Elvis. Some celebrities might have made a big PR moment out of that kind of giving, but for Elvis it was private and personal, part of the holiday season in his home.

Elvis was better at giving than receiving, and as one might imagine, he was a hard guy to pick out a present for. This particular Christmas, the guys managed to come up with something he really appreciated. Elvis had recently had a "Meditation Garden" constructed off to the side of the house past the swimming pool. It was designed to echo the feel of the Self-Realization Fellowship grounds, and we guys figured the perfect Christmas gift for Elvis would be a statue for the garden. Marty and I got in contact with my old art teacher, Bitter Lemon proprietor and reigning Memphis bohemian John McIntire, and commissioned a four-foot statue of Jesus in his robes, with his arms outstretched offering solace to all seekers. We put it up on a pedestal on a walkway in the meditation garden, and when we took Elvis out to show him he was visibly moved (visitors to Graceland can still see it in the same spot today).

Not all the rituals we went through that Christmas were quite so traditional. After a great deal of reading up on the subject, and a great deal of psychological preparation, Elvis had decided that he wanted to see what inner knowledge might be gained from an experience with LSD. I had no strong desire to experiment with drugs, but Elvis really approached it as a means of enlightenment—not just as a way to have kicks. Elvis had read some of Timothy Leary's writings, and he'd been very excited about Aldous Huxley's *The Doors of Perception*, and I think he hoped that acid might provide the shortcut to the insight that he'd been after. I figured that whatever method he was going to use to better himself was worth a try from me also. And I still felt that whatever I did with him, I'd be safe.

A few days after Christmas, Elvis, Priscilla, Larry Geller, and I split up some tabs of acid upstairs at Graceland (Larry had managed to procure the LSD). Sonny West was with us, too, to serve as a non-indulging assistant and security detail if any of us needed help along the way.

We took the tabs, then sat around the big table in the conference room up there and just talked for a while. At some point, it seemed that no matter what anybody said, everybody else started laughing. I looked around at the people with me, and felt like I was not just seeing them, but seeing into them—really knowing them for the first time. I figured maybe they were looking at me the same way, and I started to feel vulnerable, a little too exposed. And that's when the visuals started to kick in. I stared at Elvis sitting in his chair, and right before my eyes he seemed to morph into a child—a plump, happy little boy. And the more I stared, the more he shape-shifted—until I was seeing him as a great big, chubby baby smiling back at me, contented as could be. I started laughing, and Elvis started laughing, and I realized we were in for quite an adventure.

As the feelings and visions continued to get stronger and stronger, I became a little frightened. I started to wonder if the visions would ever stop, if I'd ever get back to "normal" again. I wanted to be in a safe, enclosed place, to try to get a hold on my reeling mind's eye. The spot that seemed safest to me was the walk-in closet in Elvis's bedroom, where I sat under the clothes hanging there. Once I felt properly protected, I began laughing again, and I heard Elvis laugh in response to my laugh. He was still down the hall in the conference room, but we began communicating by laughing back and forth—a call and response of rippling roars and gut-busting horselaughs. The laughter didn't feel forced or silly—it felt like a real conversation.

When the laughter finally subsided, I peeked out from under the hanging clothes around me and saw an attractive creature, half-cat and half-woman, sort of rubbing and clawing its way along the bedroom wall, and then stopping before a mirror: Priscilla, looking striking and beautiful and lost in a world of her own.

After a while, Elvis, Priscilla, Larry, and I regrouped on the huge bed in Elvis's room. Elvis flicked on the TV that was mounted from the ceiling above the bed. We looked up and were immediately sucked into *The Time Machine*, the somewhat disturbing George Pal adaptation of the H. G. Wells story, starring Rod Taylor and a cast of future-world mutants. It was a film we'd enjoyed before at Memphian screenings, but something felt a little off to me this time. The plot of the film somehow expanded around Rod and the mutants to include all of us on the bed. I felt like we were all in the movie—and that everything Rod and the other characters said applied to us.

At some point, it occurred to the group that nobody had eaten for ten or twelve hours. Pizza sounded like a good idea, and Sonny made the call to have some delivered. When they finally arrived, they smelled great, but I noticed something unusual—from the bottom of the crust to the topping, the pies looked to me to be about three feet thick. I had no idea how I was going to get my mouth around something like that. From the looks on my partners' faces as they tried to handle a slice, I could tell I wasn't the only one overwhelmed by the idea of wrestling our way through the mozzarella and pepperoni in front of us. Sonny had no problem knocking off a couple of slices, but the rest of us realized that food and LSD were not a great mix.

After a few hours, when the drug's charged edge had started to wear off, we all went outside to walk the grounds. It was a misty morning, and the drops of dew seemed set on the grass and trees like so many jewels. For a good deal of the trip I had felt set deep inside myself—my sped-up mind somehow apart from my slow-motion body. Now drops blown off the trees in the morning breeze landed on my skin and served as a cooling comedown. I felt back together, and was both relieved to be at trip's end, and thrilled at what we'd experienced. I also felt a rush of emotion for my fellow seekers. I guess everyone felt that, because I do remember that we all began to open up a bit, telling each other how important we were to each other, what good friends we were, and how much we loved being together. So much always went unsaid between all of us, but this was one of those rare and real times when everyone, even Elvis, spoke openly about our feelings and our friendship. Then, absolutely exhausted, we split up and went to bed.

I remember that as I drifted toward sleep that night, it occurred to me that I had in fact achieved a kind of enlightenment, but it had come in a way I hadn't expected, and ended up feeling more personal than spiritual. I didn't feel elevated to some higher plane, but I did feel I'd been on an amazing adventure that would always be a part of the way I looked at things. The drug didn't deliver instant knowledge or awareness, but it pulled you on a journey that felt both noble and ridiculous—a jolting mix of Self-Realization Fellowship and the Fairground's Pippin. Seeing that little boy inside Elvis was an insight I knew I'd hang on to. Pizza a yard thick—maybe there wasn't so much of a lesson there.

Allowing ourselves to experience life in such a different way and giving each sense a new power of discovery was worth the trip. At the same time, I had no desire to take that trip again (I didn't—and neither did Elvis or Priscilla). And just as sleep was finally grabbing ahold of me, I had my most enlightened thought of the night: I had a great friend in Elvis, and I was living a damned good life.

7

. . .

A MILE IN MY SHOES

The genius of Elvis Presley was in his music, but the magic was in his voice. He was never more at one with his talents than when he was in the act of singing, putting that remarkable voice to work. One of the most memorable times I got to watch Elvis at work in the recording studio was in Nashville, at the RCA Studios, in the spring of 1966. He, Red West, and Charlie Hodge had been spending a lot of time informally jamming and working out ideas for songs (I hadn't tried to make a musical contribution since the day we were all driving through Beverly Hills and some catchy song came on the radio. We turned it up and everybody started taking a harmony part and singing along. I thought we had a strong quartet going, but Elvis turned around, looked at me, and said, "What's that noise?" I haven't sung since).

Elvis was listening to newer sounds then, and had become fascinated with the work of Odetta and Bob Dylan—people who managed to apply their musical talents to the same kind of soulful questioning and search for insight that Elvis had pursued in his books. Around this time, I brought Elvis a Peter, Paul and Mary album—not a real natural fit with Memphis Mafia tastes—and I was very happy to see that it became one of his favorites. Elvis hadn't recorded a non-soundtrack album of fresh material in years, but that spring, with his mind set on finding some material of emotional and spiritual substance, he decided to record an album of gospel music. It would be titled after one of its standout tracks, "How Great Thou Art."

It was amazing to watch the work process in the studio, throughout which Elvis was confidently in charge of every detail. In this situation, he was clearly working for himself—not for an audience, or a television camera, or a film director. His music meant everything to him, and when it came to creating something he really cared about, he put himself into it completely. He picked the material. He worked out the arrangements. He went through all kinds of back and forth with the session players to work out all the subtleties of their parts. He brainstormed with his new producer, Felton Jarvis, over the general sound and setup for each track.

The *How Great Thou Art* sessions marked the first time that Elvis and Felton had worked together. The young, enthusiastic producer was a huge Elvis fan and had once recorded an Elvis tribute song of his own ("Don't Knock Elvis"). He'd had some great success with Gladys Knight and The Pips and pop singer Tommy Roe, but one of the main reasons RCA had him on this session was that he was as much of a night owl as Elvis and had no qualms about working through the night. Right away, Elvis seemed to appreciate the positive energy and excitement with which Felton approached their sessions, and the two seemed very much in synch when they discussed the kind of feel Elvis wanted in his recordings.

Of course, with Elvis in charge, the music-making process was quite a bit different than the movie-making process. On a movie set, time was strictly kept: a 7:00 A.M. call-time meant you got started at 7:00 A.M. In the studio, a 7:00 P.M. session meant that Elvis might turn up around seven, but then he might do everything but record—there might be hours of hanging out before a note was sung. He could step out of his trailer on a movie set and deliver his lines for *Harum Scarum* on demand. But when he sang he was at his most open and exposed. His singing was at the core of who he was, and to perform as well as he wanted to, he had to feel some creative spark and a degree of inspiration. That spark couldn't always be tightly scheduled.

I learned that studio hang-out time was crucial to Elvis's getting into the right frame of mind. The studio was always part social club and part sanctuary for him, and whenever he was there, that's exactly where he wanted to be. He loved spending time with the musicians, and enjoyed talking shop with them. There'd be laughing and talking and storytelling between Elvis and his players—his way of taking the pressure out of the situation. Felton himself was a tremendous storyteller with a great sense of humor, and Elvis couldn't get enough of his crazy tales of working with Fats Domino, one of Elvis's favorite performers. After the talk and the laughs, when Elvis felt things had built to just the right moment, he'd go to work.

By the time of the *How Great Thou Art* sessions, most of the other guys had sat through dozens of recording sessions, and some of the mystique of Elvis in the studio had worn off for them. As on the movie sets, a lot of the guys that came with Elvis would spend some time watching and listening, but also spent a fair amount of time playing cards. Red and Charlie, though, were often very active participants in the studio sessions. They could speak the language of the Memphis guys as well as the language of the session players, and they worked as a pair of very critical bridges between the groups. Elvis made the final calls musically, but Red and Charlie were both talented and comfortable enough to offer musical input as well as moral support.

I didn't have much to offer musically, but I had no interest in playing cards. I was interested in watching Elvis at work, and I was also fascinated by the whole studio process. I'd watch the engineer check the buttons on his console, watch the drummer set up and tune his drums, watch the careful placement of microphones. The sounds and the ambience in the studio reminded me of the sounds you'd hear coming from a Broadway orchestra pit as the players loosened up and got ready for a big opening number. That was a lot more exciting to me than any game of five-card stud.

There was magic in that voice—but there was magic in those ears, too. I was blown away at how Elvis would shape not just his own performance, but the entire track. As the players began work on a new song, Elvis would call for all sorts of changes—he'd want the bass up, or the tempo slowed. He'd work out just how the background vocals should come in, and the manner in which they'd stack their harmonies. He'd work out with Felton how present he felt his vocals should be in relation to the backing track. He was dead serious about getting his music just right (he'd learned from the best, working with Sam Phillips in those early days). In fact, although he didn't take the credit often, I believe Elvis is the most underrated producer in rock and roll. When you put Elvis Presley in the studio with some decent material, what you got was never just an Elvis Presley vocal: You got the Elvis sound in every element of the music.

Still, it was that voice—his instrument—that pulled it all together. He'd sing his vocals separately if he had to, but he liked to keep his performances as live as possible, and a lot of his takes were recorded with the band. And when he was done experimenting and was really shooting for a master take, you could feel the energy in the room.

At that Nashville session, I found a spot at a window looking into the recording room, and watched as Elvis delivered a transcendent performance while belting out the track "How Great Thou Art." All the showmanship of his stage performances just dropped away—it was just voice and microphone—but you could see in the intensity of his expressions that this one was coming straight from the soul. When he got to the dramatic finish of the song, there was a strange hush in the room— nobody wanted to break the spell. I've been in a lot of recording studios since my time with Elvis, but I've never seen a performer undergo the kind of physical transition he did during that recording. He got to the end of the take and he was as white as a ghost, thoroughly exhausted, and in a kind of trance. He was on, and everybody in the studio knew it (though no one in the room suspected that Elvis had just delivered his first Grammy-winning vocal performance).

Elvis was hunched over, almost down on his knees. He seemed shaken—like he'd been touched by a little of what he had been searching for in his spiritual readings. He happened to look up, he saw me looking back at him, and a beautiful smile spread across his face. He knew I'd seen something special. Now, if Red or Charlie had been standing where I was standing, they would have gotten that smile. If Elvis had turned his head the other way, one of the session guys would have seen it. But it just so happened that I caught his eye and I saw the smile and got to share that moment. And that moment will stay with me forever. As a guy working for Elvis, receiving that kind of smile was even better than getting a motorcycle from him.

Elvis may have treated the studio as his sanctuary, but many involved in the Elvis-business did not treat it that way. One of the regulars at the studio card games was Freddy Bienstock, the representative of the Colonel-sanctioned Hill and Range Publishing Company—owned by Jean and Julian Aberbach—through which all of Elvis's material was supposed to be supplied. The Colonel was especially proud of his dealings with Hill and Range, which had set up a pair of separate publishing firms for Elvis, Elvis Presley Music and Gladys Music. Since Elvis had signed his first RCA deal in 1955, the Colonel and Hill and Range had overseen a lucrative system in which Elvis got a piece of the publishing of every song he recorded. And at first that system worked fine—in the fifties and early sixties songwriters generally had a low profile in the music world and were willing to do anything to get a song recorded by a star, including giving up a huge share of songwriting royalties. But in the era of the Beatles and Dylan, the songwriter was the star, and top writers were no longer willing to give anything away.

Elvis had a great sense of what songs would work for him, and early in his career he had picked most of the songs he wanted to record. There was a special drawer down in the Graceland TV room where he kept some favorite records—songs he had some kind of emotional connection to, some dating back to his high school days. From those 45s and 78s Elvis would very carefully select a song or two he felt ready to take on, and he'd carry those precious bits of vinyl off to the recording session with him. If the studio was his sanctuary, that drawer was full of scripture, and everything he pulled from there was chosen, and performed, with love.

Elvis always had the freedom, and the power, to bring in a song to a session. If Elvis was excited about it, the businessmen would keep quiet and arrangements would be made. But increasingly, when Elvis was asked to pick material from a pile of Hill and Range–selected songs, he found himself listening to material he just couldn't get excited about. Elvis trusted that the people around him would be trying to get top material for him, and sadly, he was just way too trusting in that regard.

It may have been frustration over material, or frustration with the lousy script for his next film (*Double Trouble*), but, for some reason, on June 10, 1966, when we were back in Nashville for more sessions at RCA Studio B, Elvis was in a foul mood. He didn't want to go to the studio at all, so an unusual plan B was put into effect. Since one of the three songs scheduled to be worked on that night was a Red West composition, "If Every Day Was Like Christmas," Elvis decided he would stay at our Nashville lodging, the Albert Pick Motel, and Red, Marty, and Charlie would go to the studio so that Red could sing reference vocals while the session musicians laid down the three backing tracks.

I was the guy Elvis chose to stay with him at the Albert Pick, though it could sometimes be considered hazardous duty to be sitting up with a moody Elvis. His room at the Albert Pick wasn't anything special—just a small, typical motel bedroom. As usual, tinfoil was up on the windows to keep it dark, and Elvis had the air-conditioning turned up so high it felt like a meat locker. His mood was about as dark and cold as the surroundings. I did what I could to keep him distracted and comfortable, and between ordering some food and watching some TV, I tried to keep the conversation light and minimal.

Hours later, there was a knock at the motel door, and I let in Red, who was carrying a small tape machine. He asked if Elvis wanted to hear the results of the evening's work there, and Elvis gave him a not very enthusiastic OK. Red played the tapes of the three tracks, with and without his scratch vocals: his Christmas song, "I'll Remember You," and "Indescribably Blue." For the first time that night, I saw Elvis's expression warm, and he let himself relax. He sat cross-legged on his bed, nodding along with the rhythm, mouthing the words and getting lost in the music. I think he must have appreciated how strange and daunting it had been for Red to try to step into his shoes, and now, listening to Red's remarkably Elvis-like stand-in performance, I think he did get a sense of just how much his friends were willing to put themselves on the line for him.

"That's it, man, that's it," Elvis said when the tape ended. I'm pretty sure that was all Red needed to hear to make his night. But Elvis wasn't quite through with that tape. Something about "Indescribably Blue" had fanned a creative spark, and he wasn't going to let the moment pass. He wanted to make some music. Red quickly hooked up the machine's dinky little microphone and flipped a few switches so that Elvis could hear one channel while recording into the other. Elvis plumped up the pillows behind him on the bed, got himself settled against the backboard, pulled the little tape machine close, and set the mike out in front of him. Then he started playing the backing track. And he started singing.

Now, "Indescribably Blue" is no throwaway tune. It's an intense, emotional, vocally demanding ballad. And, sitting there in his pajamas at the Albert Pick Motel, with a battery-powered tape player in front of him, Elvis nailed it. But this vocal performance was almost the polar opposite of what I'd heard him do in the studio. This time, the music came out of him so easily, as naturally as breath. I sat there on the foot of the bed as Elvis moved from the song's almost whispered, confessional opening to its heartbroken crescendo, and then back down to its trembling finale. With his eyes shut, singing out to that little plastic mike with calm and tenderness, he casually, quietly packed everything he loved about singing into the two and a half minutes of "Indescribably Blue." I think, for him, the Albert Pick Motel just disappeared. He didn't know where he was, and he didn't care. He let himself get lost in that song.

And when he was through, you could see the change: The black mood had lifted. The AC was still cranking, but the big chill had passed. That little moment of music in a motel room had done something big for him—it satisfied his soul.

Life with Elvis changed quite a bit for me in 1966. Most significantly, I moved out of the Graceland basement. Sandy did come to Memphis at the end of the Christmas season in '65, and rather than subject her to the bare bulbs, dangling insulation, and seeping puddle of my room, Elvis arranged for us to have a place in the apartment building directly across the street from the estate (behind where the Graceland shops and ticket counters are today). Charlie Hodge, still single, inherited the spot in the basement. I knew I was in love, and I wanted to do right by Sandy, who was leaving a lot behind to come step into our crazy world. But I have to say it was hard to give up that ugly little room in Graceland. It was hard to have to leave at the end of the night and head back out through those gates I'd wanted so much to come through.

It felt both wonderful and surreal to be living with my Polynesian love in our own apartment. We'd fallen in love and gone through a dramatic courtship, and it was strange now in Memphis to finally settle down and really get to know each other. We'd never even spent the night together in Hawaii or Los Angeles, and now we found ourselves building a life together. Sandy was as beautiful out of her home environment as she had been in it, but where she had once been safely looked after by her family, now she was vulnerable, and it hit me just how much she was depending on me and how responsible I was for her. For her part, Sandy never complained at all about what must have been a rough transition, and day after day I was even more taken with her calm, her grace, and her loveliness.

My relationship with Sandy may have pulled me out of Elvis's house, but as a couple we had the opportunity to connect with Elvis and Priscilla on a different level. For one thing, they could see the sweetness, beauty, and honesty in Sandy as clearly as I could, and they welcomed her into their life as a new member of the family (when Grandma had first heard I was in love with a Hawaiian girl, she looked very concerned and said, "Oh, son, why don't you settle down with an American girl?"—but when Sandy finally came over, Grandma warmed up to her and eventually thought of her as family, too). Priscilla and Sandy were from very different backgrounds, but their jumps from stable family homes to the craziness of the Elvis world gave them a lot in common. Priscilla and Sandy gradually became good friends, and Elvis and I spent a lot of time together with the ladies, going for walks, going for drives, spending time in the Meditation Garden, and enjoying each other's company. There was enough of a bond between the four of us that Elvis felt comfortable taking us along when he made his trips to his mother's grave.

Life was good, but with all that was going on around Elvis, it sometimes seemed that every silver lining had a way of finding a cloud. I remember one warm evening the four of us decided to take a drive down to the Mississippi River in Elvis's newest Cadillac Eldorado convertible. We were driving along, watching the sunset over the water, when Elvis's new single came on over the radio (I can't quite remember which single it was). I was thinking that the moment was perfect: a Caddy, two beautiful women, and Elvis both at the wheel and on the radio. But suddenly the car was turned 180 degrees around and we were heading back to Graceland at about a hundred miles an hour. When we got there, Elvis jumped out of the car looking like he was ready to kill somebody. He headed upstairs and I don't think we saw him for a couple of days.

When I did see him again, it was in the back room of the house, where I was hanging out with a couple of the other guys. Now Elvis was looking more concerned than angry.

"Look, I know you guys think I'm crazy. But Jerry, go down to the record store down the street and buy that single."

I went down to the record store closest to Graceland and got the record. When I brought it back to Elvis, he took it downstairs to the TV room along with an acetate of the same song. Elvis wanted to be involved in every step of the recording process, and the last step was always for him to listen to an acetate—a kind of test pressing—of the takes and mixes he was approving, and then he'd sit through the mastering of those recordings with the engineer. He assumed, as anybody would, that what he heard and approved was what a listener would eventually hear when they bought the record.

Down in the TV room, he put his acetate on and played the song. Then he put the actual single on, and even a nonmusician like me could hear the difference—there was a marked drop in punch and volume. His voice was forward in the mix and the band and background vocals had just about disappeared. To put it bluntly, the song had lost its balls.

Elvis just stood there shaking his head, and I don't think any of us knew what to say except that we heard the difference. I remember the word that came to mind for me—a word out of my Catholic school days: sacrilegious. Here's one of the greatest talents of his time, and rather than just let him do what he did so well, the business people around him kept finding new ways to mess with his music. Sadly enough, I think one of the reasons my memory's foggy about this single is that the same scene happened more than once.

When we were all back in Memphis, there were still football games and nights at the Fairgrounds or the Memphian. There was also a new leisure activity that was undertaken with typical Elvis-style intensity: slot-car racing. Priscilla had given Elvis a beautiful track for Christmas, and he got excited enough about it that within a couple of weeks he'd gone out and bought a huge, professional, arcade-size track. He set it up in an extension to Graceland he'd built off the music room. For a while, racing those little cars was just lighthearted fun, but pretty quickly, all of us guys had our own personalized slot car, and those races were intensely competitive and treated as very serious business. Serious enough that during one heated set of qualifying laps, Marty Lacker and Red West came close to throwing punches over who'd nosed out who at the finish line, an argument that sparked probably the biggest fit of temper I ever saw Elvis unleash.

He had his frustrations over the movies, and he got understandably upset when his music was tampered with, but the one thing he absolutely wouldn't stand for was disharmony in the group. When the guys went after each other in a mean or petty way, it drove Elvis crazy, and when he got crazy, he was not the type of guy to talk through his feelings. So, as words were exchanged between Marty and Red over that slot-car track, there was suddenly another sound—the sound of Elvis erupting.

He lifted up his hefty, metal control box and smashed it down hard on the track, shattering lengths of it into pieces.

"Goddamn it—if you guys want to argue about something, argue about who's going to clean this shit up," he yelled. He smashed a bit more, then headed out of the room.

No, it wasn't a pretty picture. But I will say this—Red and Marty didn't exchange one more word about who had the faster slot car. Elvis had multimillion-dollar contracts to live up to, and he couldn't see any way to step back and figure out where it was all heading. Now his friends couldn't even race slot cars without bickering and sniping at each other. Why not smash something up? It wasn't long after that the the slot-car track disappeared entirely and the extension became Elvis's "Trophy Room," home to his gold records, plaques and awards, and fans' scrapbooks from all over the world.

Out in L.A. there had been some changes in the housing situation. By early 1966, Elvis had moved out of the Perugia house and into a new one on Rocca Place in Bel Air, and compared to the bachelor-pad feel of the former, the new home felt much more domesticated. In addition to Elvis and Priscilla, the Rocca inhabitants included Sandy and me, Marty Lacker, and Patsy Presley and her husband, Gee Gee Gambill (dubbed "Muffin" by Elvis for his easygoing nature). Elvis would star in three more films that year, first making *Spinout* and *Double Trouble* at MGM, and *Easy Come, Easy Go* back at Paramount.

Once during a lunch break on a location shoot day for *Spinout*, Elvis had Alan Fortas bring some of our motorcycles to the set, and we'd go for rides through Topanga Canyon, often with *Spinout* costar Deborah Walley sitting on the back of Elvis's Harley. I had a chance to get to know another costar—Shelley Fabares—a little better during some of the filming. In a scene in which Shelley's car goes off the road and into a little lake and Elvis wades in to help her, I was working as Elvis's stand-in. We were working late in the day, and we needed to do many takes of the characters in the water, so I had a wet suit on under my wardrobe. Shelley had on only wet wardrobe however, and I knew just how cold she had to be in that water. Alan Fortas came up with a solution—he thought a few sips of brandy might help keep Shelley warm, so he passed a small bottle to assistant director Claude Binyon, who rode a small boat out between takes and delivered it to the actress. Shelley wasn't a drinker and she may have had more than a few sips. Fighting her way through the cold and the brandy, she bravely finished the scene. We could see why she was one of Elvis's very favorite costars.

Elvis himself was quite protective of his *Double Trouble* leading lady, a British girl named Annette Day. Annette didn't have any acting experience—not even in a high school play—but the producers thought she had the perfect look to play against Elvis in a story about European intrigue. Elvis wanted Annette to feel comfortable throughout the production and tried to help her out any way he could. So when he heard that she didn't have a car of her own, he gave her one. This was typical Elvis generosity, but the trouble this time was that the car he gave her was mine—a '64 Mustang that I had purchased for Sandy and myself. One day on the set, Elvis simply said, "Jerry, you got the paperwork on that?" and the deal was done—Annette Day was a Mustang owner. Of course, Sandy and I didn't get stuck taking the bus around town—Elvis bought us a convertible Cadillac as a sign of appreciation for our unintentional generosity.

And Sandy and I weren't the only drivers Elvis put in a Cadillac—he bought several of them, all convertibles, for me, Red West, Sonny West, Joe Esposito, Richard Davis, Alan Fortas, Larry Geller, and Marty Lacker. The cars were offered to us in a great spirit of friendly giving, and Elvis explained his generosity by telling us, "Hell, we were all poor kids from Memphis—we deserve it." And just as we had ridden our matching motorcycles together as the "Bel Air Bonnevilles," we celebrated our Cadillac ownership one afternoon by putting all the tops down and caravanning along Sunset Boulevard and out onto the San Diego Freeway.

George Klein was out in L.A. to take a bit part in *Double Trouble*, and he had connections with the sensational soul singer Jackie Wilson. When

Wilson did a run of nights at a Sunset Strip club called the Trip, Elvis and the rest of us went out to catch a show. Elvis and Jackie hit it off well enough that night that Elvis invited Jackie to come to the MGM lot to watch a day's shoot. If you look carefully at a couple of the music sequences in *Double Trouble* you may notice that Elvis doesn't really move in patented Elvis fashion. There's something different about the way he snaps his fingers and twists his torso. In fact, he's doing his best Jackie Wilson impression, because Jackie Wilson is standing about ten feet away. All those smiles Elvis is directing off-screen are directed right at Jackie, and the two of them cracked up together after every take (Elvis also memorably borrowed some Jackie moves when he performed "Return to Sender" in 1962's *Girls! Girls! Girls!*).

That night back at the house, Elvis and some of us were sitting around, and talk turned to what a great performance we'd seen at the Jackie Wilson show. I mentioned that I couldn't understand how a guy that talented hadn't broken out bigger yet—why wasn't he doing bigger concerts, and film and television?

Elvis shook his head slowly. "Man, Jackie and I were talking about that today. He's in a hard place."

"What do you mean, E?" I asked.

"I told him he was a good-looking guy—he should be doing movies. He said he really wanted to, and he'd had some interest from the studios. But his manager won't let him out of his nightclub commitments— I think there's a lot of mob connections there, and Jackie just can't break out of it. They won't give him enough time away from the club dates to make a picture."

Thinking about Wilson's situation later, I couldn't help but see a parallel with Elvis. Elvis wasn't dealing with people who'd break his legs, but he was in a position where the connections that had helped get him to where he was were getting in the way of doing the work he truly wanted to do. Seemed like no matter how talented you were, somebody could find a way to box you in.

Colonel Parker had apparently been impressed enough with what he'd seen of me on the Hawaii trip that he thought I could be useful to him, so I became a loan-out to him one day a week, spending the day in one of the massive offices he had on either movie lot (his headquarters on the MGM lot was an entire dance studio converted to office space, complete with its own kitchen). Both spaces were decorated with Elvis movie posters and all kinds of Elvis merchandise. The office decor also featured a fantastic number of expensive ivory carvings and marble representations of the Colonel's favorite animal, the elephant, most of them gifts from affectionate friends and business associates.

You could never get too comfortable around the Colonel, but it was still a pleasure to watch him work. He'd call for a lunch meeting at his office with top entertainment executives—guys who were used to lunches at three- and four-star restaurants around town—and serve them his special "hobo stew," or a homely plate of cold cuts. During those cold-cut luncheons, a big plate of ham always seemed to end up in front of the Jewish Abe Lastfogel, president of the William Morris Agency and someone the Colonel considered a good friend. Whatever offense Lastfogel might have otherwise taken was probably balanced out by the fact that the only nice piece of furniture in the Colonel's office was a special leather chair with Lastfogel's name engraved on it.

The Colonel had a system of barking like a dog to summon his assistants—one bark for one particular staffer, two barks for another—which was funny unless you didn't respond promptly to the bark, in which case you might be subject to a severe talking-to. And the Colonel was a primary catalyst for pranks and hijinks on the otherwise dreary film sets of this period. One of his favorite gags was to show off some alleged hypnosis skills. He'd put Billy Smith in a trance and instruct him to go sit in the director's chair (a huge no-no in Hollywood). Or he'd pretend to put Red and Sonny and some of the other guys under his spell and tell them that they were dogs. They'd be down on the floor of the set barking and howling away, and the Colonel would puff away on his cigar with a contented smile on his face. On the one hand, he was playing the role of crazy uncle who wants everybody to have a good time. But it was also his way of reminding the cast and crew around him: I'm in charge, and will do as I please.

I remember watching those guys down on all fours howling away, and thinking "I'm not going to do that." I know the other guys felt that it was all in good fun, but it looked humiliating to me. I don't know what would have happened if the Colonel insisted I join in, because I was never tested. To the Colonel's credit, he was an expert at reading people, and instantly understood how far he could push someone. He never once tried to turn me into a dog.

One day, I was working in the Colonel's office when a young, good-looking guy came through the door with a big bag of something. He looked vaguely familiar to me, but before I could ask who he was or what he wanted, he yelled out, "Colonel—I've got some sausage from the President."

"Come on in here, George," the Colonel bellowed back from his room.

It was actor George Hamilton, delivering some Texas sausage, care of Lyndon Johnson. The Colonel and the President had met back when Johnson was a senator and the Colonel had arranged for country star Eddy Arnold to sing at a private party Johnson was throwing. They hit it off right away, with the Colonel quickly inducting the senator into an exclusive, private club—the "Snowmen's League." Snowmen were those who were expert in the art of snowing—the ability to con, charm, fool, flim-flam, or otherwise pull the wool over someone's eyes. Membership in the league was only open to those the Colonel deemed worthy (I still have my own league membership card). Hamilton was now dating Johnson's daughter, and had also become very friendly with the Head Snowman. For all the Colonel's bluster, you could never overestimate how well connected he was.

On another day at his office, I got a glimpse of the more manipulative side of the Colonel's management techniques. Elvis never wanted the Colonel around the recording studio, and the Colonel had no particular desire to be there (he'd send a representative like Tom Diskin instead). Of course, the Colonel kept tabs on everything that came out of the studio. Working in his office I overheard the Colonel talking on the phone with somebody at RCA (it was never hard to overhear the Colonel). He made a comment about a recording Elvis had just done, which had been circulated as an acetate but hadn't been put out yet: "My wife, Marie, says she can't hear Elvis with all that stuff going on," the Colonel said. "It's an Elvis record, but you can't hear Elvis."

That's how the records got changed. The Colonel would never be so heavy-handed—or traceable—as to try to override a mix Elvis had OK'd. But in his indirect way, he was making a demand. And that kind of conversation between the Colonel and RCA is what led to Elvis's records not sounding the way Elvis wanted them to sound. Looking back, maybe I should have gone to Elvis and told him about that phone conversation right then. But at the time, I felt that trying to put myself between Elvis and the Colonel was only going to make things worse all the way around.

I spent more time with the Colonel after he was loaned a house in Palm Springs by the William Morris Agency and decided that I should be one of the guys to drive him to and from L.A. These days involved a lot more than just driving, however. I had meals with the Colonel and his wife, I accompanied him for long sits in the sauna and steambath at the Palm Springs Spa Hotel, and I sometimes split a secret beer with him out in the toolshed behind his home (his wife disapproved of his imbibing). Getting that relaxed around the Colonel required a delicate balancing act. I knew that Elvis absolutely did not want the Colonel involved in his personal life. I had to be on guard as I sat in the car on those two-hour rides back to L.A., with the windows rolled up and Colonel puffing away on his cigar. Sometimes he'd sit in silence for forty-five minutes just staring out the window—you could almost hear his mind whirring away. But sometimes he would begin to ask questions, and I knew that the Colonel's most innocent-sounding questions might lead to information being passed along that Elvis would not be happy about. The more the Colonel inquired about things that seemed unimportant, the more careful I'd be about my answers. I was starting to enjoy time with the Colonel, but I was always aware that my true loyalties were with Elvis.

As much as the business and personal sides of Elvis were supposed to stay separate, the Colonel had a keen interest in having somebody he could depend on within Elvis's inner circle, and he and Vernon had discussed putting me in the Elvis "foreman" spot during the period when Joe Esposito was gone and the Colonel felt that Marty Lacker was not communicating well with him. The most I heard about this was when Vernon offhandedly remarked, "Marty's not getting the job done. The Colonel and I were talking about you." The situation was resolved when Joe returned as co-foreman, and frankly, I was relieved, knowing that Joe was the right guy for the job.

Spending time with the Colonel on those drives, I picked up a couple of insights into his mercurial character. First, for all his psychological gamesmanship and sly personal politics, as a businessman, the Colonel was not a bullshitter. He told you what he wanted, told you what he'd give you, and when he said a deal was a deal, it was done. People could always say no to him. It's just that most didn't. Second, as much as he's come to be seen as a heavy in the Elvis story—a reputation partly deserved—the odd thing is that he was fun to be around. As dominating as he could be, he was highly entertaining. Lastly, I came to realize that in some ways, Elvis and the Colonel were a lot alike: strong, smart, stubborn men who had become centers of power in worlds of their own making.

By the fall of 1966, during the filming of *Easy Come, Easy Go*, Elvis and I were living with Priscilla and Sandy in the same house, and spending just about every minute of the long work days together. I suppose it was inevitable that at some point, the mix of professional and personal lives would become combustible.

It was a day early in the shoot—maybe one of those still-photography days that Elvis hated—and he was in a lousy mood. He was sitting in his makeup chair in his dressing room, and he was being crabby to all the guys around him that day, but when he went at me something snapped. I knew when it was smart to defer to Elvis, to let him vent. But this time he brought Sandy into it. I don't remember exactly what his complaint was, but one of the guys had told Elvis that Sandy had said something to Priscilla that made her suspicious about Elvis's behavior. I knew that Sandy was too smart, and by nature too sweet, to have done that. I tried to stay calm.

"Elvis, she loves you and she wouldn't do that," I said. "You know that."

The words didn't seem to sink in at all.

"Yes, she did," he said.

I could tell that he didn't have a real gripe with Sandy—that he was just being disagreeable. But I was feeling protective of Sandy, and I just wasn't in the mood to defer. Instead, I exploded.

"No, Elvis, you don't know what you're talking about. You're just in a bad mood."

There was no faster way to move Elvis from a bad mood to a worse mood than by telling him he was in a bad mood. He got out of his chair. Fast.

We stood face-to-face hollering at each other, waiting to see who would back down first. But neither of us backed down. We just got louder. I'd been holding a briefcase when we started yelling, and now I flung it across the room hard enough to smash it open against the wall. Elvis stepped back just long enough to pick up a huge glass ashtray off an end table and hoist it up in the air. I didn't know if he was going to smash that, too, or if he wanted to bring it down on my head, but I decided I didn't want to find out. I wheeled around, and started walking. And walking.

I was so enraged at Elvis that I didn't want anything to do with anything connected to him, and that included his cars. Rage has a curious energy to it, and apparently I was angry enough to walk from the Paramount lot to the Rocca Place house—a ten-mile hike. I don't remember making the decision to do so—I just remember that by the time I hit Hollywood Boulevard and took a left toward Bel Air, it occurred to me that after twelve years of knowing Elvis, this was our very first argument. It also occurred to me that my plan not to have anything to do with him had a serious flaw in it—I was, after all, walking home to his house. If I kept on walking, I wasn't just quitting a job—I was walking away from everything I thought I'd wanted, sending myself back to square one. I guess that thought made me even angrier, because I kept on going, stomping over the stars of Hollywood Boulevard. I decided I'd pack up and get Sandy and myself out of Elvis's life as soon as possible, moving on to a big question mark of a future.

The flash of anger in my eyes must have done something for my looks—at one point on Hollywood Boulevard I was stopped by a guy who pulled up alongside the curb and announced that he was a scout for a modeling agent. I'd been in Los Angeles long enough to know a line when I heard one, and it didn't help my mood to think that I could be mistaken for a male hustler. I kept walking, though I did take note that the guy's front seat was covered with industry trade papers and head shots.

The car pulled around the corner and a moment later the driver was walking toward me, looking apologetic, saying again and again that he didn't want to give the wrong impression, but would I be interested in an agency audition? My head had cleared enough to allow a coherent thought to come through: If I had really just quit working for Elvis, I could use a job. The more the guy talked, the more legit he seemed, and when he offered to walk me over to a modeling agency down the street, I accepted. Moments later I was sitting in the reception room of the Nina Blanchard Modeling Agency, waiting to be seen by Nina Blanchard herself. The name meant absolutely nothing to me at the time, but I later found out that this was the top agency of its day, and nobody could ever expect to simply walk in off the boulevard. and get a meeting. But there I was.

Ms. Blanchard liked my look—I guess there was still enough rage in my eyes—but was a little irritated that I didn't have a head shot or résumé to give her. She wanted me to come back for a proper audition when I had all the required paperwork together. I thanked her, headed back out to Hollywood Boulevard, and kept walking to Bel Air.

When I finally got back to the house, I stewed around for a while, going over the fight with Elvis. Every time I ran it through my head, I ended up just as angry. But more and more, sadness was creeping in, too. I could find another job somewhere, but maybe I'd just lost my best friend. I started packing, and thinking about how I'd explain the move to Sandy. I'd gotten the suitcase about half full when I realized Elvis was at the door.

I stopped what I was doing. There was a very awkward moment, with both of us trying to not really look at the other, and neither one knowing what to say. But just being that close, and that quiet, I felt something shift a little. Had he been a jerk? Yes. Had I overreacted? Probably. We both had nasty tempers. But now we were both cooled down. The guy standing at the door was the guy I'd been enraged at all day, but now that he was right there, I had no desire to pick up where we'd left off. And I could tell from his downcast gaze and uneasy stance that he wasn't in any kind of fighting mood. We could both feel that the emotions in this room were a lot different from those left behind in the Paramount dressing room. We just weren't sure what to do.

Elvis was never much of a hugger—we guys were much more likely to get hit than hugged by him. But without a word he came across the room, put his arms up, and we joined for a quick, easy embrace. In a flash, I realized that I really didn't want to go anywhere.

We were still silent—I didn't feel like rehashing the fight or sorting it out, and I know he didn't, either. I just quietly started reaching into the suitcase and putting my clothes back in the drawers of my dresser. And, quietly and carefully, Elvis began to help, gently moving a few things from suitcase to drawer. This was a guy who didn't pick up his own clothes—to have him put away a pair of my socks meant a lot.

It meant that, for the moment, Hollywood was going to be short one male model.

8

. . .

RISING SUN

The phone rang at our apartment one day about a week before Christmas. I recognized the voice right away.

"Jerry, come on over. Meet me in the dining room for breakfast."

Typically, everybody around Graceland just grabbed breakfast whenever and wherever they were in the mood for it. An invitation to a breakfast in the dining room was unusual. But a little while later, I was sitting there with Elvis, digging into eggs and bacon. I could tell he had something to say that he felt was important, but I had no idea what it might be. We talked about nothing in particular for a while, and then he got to his point.

"Jerry, I want to buy something special for Priscilla for Christmas. I want to surprise her with a horse."

"That's a great idea, Elvis."

"Well, do you mind if I buy Sandy one too, so the girls can ride together?"

"Man, are you kidding? Sandy would love a horse. Sure, go ahead."

He drained the rest of his coffee cup. His face lit up with a big smile.

"You ever gone horse shopping?"

An hour later we were heading out toward the Memphis airport on a horse-buying mission. Elvis was at the wheel of a big old pickup truck he'd bought for Graceland, and we headed out to see a local horseman, William Spence, who had a wide variety of horses for sale (Spence had a Graceland connection—he'd managed the horses there for the previous owners, and ran the Graceland Farms Saddle Club on some adjacent property). When we got to Spence's place, I discovered that Elvis had another reason for bringing me along on this trip. I wasn't just there to OK a gift to Sandy—I was going to be Elvis's official jockey.

I didn't know a damn thing about horses at the time, but Elvis had been badly spooked by a runaway ride during one of his early films, and he wasn't eager to get up in the saddle again. So I was the one who got up on each of the potential gift horses. I quickly learned some of the crucial, equestrian basics: a Western saddle gave you something to hold on to, while an English saddle left you no choice but to pray that the horse didn't hate you. I was sitting on horse after horse at farm after farm, just getting bounced around and trying like hell to stay on. And the harder I tried to stay on, the harder Elvis laughed. I started to get the feeling that he wasn't even really looking at the horses anymore—he was just laughing his head off watching me.

Eventually, we found the two perfect gift horses—a beautiful black quarter horse for Pricilla and a chestnut sorrel horse for Sandy. And our brief, exciting life as cowboys began.

Elvis had come up with a perfect gift; Priscilla and Sandy were thrilled with their horses and began riding together frequently. Petite Priscilla was deceptively athletic and a real natural rider—she often rode bareback on her horse, Domino. One of the loveliest sights around Graceland at the time was that of Priscilla and Sandy riding together, both of them with beautiful long black hair that blew in the wind and bobbed to the rhythm of the ride.

The Graceland property included a run-down barn, stables, and corral fences, and Elvis decided that he wanted it fixed up so that he could keep horses on the property. But he wasn't just going to write a check and have all that taken care of—this was going to be a hands-on project. He'd be the carpenter. He'd be the painter. And, in the case of some extra buildings on the property that needed to be taken down to create a riding area, he'd drive the bulldozer.

So, between trips to the local tack shops to pick up harnesses, saddles, ropes, and everything else we needed for the horses, Elvis and I began spending time together hammering away at planks in the barn and mending fences. And Elvis being Elvis, almost every day we were taking another trip somewhere to buy another horse. (A quick note on the bulldozing that tells you just how "Elvis" Elvis could be: Vernon had already purchased a little bulldozer for work around Graceland, but that wasn't big enough for Elvis's tastes. I came back to Graceland one afternoon to find Red West riding the little bulldozer and Elvis wearing a football helmet and sitting at the controls of a monstrous D9 industrial-grade bulldozer, looking pleased as could be as he flattened everything in his path, which, at one scary moment, almost included Red.)

I was still doing the test-riding, and when Elvis encouraged me to find a ride for myself, I found a big, friendly black horse. With all the barn renovations going on, there was room for plenty more horses, and since Elvis was in a buying mood, pretty soon the whole inner circle formed its own unofficial Graceland riding club. Billy and Jo Smith had horses, Alan and Jo Fortas were up on their mounts, and Richard Davis had his own horse, too, but always got a laugh settling his lanky frame atop one of the little ponies the Colonel had sent to Elvis as a gift. The horses pulled us together in a very happy way, and it started to feel as if some of the fun and games and good times from the Fairgrounds had been moved right to Graceland.

Elvis proved to be the hardest rider to find the right horse for. The daredevil side of him wanted an animal that was the strongest and fastest of all. But he was still battling his nervousness about being back in the saddle and needed a very well-trained, dependable horse that wouldn't fight him. The first horse he bought for himself was easy to handle, but was too tame. So we went out looking for another.

I guess word of all the horse-related purchases at Graceland spread pretty quickly, because one day, when Elvis and I were out looking for horses, I was approached by a man named Robert Boyd, who said he had the perfect horse for Elvis. I was a little wary—in our short time as horse buyers we'd discovered that horse traders could be as snaky as used-car salesman. But Boyd got my attention by showing me a picture of a huge, beautiful horse, with his twelve-year-old daughter in the saddle, proudly wearing the blue-ribbon sash she and the horse had just won. He told me that his daughter had ridden this particular horse in shows and equestrian events and had never had any problems—the horse was strong, smart, and impeccably trained. Boyd said he was more interested in finding a great home for the horse than in making a big profit from a sale, and went on to say that just about anybody else who wanted to sell a horse to Elvis was going to rip him off.

I pulled Elvis aside and showed him the picture.

"Let's go," he said.

The horse was a gorgeous, golden palomino, just as powerful and well-trained as the man had said. Elvis was taken with it right away. He bought it on the spot and soon renamed it "Rising Sun." (The barn got renamed, too—when I pointed out to him that the structure was now "the house of the rising sun," he liked the idea enough to paint HOUSE OF RISING SUN on the side of the barn.) It took Elvis a while to get comfortable as a rider, and it was interesting to watch him push himself. The first time he climbed up on Sun he was clearly still uncomfortable, but he rode a little longer and a little harder every day until after a couple of weeks he looked as natural in the saddle as he did behind the wheel of a Lincoln.

I'd become comfortable with the horses pretty quickly, too, so I decided to push myself toward mastering an even scarier form of transportation: I was going to become an airplane pilot. Even aside from the Paramount shouting match, something had been bothering me for a while about the mix of my professional and personal life with Elvis. I was thrilled to be his friend, but it seemed awkward to think of that as a career. What exactly was my line of work? Something had clicked for me when I'd watched all those talented, qualified movie people around the sets, each contributing to the overall process as a master of their own craft. I guess it was a mix of Catholic guilt and Protestant work ethic, but I started to feel that if I was going to be on Elvis's payroll, I wanted to offer some clear, constructive service to him, like being his personal pilot. I'd be his friend for free.

I began spending mornings over at the Memphis Airport, taking some flight lessons from a guy who'd done time as a fighter pilot over in Vietnam. He put me on an accelerated lesson plan, and after only nine hours of instruction, he let me take my first solo flight piloting a little Cherokee 140.

It was an easy takeoff—it seemed like all you had to do was give the plane some speed and you couldn't go wrong. But being alone for the first time up there, I became very aware of all the noises around me. The wind was roaring, and I started hearing all sorts of cracks and creaks from the plane—noises I wasn't sure I'd ever heard an aircraft make before. I tried to keep my rising nervousness in check and contacted the airport's control tower, identifying myself as a student pilot and requesting clearance for a touch-and-go landing. A voice from the tower asked me to repeat what I'd said, and I did. But when the voice answered back, what I heard was a crackle of static, and maybe every fourth word the guy was saying. The radio wasn't working.

I started to break a nervous sweat. I radioed in again and tried to make it clear that I was requesting a runway with no crosswinds—I hadn't yet been instructed on the tricky art of crosswind landings. Apparently, the guy in the tower was hearing only every fourth word I was saying, and thought I was asking for a place to practice my crosswind landings. I was directed to the runway with the strongest crosswinds on the field.

I started to come in for my landing, but the powerful winds kept pushing the plane sideways, off line with the runway. The only way I could get the plane lined up again was to increase my speed, and when another gust blew me sideways I had to go even faster. This during the time I was supposed to be slowing down to land the plane. But speeding up and slowing down became a moot point—my palms got so sweaty that I couldn't even keep my hands on the throttle.

I hit the runway way too hard, and the little plane bounced up into the air with a terrible groan. The wind hit me and blew the plane off the runway. When I hit the ground again I was out on the grass of the airfield. I tried to steer the plane back to the runway, but as it dipped into the turn the left wing caught the turf and the plane slammed propeller-first into the ground.

Suddenly things were a whole lot quieter, and I found I was upside down, strapped into my seat, listening to just two sounds—my heart pounding in my chest, and the fuel pump clicking away. I guess the thought of imminent explosion focused my mind, because I got myself unbuckled and out of the plane before the fire trucks and the airport police showed up.

I don't remember leaving or driving back to Graceland—all I remember is getting to the barn, walking past Elvis, hopping on my horse, and going for a full-gallop ride around the property. I needed an outlet for all that nervous energy, and I think I also needed to prove to myself that I could pilot something without crashing it.

When I got back to the barn, Elvis looked at me hard and said, "What happened?"

"What do you mean?"

"Jerry, when you got on that horse, you had the wildest eyes I've ever seen on a man. What happened?"

I told him.

"Jerry, forget about the airplanes. You're too young."

"There are pilots younger than me, E."

"Yeah, but I don't want a young pilot. Anything we run into up in the air, I don't want a pilot who hasn't dealt with it before. I'll stick with an old-timer. You know what I mean?"

I did. I gave up the plane lessons for a while and stuck with the horses.

As more horses joined the Graceland herd, more work needed to be done on the barn and on the fences. And when I think about favorite times with Elvis, this period always jumps to mind. Here was Elvis Presley, finding satisfaction in wiping cobwebs out of an old barn, in nailing up planks and painting fence posts. We'd spend hours together in the afternoon, just going through all the basic chores of horse care: checking their water, forking over their hay, brushing out their coats.

Sometimes, walking through the Graceland kitchen, I'd find a yellow legal pad on the counter with personal notes from Elvis making me aware of what job needed to be handled next: "We need to get three bridles," "We need more horse blankets," "We need stirrups to match the bridles" would be written out in red. Elvis wasn't a guy who usually left notes for anybody—but the last thing he'd do each night was write these out, so that every detail he thought of would get taken care of.

After working all day, we'd often go back out to the freezing cold of the barn bundled up in our jackets and cowboy hats. We'd sit around a little bucket of fire out there, with our feet up, passing the time away. Sometimes Priscilla and Sandy—whose gift horses had started all this— were down there with us. One of them would make coffee and we'd huddle together and sip from our mugs. Sometimes a few of the guys would hang out together down there, having a laugh. And sometimes it was just Elvis and me next to the fire, talking away like we had on that very first cross-country trip. Sure, I loved the limos, and the mansions, and the movie life, and the VIP treatment everywhere we went. But this simple cowboy life was just as satisfying, and everything I loved about our friendship was right there in that freezing, freshly painted barn.

I felt Elvis had created something great with the barn and the horses— he'd given himself a perfect way to escape the pressures and burdens that built up on him outside of those stables. But it was just impossible for him to say "This is just right." Instead, he must have felt that if having ten horses was a good thing, having twenty would be even better, and having thirty would be even better than that. We kept going out and buying more animals and more gear, and our trips started happening during typical Elvis hours—we'd often be down in Mississippi somewhere riding potential purchases at three in the morning.

On one of those trips, Elvis and Priscilla, Sandy and I, and Alan Fortas went out, driving down to the renowned Lennox Farms in Mississippi to find a Tennessee Walker for Vernon. It was just about daybreak as we headed back toward Graceland piled together in that big old double-cab pickup truck. Alan was driving, and all of a sudden Elvis told him to pull off the road. When Alan did so, Elvis pointed out the passenger window. Right away we all saw what he saw—a huge white cross towering over some rolling green hills as pristine as a golf course. The first rays of sunlight were glinting off a rippling lake in the center of the property, and there was one perfectly quaint little farmhouse close to the road. There was also a FOR SALE sign up. Elvis got that look in his eye—the one that meant he'd just put a plan together.

"Alan," he said. "Go knock on the door of that house. Tell them you want to buy this place. But don't tell them it's for me."

The place was called Twinkletown Farm, and was owned by Jack Adams, a retired TWA pilot who'd made a fortune as a used-aircraft salesman. Within days, it belonged to Elvis, and was promptly rechristened the Circle G Ranch. Elvis's plan of having Alan pose as the buyer didn't save much money, as Elvis agreed to Adams's asking price without even a pretense of negotiation. What had started as a humble, hands-on pleasure in back of Graceland had now become a massive, money-gobbling endeavor. And what had begun with such a sweet impulse—to give a wonderful gift to Priscilla and Sandy—turned into an almost unquenchable desire to accumulate. Within weeks the 160-acre Circle G was home to forty horses, along with trucks, tractors, trailers, and all sorts of expensive ranch gear. In addition, there were a hundred head of Santa Gertrudis cattle that came with the price of the ranch.

Elvis loved to take on a challenging project, he loved to spend money, and he loved to have the people he loved around him. The ranch gave him a chance to have all of that at once, and as things settled down a bit, there were some good times. Elvis was active and having fun, and Priscilla, Sandy, and I, along with Alan, Marty, Red, Larry Geller, Mike Keaton, Richard Davis, Joe and Joanie Esposito, and Billy and Jo Smith got into the spirit, too, spending a lot of time on horseback. The horses were trained and looked after by Mike McGregor, a professional horseman and saddler who became a well-liked and much-appreciated member of the group—the Circle G's answer to the Marlboro Man. There were picnics, barbecues, target shooting, snake hunts—a lot of nice, easygoing, outdoorsy moments.

I even got back up in a small plane—Jack Adams turned out to be a real friendly guy, a dignified gentleman with a warm, open manner. When he heard about my training—and my crash—he took me out to Twinkletown Airport, about five minutes away from the ranch, and got me to agree to copilot a plane with him. He felt it was important that I get up in a plane again soon and get over the fear of what had happened. We had a nice, smooth flight, and I had no fear at all as long as Jack was piloting. When we landed, I was about to get out when Jack said, "You can do it solo now. You won't feel satisfied if you don't."

I took the plane up, feeling a little nervous at first, but Jack had gone over things with me enough that my confidence started to come back. I made it back down, and this time, managed to avoid any crosswinds. And, with some further encouragement from Jack, went on to log another forty hours of solo flight time.

For all the activity at the ranch, something about it didn't feel right to me. It just seemed like too much, too fast, with Elvis spending way too much money. I was perfectly content with those late-night talks in the old Graceland barn, but that wasn't enough to satisfy Elvis. He liked to do things big, but it seemed to me that things at the ranch had gotten so big that they weren't special anymore. I know Elvis's impulse to buy came from a heartfelt generosity—he wanted to buy so that he could share with the rest of us. But I could also see something desperate in all that buying.

Part of Elvis's plan was to deed over an acre of ranch land to each of the guys—I think he wanted to create a sort of cowboy commune for all of us. At first Vernon was very supportive of the idea, but I'm almost sure the Colonel got to him and soured him on the deal—the Colonel was not at all excited about the prospect of having Elvis regularly sequestered away on a Mississippi ranch surrounded by his guys and well out of reach of the Colonel's influence. When Vernon steered his son away from handing out the land parcels, Elvis instead decided to buy a few house trailers so that there would always be accommodations for a few members of the inner circle to stay at the ranch with him and Priscilla. Elvis approached a few of us about buying these trailers—he'd arrange everything and put up the down payment, and then we'd take on the rest of the payments. He thought it was a great way for us to own a piece of his ranch.

I'd agonized over taking on payments for my own motorcycle, and I really didn't want to be putting money into a Mississippi house trailer. Elvis and I had some frank discussions over this, and he just couldn't understand why I wouldn't jump at the opportunity. Resistance didn't accomplish much—Elvis had already arranged for trailers to be leased and delivered. I put up the money, and started making the payments—some of the other guys did, too. But, as usual, Elvis ended up paying off everything.

I put up some stronger resistance over the issue of a brand-new truck. We had the horses, we had golf carts, we had some old trucks—there were plenty of ways to get around the ranch property. But Elvis, still in full spending spree, decided that everybody needed a brand-new Ford Ranchero pickup truck. I think I was out doing some work on the house trailer I hadn't wanted when Elvis came by and tossed me some keys.

"That's for your truck."

The bigger the gift, the more casual he liked to act about it. So it took me a moment to understand what he was giving me.

"Elvis, I don't want a truck. I don't need a truck."

That was a reaction he hadn't expected, and it stopped him in his tracks. He looked a little puzzled, a little pissed.

"It's your truck, man. Drive it."

For the first time, receiving something from Elvis didn't feel special at all to me. He didn't care whether I wanted it or needed it. It didn't even matter that it was for me—he was handing them out to everybody. And the giving didn't seem to mean anything to him. When he'd bought me and the guys our convertible Cadillacs, the act seemed so personal and loving that some of the guys got choked up over it—the feeling behind the gift meant so much more than the cars themselves. But this brand-new truck had no meaning at all, for Elvis or for me. He was just spending money. The motorcycles and the Cadillacs were extravagant gifts, but they had, in some way, pulled the guys together. Elvis's unlimited spending and gifting was now creating more pettiness among the guys. Somebody was always upset that so-and-so had the nicer trailer, the fancier saddle, or the better-color truck.

He could tell that the Ranchero left me cold, but he barely reacted. He just walked toward an electrician who happened to be there that day, working on some of the power lines to the trailers. Elvis called out to this guy, a stranger to all of us.

"Hey, man, you want a new truck?"

"Sure!" said the electrician.

"It's yours."

The electrician got the keys.

Elvis spent nearly a million dollars over the space of a few weeks, acquiring and gearing up that ranch. And, actually, there was a very understandable explanation for all that spending. Just before we began our horse-buying spree, Elvis had been sent the script for his next film, *Clambake*, which had every indication of being his lousiest production yet. I know it just bothered the hell out of him—his music was being messed with, his once-promising film career had been turned into a joke, and he didn't see any way out. He knew he wasn't looking his best—he'd put on some weight over the last couple months and this time was having a hard time dropping it. The idea of turning a ranch into a refuge for himself had to be appealing. His spiritual readings and his LSD trip hadn't gotten him to the peaceful state of mind he was after—maybe he could spend his way there at the Circle G.

He really did not want to go back to Hollywood this time. And as the deadline for returning to L.A. for filmwork loomed, Elvis announced that he needed a postponement in the production schedule because he'd ridden hard enough and long enough to develop some painful and incapacitating saddle sores. George Klein's girlfriend, Barbara, worked for a medical group, and recommended a doctor from the group to come out to the ranch, examine Elvis, and provide prescription ointments for treatment. That doctor was George Nichopoulos, who would soon be more familiarly known as "Dr. Nick" and would become an integral member of Elvis's inner circle.

Elvis's attempt at seclusion got the Colonel's attention. He was furious that Elvis was going incommunicado and messing with business-as-usual. He put a good deal of pressure on Marty Lacker to guarantee that Elvis would follow through on the schedule and responsibilities that his film contract demanded. Elvis Presley was not going to be able to escape being Elvis just by riding horses, and he knew it. The more he thought about what he would be leaving the ranch to go back to, the more it must have torn him apart inside. But when he took enough of some of the pills prescribed to him, he didn't have to think about anything at all.

Late one night, Sandy and I were in our trailer, listening to a winter rainstorm pound away at the roof. At first I didn't realize there was a knocking at the door. When I answered it, there was Elvis, standing in the pouring rain, looking confused and disheveled, and holding, somewhat improbably, a loaf of bread.

"Jerry, I need you to come with me."

It was late, and I would have rather stayed in, but there was no way I could say no to Elvis when he was looking so vulnerable. I grabbed a coat, we got to his truck and headed off the ranch. We headed all the way back up to the Memphis suburbs, and Elvis seemed to know exactly where he was going. He got to the neighborhood of Southaven, turned down a street, and pulled up in front of a modest home. He told me it was the home of the pharmacist we dealt with most often in Memphis. He was there for a personal pickup. I'd known for a while that Elvis was taking too much medication, but I had no idea he knew where our pharmacist lived. We'd all been using the prescribed uppers and downers to keep up with the lifestyle we were in, and there had been a few scary moments: Alan Fortas, who had refused to give me any sleeping pills when I started with the guys because he knew the damage they were doing to his system, spun out of control one night in L.A. and had to be taken to the emergency room. He became so violent with the doctors and nurses that it was up to Richard Davis and me to restrain him so he could be sedated.

But Elvis always seemed to be in control; you didn't see him get sloppy or wild. And his usage always seemed tied to some work-related purpose—trying to keep his weight down, or trying to get himself to sleep so he could be up for one of those seven A.M. film-set calls. He thought of his pills as helpful medicine. But seeing the state he was in on that rainy night, and seeing how important getting ahold of some relief was to him, I became worried.

Elvis gave everyone cause for concern when we got back out to L.A. One night at the Rocca Place house, Elvis fell in his bathroom and banged his head hard enough to give himself a concussion. It was pretty clear to everyone that the reason for the fall was not simply a loose electrical cord on the floor. Whatever Elvis was taking to try to blot out his frustrations was starting to have a clear, negative effect on him.

Doctors treated Elvis at the house, and a day later the Colonel came over for a short, private meeting with Elvis, and then a group meeting with Elvis and all the guys. Despite the Colonel's stated policy of not getting involved in Elvis's personal life, when the personal interfered with the business, he stepped right in. At the group meeting, he took charge and ripped into us. Right off the bat, Marty Lacker was told that he would no longer be co-foreman with Joe Esposito—Joe was now solo top man. And it was made clear that anybody who insisted on getting Elvis's head "all fogged up" with talk of religion and spirituality would no longer be welcome—the Colonel's way of dismissing Larry Geller. He went on and on, making it sound like it was us guys who had been wasting Elvis's money, and making it clear that there would be cutbacks in payroll and expenses and that several of us would be let go after the current film was finished.

The most disturbing part of the meeting was that Elvis was sitting right there, looking down at the floor, letting the "fat old man"—as he so often referred to the Colonel—cut us down. There's no way this could have happened when Elvis was at full strength. Elvis truly needed the Colonel just then to make things right with the studio and get a messy situation under control. But the Colonel was also asserting himself in Elvis's personal life in a way he had never dared to before. It's one of the very few times I saw Elvis let the Colonel get away with that kind of power play, and it was depressing to watch.

I went back to my room after the meeting and began packing my old suitcase again. I liked Larry Geller, I liked having discussions about spirituality with Elvis, and I knew I was seen as more of an independent spirit in the group. From what the Colonel had said, I assumed that I was one of the guys no longer wanted, and I wasn't going to hang around if that was the case. Then Elvis walked in, still looking dejected. He seemed a little surprised to see me packing again, but there was no hug this time. He simply shook his head and said, "He wasn't talking about you, man. He wasn't talking about you."

In the midst of this strange and strained time, one thing was clearer than ever to me: I loved Sandy. We flew out to Las Vegas just a couple of days after that tense meeting with the Colonel and got married. I would have loved for Elvis to be my best man, but he was in Palm Springs still recuperating from his concussion (he'd asked for a second postponement in the *Clambake* shooting schedule because of his fall, and it wouldn't have gone over well if he'd turned up in Vegas). Sandy and I had a simple, low-key ceremony with Joe and Joanie Esposito standing with us as best man and maid of honor, and we spent a weekend on the town as our honeymoon. Elvis paid for all of it as our wedding gift. Of course the weekend was all about the celebration of love between Sandy and me, but it was also nice to share the occasion with Joe and Joanie. Elvis had always been at the center of anything we did together, but here we were away from all that, and the time the four of us spent together felt very special.

Back in L.A., we went to work on *Clambake*, which turned out to be just the kind of by-the-numbers production that Elvis now dreaded. Some of the guys tried to lighten the mood with some favorite on-set mischief—setting off firecrackers and tossing water balloons. But it started to look to me like we were a little old for balloon fights. And even though a well-timed firecracker might get a laugh, it was becoming harder to tell if people were actually having fun or just acting like they were having fun.

On May 1, 1967, a few days after production had wrapped, Elvis and Priscilla became a married couple. It's understandable that Elvis's wedding would be treated with some secrecy—nobody wanted it to turn into a circus. But on this most personal of days, the Colonel did not hesitate to run the show. His idea of a smooth event was one in which the guys were minimally involved. In fact, when the whole entourage finally got to the site of the wedding, the Aladdin Hotel in Las Vegas, the Memphis Mafia found itself disinvited.

The Colonel planned for Elvis and Priscilla's ceremony to be held in a hotel suite, and announced that there was room for only Joe and Marty—doing their last co-foremen duty as co-best men—and George Klein, who had flown in from Memphis for the wedding. There was room for the Colonel's friend, Aladdin owner Milton Prell—a stranger to Elvis. But not for us. Myself, Red West, Alan Fortas, Richard Davis, and our wives were expected to turn up only at the reception. Larry Geller was not even invited to that. Red was angry and hurt enough to kick in the door to his room, and simply skipped the whole thing, heading back to L.A. The rest of us were upset, but nobody wanted to do anything to spoil the day for the couple.

Elvis, though, tried to make up for some of the hurt feelings by essentially inviting us along on his honeymoon. When he carried Priscilla across the threshold of their new Palm Springs home—the so-called Honeymoon House—the first thing Priscilla saw on the other side of that threshold was us: me and Sandy, Joe and Joanie, and a couple of others. We were courteous enough to come in through a back door rather than trample the threshold before the newlyweds did. And after a day or two, when the beautiful couple headed off for their real honeymoon getaway, we were all right there with them at the Circle G Ranch.

Maybe it was because the buying was all out of the way. Maybe it was because, having frightened himself with his fall, Elvis had gotten himself healthy again. Maybe the Colonel's coming down hard had made him more determined to take back life on his own terms. Maybe it was because he was just so much in love with Priscilla. But whatever the case, when we all went back to the ranch again, it really was a magical time. Elvis was calm and contented. Priscilla was thrilled to be away from Graceland or the big L.A. houses. She was happy to be in a simple place where she could cook breakfast for Elvis and make his coffee—happy to be an attentive wife for her loving husband. She and Elvis actually moved out of the ranch farmhouse, giving it to Alan Fortas and his wife, Jo, so that Priscilla and Elvis could enjoy the closer intimacy of one of the house trailers. Sandy and I still had a honeymoon glow, too, and were thrilled to be in our little trailer. All the guys and wives were getting along with each other, and we really did start to feel like a big, happy family. A strange family, but a happy one. Somehow, after a false start, Elvis's dream of a cowboy commune seemed to be working perfectly.

My daddy came down to spend a little time at the ranch, and I think one of the sights that Elvis enjoyed the most was my father up on a horse. We'd all learned pretty quickly that the key to riding was to yield to the animal—to loosen up and let yourself move along with the horse. My daddy was never what you'd call a loose or yielding guy, and the sight of him sitting solemn and stiff-backed in the saddle, trying to maintain control of a Tennessee Walker, had Elvis laughing hard.

There were more cookouts and picnics and frog hunts and football games, and this time the vibe at the place was just right. The days were easy and lazy and fine, and I didn't get summoned for any more late-night trips to the pharmacist's house. Things went well enough that a month later, when it was time to head back to Los Angeles for another typical film (*Speedway*), Elvis made a very surprising decision. Instead of kissing wives and girlfriends good-bye and heading to work on the usual cross-country drive, this time we would keep the good times rolling with a family caravan to California. The Schillings, Espositos, Smiths, Lackers, and Gambills become a happy-go-lucky motoring tourist group—the only such group to include Elvis Presley as its bus driver.

I don't remember anything especially dramatic happening during the production of *Speedway*, but by the end of the shoot, I'd made one of the biggest decisions of my life: I was going to leave Elvis. Not in anger, and not really because of anything about Elvis at all. I was happy being one of Elvis's guys, but I was going to leave to answer a question that had been gnawing at me: Could I be something other than one of Elvis's guys?

During the film production, I started spending a lot of time with Bill Saracino, a top music editor at MGM. I remember being awed by the look of his workroom, with all the various reels of dialogue, sound effects, and music recordings spinning away, and I was greatly impressed with the skill and craft Bill applied to his work. I got excited by the mix of hands-on mechanics and artistic creativity that went into the film-editing process. I also thought it might be nice to have a job that depended solely on my own skills—that wasn't tied to somebody else's moods or impulses. Finally, I figured that if I couldn't be Elvis's pilot, maybe I could be his film editor.

I sat up with him at the Rocca house one night, beating around the bush enough that he realized something was up.

"Jerry, what's on your mind? Just say it, man."

I was nervous. If Elvis fired somebody, he might later change his mind and hire them back. But I'd never heard of anyone telling Elvis they were leaving him and staying in his good graces. With the premium he put on loyalty, it seemed like if you chose to step out of the circle, you'd be gone forever.

"I appreciate everything you've done for me Elvis. I can't tell you how much. But I feel like I've got to do something else. I want to stay out here and work. For myself."

He nodded appreciatively.

"I got it, Jerry. Tell me what you want to do. We'll make a call or something."

"No, Elvis. It's all right. I've been talking to some guys at the studio. I think I'm gonna take a shot at becoming a film editor."

He nodded some more, slowly, staring out the window.

"Film editor. That's a good move."

No explosion. No ill will. Nothing petty. It felt like maybe he was just a little sad that I wouldn't be around. And walking out of that room became the hardest thing I'd ever done in my life.

"Thanks for everything, Elvis. I really mean it."

He didn't say anything. I knew he wanted me to stay, but—as a friend—he wasn't going to stop me from doing what I felt I had to do.

Life was suddenly a lot smaller, and a lot harder. But not unpleasant. Sandy and I moved out of the Rocca Place house and into a small one-bedroom apartment in Culver City a block away from MGM (I figured being close to a studio couldn't hurt my career transition). I didn't have any illusions that breaking into the editing profession would be easy, but I knew I was smart enough and hardworking enough to support us somehow. Sandy was entirely supportive of the move, and I think she was actually happier to be in a place, however humble, that we had to ourselves. A place away from the guys' world around Elvis. And I don't think either one of us really missed the luxuries of Bel Air—there was something very satisfying about stocking our own refrigerator, cooking our own meals, and paying our own phone bills.

We would survive—I didn't have any doubts about that. The only doubt that nagged at me concerned Elvis. We'd made it through fights and all kinds of friction, but I wondered if I could step away like this and still be considered his friend. He'd built a world where his friends, the people he cared about, were close around him. If I wasn't right there with him, was I going to be a part of his life at all?

A couple weeks later, on a Friday evening, I hadn't made much progress in my editing career, but Sandy and I were starting to get very comfortable in our small apartment. The phone rang.

"Jerry—you do that editing on the weekends?"

"No, E. Actually I haven't really started yet."

"OK. I'm coming by to pick you up. We're going to Palm Springs."

The biggest fear of my life—losing Elvis's friendship—just disappeared as we spoke. I was still a guy he wanted to share a weekend with. An hour later he did come by, and with Sandy's very understanding blessing, Elvis and I were off to the desert. I had a loving wife, a wide-open job future, and a great friend. I could certainly live with that.

Being a friend of Elvis didn't help me get a job as an editor—there were some strict union rules in that line of work that weren't going to bend for anybody. However, some of the friends I'd made on Elvis sets—first and second assistant directors, stunt coordinators—were willing to get me some gigs on other sets. I began a brief but exciting career as Jerry Schilling, Actor. Over the next several months I put together a list of credits that included extra work on *Rat Patrol* and *The Man from U.N.C.L.E.*, and photo-double work on *The Outcasts* for actor Don

Murray (probably best-known for costarring with Marilyn Monroe in *Bus Stop*). I was a two-faced alien on *Star Trek*, and a muscle-bound policeman on *Get Smart*. I got chewed out on that set by guest star Don Rickles when a karate chop I hit him with was a little too realistic for his tastes. He scared the hell out of me, but ended his tirade by flashing a big smile and letting me know that he was just putting me on. I began taking acting classes with Paul Mantee at the Melrose Theater, and had the honor of sitting through a master class with Rod Steiger. Finally, some connections on the MGM lot—particularly through assistant director Claude Binyon—got me a chance at a few speaking lines and some actual acting in *Ice Station Zebra*.

It was on that set that I got a taste of everything Elvis had been missing in his films. I watched director John Sturges sit with his stars—Rock Hudson, Ernest Borgnine, Patrick McGoohan—and discuss how a scene was going to work and how they'd approach it. Everyone took their roles seriously and obviously cared about doing great work. I realized what a raw deal Elvis had gotten—how often he was treated as if his talent didn't matter, and how often things were just rushed through on his set.

I really enjoyed watching Rock Hudson work—he had that same kind of ease and natural talent as an actor that Elvis had as a performer. Rock had a powerful star presence, but he always came across as a regular guy—tough, funny, charming, and much more comfortable playing poker with the crew and the stunt guys than talking with the studio suits. Elvis looked great all the time, but he made sure he looked great. Rock looked great without doing anything—whether he was neatly put together in a Navy uniform or in jeans and a T-shirt with his hair messed up. He also loaned me his car so that I could get to the dentist to have a cracked tooth fixed.

The acting job that meant the most to me in this period didn't offer me any lines, or any chance to showcase my dramatic skills. In fact, it was a film that gave me only about a second and a half of screen time. It was called *Stay Away, Joe*—the first film Elvis did after I set out on my own. He called me up to offer some work on the location shoot in Arizona, and said he'd take care of everything. So I became one of the few struggling actors to have a limo and chartered plane at my disposal, and before long I was palling around with Elvis and Joe and Red and Sonny West. It meant a lot to have him reach out to me so that we could spend some time together out in the Arizona desert. As far as my friendship with these guys was concerned, it didn't feel like I'd lost a thing.

In fact, I even found a way to push my new hoped-for film-editing career forward. I'd had a hard time getting in the door at ABC Television, where I'd tried to sign on as an apprentice editor but didn't have enough background in the field to justify their taking me on. So I decided to build up that background as much as I could. After a day's shoot on *Stay Away, Joe*, I'd hang out with the director, Peter Tewksbury, and his editor, George Brooks, a couple of talented guys who were happy to let me watch their work process and to offer me a free tutorial on the tricks of their trade. The more I watched, the more I was hooked, and the more I felt that, despite ABC's resistance, and despite the success I'd had earning a SAG day rate to menace Captain Kirk or tackle Don Rickles, editing was the right line of work for me.

It seemed that stepping away as an employee of Elvis only brought us closer as friends. By December of 1967, Priscilla was seven months pregnant (if you do the math, you can see how happy those honeymoon ranch times were). When she and Elvis decided to take a drive up the coast to visit her parents at Fort Ord, Sandy and I were invited along for the ride. Elvis wanted to tend to his expectant wife as much as possible, so I became the wheel man, driving a Caddy limousine so that the four of us could ride in maximum comfort. The plan was to drive up around Monterey, spend the night in a motel, and then make it over to the nearby military base.

On that drive, we took a very interesting side trip together. Elvis had decided to take advantage of an invitation that had been offered to him by George Stoll, the longtime genius conductor over at the MGM soundstage. He and his wife owned the Crocker Marble Palace on 17-Mile Drive near Pebble Beach, and were very eager to have Elvis come by for a visit. We found the place just around the bend from the drive's famous landmark—the Witch Tree. That tree apparently set the tone for the palace—it was a damned spooky mansion. Spooky enough that the Stolls were having a hard time getting gardeners and housekeepers to work there—the woman doing the weeding out front turned out to be Mrs. Stoll. We were all a little creeped out by the place, but the Stolls were completely at home—they'd fully embraced the spooki-ness and filled the place with macabre collectibles, such as three actual shrunken heads, which included what they proudly claimed was the only white shrunken head in North America. They also had an elabo-rate electric train set that ran between bedrooms, and a special stretch-ing machine that George believed would counteract a loss of height due to nighttime shrinkage.

Apart from the strange collectibles, the Stolls were wonderful hosts—George was a crazy, endearing mix of Toscanini, Einstein, and hepcat, and nothing meant more to him than showing his guests a won-derful time. And part of that wonderful time included some energetic sampling of his extensive collection of aged bourbons. Elvis was not a drinker, and neither was I. But when you've got a bourbon enthusiast leading you through a tasting, pointing out the hints of wood and smoke and honey in the various blends, it's very difficult not to get excited about the stuff. I was hyperconscious of the fact that I was the driver for a very pregnant woman, so I declined to partake of most of what was of-fered to me. But Elvis sampled just about everything he was offered, and enjoyed it, too. After a while we went out to have our dinner over at the posh, exclusive Pebble Beach club restaurant, The 19th Hole.

As we got to our table, all that bourbon tasting seemed to suddenly catch up with Elvis: He got groggy, and very sleepy. He wanted to lie down on the restaurant floor for a quick rest, but after we discouraged that idea, he instead reclined on a couch against the wall. That turned out to be not such a great idea, either—the restaurant management in-formed us that our behavior was unacceptable and that our business was no longer appreciated. I can say that I'm the guy who helped Elvis leave the fanciest joint he was ever thrown out of.

The next day we finished our drive up the coast and made it over to the base to visit Colonel and Mrs. Beaulieu, and Priscilla's four brothers and her sister, Michelle. The Beaulieus were friendly, generous people who clearly loved both Priscilla and Elvis a great deal. And it was inter-esting to see Elvis as a son-in-law—he was polite, charming, respectful, and seemed to be Colonel Beaulieu's favorite audience for his ready supply of Air Force stories. Elvis also enjoyed getting into some esoteric conversations with Michelle, a fourteen-year-old free-spirited thinker who sported bright green nail polish.

Elvis had become close with *Speedway* costar Nancy Sinatra, and wanted all of us to watch her NBC television special, *Movin' with Nancy*, which was airing that weekend. But he wanted to see the show in color, and the Beaulieus' TV set was a black-and-white model, so when we went off to check into a nearby motel, he made some calls and ordered up a big color TV to be delivered as soon as possible to the Beaulieus' address on the base. We headed back to their house just in time to see Colonel Beaulieu—having no idea why a pair of deliverymen were try-ing to wheel a new television into his home—emphatically turning them away, insisting that there was some kind of mistake. Elvis straight-ened it all out, and we had a fine time together watching Nancy's special that night on the new set.

The next day, Elvis had an idea for a road trip we could take with the Beaulieus—he had me drive the limo back down to the Stolls' place, so the Colonel and Mrs. could get a look at some of the collected oddi-ties there. On second look, the castle was just as creepy, but the Stolls were again fun to be with and it was a great day for everybody.

At the end of our trip up and down the California coast, Elvis ex-tended a further invitation to Sandy and me—he wanted us to spend Christmas with Priscilla and him in Memphis. The Schillings had a choice between spending the holidays in a one-bedroom apartment in Culver City, or spending the holidays at Graceland. It was an easy call to make. Again, our time together was warm, easy, and wonderful. And after New Year's, when we got ready to leave as scheduled, Elvis ex-tended his invitation.

"How can you leave now? It's my birthday in a couple of days—you're gonna stay for that, aren't you?"

We stayed for his birthday—a beautiful dinner at Graceland followed by a night of movies at the Memphian. A week later, Sandy and I got ready to leave again, but Elvis had other plans.

"I got a session to do, Jerry. Nashville. You better come along for that."

So I joined Elvis and some of the guys again for a drive to Nashville, where he was supposed to record some tracks for the *Stay Away, Joe* soundtrack, and to try to get some material done for another RCA al-bum. This time in the studio, it was sad to watch Elvis wrestle his way through the less-than-impressive movie material that needed to be done. Things didn't pick up much when he turned to the material that had been pulled together for possible album tracks, and I could see that Elvis was getting more and more frustrated—he was willing to work, he was in the studio, and he couldn't get a decent song to sing.

One element of the session that had kept him hopeful was the up-beat energy supplied by guitarist Jerry Reed. A couple months earlier, Elvis had been thrilled to bring Reed into a session so that a cover of Reed's song "Guitar Man" could be properly recorded. Reed's song-writing had guts and smarts, and his guitar sound was gritty and dirty, and Elvis had responded well to that shot of musical adrenaline in the studio. He knocked out a killer version of "Guitar Man," but then the whole deal was almost squelched when Hill and Range came down hard on Reed, pressuring him to give up a huge chunk of his publishing rights. The Colonel had set up a system that had made Elvis one of the richest entertainers in the world, but now that system was turning Elvis into an artistically starving artist in the name of adding a few more dollars to his bank accounts. Jerry Reed was in no mood to give up his song, though, and he was tough enough and smart enough to say "screw you," to Hill and Range, who consequently couldn't quite figure out a way to tell Elvis that they wouldn't go forward with a song he had gotten so excited about because it wasn't cheap enough.

At this Nashville session, Jerry Reed had been called in not as a songwriter but simply as a session guitarist—Elvis wanted to keep some of that dirt and grit in the band sound. But when he cut short a take of one uninspired number and yelled, "Doesn't anyone have some god-damn material worth recording?" Jerry came forward, a little reluctantly, with another tune, titled "U.S. Male." He handed Elvis a demo, which Elvis took back to the studio's listening room. Felton Jarvis, Freddy Bienstock, Joe Esposito, Lamar, Charlie, Red, and I were there, listening along with Elvis. He had to hear only about twenty seconds of the song before his energy shot right back up. "Let's cut it," he said. He was finally hearing something he could grab ahold of and get excited about. Freddy and Lamar, who was now working for Hill and Range, left the room, while Elvis and Felton worked out some details of the arrangement.

The song should have been good news for everyone at the session, but apparently Freddy was not happy about doing business with Jerry Reed again. As I left the listening room and headed down a hall toward the studio, I saw Reed just about pinned to the wall by Freddy and

Lamar. From the bits of growled threats I picked up, the message was clear: Don't you ever, ever pitch a song again at an Elvis session. The guitarist wasn't going to back down, but he didn't have much of a chance to respond, because just then Elvis came around the corner, still looking up and energized. Freddy and Lamar backed off quickly, trying to make it look like they were shaking Reed's hand.

"Great tune, man," Elvis said to Reed as he passed by. "We need more of that around here."

A few months later "U.S. Male" came out, and was a big enough hit to make plenty of money for everybody.

Back at Graceland, Sandy and I again prepared to head to L.A., but again, Elvis had other plans.

"Jerry—you're not going to stay for the birth of our child?"

We stayed. And Elvis let me know that I would serve a very important role in the baby proceedings. Perhaps because he liked the way I handled the big old limo on 17-Mile Drive, Elvis gave me the daunting responsibility of driving him and his wife to the hospital. As Priscilla's due date approached, Elvis and I went over the plan again and again, reviewing just how things would unfold, and which entrance I should drive to at Methodist Hospital. I even took Elvis and Priscilla on a couple of practice runs to the hospital, so that our trip there would be as quick and smooth as possible.

On the morning of February 1, Sandy and I were just barely awake out in the Graceland annex when the intercom buzzed. It was Elvis.

"Hey, don't get yourself all excited, but meet me in the kitchen. Priscilla's ready to go to the hospital."

I got there as fast as I could, meeting the father-to-be and Charlie Hodge. Grandma and a lot of the staff were up as well, and were buzzing about from room to room in excited anticipation. I felt nervous, and Charlie looked nervous. Everybody looked nervous except for Elvis. As excitement built around him, he looked as cool and as calm as could be. So damn cool and calm that I knew he'd never been more nervous in his life—his response to this kind of anxiety was to slow himself down and act as if there were absolutely nothing in the world to worry about. Slowly, almost casually, Elvis went over the plans once more. Then we heard the yell.

"Elvis—HURRY UP!!!"

Priscilla was out in the front drive, trying to get herself into the car. I saw Elvis go a little pale—there was no way to slow-talk through this. He and Charlie Hodge and I snapped into action and got Priscilla comfortable in the backseat. Elvis sat with her, holding her hand and trying to keep her calm. I got behind the wheel and Charlie jumped in to ride shotgun. I got us quickly and safely to the right entrance of Methodist Hospital, just as we had planned.

"It's the wrong hospital," said Charlie.

I didn't know what he was talking about and ignored him. I was about to spring out of the car and get help for the mother-to-be when I heard Elvis's voice from the backseat.

"It's the wrong hospital, Jerry. I forgot to tell you—we switched it over to Baptist."

"Oh no," said Priscilla quietly, in a strained low voice. "Hurry."

After all those careful plans for birth-day transportation, I hadn't been told of the change in destination: Baptist Hospital rather than Methodist Hospital. Luckily the two weren't far apart, although I did break a hell of a sweat trying to get over to Baptist before the backseat of the Lincoln became the delivery room.

Priscilla was whisked away by nurses, and Elvis, Charlie, and I were led to a special waiting room that the hospital had set aside for Elvis. We weren't there long before we were joined by Vernon and then Joe Esposito, who'd flown in from L.A. for the occasion. Throughout the day, we were joined by a few more of the boys. At first, Elvis was still keeping things calm, keeping himself cool and collected. But the more he got status reports from the doctors, the more he started to give in to the emotions of the day. You could see in his eyes how excited he was, and by the middle of the afternoon, when the rest of us were trying to stay as comfortable as we could in our chairs, Elvis couldn't keep still. He paced and bounced around the little room, hot-wired with nervous energy.

At 5:00 P.M., he got the word—he was the father of a beautiful and healthy daughter, whom he and Priscilla named Lisa Marie. Elvis left us to spend time with mother and child, but a while later he came back grinning and led us to the hospital's nursery window so that he could proudly point out his baby to us.

Priscilla and Lisa Marie were going to stay over at the hospital, and by the time Elvis was ready to go home that first day, word had gotten out about the birth and a huge corps of press had gathered around the hospital. So another special transportation plan was put into effect: Elvis, Joe, Charlie, and I slid down laundry chutes into the hospital basement, and then rode home in an anonymous-looking panel truck that Elvis thought would be right for the purposes of an undetected getaway.

I drove Elvis, Priscilla, and Lisa Marie home from the hospital a couple days later, where we were greeted by Vernon, Grandma, and the Beaulieus. In the house, I had the chance to watch Elvis hold his tiny daughter. I got the feeling that whatever he'd been searching for in his spiritual explorations, he had finally found a piece of right there in his arms. Whatever emptiness he'd been feeling inside him was suddenly filled up by his own small family. Standing beside his beautiful wife, holding his baby, he looked like a proud husband and a natural-born dad. At some point, down there in that little kitchen, Elvis caught me looking at the baby and decided he'd share some of his happiness.

"Here," he said, holding out little Lisa Marie, "You want to hold her?"

I think I did say no, but it was too late—he'd already put the hand-off into motion. Lisa was the first infant I'd ever held, and I stood there awkwardly cradling this little creature, hoping like hell I didn't drop her or damage her in any other way. My heart was pounding like a jackhammer, and though I tried to smile, I couldn't wait for the moment to be over (I'm much more comfortable around Lisa these days). I handed this incredible little package back to Elvis, who scooped her into his arms and stood there beaming down at her.

He looked about as contented as a man could be.

9

. . .

A LITTLE MORE ACTION

1968 was a year of extremes, a year of turmoil, and a year of enormous—often violent—change. Police were beating student demonstrators on American streets. Racial clashes were erupting into riots. And the war in Vietnam was starting to look unwinnable. The chaos of the headlines was reflected in the culture around us: Jimi Hendrix played his Stratocaster louder and wilder than any guitarist before him, and the Beatles, who had achieved an artistic triumph with *Sgt. Pepper*, were now at work on their *White Album*—and with beards, mustaches, and shoulder-length hair, they bore almost no resemblance to the guys that had hung out at Elvis's Perugia Way house. Muhammad Ali had been stripped of his heavyweight title and brought up on federal charges for refusing his draft induction. Down on Sunset Boulevard, the hipsters in suits had been replaced by hippies in tie-dye. In Stanley Kubrick's *2001: A Space Odyssey* the future looked to be even more confusing than the present.

Old rules were being challenged, and new answers were being sought out. Thousands of people were turning to Eastern religions and philosophies, embracing some of the very same works that Elvis had read so fervently. And the enlightment-through-chemistry experiment we'd quietly attempted in the Graceland conference room had been embraced by a much wider population—"psychedelia" was turning up in music, in fashion, and even on Broadway (*Hair*).

We had a personal connection to the war effort through Priscilla's father, Colonel Beaulieu, who headed over to Vietnam shortly after the birth of Lisa. Elvis had recently seen the national TV news reports of the attacks on the U.S. Embassy in Saigon during the Tet Offensive, and had learned that a military attaché at the embassy had found himself out on a balcony unarmed during the assault—military personnel below had to toss a weapon up to him so he had some means of protection. Before Colonel Beaulieu shipped out, Elvis told him, "I don't want that to ever happen to you," and gave him a snub-nosed Colt Python revolver to carry with him. In photos that Priscilla and her sister, Michelle, later showed us of their father overseas, it looked like he always had Elvis's gun at his side.

I was standing with Elvis in a trailer on the MGM lot when we learned of one of the year's most heartbreaking events. I was still looking to get into film editing, but had continued taking on acting roles and extra work to make some money. When Elvis began work on *Live a Little, Love a Little* over at MGM, he hired me as his stand-in and photo double. Again, the script was uninspired and the production was hurried. The most notable details about the film are that Vernon made a cameo appearance as a high-class subject for the commercial photographer Elvis played, and I had another chance to get wet with an Elvis costar—that's me in the Paradise Cove surf with Michele Carey at the end of the film (also of note—a little throwaway song Elvis sings to costar Celeste Yarnall, "A Little Less Conversation," became a global number-one hit thirty-four years later).

But what I remember most about the production is that on April 4, I was with Elvis in his trailer, hanging out between scenes. He had a little TV in there that was usually on in the background, and the set grabbed our attention when a newscaster interrupted the programming with a news bulletin from Memphis. Martin Luther King Jr. had been shot and killed.

I was confused at first. We knew that the mayor of Memphis was refusing to meet with striking sanitation workers, and that Dr. King had gone to the city to try to mediate the situation. But how could something so awful and wrong happen in the city we loved? The confusion quickly gave way to sadness. This had happened in our town. And in a terrible way, it made sense—we were well aware that beneath all the good music for good people that had come out of Memphis, there had always been an ugly racial tension. It had been there in the separate drinking fountains, in the separate counter at John's Little Kitchen, and in the struggles of Sam Phillips. It had been there in Mrs. Doolittle's re-action to "Sixty Minute Man," and in the early, angry reactions to Elvis. Now, with one hateful bullet, that sort of ugliness was being exposed for the whole world to see.

Elvis didn't often speak openly about race or politics, but he had been greatly inspired by Dr. King's "I Have a Dream" speech and had committed much of it to memory. I'd heard him recite those beautiful, hopeful words many times. I looked over at Elvis now and saw that he was staring hard at the TV. There were tears in his eyes.

"He always spoke the truth," he said quietly.

By the end of April, I'd finally gotten a chance to work as a film editor—or, more accurately, in an editing department. I found myself reporting to the basement of one of the post-production buildings at ABC Television, where it was my responsibility to scrape the labels off the cans of film that had come back from overseas syndication runs. I'd been trying to get in over at ABC for months and the guy who finally hired me, Jim Taylor, admitted that he'd been reluctant at first to give me a job. "I knew you were one of Elvis's guys," he said. "I didn't think you could be serious about working as an editor."

Scraping labels in the basement wasn't exactly the mix of artistry and craft that had attracted me to editing in the first place, but I liked the routine of a steady day job and enjoyed earning my living through my own hands-on work. Sandy took a job at the Casual Corner, a women's clothing store in Century City, and we started to settle into a happy, humble domestic life. And after a couple months of scraping, I got bumped up to a position with a team of assistant editors, cutting to-gether the footage for the network news. I got to put some of my old backfield moves to use, running fresh footage from cameramen's heli-copters down to the editing bays.

I didn't see much of Elvis for a while, but I stayed in touch with Joe Esposito and some of the other guys. I heard that Elvis had taken them back to Hawaii for a vacation trip. I also heard that he had signed on to do his first television special, which was being shot all through June over at the NBC studios. I couldn't get away from work for any of the

tapings, but I felt like I was represented by Sandy, who went one afternoon with Priscilla, Pat Parry, and Joanie Esposito. Sandy reported that
Elvis looked great and sang some of his older hits. I hoped that Elvis
was having a better time making his special than he had making his last
few films.

"Come on out to Arizona. And let your beard grow."

The call from Elvis was an invitation to join him on location for
production of a film that sounded like it might actually be exciting—a
gritty cowboy tale in the mold of Clint Eastwood's spaghetti westerns,
to be titled *El Charro!* He wanted me to work again as his stand-in and
photo double. It meant a lot that he was keeping me a part of things,
and I had to admit that even though I liked working on my own, it
wasn't easy to hear about something like that Hawaii vacation trip without wishing, just a little, that I'd been a part of it.

At ABC, I was moving up again, joining editor Bud Tedesco's staff
to assemble preview footage of the network's upcoming shows so that
they could be introduced, and sold, to the network's affiliates. That
work didn't start until the fall. And I used vacation days and some favors
from my bosses to get enough time off to accept Elvis's invitaion and
become a bearded cowboy that August at the Apacheland Movie Ranch
in Apache Junction, Arizona.

When I got out to the location, I could see that the production was
in trouble. This hadn't been set up as the typical soundstage shoot, and
a better-than-usual cast had been assembled for the film, including Ina
Balin, Victor French, and Barbara Werle. Elvis had had some hope that
this might be a meaningful film. But the edgy script that had caught
Elvis's interest was being rewritten and toned down, the crew seemed to
be broken into factions, and, to top it all off, the stuntmen had gone on
strike—a pretty big problem for a film full of gunfighting, fistfighting,
and horse-riding.

I was asked if I wanted to do some stuntwork in addition to my
photo-double duties. Thinking of the much higher day rate that stuntmen made, and all my experience in the saddle at Graceland and the
Circle G, I said yes. I was part of a big scene in which a group of desper-
adoes on horses try to cross a river while being shot at by a cannon. We

were to ride through the water as two large, precisely timed charges of real dynamite buried in the river went off to create the effect of incoming cannonballs. Everything about the scene was carefully thought through—except the strength of the river's current. On "action," we charged into the water, and the first blast went off right in front of us—it was much bigger than what had been described to us, and spooked both horses and riders. While everyone tried to rein in their mounts, the river pushed us toward the second charge, which turned out to be not so precisely timed—it didn't go off until we were right over it. The scene was a disaster—with both people and horses getting hurt. But with our schedule and budget, there was no chance for a second take. The scene made the final cut.

As the shoot days limped along, it was still great to spend time with Elvis and some of the guys (Charlie Hodge had a role in the film as "Mexican Peon"). One morning, I was up at dawn, before any of the other guys, for an early call. I headed over to the ranch cafeteria for a quick breakfast, and saw that one other person had gotten there before me. He was an older man with long silvery hair, dressed all in black. I'd never met him before, but I knew right away that this was Billy Murphy, a semilegendary character actor and buddy of John Wayne's and Robert Mitchum's, who had spent a lot of time with Elvis in the early L.A. days. Seemed like everybody that had met Billy Murphy had a great, oddball story about him, and I'd heard Elvis tell enough Billy stories that I had no doubt about who I was looking at. I walked over to his table.

"Mr. Murphy?"

"Sit down, mister," he said, almost as if he'd been expecting me. There was no mistaking that "mister"—I'd heard Elvis say it just the same way countless times.

"What are you doing here? How'd you get here?" I asked.

"Got in the Saint. Followed the sun," he said. This was pure Billy—part philosopher, part poet, all cowboy. It was a while before I learned that "the Saint" was his trusty, beat-up old car.

Billy hadn't made any arrangements with Elvis—he'd just shown up on the set, on his way to another Arizona location where a Robert Mitchum film was being shot. As soon as I had a chance, I got over to the location house where Elvis was staying and told him Billy was out here. Elvis was excited by the news. As always, he loved a character, and Billy was much more than that—he was a truly unique personality that Elvis enjoyed spending time with. Elvis asked me to make arrangements with the assistant directors to get Billy into a few scenes of the film.

A couple days later we were shooting a night scene, and Elvis was in a director's chair off to the side, watching the action. He called me over, and pointed to Billy, who, in the scene, was walking down the Western street with a distinctive cowboy strut.

"Jerry—take a look at Billy over there. You see that walk?"

"Yeah, E."

"I used that walk in my TV special."

From the Memphis truckers' neckerchiefs to James Dean's up-turned collar to Billy Murphy's strut, Elvis always had a knack of borrowing from the best—and the most unlikely—and making it his own.

After *Charro!* wrapped, Elvis wanted to head to Las Vegas for a couple days of fun, and he asked me to come along. We still had matching beards, matching hair, and, quite frequently, matching miniature Villager Kiel cigars. Our first night in Vegas we went down to a blackjack table, and when management spotted us, they put up some red velvet ropes around us. Of course, this only called more attention to us. And I guess maybe the matching beards confused a few people, because suddenly there was a woman at my side asking me for an autograph. I don't know who she thought I was, but I was trying to ignore the request. I figured I didn't need to be signing autographs when I was standing next to Elvis Presley. The woman was insistent, though, and it seemed like the situation might get uncomfortable. Suddenly, Elvis gave me a nudge, and, with his cigar held in this teeth, said, "Go ahead. Sign it." I turned to the lady and signed the first "Jerry Schilling" autograph of my life. Turning back to Elvis, I think I saw just the barest hint of a smile as he pushed his next stack of chips out on the table.

Tanned. Thin. Dangerous. And singing straight from the soul. Elvis was back, with a vengeance. I was sitting in a small conference room at NBC, watching a rough cut of Elvis's TV special. It was just Elvis, my-self, Joe, and Charlie, along with producer/director Steve Binder and a network executive. I don't know what I'd expected this show to be, but from the first moment to the last it was obvious that Binder had allowed it to become the kind of artistic challenge Elvis had been so hungry for. For the first time in a long time, somebody had let Elvis be Elvis— rather than the tame, nice-guy-next-door he'd had to play in so many films—and he rose to the occasion in a spectacular way. The special's loose story line was guided along by Jerry Reed's "Guitar Man," and the set pieces combined gospel music, modern dance, karate moves, and— always—Elvis in peak voice. There was an informal jam that teamed Elvis with Scotty Moore, D. J. Fontana, Charlie Hodge, and Lance LeGault, as well as Alan Fortas, who contributed what he could by tapping on the back of a guitar case. There was also a solo performance, during which Elvis ripped through some of his old favorites. In both sequences, Elvis was in black leather pants and jacket, and, at thirty-three, looking better than ever. This show didn't have a studio feel, a network feel or a Colonel feel—the whole thing had a true Elvis feel to it. And yes, there was a little Billy Murphy in his walk.

The special ended with a song written for the occasion, a plea for peace and brotherhood called "If I Can Dream." The shock and hurt of the loss of Dr. King, and then Robert Kennedy, was still heavy in the air, and Elvis gave himself over completely to the stirring music and the simple message of hope. It was a breathtaking performance, and the pain, the power, and the heart that went into it made one thing very clear to me in that little conference room: The guy who had created all that excitement back in the fifties could still, in the turmoil of 1968, move you to tears with his awesome, undimmed talent. Nobody had originally talked about this as a "comeback special," but Elvis had turned it into one.

We all shared our positive feedback with Elvis after the screening, and I know that meant a lot to him—I don't think he really knew how good the show was until he'd seen it cut together that night. But he was still a little pensive. It had been a long time since he'd put himself out like this to the public, and I think he was actually nervous about what the public's reaction would be.

His nerves probably weren't helped much by the Colonel's opinion of the special. Right from the start, the Colonel had disagreed with the approach Elvis and Binder had taken, and he still wasn't won over by the results of their work when he had his own screening at the network. Originally, he'd envisioned the program to be more along the lines of a traditional Christmas special—Elvis singing holiday standards à la Bing Crosby. But Elvis and Binder had stuck to their guns. And when the show aired in early December, it was a critical success and a ratings smash that delighted old-time fans and let a whole new generation of fans see what really made Elvis "Elvis."

Through the fall and winter of 1968 I went back to steady work as an editor at ABC, though I did take advantage of a couple of days off to walk from my apartment over to the MGM lot, where Elvis was working his way through his final film for the studio, *The Trouble with Girls* (I couldn't get the time off to be a stand-in, but I did score a couple of days' work as a "Deputy Sheriff"). Soon after that production wrapped, Elvis headed back to Memphis to begin some new recording sessions. Reenergized by the reaction to the special, Elvis was now eager to start making quality records again and, after some encouragement from George Klein and Marty Lacker, he decided to shake things up. Rather than lining up another round of the usual recording process in L.A. or Nashville, he teamed with a young, hot producer named Chips Moman at Moman's low-budget American Studios in North Memphis. In that small, run-down facility—not so far from Humes High and Leath Street—Moman, who'd been a creative force behind many successes at Stax Records, quickly proved that he also knew how to let Elvis be Elvis. Those North Memphis sessions would produce some of Elvis's best work, including "In the Ghetto," and "Suspicious Minds."

In the spring, Elvis was spending a lot of time in Palm Springs, and I developed an interesting weekend ritual—I'd spend the week as a hardworking, low-paid apprentice editor, but at Friday quitting time I'd drive over to Santa Monica Airport to be flown out by private plane for a weekend in the desert with Elvis and the guys.

The Colonel had been the first big advocate of weekends in Palm Springs—he was out there doing business, and encouraged Elvis to come out for weekend getaways. The idea of being able to keep a close eye on Elvis had an appeal to the Colonel, but the appeal of Palm Springs wasn't so clear to us guys at first. It seemed like a town of old folks that didn't have much to offer. The desert destination grew on us, though. There was fun to be had out there—everything from an active nightlife to a shooting range to a run of giant sand dunes that we used for afternoons of wild dune buggy rides. For a while, Palm Springs was a great getaway for all of us, with Elvis and Priscilla and the guys and their wives enjoying the place as a mix of romantic hideout and family resort. Sometimes, Elvis, Priscilla, Sandy, and I would go over to the Colonel's house in the late afternoon to spend some time with him and his wife. These get-togethers were generally pleasant—unless Elvis and the Colonel decided they needed to head out by the pool for a private meeting, in which case I'd be stuck playing Yahtzee with the girls, watching Marie Parker cheat her way through game after game and listening to her constantly reprimand Priscilla for dressing too sexy.

We traveled a little farther for a getaway in May of 1969, when Elvis and Priscilla invited Sandy and me and several other couples to join them for a Hawaiian vacation. I lined up some days off to make the trip, and was very happy to find myself back at the Ilikai Hotel, where I'd been staying when I first met Sandy. In between our nights at the Ilikai, we also stayed in some beach houses on the other side of the island. By the end of May, the Circle G Ranch would be sold, but that Hawaiian trip had some of the easy, carefree feel of some of the best ranch times. One night, Priscilla, Sandy, and Joanie Esposito decided to make a taco dinner for everyone over at Elvis's beach house. Something must have sparked that competitive spirit in Elvis and me, because we decided to have a taco-eating contest. I thought I had him beat when I wolfed down twelve of them, but he went on to edge me out by putting away a thirteenth.

Toward the end of the trip we decided we needed to treat the wives to something a little fancier than competitive eating. We wanted to give them a special night out and a chance to get dressed up, so we made plans to dine at the Ilikai's rooftop restaurant, Top of the "I." We had a great meal in a private alcove in the dining area up there. There was good food and a lot of laughter, and even though he was out in a fairly exposed public place, Elvis was relaxed and enjoying himself.

Toward the end of dinner he got up to use the restroom and asked me to come along with him (even back at the Memphian, he always brought someone along on a bathroom trip—he didn't want to get cornered when he was at his most vulnerable). We were on our way back to the table when he suddenly left my side and headed for the maître d's station. Apparently, he'd noticed that there were a number of people lined up there, waiting to be seated. Elvis walked directly over to the station and addressed the first person in line.

"Yes? Party of?" he asked.

"Miller. Party of four," said a well-dressed middle-aged woman.

"Table for four," said Elvis. He picked up a pen and made a note in the reservation book, then began to look around the restaurant for an open table.

The woman had a puzzled expression on her face. "Excuse me—are you . . ."

"I get that all the time," said the pinch-hitting maître d'.

The other people waiting to be seated started to realize who was now handling their reservations. The real maître d' now hurried back to his station, looking a little surprised that a VIP guest had found it necessary to step in for him.

"This man will take excellent care of you. Enjoy your dinner," said Elvis with a devilish grin.

Slowly, the Palm Springs weekends began to shift away from the couples and families, and the stays in the desert started to have more of a boys' club feel. At Elvis's Palm Springs houses—he went through a few of them—we kept late hours, and the weekends took on the feeling of a more adult version of the old Graceland parties or the nights at the Perugia Way house. Along with Joe and Charlie, the guys at this point included Sonny West, Richard Davis, G. G. Gambill, and a few others. L.A. friends like Pat Parry might come down and join us, and just as a few pretty girls had made it through the Graceland gates, there were some L.A. and Palm Springs women who'd come hang out with us. There was still very little drinking—I don't remember a stocked bar at any of the Palm Springs houses. There was some music, some storytelling, some laughs, and, with our new guests, some new relationships.

When we got out of the house, the boys had some interesting encounters with the Palm Springs locals. We'd find ourselves hanging out for a night at Liberace's house, or riding around in a Rolls-Royce Elvis had borrowed from Sammy Davis Jr., at Sammy's insistence. One night around midnight, Elvis was driving the Rolls along Palm Canyon Drive when he spotted the silhouette of someone walking across the road up ahead, holding a golf club. "I think that's Bob Hope," he said. And as he pulled up to the pedestrian, we saw that it was indeed Mr. Hope, accompanied by his valet. Elvis got out of the car and talked with Bob for a while, and made a point of introducing me and Joe to him. Just another night out for all of us.

I felt like I was back to leading a double life: on Sundays I'd be riding around in Liberace's dune buggy (equipped with a pair of chandeliers) and on Monday morning I'd be punching the clock for a day of film splicing. I'm pretty sure I was the only apprentice editor whose Monday morning commute included limos and charter planes.

By the middle of 1969 Elvis and I had both made important career moves. After putting in my year of apprentice work in television editing, I was hired at Paramount as an apprentice editor on feature films. This meant that I now spent my days lugging around the heavy cans of 35 mm film from the lot's film library to projection rooms for directors' screenings. It wasn't exciting work, but the days were sometimes broken up with some interesting encounters—I helped *The Brady Bunch*'s Maureen McCormick carry her bags of fan mail to her dressing room, and I sometimes worked the heavy bag in the studio gym alongside *Bonanza*'s Michael Landon.

Elvis's career move may have been a little more exciting—after more than eight years away from the concert stage, he decided to make a return to live performance at the end of July with a monthlong concert engagement at the brand-new International Hotel in Las Vegas.

At that point, it had become a part of the rhythm of our friendship that, even though I wasn't working for him, I'd be involved in what was happening around him. So I was there at the RCA studio in Hollywood for most of the band auditions as Elvis carefully selected the players who would back him in Vegas. He started by picking guitarist James Burton, a masterful player whose credits ranged from Ricky Nelson to *Shindig* to Frank Sinatra sessions. Then, with Burton as a musical anchor, Elvis built up his band, musician by musician. With the TV special still fresh in people's minds, and "In the Ghetto" now at the top of the singles charts, Elvis could have his pick of the top players in the business. But he didn't just automatically go after the players generally considered to be the number-one session guys—he wanted musicians who played with some character, too. After so many years of slickly recorded soundtrack sessions, he now wanted a band that would surprise people. After all those years of having his voice pushed up in the mix and the instruments pushed back, Elvis wanted a band that would kick some ass.

The key to the band's power would be the rhythm section. Burton brought in a guy named Jerry Scheff, who played what Elvis would always describe as a "thundering bass." But the band still needed a drummer. With just a few weeks to go until opening night, it was assumed that Elvis would go with one of the top L.A. session drummers who had already auditioned. But on the last day of auditions, another drummer showed up. He was a big, bearded guy named Ronnie Tutt, who'd just come to L.A. from Texas—in fact, he had his family, his station wagon, and a trailer full of all his earthly belongings parked outside the studio. I don't think anybody had high expectations for Ronnie—he didn't have anything close to the kind of concert and recording credits the rest of the band had. And when he first played with the band, it didn't seem like he impressed his bandmates all that much.

But Elvis heard something. And he wanted to hear more of it. He told the drummer they were going to run through some more songs, and this time Elvis wanted him to use the drums to accentuate the moves he made while he sang. They started a song, Elvis started moving, and you could see Ronnie trying to keep the beat solid while punching drum licks to accent what Elvis was doing. Elvis kept calling out more directions to the drummer, telling him to follow the moves and hit the accents harder. Ronnie's brow started to furrow and a dark look showed up in his eyes. He was keeping the songs rolling and doing his damnedest to bash out those accents. He started to look like he was playing angry. The whole band's energy seemed to jump, but when the song was over the other players probably still assumed that they'd be working in Vegas with a dependable session ace behind the drums.

Elvis came over to where I was standing with Joe and Charlie and some other guys. Somebody asked if he was going to go with a well-known, established drummer. It seemed obvious that the answer would be yes, but Elvis surprised us.

"I need somebody on stage who plays with my temperament," said Elvis. "And the guy with the beard's got it."

As usual, when Elvis was allowed to make his own decision about his music, he made the right one. Ronnie Tutt could match Elvis's temperament—and temper—move for move, song for song. And he'd go on to be recognized as one of the most powerful drummers in the business.

My work schedule at Paramount prevented me from being in Las Vegas for the big opening night on Thursday, July 31. But I'll never forget the report I got from Joe Esposito when I called him to make arrangements for Sandy and me to be there the next night. Joe said Elvis was phenomenal, and the sold-out crowd loved every second of it. But the detail that stood out the most to me was this: After the show, the Colonel had come backstage with a tear in his eye. Without saying a word, he'd walked up to Elvis and the two had embraced. You could see, Joe said, that the Colonel was shaking. And Elvis looked just as moved. The Colonel got what Elvis was doing, and for that moment, they'd looked closer than they ever had before.

Sandy and I were there the next night to see the show for ourselves, and it was just as thrilling as Joe had indicated. Elvis was in a striking, white-on-white suit that had the look of a tailored karate *gi*, with a low collar and a loose cloth belt tied around his lean frame. As he kicked things off with a rocking version of "Blue Suede Shoes," I could see right away that everything I had always admired about Elvis as a performer was still there. The jungle-animal-on-the-prowl instincts I'd seen at Ellis Auditorium back in 1956 were right back up on the Vegas stage, but that raw energy had now been channeled and choreographed into a more powerful, physical display of athleticism, including a lot of explosive karate moves. The wild animal had been trained, but not tamed.

The band I'd seen Elvis put together did in fact kick ass, but he also had a string and horn section up on stage with him, along with a pair of backup singing groups—a quartet of white gospel singers called the Imperials and a quartet of beautiful, black female singers called the Sweet Inspirations. It occurred to me that on this one stage, Elvis had brought together elements of every musical influence that had in some way shaped him: black gospel, white gospel, country-guitar licks, the earthiness of rhythm and blues, the drive of rock and roll—even the orchestral sweep of the Mario Lanza records he'd loved as a kid was part of the act now. That was a lot to try to hold together, but he did it, and the timing, pacing, and dynamics of the show were unbelievable. The show moved with a steady, natural flow from the high-energy opening of "Blue Suede Shoes," to the power of "Suspicious Minds," to surprises like Del Shannon's "Runaway" and the Beatles' "Hey Jude," right on through to the emotional finale of "I Can't Help Falling in Love with You."

It wasn't until that Vegas show that I realized how much I'd missed watching him do what he could do on a concert stage. His performance had all the enthusiasm and intensity that he'd brought to his TV special, but the stage gave him a freedom that he hungrily seized upon. He wasn't just the rebel anymore, singing to an underground audience. He was more in charge and more exciting. A master performer. Back at Ellis, he had dragged his mike around as if it were putting up a fight for its honor. Now there was no question that Elvis was the triumphant seducer. The bad scripts and the gimmicks and the interference had finally been swept away. This was his room, his band, his show, and his music. Against all odds, the tiger was back—strong and sleek and ferocious as ever.

In the fall, Elvis and Priscilla headed to Hawaii for an island vacation. The trip was paid for by the International Hotel as a thank-you for Elvis's engagement, which had set new attendance and box office records in Las Vegas. The couple took the Espositos and Gambills along with them. I was back to my day shifts at Paramount, but a few days after the group had left for the island, I got a call at home.

"You got a passport, Jerry?"

"No, Elvis. Why would I need one?"

"The island's real nice. But we've been talking. We need a real vacation. We're all going to Europe in a couple of weeks. I want you and Sandy to come."

The idea sounded great. But I'd known Elvis long enough to know that sometimes his great ideas weren't thought through all the way.

"I can probably get the time off to do it, E, but—are you sure the Colonel's going to let it happen?"

"He ain't got a goddamn thing to do with it. None of his goddamn business. We're going to Europe—are you coming?"

"Sure, Elvis, yeah. It sounds perfect."

I put in the request to use up my two weeks' worth of vacation days for the year at Paramount, and when Elvis and the rest returned from Hawaii, we all set about getting expedited passports. There were a few days of high spirits as the wives began to plan the cities they wanted to visit and the sights they wanted to see. But predictably, a European vacation didn't sound so perfect to the Colonel. As soon as he heard about Elvis's plan, he came down hard on him, insisting that it would be a terrible insult to European fans to take a vacation there before he'd ever performed there. This didn't make a lot of sense to anybody, and at first it seemed like Elvis—charged up and riding high on his new string of career successes—would simply ignore the Colonel.

But before our European itinerary could even be set, Elvis announced that there would be a change in plans. We wouldn't be heading to Europe—we'd be heading to the Bahamas. The Colonel knew the owner of the main hotel on Paradise Island off Nassau, and had arranged for us to have a spectacular vacation stay there. Elvis was a strong, smart guy, but he also hated conflict. I'm sure that once the Colonel was on him, telling him that he was making a thoughtless mistake, at some point it just seemed a lot easier to stop arguing back and head off to the Bahamas. We all tried to get over the disappointment, and tried to concentrate on the chance for all of us to have a great time together. After all, how bad could a place called Paradise Island be?

We flew in to the island's small airport at sunset and checked into the hotel. Then Joe and I went down to the nearby docks to rent some boats we could use the next day—Elvis wanted to water-ski. We had a nice dinner together in the hotel restaurant, then headed off to our separate rooms.

The room phone woke me up the next day, and I was surprised to hear Elvis's voice on the other end—in all the years I knew him, there weren't many mornings when he was up before me.

"You ready to hit those boats?" he asked. Despite the early hour, he sounded like he was in a great mood.

"Uh, yeah, Elvis. Just waking up over here, but yeah."

"Well, take a look out your window."

I put the phone down, walked over to the window, and parted the heavy drapes. The sky was dark and angry-looking, and the wind was so strong it was whipping bullets of rain sideways through the sky. Half the palm trees on the beach had been knocked over. And down at the dock, the boats—including the ones we'd rented—were tangled and tossed and smashed together. We'd come to the island just in time to sit in the middle of a brewing hurricane—a violent stormfront that didn't let up for days. We ended up hitting the casinos instead of the beach, and managed to have some fun together, but we came back to L.A. a week early, all very conscious of the fact that our grand plan for two weeks in Europe had been reduced to six days of Bahama hurricane. My new passport was still unstamped, and a combination of bad weather and Colonel Parker had wasted away my hard-earned Paramount vacation days.

In early 1970, Elvis was as free as he'd been in a long time—he'd finally fulfilled all the obligations of his film contracts, and didn't have any upcoming recording sessions. He also had a number-one hit single: "Suspicious Minds" had made it to the top of the pop charts in November. For the first time in a long while, I got the sense that he was really enjoying what he was doing, and it didn't surprise anybody when he booked another monthlong engagement at the International in Vegas.

I'd worked myself up to a higher position at Paramount. Instead of just moving film cans around, I was now doing some hands-on editing. I was working with the syndication department, splicing out the foreign commercials that had been spliced in when the features aired on overseas television, and making sure that the prints were in good enough shape to be sent out again. I enjoyed the work and loved putting my skills to use cutting and restoring those 16 mm feature prints. And I still felt like I had the best of both worlds—most of my Paramount workweeks ended with an Elvis-hired plane whisking me off to Las Vegas.

Elvis knew me well enough to know that I didn't want to feel like I was getting something for nothing, so he started giving me some unofficial duties when I was out in Vegas with him. I became a kind of personal PR man, helping with special arrangements for stars that wanted to come see the show, and making sure that certain guests got an introduction to Elvis. I was also put to use as an extra member of Elvis's security team. Among the guys working full-time for Elvis, Joe Esposito handled the VIPs and Red or Sonny West was always in charge of security. But when things got crazy and those guys got busy, I was there to help as an all-purpose utility man.

One weekend in this period I found myself back out in Palm Springs with the Colonel, rather than with Elvis. The Colonel had invited Sandy and me out for a visit. He was putting us up in the Palm Springs Spa and wanted us to come to a dinner there with him and Marie and another couple, a Los Angeles promoter, manager, and former talent agent named Jerry Weintraub and his wife, the singer Jane Morgan. The invitation was a little unusual. The Colonel and I had stayed on good terms, but it seemed strange that he'd have me be a part of a business dinner, and I knew there was no such thing as a purely social dinner with the Colonel—if he was talking, he was doing business. Elvis's incredible success in Las Vegas had gotten the entertainment world very excited, and now there was a buzz about his heading out on the road for more concert appearances. If and when that happened, the Colonel was going to need some help to help mount a tour. Jerry Weintraub wanted to be a part of that venture. I'd seen that the Colonel usually liked to have a staff guy like Tom Diskin or George Parkhill at any business meeting to serve as a friendly witness. I felt that at this dinner, I was in that role.

It was actually nice to spend some time with the Colonel, and as usual, though he didn't talk in direct business terms at the dinner table, you got the feeling that everything he said had some strategy behind it, and that everything Weintraub said was being very carefully assessed. Weintraub was an outgoing and charismatic young guy, and we got along well enough that before he left he asked me to get in touch with him back in L.A. It seemed like a good contact—I was trying to catch a break in the business, and knowing a guy like Weintraub couldn't hurt.

The Colonel thought otherwise. No sooner had Weintraub's car sped away than the Old Snowman came up next to me, took a puff off his cigar, and said, "Stay away from that guy. You don't need to get together with him." I didn't know if the Colonel was looking out for my interests, or if he wanted to keep me out of his. I was pretty sure it was the latter.

Elvis did get on the road again, and he restarted his touring career in a typically big way: on the last weekend of February, 1970, he did six shows at the Houston Astrodome, headlining the annual Houston Livestock Show & Rodeo. The huge venue, just a few years old at the time, was the first indoor baseball/football stadium—air-conditioned against the Texas heat—and was still being billed as "The Eighth Wonder of the World." I flew in to Houston to be a part of the team for the weekend, and got over to the Astrodome Hotel, where I met up with Elvis, Vernon, and the guys. There was a bit of the usual kidding around, but the atmosphere was more strained than usual—it was clear to everybody that Elvis was extremely nervous about the shows. Band rehearsals had been difficult because of the cavernous acoustics of the Astrodome, and the size of the crowd—the place could hold nearly 50,000 people—made it a huge jump from the Las Vegas gigs.

We were taken to the Astrodome on a bus driven by the legendary race-car driver A. J. Foyt, a surprise the Colonel had arranged. The bus pulled into the loading area of the venue and drove up a tunnel that was curtained off from the field and the seats. A part of the rodeo had just finished, the lights were down, and we could just barely see what we were about to head into. Elvis was at the front of the bus, getting ready to disembark, when the curtain before us was pulled open and the lights came up inside. Elvis was overwhelmed. I was standing close to him, and I could see that he was physically shaken—he went pale and came very close to being physically ill. The stage was out in the Dome's center field, and nobody in the audience was going to have a chance to see the show up close, so the plan had been that Elvis would do a kind of preshow victory lap—he'd stand in a Jeep and be driven near the seats so that he could make some personal contact with fans before performing. Sonny, Red, and Vernon were going to ride in the Jeep with him. Now, looking out at this space, and this crowd, he wanted a little extra support.

"Jerry, you better ride with us," he said quietly, still looking white as a ghost.

We took our places in the Jeep—Elvis standing and holding on to the top of the windshield—and began our slow drive around the edge of the seating areas. The crowd immediately came to its feet and greeted Elvis with a roaring ovation. Elvis was high enough in the vehicle that as we drove, he could reach out and shake hands with people and they could reach out and touch him. I was hunched down next to him, helping him stay up, and as I listened to that crowd roar, I had the sensation that I was in the Roman Colosseum, hanging on to the leg of a Caesar. Hearing that roar and seeing the excitement he created, a single thought kept coming back to me: "Oh my god—I forgot who this guy was."

Despite the welcoming, Elvis was not at all happy with that first Friday matinee show. He went directly from being nervous beforehand to being dejected afterward. Once we'd gotten out to the center-field stage, we could see that the venue was only half full. In addition to that discouraging fact, Elvis felt he hadn't been able to deliver the kind of performance he wanted to, partly due to the unpredictability of the event's revolving stage ("I finished 'Love Me Tender' and I was singing to a cow," he muttered back at the hotel).

In the hotel room between the afternoon and evening shows, Elvis started being hard on himself, saying that not only was the afternoon show a failure, but telling us that it was a mistake to think he could pull in a crowd big enough for a venue this size. A Vegas engagement was one thing, but as far as grassroots fans were concerned, he just didn't have it anymore. We tried to tell him that you couldn't expect much from a Friday afternoon show—people who wanted to be there were still at work. That didn't do much to lift his spirits. But then somebody called him over to his room's window. From our vantage point at the top of the hotel, we could see that traffic was streaming in from every direction to get to the Astrodome. He watched for a while, and then he started smiling. You could see all his uncertainty slip away, replaced by the confidence he'd been bringing to the Las Vegas stage. Obviously a guy who could create a traffic jam that size still had a few fans.

He did a great show Friday night for a crowd that set attendance records, and he did more great shows and set more records throughout the weekend. Even the cows must have been impressed.

By the end of the summer, Elvis was back in Vegas for his third engagement at the International, and I was spending more weekends at home in L.A. either enjoying time with Sandy or putting in longer hours at

Paramount. One Friday afternoon I got a call at work from Joe Esposito. He told me that Elvis wanted to speak with me. In a moment, Elvis was on the line.

"Jerry, I need you out here tonight. I've sent a plane. I'll explain it to you when you get here."

I didn't know what was going on, but from the sound of Elvis's voice, I knew it was serious. I bolted out of work and drove over to Santa Monica Airport, where a Learjet was waiting to take me to Vegas. I got to the International about ten minutes before Elvis was to go on and was immediately led backstage. He was in a little dressing area, in front of his makeup mirror, and when he saw me I detected some conflicting emotions in his expression. He was glad I was there, but he was also clearly angry and upset. Something had gotten to him. It wasn't common for us to make a big deal about greeting each other, but this time we embraced. Suddenly it felt incredibly important to be standing there with him, to be right here beside him when he needed help.

"Let me show you what's going on," he said.

He picked up a piece of paper. It was one of the promotional menus for the engagement with his picture on it, except that on this one Elvis's face had been crossed out and something unreadable was scrawled across it.

"Read it backwards," he said.

The scrawled letters spelled out "I am going to kill you."

"Some son of a bitch slid this under my door. The FBI says it looks like the real thing and we have to take it seriously. The hotel said I didn't have to do the show, but I'm not going to let this motherfucker push me off the stage. I wanted you and Red and Sonny here to watch my back."

"I'm here, E."

Elvis stared down at his defaced picture, and his anger seemed to push his fear out of the way. "Listen to me, Jerry. I don't want anybody going around saying they killed Elvis Presley. If anything happens out there, forget about me. You go get the son of a bitch and rip his eyes out."

Elvis wanted Sonny and me on stage with him. I was going to take a position behind the piano, with Sonny behind the backup singers on the other side of the stage. Red would be out in the audience along with Ed Parker, a dynamic karate instructor Elvis had become friendly with. All of us would be carrying our own guns, and Elvis would have a small pistol packed into his boot. There were also FBI agents out on the floor. Sonny and I talked briefly about what our best plan of action would be if we heard a shot—we decided that the first guy who could get to Elvis would bring him down fast to the floor, and the second guy would drop over him.

The backstage area was below stage level, and as we made our way up the stairs toward the stage just a minute before showtime, I noticed that one of Elvis's personal doctors, Dr. Thomas "Flash" Newman, was there, which was not part of the normal routine before a show. As we continued walking, Elvis nodded over to the open doors of the loading bay at the back of the building, where an ambulance and a crew of paramedics waited.

The show started on time, and the band members were understandably a little tense—everybody knew what was going on. They were also trying to get used to the fact that Sonny and I were now armed members of the orchestra. Elvis put on a strong performance, though he never stayed in one spot long, and he tried harder than usual to see past the stage lights and keep an eye on the crowd. Somewhere toward the middle of the show, there was a quiet moment before Elvis was to sing one of his ballads—the lights went down on stage until the orchestra was in darkness and Elvis was lit with a single spotlight. Just before the song began, the quiet was pierced by a male shout from the balcony: "Elvis!"

I reached for my gun, and was ready to make my move toward Elvis. I saw Sonny was ready to do the same. Down in the front of the house, Red was looking toward the voice from above, ready to go for his gun. Elvis immediately dropped to one knee and turned his body sideways—using a defensive karate strategy to make himself the smallest possible target.

"Yeah?" he growled back angrily at the balcony voice. If this was the son of a bitch who had threatened him, he wasn't going to give him any satisfaction.

"Would you sing 'Hound Dog'?" the balcony voice asked.

I don't think I've ever seen Elvis take a request so quickly, and I don't believe I've ever heard "Hound Dog" played any faster than it was that night. We made it through the show without any further incident, and the menu-mangling potential assassin was never heard from again.

Not every moment around Elvis was quite that exciting, but even a quiet night at his home could turn into an interesting adventure. I was visiting Elvis and Priscilla at their latest home, on Hillcrest Drive in Beverly Hills, after Elvis had completed a six-city mini-tour. I was in the den talking with Patsy and Gee Gee, who also lived there, when the in-house phone rang. I picked it up—Elvis was on the other end.

"Jerry, come back to the bedroom. I want to show you something."

I headed to the room, and found Elvis and Priscilla standing side by side, looking at a piece of paper that Elvis was holding. I knew it couldn't be another death threat, because Elvis had a great big uncharacteristic grin on his face—he was clearly thrilled with whatever he was looking at. He carefully handed me the paper and said, "What do you think?"

It was good to see Elvis this enthusiastic, to see him full of almost boyish excitement. I didn't want to say anything to sour that mood, but frankly, I had no idea what I was looking at on this paper. It was a drawing of something—a lightning bolt with letters on it.

"God, Elvis, this is great. What is it?"

"It's a TCB," he said proudly. He and Priscilla looked at each other and smiled.

"Oh!" I looked a little harder at the drawing. "Uh, what's a TCB?"

"Takin' care of business. Picture it in gold, on a chain. Priscilla sketched it out on the plane from Memphis. You're going to get one—all the guys will get one. It'll be our thing."

Now I could see it—and the lightning bolt with the "TCB" around it did make a striking jewelry design. Elvis had a favorite jeweler in Beverly Hills, Sol Schwartz, from whom he had purchased a number of pieces. I knew he'd want Schwartz to make up these, and I offered to bring the design to Sol's shop the next day. That wasn't good enough for Elvis. It was already past midnight, but he wanted to meet with the jeweler immediately.

Elvis had done enough special-order business with Schwartz that he had his home numbers, so I gave him a call and asked if he'd come meet us at the shop. Mr. Schwartz didn't seem too upset about having his sleep interrupted, especially for an Elvis request, and a short while later I was with Elvis and Priscilla outside the shop on Beverly Drive as the jeweler turned the alarms off and the lights on. Elvis and Priscilla presented the sketch to him and explained the design. The jeweler made a few notes, then took the order for the very first dozen fourteen-karat gold TCBs. And while the TCBs may have started as a late-night whim, they would become the most cherished of inner-circle possessions.

10

. . .

ALL THE WAY FROM MEMPHIS

I'd gotten used to the fact that my life could change very quickly with a call from Elvis: calls to come join him on a movie set, invitations to Palm Springs and Las Vegas, an intercom call to come check out a jewelry design. Still, nothing quite prepared me for a call I got one Saturday night just before Christmas 1970, or the events it led to. I guess the work at Paramount and some of those Elvis weekends had caught up with me—I'd fallen asleep early, and the phone woke me up. I mumbled some sort of hello into the receiver.

"Jerry."

For once, I was caught off guard.

"Who is this?" I asked, already suspecting the answer as I said the words.

"It's me," he said. Of course it was.

"Elvis, where are you?" Last I'd heard he was going to be in Memphis through the holidays.

"I'm in Dallas. Texas. Changing planes. I should be out there pretty soon."

"E, who's with you?"

"Nobody," he said. He sounded proud of it.

"You're at the Dallas airport—by yourself?"

"Yeah. And listen, Jerry—I don't want *anybody* to know where I am. It's important. Can you meet me at the airport?"

I asked him what flight he'd be on. For all the traveling Elvis had done in his life, he'd never had to worry about flight numbers and gate numbers and terminal numbers. We guys worked out the details—Elvis just got on a plane and assumed it would get him to where he was supposed to be. But here I was on the phone, listening to Elvis rustle through his papers to figure out the flight number of his American Airlines connecting flight from Dallas to L.A. When I was sure I'd gotten the right numbers from him, I told him I'd bring my own car so as not to attract any extra attention.

"Well, I think we can trust Sir Gerald," Elvis said. "Why don't you give him a call. But tell him I don't want anyone to know I'm here."

Gerald Peters was Elvis's favorite limo driver in L.A., an older, dapper, exceedingly trustworthy Brit. He had never actually received a knighthood, but when Elvis discovered that he had been a driver for Winston Churchill, Elvis immediately titled him "Sir Gerald." A few hours later, just after 2:00 a.m., I was in the back of a limo driven by Sir Gerald, and we drove right up to the American Airlines plane from Dallas (back then, you could make arrangements to pick up VIP passengers that way). I watched as passengers streamed off the plane, and I began to worry about what might have happened to an unattended Elvis since he made the phone call from Dallas. But after all the others were off, there he was at the top of the steps. I got out of the car and waved him over. As he approached, I saw he was holding a little cardboard box.

"Hey, E, you OK?"

"Yeah. Thanks for coming out."

"What's in the box?"

"That's my luggage."

Back then, a first-class passenger got a little container with a facecloth and a comb and toothbrush inside. Not only was Elvis traveling by himself, he was traveling light. I also noticed that he had some angrylooking red welts on his neck and face.

"What's the matter with your skin, E?"

"Oh, I took some penicillin for a sore throat. I guess I'm having an allergic reaction. Maybe we can get a doctor to the house."

"All right, I'll make the call. Sir Gerald, let's go."

"Wait a minute, Jerry—I promised the stewardesses that I'd give 'em a ride home."

He nodded over his shoulder and I saw that we were being joined by a pair of stewardesses from the flight. Apparently Elvis's desire to travel secretly didn't stop him from charming the flight crew—and while I made arrangements for a doctor to meet us at the house on

Hillcrest, we drove across town, dropping off the very impressed girls at their apartments.

We finally got to Hillcrest, and a doctor I'd gotten through a referral service was waiting for us at the gate. We got inside and the doc gave Elvis an examination and agreed that it looked like an allergic reaction. It was getting close to dawn, Elvis was already looking pretty tired, and the doctor gave him something to relieve the skin irritation that just about knocked him out. The doctor left and Elvis went off to bed. I called Sandy to let her know what was going on, and as I hung up, the crazy, scary truth of my situation hit me hard: Elvis Presley was my responsibility. His wife didn't know where he was. His father didn't know where he was. The guys didn't know where he was. The Colonel didn't know where he was. For the first time in fifteen years, nobody close to Elvis knew where he was. Except me.

I was tired, but I stayed awake, watching the morning sun light up the sky. Taking care of Elvis had brought on a surge of adrenaline, and while he slept, I stayed in the living room, trying to figure out the most sensible way to handle the situation. By Sunday afternoon, I still hadn't come to any firm conclusions, but Elvis was wide awake. Whatever had gotten him out of Memphis didn't seem to be bothering him now—he was in a great mood. We made some coffee and sat there staring out at the home's spectacular view of the city. We caught up with each other and talked about Priscilla, Sandy, and little Lisa. We talked about which guys were doing a good job for him and who was getting into trouble. Eventually he let me know why he'd left Graceland.

"I'll tell you why I didn't want anybody to know where I was," he said. "It's because Daddy and Priscilla were complaining about the way I spend my money. The way I spend my own damn money. And they went and brought the fucking Colonel into it, too. I wasn't going to sit around and listen to that."

He'd stormed out of the house in the past after various arguments, but this time he simply walked out of the house and left town. He'd gotten on the first commercial flight out of Memphis he could, which took him to Washington, D.C. He'd checked into a hotel there, but then decided he'd be better off making his way to L.A.

I'd learn later that Priscilla and Vernon had some reason to be upset. Over the last month or so, Elvis had gone on a spending spree amounting to tens of thousands of dollars, and there was no sign of him slowing down. The gold TCBs had only been the start. After the death threat in Las Vegas, he'd become very concerned with personal protection and had spent thousands on new guns. At the beginning of December he had completely bankrolled George Klein's wedding, flying all of us to Las Vegas for a weekend. At the end of that weekend, he decided to put a down payment on a house for Joe and Joanie Esposito, and he bought several Mercedes as gifts, one of which went to Sandy and me (Elvis told me he was going to put a down payment on a house for me, too, but Joe talked him out of it, explaining that I wouldn't be able to make mortgage payments on my apprentice editor's salary).

Elvis and I spent the whole day up at Hillcrest just sitting around talking. He was very excited about all the adventures he'd managed to pack into his solo trip so far, and wanted to relay all the details. In the wake of the death threat, Elvis had gone about qualifying for a Shelby County deputy sheriff badge—a credential that allowed him to carry a concealed weapon. But he explained that "a little uppity mustache guy" steward on the flight to Dallas wasn't going to let him bring his gun on the plane, even after Elvis showed him the new badge. After Elvis angrily left the plane, the pilot himself came running out to get him, apologized for the inconvenience, and insisted it would be all right by him for Elvis to have his registered firearm on board.

Since I'd stopped working for Elvis, it had become harder for us to spend this kind of time together. But it felt easy and satisfying to be sitting with him again, sipping coffee and talking friend to friend. It was getting close to sunset when he told me that his weekend trip wasn't over.

"Jerry, I'm going back to Washington. Tonight. I need you to come with me."

"Elvis, I've got a job. I have to be at work tomorrow."

"I'll charter a Learjet to fly you back."

If his spending habits were getting him into trouble, I didn't want him hiring a jet just for me.

"Look, Elvis—a chartered plane won't get me back any faster than a commercial flight. There's no use in spending that kind of money."

For the first time that day, his warm expression darkened. "All right, I'll go by myself," he said. He sounded equal parts defiant rebel and pouting little boy.

I still felt responsible for his safety, and I thought about him carrying his gun onto another plane, maybe one with a pilot who wasn't so understanding. There was a chance I'd lose the job at Paramount I'd worked so hard to get, but I decided I'd help get Elvis through the next part of his trip.

"Listen, E, if I go with you, you have to let me make a call. People may think you're hurt, or kidnapped. Your family's probably worried sick. Let me tell your dad and Priscilla you're OK. And let me have Sonny or Red come up and meet us in Washington, so I can fly back."

He agreed I should make the call, and said I should have Sonny come up and meet us. I phoned Graceland right away, and Sonny answered the phone. I explained to him what was going on, then took some time to explain to Vernon where Elvis was and where he was going, and that he should let Priscilla know that Elvis was all right. After that call, I had to snap into action to work out all the details for Elvis's return trip to D.C.—lining up our airline tickets, making pre-boarding arrangements, booking our hotel rooms, and hiring limos to get us to and from the airports. There was no way to do this without spending some more of Elvis's money—I charged most of it to his American Express card.

A short while later, with Sir Gerald again at the wheel, we were driving back to LAX. It had occurred to me that we might need some cash during the course of the trip. I didn't have any (not an unusual situation for me back then) and Elvis didn't have any, either. All we had was his credit card and a checkbook that I'd found in his desk at Hillcrest. The ever-resourceful Sir Gerald spoke up and said that he knew someone at the Beverly Hilton Hotel who might honor a check for $500 on a Sunday night, so we made the stop there and succeeded in getting the money. Elvis handed it to me for safekeeping.

We got to the airport and were the first to board our red-eye flight. As the rest of the passengers boarded we noticed that there were an unusual number of soldiers on the plane—guys coming home from Vietnam who had first stopped in L.A. and were now heading back east to their homes, just in time for Christmas. Many passengers recognized

Elvis, and he was cordial with everyone who said hello. Before the plane took off, one of the soldiers came up the aisle to stand next to Elvis and talk with him. He told Elvis what a big fan he was, and Elvis took an interest in the young guy, asking him where he was coming from and where he was heading. I saw that the two were having a very friendly conversation, and my attention drifted after a while. It was refocused when Elvis put a gentle elbow in my ribs.

"Where's that money?"

"What money?" I asked. But I'd seen enough of Elvis's gestures of generosity to suspect what was coming next.

"The $500."

"That's all we've got, Elvis."

"You don't understand—this guy's just come home from the war. He's going home to see his family. I want him to have the money."

The soldier got the $500, and I was suddenly in the strange situation of traveling across the country with Elvis Presley, absolutely penniless.

Once the flight was in the air, Elvis struck up a conversation with the stewardess who was tending to us. From her he learned that there was a government VIP on the plane: U.S. Senator George Murphy of California. Elvis was very interested in meeting the senator, and headed back to introduce himself. I looked back a couple of times to see that the two seemed engaged in a very serious conversation.

When Elvis returned to his seat, I got another elbow.

"Jerry—you think they have some stationery on this plane?"

We called the stewardess over and got ahold of several sheets of airline stationery and a pen. And there in the first-class cabin, Elvis Presley began to write a letter. This might have been the most surprising development of the trip so far—I'd certainly never seen Elvis write a letter before. He worked diligently for quite a while, and when he was finished, he handed me the pages.

"Jerry, I just wrote a letter to President Nixon. Would you proofread it for me?"

Here was a letter from the biggest star in the world to the leader of the free world, being given to me—the guy who flunked first grade—for proofreading. But I was touched by how readily he trusted me with it.

The pages weren't pretty—Elvis's penmanship was somewhere between a doctor's and a grade-schooler's—but right away I was impressed with the tone of the writing. Elvis was being humble, respectful, and sincere, and was offering his services to the President to work as a kind of ambassador between the rock-and-roll subculture and the government. After describing "The Establishment" that so many young people were finding fault with, Elvis had underlined a thought: "I call it America, and I love it." I felt a mix of feelings as I read that; I felt protective toward Elvis, and didn't want him to come across as a right-wing extremist. But I also knew where his heart was, and had always felt that the truest expression of his politics was in a pair of his records, "If I Can Dream" and "In the Ghetto." And reading the letter I could see that when he talked about loving America, it wasn't part of a political agenda—it was because he had lived the American dream and wanted desperately to be able to give something back to the land that had made his wonderful life possible. He didn't consider his years of army duty to have settled the debt. He was going straight to the highest authority in the country to try to find a way to use some of his power in a constructive way.

He did want something in return. "First and foremost, I am an entertainer, but all I need is the Federal credentials." Elvis was making a sincere offer of services, but if he was going to be of some use to the government, he wanted official recognition. He wanted a badge.

To me, this didn't seem crazy or unusual. From the earliest period of Elvis's career, he'd felt a strong kinship with the policemen who protected him during concerts and public appearances, and greatly enjoyed hearing about their lives and their work. And it seemed that no matter how tough the cops were, they always enjoyed their connection to Elvis. At some point, he began asking if he could have credentials from the police departments he worked with, and began accumulating honorary badges. His badge collection became a passionate hobby of his—he'd show them off the way someone else might show off their prized coins or stamps. After the threat in Las Vegas, though, the honorary badges weren't quite as exciting or useful anymore. He wanted credentials that gave him a real, working connection to the police forces he dealt with, and he wanted to be able to travel with the guns he felt he needed for personal safety. He, along with some of us guys, had received Shelby County deputy sheriff badges back in Memphis, and we had also been officially deputized in Palm Springs after proving ourselves capable on the police shooting range.

I'd been with Elvis a month before when he'd gotten a glimpse of the ultimate prize—a federal badge. Elvis had asked me to come along with him to a dinner at the renowned Beverly Hills restaurant Chasen's. The dinner had been set up by John O'Grady, a tough, gruff, ex-L.A. narcotics cop. O'Grady had been referred to Elvis by his attorney, Ed "The Hook" Hookstratten, to work for him as a private detective, helping him get to the bottom of what turned out to be a baseless paternity suit against him. Elvis had no interest in dining in upscale hot spots, but he couldn't say no to O'Grady's invitation—the detective promised to introduce him to a fully credentialed federal undercover agent.

That agent turned out to be Paul Frees, an unremarkable-looking guy who was well known as a cartoon voice-over artist. Frees had done undercover narcotics work for the Bureau of Narcotics and Dangerous Drugs, the precursor to the DEA (given his government work, it's interesting that one of his best-known voices was that of evil spy "Boris Badenov" from the *Bullwinkle* show). With some encouragement from O'Grady, Frees showed Elvis his federal badge, and I saw my friend's eyes light up. He was going to have to figure out a way to get his own BNDD badge.

And this letter was a brilliant way to make that badge a possibility. Elvis cited Senator Murphy in the body of the text and had him listed as a messenger—it would be delivered "via Sen. George Murphy." A couple other things struck me about the letter. First, though I had long stopped being impressed that Elvis knew my name, I was a little surprised to see that he could spell my surname perfectly—he mentioned to the President that he was traveling with me. I was also amused when I read one of Elvis's final points—that he'd be glad to help his country "as long as it is kept very Private." I didn't see how anything around Elvis could stay private for long, especially a government credential. The letter ended with a request for a personal meeting with the President.

When I finished reading the letter, I felt that these pages couldn't capture the spirit of Elvis any better. It was a work of warmth, sincerity, innocence, and skillful strategy that conveyed both a successful man's generosity and a little kid's desire for a special prize. Frankly, I didn't think we had a chance of getting into the White House—I'd read that, with the Vietnam war effort in a state of turmoil, even senators were having a hard time meeting with the President. But I wasn't going to change a word of Elvis's heartfelt writing.

"Great letter, E. I think you should send it as is."

By the time we landed in Washington and climbed into a limo, Elvis had changed his mind about delivering the letter—he didn't want to send it via the senator, he wanted to deliver it in person. I'd been up for two days, and had been looking forward to a shower at the Washington Hotel.

"Elvis, it's barely daylight. Shouldn't we check into the hotel first and clean up?"

"Jerry, I want to get this to the White House."

Of course, we headed to the White House. And I guess it hadn't really occurred to me how out of place we'd be in official Washington until our car pulled up to the northwest guard gate at the White House and Elvis jumped out to deliver his letter. He'd been wearing clothes that made perfect sense in any Elvis setting—a navy-blue gabardine, karate-style two-piece suit over a high-collared shirt, with a topcoat draped over his shoulders, accessorized with a gold medallion, a thick gold belt, and a gold-handled walking stick. At Graceland or in L.A., this was simply Elvis dressed up. But as he strode purposefully toward the White House security guards, I feared he might be taken for some kind of gabardine invasion force.

The guards certainly didn't appreciate being startled this way, and went into a high-alert mode—they wanted the car moved and the guy in the topcoat gone. I could see Elvis wasn't going to come this far to be turned away, and the situation had the possibility of turning ugly, so I ran out to do some diplomatic work. I began to calmly explain that this was Mr. Elvis Presley and that he had simply written a letter to the President that he wished to deliver. The guards took another look at the security threat beside me and all of a sudden understood who was in front of them. Happy to be of service, they took the letter and promised to get it to the President within the hour.

We finally got over to the hotel and cleaned ourselves up, and I assumed Elvis and I would hang out until Sonny got there. It would be my job to keep him from getting too disappointed about the White House not calling. But Elvis had some other angles to work. He wanted his meeting with the President, but he'd also done enough research to know that the deputy director of the Bureau of Narcotics and Dangerous Drugs was a guy named John Finlator. Elvis was going to Finlator's office to make a direct request for the badge.

"Jerry, you stay here and wait for the President's call," he told me. "Here's the number at Finlator's office. Call right away when you hear something."

And he left. I'd been reading stuff about some of the people that worked for Howard Hughes—how they'd be left in a hotel room waiting for some urgent, top-secret call that never came. I had visions of growing another beard for Elvis, as I waited in vain for the phone to ring. But about a half hour later, just as I was thinking about keeping my strength up with a room-service order, the phone did ring. It was the White House.

"Mr. Schilling, this is Egil Krogh, of the White House staff. The President has read Mr. Presley's letter and would like to meet with him in thirty minutes."

I explained that Mr. Presley wasn't there at the moment but that I'd get in touch with him and relay the message. I dialed John Finlator's office number as quickly as I could.

"Hello is—is Mr. Elvis Presley there?"

"Who is this?"

I explained my connection, and in a moment Elvis was on the line. He sounded down.

"I'm not doing any good here, Jerry. Can't get the badge. What's going on?"

I told him that the President wanted to see him in twenty-five minutes and counting. Knowing how badly he wanted this meeting and the badge, the easiest thing would have been for him to make a beeline to the White House by himself. But he wanted me to come with him.

"Jerry, you stand out in front of the hotel—we'll swing by and you jump in."

I got down in front of the place just in time to see Sonny get out of his cab from the airport and grab his bags.

"Sonny," I shouted, "Leave your bags with the bellman. We're going to the White House."

With perfect movie timing, Elvis's limo pulled up right then, and Sonny and I jumped in.

This time, the gate guards were prepared for us, and we made a smooth entrance to the White House grounds. We were met by Egil "Bud" Krogh, a friendly, professional-looking guy who had an aura of can-do competence about him. He had us sit in his office for a moment so that he could put us through an official pre-Presidential meeting interrogation, making clear exactly what our purpose was in requesting the meeting with the President. Elvis got comfortable on the couch in Krogh's office and went over some of the same points he'd made in his letter. Krogh had read the letter, and he and Elvis discussed some of the ways he might help the administration deliver an anti-drug message to kids and teenagers.

The meeting didn't last too long, and ended with Krogh telling us that White House Chief of Staff Bob Haldeman had approved the meeting of Mr. Presley and President Nixon. There was just one complication—because of Secret Service precautions, only Elvis would meet the President—Sonny and I would have to wait for him in Krogh's office. Krogh and a very contented-looking Elvis got up to head to the meeting. And I couldn't believe that what had started out as a crazy idea on some American Airlines stationery was now going to end in the Oval Office. Sonny and I hung out with a young White House staffer, who I seem to remember had just started dating Nixon's younger daughter. We talked about some of the complications of a romance like that, and we talked a little bit about our experiences working with Elvis. After a while, the phone in the office rang, and the staffer went to answer it. He came back with a very surprised look on his face.

"Uh—the President wants to meet Mr. Presley's friends."

Elvis had gotten his meeting, and the leader of the free world was, understandably, on a rigidly controlled time schedule. But Elvis was thoughtful enough to ask if Sonny and I could come join him. And he and the President had gotten along well enough that the President said yes.

We were led down the hall to the Oval Office, and I remember thinking: I'm the guy who wanted to be a history teacher, and now I'm about to step into a room where history is written almost every day. I'm about to step through a door into the office of the most powerful man in the world. But when we got to that door, it was opened by maybe the second most powerful man in the world: Elvis.

"Come on in, guys," he said. "Meet the President." I don't think he'd ever been in a better mood.

I stepped in and froze for a moment. My first thought, admittedly not a profound one, was, "Wow, the Oval Office is really an oval." Elvis may have thought I was scared to come further in, so he pushed me a little, and started laughing.

"It's OK, Jerry. You don't have to be afraid."

President Nixon was by his desk at the far end of the oval, signing something, and he moved to welcome us as we stepped forward. After we shook hands, the President gave me a light punch in the arm. "You've got a couple of big ones here, Elvis," he said. "You boys play football?"

I hadn't been a fan of Nixon's, and in person he seemed as uncomfortable as he looked in photos and on television. But there was something open and—surprisingly—honest about him, too. He really had been moved by Elvis's letter, and seemed genuinely pleased to have us all there for a visit. We were probably the most unusually dressed visitors he'd had in some time—along with Elvis in his gabardine, Sonny was wearing a dark suit fit for a Hollywood nightclub, and I was in a leather jacket. But that didn't seem to faze the President a bit. So, we talked some football with him, handicapping the college season. There was a White House photographer in the room, and we all had our pictures taken with the President. As the photos were snapped, I couldn't stop thinking about just how far Elvis had taken me in all our years and all our travels: from Guthrie Park to the White House.

By the end of our audience with the President, he and Elvis were talking like old friends, and exchanging thoughts on how Elvis's offer of service might be put into action. Here were two great men, but great men who had found their success to be extremely complicated, and as different as they were, I think there was a mutual understanding between them. From some of their conversation, it also became evident to me that President Nixon had overridden Deputy Director Finlator: Elvis was going to get his badge.

As our time in the Oval Office came to an end, the President made what was probably the customary gesture of goodwill for visitors: He gave us each a pair of Presidential cuff links. To Sonny and me, these were as good as our own badge, and we thanked the President. But Elvis was thinking that we shouldn't go back to our families empty-handed.

"You know, sir, these men have wives," he said.

"Of course," said the President. "Let's see what we can find for the ladies."

The President went to his desk at the end of the room and pulled open a drawer. Elvis stood right at his side, and when the President began rummaging through the drawer for more gifts, Elvis stuck his hands in and rummaged right along with him. By the time they were done, they'd come up with gold pins bearing the Presidential seal—a perfect gift for Priscilla, Sandy, and Sonny's wife, Judy.

"Thanks for coming by, fellas." said the President as we moved through a final round of handshakes. We all thanked him, then exited the Oval Office, guided again by Bud Krogh.

Sonny and I were awestruck by what had just happened. The lesson for me was to never doubt what my friend Elvis could accomplish. He was beaming, extremely satisfied with the way things had worked out, but I had the feeling he wasn't going to leave the White House until he had his promised badge and its accompanying credentials in hand. When Bud suggested that we could have lunch in the White House mess hall, Elvis quickly took him up on the offer.

On the way to lunch, Krogh gave us a private White House tour. We started in the Roosevelt Room across from the Oval Office—which featured a striking portrait of Teddy Roosevelt in his "Rough Rider" uniform—and then down hallways past all kinds of offices. Apparently word was out that Elvis was in the building, because I think every secretary on duty came to their door to get a look at him—one even ran up and gave him a kiss (what visiting head of state would get that reaction?). We made our way to the basement of the West Wing, past some stunned special-duty police officers and some Secret Service agents trying not to look stunned. Elvis hadn't been too impressed with the plates, portraits, and White House trivia Bud pointed out along the way, but he was very excited when Bud showed us the door that led to the actual "Situation Room"—where global crises of all sorts were regularly taken care of.

"No fighting in the War Room," Elvis said—referring to a favorite moment from *Dr. Strangelove*.

We went down a few more basement hallways to get to our lunch destination. The White House mess was officially run by the navy, and had the look of a grand dining room: dark-wood paneling, heavy, dark-wood tables and chairs, and a thick carpet on the floor. Just the kind of formal place that usually made Elvis uncomfortable. But this day he didn't mind the formal setting or the attention he drew. We took a table right in the middle of the dining area, and saw turning heads and amazed stares from all over the room—princes, presidents, and power players of all kinds walked into that room every day, but an Elvis Presley sighting was obviously a bigger deal than that. We had our lunch, and afterwards, back at Krogh's office, Elvis got his BNDD badge and his credentials appointing him a "Special Assistant." He was happy that he'd gotten what he was after, but I could see he was also quite sincere about trying to do something positive with his position.

After we left the White House, we drove straight to the airport to catch our respective flights. I wanted to catch the first flight back to L.A. to make it to work on Tuesday, if Paramount still had me on the payroll. As we drove along, Elvis made it pretty clear that he wanted one other thing out of this weekend: He wanted me back working full-time for him. Elvis didn't ever have to put himself in the position of pitching someone a job with him, but I think he really liked the way I'd handled his escape to L.A. and our White House adventure. I'd passed some kind of a deep loyalty test that he hadn't even realized he'd been putting me through. And he knew I wanted work that felt like a career—work that made use of my own abilities. So he pitched me.

"Jerry, how'd you feel about being my personal public relations man?"

"I don't know, E—what would that entail?"

"Well, I was talking with GK, and he had an idea about helping to get my records to sell. RCA doesn't give them enough push, so George said maybe I could use somebody like you as a personal PR man. Have you meet with radio program directors, make sure they get the records. Set up some interviews. All that type of stuff. What do you think?"

If it were just between Elvis and me, I thought it sounded great. But there was somebody else to consider.

"Elvis, I'd love that job. But I don't think the Colonel would let it happen."

"Hmm. You'd be interested, though?"

"It'd be a great job, Elvis."

We left it at that. I made it back to L.A., where I discovered I was still employed at Paramount. A couple weeks later, though, when I got home from work, Sandy handed me a large package from Memphis. I opened it to find stacks of hundreds of shiny red business cards, lettered in black with my name and a new title: "Jerry Schilling—Personal Public Relations to Elvis Presley." I had every reason to believe that once the Colonel heard about this, these cards would be a waste of paper. But if Elvis was working this hard to get me back, what exactly was I doing splicing German Coke commercials out of Paramount features? I made up my mind. Whether the new title held or not, I was heading back to Memphis.

11

. . .

PROMISED LAND CALLIN'

In January 1971, I was sitting in Ellis Auditorium, just like I did back in 1956, watching Elvis Presley headline. Except this time, Elvis wasn't sharing the bill with country and western stars, but with a cancer researcher, a civil rights activist, a highly decorated army captain, and, from the Nixon White House, Press Secretary Ron Ziegler.

Elvis had been named one of the Top Ten Outstanding Young Americans by the national Junior Chambers of Commerce (the Jaycees)—an award that over the years had gone to such notables as Orson Welles, Jesse Jackson, Leonard Bernstein, Ted Kennedy, Howard Hughes, and Richard Nixon. As one of those outstanding Americans, he was required to make a speech. For all the stages he'd been on, and for all the press conferences he'd handled, he'd never appeared anywhere as a public speaker, and was incredibly nervous about doing so at this event. But when Elvis got up to accept his award, he delivered a humbly eloquent speech that, in a few brief lines, managed to say everything about how he saw himself. I could hear the nervousness—his voice was soft and his delivery halting. But his message still rang out in that auditorium: "When I was a child, ladies and gentlemen, I was a dreamer. I read comic books and I was the hero of the comic book. I saw movies and I was the hero in the movie. So every dream I ever dreamed has come true a hundred times."

He took a moment to graciously recognize the achievements of the other nominees, then finished with some lines from a favorite song of his childhood—one he knew best as a 1955 hit record for R & B singer Roy Hamilton—that, in this context, sounded simple and insightful:

" 'Without a song, the day would never end; without a song, a man ain't got no friend; without a song, the road would never bend. Without a song.' So I keep singing a song. Good-night. Thank you."

Yes, I was back with Elvis and back with the guys (which at this point included included Red and Sonny, Joe Esposito, Marty Lacker, Charlie Hodge, Billy Smith, and Dick Grob, a former Palm Springs policeman now assisting with Elvis security). It felt good to be back in that circle, not having to worry about jetting back to L.A. to punch a time clock every Monday morning. As much as I'd enjoyed my editing work, I'd been watching Elvis's career pick up momentum and excitement, and if he was willing to look for ways to give me more to do, it seemed an easy call to step away from the Moviola editing machines and get back with him. My beautiful wife was, again, completely supportive of the career change, which turned out to be not quite what Elvis had pitched. Just as I had suspected, the Colonel, in his indirect, nonconfrontational, but absolutely final manner, had shot down any chance that I'd be working as an independent, personal record promoter for Elvis. No matter how ready I was for a promotion, the Colonel was not going to let me get between him and RCA. That was disappointing to me, but I understood that the Colonel was doing his job as a manager.

The circle of guys had been particularly tight lately. Elvis's interest in badges and credentials had spread to the rest of us, and we'd all done the required work to earn official Palm Springs police badges and Memphis deputy sheriff badges, taking all the required courses and written exams for both, and proving our abilities on the respective firing ranges. We'd also all been together for George Klein's wedding in Las Vegas, and for Sonny West's wedding in Memphis (Elvis was the best man at both).

The Jaycees award meant a great deal to Elvis. It honored him as an entertainer, but it also recognized his years of often unheralded generosity of time and money to so many charities. I think this humanitarian aspect of the award made it more meaningful to Elvis than any musical award he ever received. A gold record or even a Grammy was a "win" that satisfied his competitive spirit, but to be honored as a person of substance and good works was what he'd always been after. He actually carried that Jaycees award around with him for years, proudly showing it off (sort of the way he'd carried my gift gun around years before, though the gun couldn't exactly be considered a symbol of humanitarianism).

It was a little strange that Elvis was now being honored by the sort of people who, years before, had been afraid of him, even disgusted by him (although he'd been nominated for the Jaycees honor by former Memphis Sheriff and future Shelby County Mayor Bill Morris—one of the very few local politicians who had always approached Elvis as a friend rather than a threat). Elvis had reached a point where both the politicians and the good ol' boys appreciated him. In light of that fact, I found it a little curious that our recent trip to the White House had managed to stay secret—Sandy and I sat at a small table with Mr. Ziegler at a dinner Elvis hosted at the Four Flames restaurant before the Ellis event, and the press secretary didn't say a word about it. The biggest summit meeting between the worlds of politics and rock and roll wouldn't be reported on at all until it turned up in a *Washington Post* column almost a full year after it happened. And though the government never put Elvis to any use as an agent, a representative of the Bureau of Narcotics and Dangerous Drugs would call him every six months to make sure that he still had the federal badge in his possession.

Elvis had once been seen as a dangerous rebel, and was now a respected, if very flashily dressed, member of the establishment. But a lot of what was at the core of Elvis hadn't changed so much. I got to see that as Sandy and I walked with him into a Jaycees luncheon at the Rivermont Hotel before the awards ceremony. One of the first guests Elvis recognized was Marion Keisker—who had served for years as Sam Phillips's right-hand woman at Sun Studios. It was Marion who had first met with Elvis at Sun, and she gave him some very important early encouragement. Marion had left Sun in 1957 to join the Air Force, and she was in full dress uniform at the Rivermont event. Elvis hadn't seen her in more than ten years, but when he spotted her on the way into the luncheon, his eyes lit up and he looked like the thrilled kid he must have been after many of those Sun sessions. When he turned to Sandy and me to introduce Marion, he explained who she was by simply saying, "This woman was there when it all started."

. . .

By the end of January, Elvis was back in Las Vegas, beginning another monthlong run at the International Hotel—the first engagement of several, during a year in which Elvis would also continue to record and tour. I quickly discovered that even though the business cards Elvis had printed up for me weren't going to get used, I did have some new responsibilities.

Elvis liked to take the stage the way a prizefighter steps into the boxing ring—physically pumped and with a single-minded intensity. Part of what helped him do this was his timing before a show—he didn't like to be at a venue more than fifteen minutes before he was scheduled to go on. He sometimes enjoyed socializing after a show, but never before. Once he was in his stage wardrobe he wanted to stay strictly focused on the performance at hand—putting on those clothes was the equivalent of the fighter getting his hands wrapped and his gloves on just before the fight. And those clothes had been designed to hold up throughout a fighter's workout—after his return to live performance, Elvis had quickly discovered that he couldn't move as freely and energetically as he wanted to wearing shirts and pants. Beginning with his second run at the International, he began wearing karate-influenced one-piece jumpsuits created by designer Bill Belew.

To get him in a state of maximum physical and mental readiness, he and I had worked out a move that was a cross between a karate exercise and some old-fashioned Indian wrestling. Just moments before he took the stage, he and I would stand sideways facing each other, arms locked and front legs pushed against each other's, and we'd try to pull each other off balance, slowly applying more force until we were pulling as hard as we could. We'd build up the intensity, as, behind a closed curtain, the band played its "Thus Spake Zarathustra" intro. The curtain would sweep open, and just as it got to the place where we were standing, the music would shift into Elvis's powerful vamp and he'd break away, and storm out on stage pumped-up like a weightlifter who's just done his top bench press. There were some nights when we pulled at each other so hard I thought he might pull me out on stage with him, and frankly, the music and our move got my adrenaline so pumped up that I felt like I was ready to do the show, too.

Along the same lines, Elvis began to use me as what would today be called a personal trainer. His weight had been up and down over the years—his diet and the hours he kept had always made it easy to pick up pounds, while his metabolism, sometimes kicked along with diet pills, had made it easy to get the weight off. Now, at thirty-six, Elvis knew he didn't have the same frame he'd had when he was eighteen—who ever does? It was more of a battle to keep the pounds off, but it was a battle he was winning. He was still a very physically active performer, and his performance schedule—two shows a night, seven days a week—kept him strong and lean. But he also wanted to develop an exercise regimen to keep him in top shape. So I became his exercise partner.

In so many other areas, when Elvis said he wanted to do something, he did it in a big way, ignoring limits and pushing further than anyone thought possible. That wasn't quite his approach to exercise. For all his success, Elvis had a fierce competitive streak, but he generally liked to compete at things he knew he was good at. Exercise presented two problems: first, by nature, it wasn't competition. And, second, Elvis just wasn't a very good exerciser.

We were supposed to get in a good session before the first show each night, so every day, after I heard that he was awake and had ordered his breakfast—usually in the late afternoon—I'd go up to his suite. Elvis started his days slowly and quietly—you didn't push him to do anything before he'd had some food and coffee. So, once he'd had his meal and the time seemed right, I'd ask if he was ready for a workout. More often than not, the answer was no, he wasn't ready. Or he'd tell me flat out that he wasn't going to exercise that day—he didn't have time. I'd sit with him awhile to talk and sometimes take one more try at it: "You sure you don't want to exercise, E?" The look in his eyes when he said, "Are you kidding?" meant that the discussion was over.

Sometimes, I'd go ahead and do my own workout in my room—I think I may have done some pioneering work turning desks and chairs into personal gym equipment. Then I'd go about my day, helping the guys take care of whatever needed to be taken care of before a performance. Finally, I'd change out of my casual clothes and get cleaned up and dressed for the night. I'd go down to the hotel restaurant and hang out with Joe Esposito, Dr. Nick (who now traveled with us as Elvis's personal physician), promoter Tom Hulett, and Joe Guercio—

the fast-talking, fast-witted music director for Elvis's band. Many times we'd be seated, with our food ordered and on the way, when I'd get a call from Charlie Hodge upstairs: Elvis wants to exercise.

I'd go up to his room, often to find that even though I was in my evening clothes, Elvis was still in his pajamas. I'd try to give him the best workout I could for a trainer in British designer jeans and leather boots. I'd put on some music and we'd run in place, I'd do some sit-ups with him holding my legs, and then he'd do sit-ups with me holding his legs. But it seemed that whenever it was his turn to do sit-ups, he'd always come up with just the right comment to get me laughing and make me lose count. And if I lost count, then he started laughing. The truth was, he could do karate all day long, but he couldn't get through our exercise routine fast enough. There was no competition to it, except that I could do more sit-ups than him, and he didn't like that at all. So by the end of our sessions, he'd still be cool and calm in his pajamas, while I'd have sweated through my dress clothes.

The halfhearted workouts didn't diminish in any way what he could do on stage at the time, and I never got tired of watching him from the wings. And, to his credit, he never quite gave up on our fitness program. It became fairly predictable that each night, just as I sat down to dinner, I'd get the call: Elvis wants to exercise.

Elvis would often stay in town a few days after a Las Vegas run—sort of waiting out his fans—before he'd go out and see some of the other shows on the strip. Sammy Davis Jr., Tom Jones, Fats Domino, and Ann-Margret were particular favorites. In the right mood, he'd jump on stage to join Tom in a song or two, and I remember him doing a Valentino-style slide across the stage on his knees to make a surprise entrance during one of Ann-Margret's shows (Ann and Elvis were both married now, but remained very close friends). And one of my fondest Vegas memories is a night when Elvis was bringing Sammy back to his suite after a show. He and Priscilla, Sammy and his wife, Altovise, and I were making our way through the lobby when from the lounge we heard some unmistakable guitar riffs. Elvis looked at Sammy. Sammy smiled. Elvis said, "Let's go."

The five of us strolled into a nearly empty lounge—this must have been a final three A.M. show—and saw Chuck Berry up on stage, finishing a tune. We got into a booth right up front. Chuck was extremely happy to have Elvis and Sammy in the room, and started addressing them directly between songs. "Hey, Elvis, remember when you were number one with 'All Shook Up' and I was trying to catch you with this one," he said, hitting the opening riff to "School Day." Elvis loved it. When he was watching a show he enjoyed in a comfortable setting, he was not a quiet audience, and this night he was hollering all kinds of encouragement to Chuck. He also had a great camaraderie with Sammy—an easy friendship that grew from their respect of each other's music and talents. It was Chuck up on the lounge stage, but the real show was in the great, loud interaction between him and Elvis and Sammy (Priscilla and Altovise were also enjoying the show, but had a little more ladylike poise).

"Play 'Promised Land,' Chuck," Elvis shouted out at one point, and Chuck went right into the tune, the story of a poor Southern boy making his way to California that was one of Elvis's favorites (in 1974, Elvis would reach the Top 20 with his own version of the tune). Elvis and Sammy started singing along from the booth, shouting out "Yeah's" as Chuck name-checked his way through Norfolk, Charlotte, Atlanta, and Birmingham. When Chuck got to the line about buying a "through train ticket" so that he could be "Ridin' cross Mississippi clean," Elvis and Sammy cracked up, both of them understanding completely why Chuck, or any black person, wouldn't have wanted to make any stops within those state lines back in the 1950s. It was another of those reality-check moments for me: I was sitting in a Las Vegas booth with Elvis and Sammy Davis, watching Chuck Berry do a private concert for us. That's a good night out.

The showbiz personality that Elvis became closest with was Tom Jones, who he considered a trusted friend. They'd crossed paths several times through the sixties and had hit it off with each other right away, and eventually spent some together in Hawaii. When they were both in Las Vegas, they enjoyed hanging out and partying after each other's shows, and I can vividly remember Tom's stunned-but-game reaction the first time Elvis offered to put on a karate demonstration for him up in his suite.

Tom had come several times to see Elvis at the International, and one night after Elvis's run was done, Elvis, Priscilla, and some of us guys went to see Tom's show at the Stardust. We went ahead and worked out the usual arrangements for a visit like this with the Stardust maître d'— Elvis and our group would be seated after the lights went down and escorted to the backstage dressing room before the end of the show to avoid being a distraction. But Elvis was still in the habit of drinking bottle after bottle of Mountain Spring water, and in the middle of Tom's show, he had to go to the bathroom. I got up to go with him. At this time, Elvis often carried a cane with him, both for its looks and its potential as an emergency weapon. But his best defensive move was speed—Elvis had learned to do a very fast power-walk through the lobbies and casinos and showrooms just to avoid being stopped, and I'd do what I could to keep up with him.

On our way back from the bathroom, we were walking even faster than we had before. We passed a little lounge where a cover band, an Irish "show band," was playing. Their lead singer was a big burly guy who happened to be in the middle of singing an Elvis Presley tune. The big guy wasn't bad, but he was overdoing the Elvis vibrato just a bit. Without breaking stride, Elvis said, "Jerry, wait here," and stormed into the lounge. He walked right up on stage, hoisted his cane like he was going to clobber this guy and said, "If you're gonna do it, do it right." He gave the crowd in the lounge a great big wink, hopped off the stage, and zoomed right out of there. But the big singer didn't see the wink— he'd been so startled that he'd fallen over on stage.

We were cracking up about it all the way back to our table. But no sooner did I get settled in to see the rest of Tom's show than Elvis leaned over to tell me: "Jerry, go back and invite that guy and his band to come up to the suite after the show."

Elvis loved a laugh, but he didn't want to be the superstar bully who'd left some poor, hardworking lounge musician feeling humiliated. I delivered the message to the guy, and I was up in Elvis's suite that night when the singer showed up. He mingled with the rest of us, and Elvis talked with him for a while, and from the huge grin on the big guy's face you could tell how much it meant to him to be where he was. In the space of a few hours, he'd gone from having an onstage nightmare come true to having the night of his life up in Elvis's suite.

· · ·

In the spring and early summer of 1971, Elvis had that rarest of luxuries—some time off. He made use of that time to further develop a couple of his passionate pursuits. In Memphis, he began to receive karate instruction from Master Khang Rhee, a slight, quiet martial arts master with a studio near Graceland. Elvis liked the no-frills setting of the studio, along with the fact that Master Rhee seemed uninterested in his new student's fame outside the studio. Pretty soon Elvis had some of us guys working out there while we were in Memphis (in Los Angeles, I had already begun studies with Ed Parker). Master Rhee came up with the idea of fitting each of us with a nickname that somehow reflected our approach to the discipline: I was "Mister Cougar," Red was "Mister Dragon," Sonny was "Mister Eagle," and Charlie was "Mister Cobra." Elvis, of course, was "Mister Tiger." Priscilla began working with Master Rhee, too, and though I'm not sure she received a nickname, she ended up with a lightning-fast reverse kick that put us all to shame.

On the domestic front, Priscilla had spent months renovating and redecorating what she hoped would be her and Elvis's longtime home in Los Angeles—a large house on Monovale Drive, formerly owned by director Blake Edwards, that offered much more privacy than the Hillcrest house.

There were still a lot of boys' weekends in Palm Springs, but in his own way, I know that Elvis still wanted to think of himself as a devoted family man. And whatever strains his schedule and his actions might have put on his relationship with Priscilla, it was always clear that he still loved being a father. I remember getting off a private plane with Elvis at Santa Monica Airport, when Priscilla had brought Lisa Marie to meet him at the airport. We came down the steps of the plane, and Lisa broke free and just came running to her dad as fast as her little legs would carry her. She had tears in her eyes, she was so happy to see him. And he scooped her up and held her like he didn't need anything else in the world. You couldn't doubt for a second that she adored him and he adored her.

By the end of 1971, the domestic situations for all of us were harder to maintain. Elvis began touring again, and for the better part of the next year I was on the road with him, hitting everything from a Kentucky State Fair to New York City's Madison Square Garden. The road can be awfully punishing—it takes a toll physically and psychologically. On a tour, it doesn't take long before you're disconnected from anything resembling the "real" world, and you're just living from city to city. You don't eat right and you don't sleep right. You lose track of what time of day it is, what time of year it is, what part of the map you're on. Still, I loved being on the road with Elvis Presley.

Working with Elvis, I'd eventually found that soundstages and studio lots could become pretty boring places. But concert tours never felt that way. I loved getting on the planes, smelling the jet fuel, and hearing the roar of the engines, I loved hopping into limos, with police lights around us as we drove to or from an airport. I loved being in the wings to watch a show, and I loved the adrenaline of running off the stage with Elvis at the end of a show, geting back into the limo and trying to beat the rush of fans. Hearing Ronnie Tutt's drums rumble at the end of the show, and Al Dvorin's famous "Elvis has left the building" announcement. I loved using the back entrances to the hotels, the secret elevators. I loved hanging out in the hotel rooms with the guys and the band, watching Elvis laugh and entertain and sometimes even do a little impromptu singing.

As undisciplined as Elvis may have been with something like a checkbook (or sit-ups), he was masterful at putting together and maintaining a smooth-running touring operation. And he took a great deal of pride in his organization. I think it was on tour that I finally realized the true value of what we guys did for Elvis. He never hired an outside accountant or road manager or security chief—he had us to take care of all that. Everybody had a job to do, from Red West handling security to Lamar Fike running the stage lights. When people wondered about the value of the Memphis Mafia, Elvis used to say, "You don't think these guys are important? I'm a multimillion-dollar operation, and I can't do this on my own."

On the road, we developed an "us against the world" camaraderie, and though a good portion of the world loved Elvis, we never let our guard down. One of our prime responsibilities was to make it possible for him to relax and be the entertainer he wanted to be. Because I was an ex-football guy, I was sometimes in the position of a "bodyguard" for Elvis. I worried about that at first—that wasn't the job I'd stepped away from my own career for. But I knew it was part of the job—it was for all of us—and on tour, I felt especially protective of Elvis. It felt good to take care of him, and to know that he felt more secure having me around.

I didn't learn much about the country, or get a feel for any new places I was visiting—one city had the same trash cans around the back entrance of a hotel as the next. But—just as I had on those film sets—I tried to learn as much about the process and mechanics around me as I could. I'd watch how the gear got moved and set up, and see how the sound equipment was handled. There was as much craft in that work as there was in what was going to be presented on stage, and I felt I was getting another great education watching it all happen. With everybody doing their part, we got our city-to-city hops down to a science. The Colonel would fly to a city with his staff and maybe one Elvis guy (usually Sonny West) the night before a show. The Colonel would make sure that all the promotions and preparations were being properly handled, while Sonny would work on security at the hotel and inside venue, figuring out the best entrances and exits and making sure that access to Elvis's dressing room could be controlled.

Right after a show, Elvis would be ready to head to that next city. Given his sleep habits, and the rush of adrenaline after a show, it made more sense for him to get to the next city late at night than to try to get him up for travel the next morning. When Al said "Elvis has left the building," he was telling the truth—we were already on the way to the airport. This meant that there was never much of a backstage scene with Elvis on the road—six Cokes and six Pepsis was as elaborate as our backstage ever got, and sometimes that didn't even get touched. But when Elvis and a couple of us were invited to meet Johnny Carson after one of his Vegas stand-up appearances, we discovered an even tamer backstage scene. Elvis was a huge fan of Johnny's and wouldn't leave for screenings at the Memphian until after Johnny's monologue was over, so he was very excited to meet him. We didn't quite expect a raging, Rat Pack–style party in Johnny's dressing room, but what we found was Johnny sitting by himself on a couch with a glass of water and a legal pad on a table in front of him. We sat with him awhile, made small talk, and left. Johnny hadn't left the building, but his backstage was quieter than ours.

After a show, we flew with Elvis on his chartered plane, and when we got to the next town, no matter what time of night it was or what the weather conditions were, the Colonel would be waiting for us at the bottom of the steps off the plane, ready to brief Elvis. Looking back, I think the Colonel was as energized by the touring as Elvis was—I've never seen a big act's manager do so much hands-on work with so much dedication.

The band followed later that night or the next morning on another plane. One of two sound systems would have been trucked in, while the second was sent ahead to an upcoming destination. The big details of security and travel plans had to be taken care of, but the small ones were important, too—Elvis's room would be prepared by some of the newer guys, who would eventually include Dr. Nick's son, Dean Nichopoulos, Vernon's stepsons, Rick and David Stanley, and Al Strada, a private security guard who worked at Elvis's L.A. homes before Elvis made him a part of his personal staff. Room preparation on the road was a process that still included blacking out the windows with aluminum foil and making sure that the AC could keep the suite just shy of freezing cold. The next day, the Colonel would head off to the next city, Elvis would do his show, and the whole routine would repeat itself.

There was just one big problem with life on the road, and that was that we all had lives off the road, too, and those lives suffered. Inside the bubble of our traveling organization, things could feel balanced and right, but outside that bubble, we were, for the most part, absent husbands and family members. As much as Elvis wanted to think of himself as a family man, he and Priscilla had begun to pull apart. In a strange way, Elvis was a one-woman man—it's just that he had a number of those one women. Priscilla was the most important woman in his life, but he felt he could be loyal to more than one person at a time—admittedly not a very traditional view of marital fidelity. In the years I knew him, he was never particularly interested in meaningless groupie encounters. He had a real romantic streak, and he wanted companionship—someone to talk with, read with, and relax with. When he was with Priscilla, he had all that. But Priscilla, now the devoted mother of a small child, couldn't travel as freely as she once had. And since Elvis couldn't always be with Priscilla, he developed friendships and relationships with women who would be part of his life for weeks, months, or even years sometimes. He was living a one-of-a-kind life, so maybe ordinary rules of romance and commitment didn't apply to him. But that certainly wasn't fair to Priscilla. She had been a little girl when she first stepped into Elvis's world, but now she was becoming a stronger, more aware, more independent woman, and she wasn't living anything close to the kind of life she wanted with Elvis. Something had to give.

In February of 1972, Elvis finished up an engagement at a familiar showroom with a new name—the Las Vegas International was now the Las Vegas Hilton. Priscilla was there for closing night, and between Elvis's two final shows, she and he spent a long time in his dressing room together. When they were done talking, Elvis asked me to walk Priscilla back up to his suite. I got her to the elevator and up to the room, and I don't think we talked much on the way. Before I left her in the room, I asked if there was anything I could get for her. She turned, looked at me a moment, and said quietly, "Jerry, you've always been a good friend." This was unusual. As close as we'd become over the years, and for as much time as we'd spent together with Elvis and Sandy, Priscilla didn't normally say things like that. And I couldn't think of anything to answer her with. I just smiled, said good night and left. But I knew something felt very different. It all came out the next night: She was leaving him.

Elvis stayed in Vegas for a while after the Hilton shows. It was obvious that he was hurt, and angry—with himself as much as with Priscilla—and it was also pretty clear that he didn't want to talk about his problems much. He stayed up in his suite a few days, and each night one of the guys would be with him. One night it was just me sitting with Elvis up there. I casually asked if he was in the mood to go downstairs and play blackjack—knowing full well that the answer would be no. Elvis wasn't a big gambler to begin with, and in this situation I thought he'd be in no mood to be around people. But he surprised me. "Yeah, let's hit those tables," he said.

We changed our clothes and went downstairs to the casino. We started playing, and, of course, began to draw some attention. The casino put the usual red ropes around us, but after a while I started thinking we should move along before we drew a real crowd. We headed back to the hotel lounge, which was bigger than most showrooms at the time, and when we saw that the Righteous Brothers were up on stage there, we decided to hang out at a small casino bar just outside the lounge entrance. Elvis and I basically were not drinkers, and I think we probably intended to order one cocktail and nurse it for the night. But as people noticed Elvis, they'd come over and say hello and offer to buy us a drink. Norm Crosby was one of the first well-wishers who wanted to pay for a round, and to be polite we said yes. The drink went down easy. And our place at the bar started to feel very comfortable—Elvis didn't feel like he was in a spotlight, and it felt normal and natural to be hanging out to have a drink. The people who stopped by didn't over-react either—they'd stop, say hello, buy us another drink, talk for a moment, then move on. We must have had four or five drinks apiece that way. We drank clear through the Righteous Brothers' set and then some. Finally one of the Brothers himself, Bill Medley, showed up with his girlfriend Darlene Love of the Blossoms, the group that had backed Elvis in the '68 TV Special. We had a drink with them and those went down even easier.

By three A.M., we were by ourselves again at the bar, and I realized that it was time for me to be the responsible party.

"E, we better get out of here." It took a little extra work to get the words out.

"Yeah, OK. That's about all the damage we can do here." He was having a little trouble enunciating, too.

We made our way across the casino floor and out the front doors. I went into responsible-party mode, keeping an eye on Elvis while I hailed a cab for us. We flopped into the backseat of the first one that pulled up.

"Hilton Hotel, please." I said to the driver.

He turned and gave Elvis and me a very curious look.

"Sir?" he said.

"Yeah?" said Elvis.

"You're at the Hilton Hotel."

Yes we were. We were at the Hilton Hotel, and we were drunk enough not to know it. We laughed our way back in and up to our rooms, and then, over the next day, fought off a pair of monster hangovers.

. . .

Joe Esposito and I were with Elvis at the RCA Hollywood Studios, where he'd just spent an all-night recording session with Felton Jarvis and most of his Vegas band. It was Elvis's custom to OK a preliminary mix in a listening room, and it wasn't uncommon to be in the room when Elvis was doing this kind of listening. But this night he made a point of having Joe and me listen to one particular new track with him. He knew there was something about this one that we could all relate to in a stronger than usual way.

The song he was listening to was one that Red had written for him—a song called "Separate Ways." While Elvis had a good time performing his rockers, he was also drawn to emotional, storytelling ballads. Red had come up with this song about a disintegrating marriage well before any of us knew the full extent of the troubles between Elvis and Priscilla. But now Elvis, with Red's words, seemed to be singing a piece of heartbroken autobiography.

> *Love has slipped away,*
> *Left us only friends*
> *We almost seem like strangers . . .*

There was even a verse about a child trying to make sense of her parents' divorce. And a chorus that said there was nothing left to do but head out in separate ways and hope that a new love might be found somewhere in the future.

Elvis could sing a ballad with as much power as he used on the rockers, but on this track there was something subdued in his voice. You could hear how sorry this singer was to be singing the words of this song.

The track hit home with Joe and with me. Hearing Elvis's voice, we thought of our own marriages, both crumbling from neglect. I still loved Sandy, but how could I tell her she was the most important thing in my life when I'd committed myself to a life that barely included her? It hurt a lot to think that we, too, were starting to feel like strangers. As Joe and I listened with Elvis, he stayed expressionless, but each time the song ended he'd cue it up, start it again, and look over at us. Then he'd look down, and shake his head a bit. You could almost hear the question hanging in the air: "What the hell have we done to the women we loved?"

The next night we were all back at the same studio for another session, one of the few times I'd ever see Elvis's musical instincts off the mark. With all the emotions that had been stirred by "Separate Ways" still fresh, Elvis was definitely not in the mood to rock. He wanted to sing more songs that would help him express the sadness and loss he was feeling. But Felton had an up-tempo song he felt sure was going to be a hit. Elvis heard it and dismissed it. Felton didn't push, but he eventually got Elvis to give it another listen. I heard the demo, too, and though I knew where Elvis's head and heart were from the night before, I could also tell that Felton was right—the song sounded like a hit. I knew not to push, but I supported Felton and encouraged Elvis to give the song a shot.

Eventually, he did, and sang "Burning Love." There wasn't any way he could truly put his heart into it, but you couldn't tell that from listening to what was recorded—he did a great, convincing job of sounding up. When he later began to sing the song in concert, he had a kind of psychological block toward it. Elvis—who had close to a photographic memory when it came to books, scripts, lyrics—always insisted that he needed a lyric sheet to perform "Burning Love." He might not glance at the sheet he was holding on stage, but he needed to have it with him. He didn't get excited about the song until it turned out that Felton had been right—the song was a hit. And, interestingly enough, with "Burning Love," Elvis found himself battling up the pop charts with an old friend. By the fall of 1972, "Burning Love" had made it to number two, but couldn't go higher—the number-one spot was held by Chuck Berry's "My Ding-A-Ling."

When Elvis began a new national tour in the spring of 1972, there was one significant change in the touring machinery: Now, many of the concerts would be filmed, and the resulting footage would be shaped into an MGM rock-and-roll documentary feature. This would be the second documentary based on Elvis performances—the first, an MGM production titled *That's the Way It Is*, had used footage of rehearsals and performances shot during Elvis's August 1970 Las Vegas engagement (when I was still a full-time Paramount employee).

The filmmakers undertaking this new project were Bob Abel and

Pierre Adidge, a pair of young, serious-minded music lovers who'd recently completed *Mad Dogs and Englishmen*, a film that followed Joe Cocker's 1970 American tour. The pair, whose production company was known as Cinema Associates, had been suggested to Elvis and the Colonel by MGM, and they impressed Elvis enough with their sense of purpose that they got the job. Elvis was excited about the project, but I think I was probably more excited. Having Elvis shows and serious documentary work come together in this way seemed like a situation full of possibilities for me.

We got used to having cameras rolling around us pretty quickly, and the tour got off to a good start. Elvis was continuing to deliver strong performances before sellout crowds. But with all that going right, there was one career move Elvis wanted to make that didn't ever seem to get any closer to being a reality: Elvis wanted to tour internationally. I sat up with him one night and listened as he talked about how much he wanted to go overseas—how he wanted to perform for fans in England, throughout Europe, and in Japan. He'd seen so many Japanese fans make the trip to Las Vegas to see him—why couldn't he go over there? He felt a responsibility to his fans around the world, and when he talked about wanting to tour internationally, it was with a real passion—and an anger that it hadn't happened sooner. "These people have a certain image of me," he said at one point. "I don't want to wait until I'm forty goddamn years old to get over there."

For years I'd seen Elvis's talents hampered by the people around him making decisions based on business and finance, and it seemed like now, finally, he should be free to make his own artistic decisions. He was excited to be performing again, but how many times was he going to be able to put his heart into singing his songs night after night in Las Vegas, or in the same U.S. cities he'd been to the year before? He needed to stay challenged. And touring internationally seemed like precisely the challenge he would rise to. The next day, I was scheduled to have a lunch with the Colonel—at his "invitation"—and I decided to bring the issue up. It still felt dangerous to step in between Elvis and the Colonel, but I also knew how deeply Elvis felt about this, and I felt I owed it to him to get some kind of a discussion started. When I told the Colonel what Elvis and I had talked about all night, he was irritated, and clearly didn't want to have the discussion with me.

"Jerry, you know Hulett," he barked. "He knows the situation over there. Why don't you ask him?"

Promoter Tom Hulett had become part of the Elvis world as a partner of Jerry Weintraub's, and their company, Management III, now handled Elvis's tours. Hulett was the partner we dealt with most often and most directly, and he and I had become close, usually finding time for a talk together after a show. He was a hip guy, but a tough businessman, too—a former athlete who, in working with Jimi Hendrix and then Led Zeppelin, had just about pioneered the art of putting on a large-scale rock-and-roll tour. Tom had been brave enough to go up against the old showbiz promotion syndicates on the East and West coasts, and smart enough that he'd become a great success. I was impressed with the way he carried himself, and the way he conducted business, and saw his knowledge and experience as a tremendous asset for Elvis.

So that night, after the show—following the Colonel's "suggestion"— I brought up the matter of international touring with Tom. The Colonel had always made it sound like it was just too complicated to ever be resolved—too difficult to work out the travel and promotion and security and guarantees. But Hendrix and Zeppelin and other acts Tom had worked with hadn't seemed to have had any trouble touring all over the globe. I asked if, theoretically, we could work out all the arrangements—and especially the security—for Elvis to perform an engagement in London that could be promoted in other European cities. Tom thought for a moment, then said, "Yeah, I think so." We talked awhile about how some of the scheduling would work, and it seemed that, by the end of the night, some forward progress toward Europe had been made.

The next day, the Colonel and I were walking together down a hallway in the Hilton Hotel in San Antonio when I told him about my conversation with Tom.

"Colonel, Tom said we can do it. He thinks we can work it out if Elvis wants to tour overseas."

The Colonel stopped in his tracks, hurled his cane down the hall, turned on me, and hollered, "Goddamn it, then—you handle him."

There were two messages that became very clear to me in that hall-

Above: President Nixon, Delbert West, me, and Elvis at the White House.

Below: The Memphis Mafia, with badges. Standing, left to right, are Billy Smith, Bill Morris, Lamar Fike, me, Roy Nixon, Vernon Presley, Charlie Hodge, Sonny West, George Klein, and Marty Lacker. Kneeling are Dr. Nichopoulos, Elvis, and Red West.

Colonel Parker with Elvis. I'm in the background.

Above: Elvis in his karate uniform, about to board the *Lisa Marie*. Dick Grob is in the foreground.

Below: The *Lisa Marie*, a Boeing 707 which Elvis completely gutted and rebuilt to his liking. Note the TCB logo on the tail.

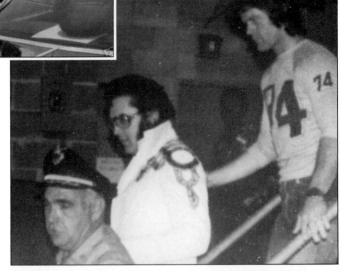

Above: Elvis and me leaving a private jet while on tour.

Right: Elvis and me leaving the stage.

Below: Elvis performing as I attempt to hold back the crowd.

Tell Ed

Elvis Mentioned about not being able to talk to him or anyone in that he told Col Parker, and that kinda hurt his

Feelings plus when Elvis called the Col to ask him who told his father Col said he was resting.

When Elvis tells someone something he expects it to be in strictest confidence

Handwritten notes from Elvis.

Me working for Elvis, wearing my TCB necklace.

Above: Linda Thompson, Elvis, and me on tour.

Left: Our trip to Vail, Colorado, in 1976 for Elvis's forty-first birthday.

Below: Me with the Beach Boys on tour in 1977.

Above: Me with Lisa
Marie, age twelve.

Right: Me with Joe Esposito
at Graceland. In the
foreground you can see
our names on the eternal
flame monument.

way: I was not actually being requested to "handle" Elvis in any way. And we wouldn't be going to London anytime soon.

Having a documentary film crew around while on tour with Elvis, I felt I was in the middle of everything I wanted to be a part of. The dream of being an editor on an Elvis film—working with him on some kind of creative level—seemed entirely possible now, but it required patience and some careful steps. As tight as Elvis and I had become on the road, I didn't want to give him the impression that I would jump ship easily. And I knew that, after making their way through all the Colonel's hoops and hassles, the filmmakers had no desire to invite an Elvis guy into their offices.

But when the filming was done, and we'd finished a second leg of the tour, I did talk to Elvis about trying to get involved with the film. I think he'd gotten used to having these kinds of talks with me by then, but this felt a lot different from the last time I'd asked to part ways with him. This time, I was secure about my abilities to fend for myself in the world at large, and I was also secure about the strength of the friendship between Elvis and me. I didn't feel like there was any chance this would be a permanent good-bye (I'd thought that might be the case the first time, but had found myself right back at Graceland for Christmas, New Year's, and the birth of Lisa Marie). But again, it meant a lot that he gave me his blessing to follow my heart.

It wasn't as easy to win over Abel and Adidge. I went to their offices one afternoon to formally offer my services as an assistant editor, but was not met with much enthusiasm. I could sense that they were very hesitant about having a member of Elvis's inner circle working on an Elvis project. I liked these guys and the way they'd worked with Elvis, and I didn't want to push too hard. So I told them if my connection with Elvis disqualified me from the Elvis film, maybe they could let me work on their other film project—a celebration of fifties rock and roll called *Let the Good Times Roll*. Somehow, that request changed the way they looked at me. I guess they figured that if this Elvis guy wasn't necessarily looking for work on the Elvis film, he had to be serious about the film side of things. And it must have struck them that, given the fact that I had some real editing experience, I was probably not just a "spy" sent by Elvis or the Colonel. Finally, I suppose they saw the value of having a way to get to Elvis other than going through the Colonel. Within a few days, I completed my next career turn and began as an entry-level assistant editor with Cinema Associates, working on *Elvis On Tour*.

Almost immediately, I had a chance to serve Elvis and the film in a unique way. A young filmmaker named Marty Scorsese was working as an editor on the film (he'd already done a brilliant job as part of the editing team on *Woodstock*), and one of the special sequences he was overseeing was a montage of early photographs of Elvis—a flowing, visual history of his career. When the Colonel heard that this was a part of the film, he nixed it, telling Abel and Adidge that Elvis did not want any old photographs of him to be a part of the project. I knew that the facts were a little different—Elvis had complained to the Colonel about the use of old photographs, but he was talking about their use on new album covers. I had a feeling that if Elvis got a sense of how the montage fit into the film, he'd have no problem with it.

I went over to the Monovale house one night and, when the time seemed right, explained to Elvis how the montage worked shot by shot—how it fit with the music and built up to the tour footage. He got it right away. "Sounds good. I don't have any trouble with that," he told me. I brought his OK back to the filmmakers, the Scorsese montage was in, and the film was better off for it. Over that one film sequence, I'd taken the huge step of being able to approach Elvis as a fellow creative. Not a creative equal, of course, but it felt huge to be with him discussing film edits rather than sit-ups.

Abel and Adidge were talented pioneers in bringing visual sophistication and state-of-the-art sound quality to to the genre of the rock-and-roll documentary. Adidge was an even-tempered giant of a guy with a keen sense of image and story, while Abel was a gregarious personality with a strong command of the latest audio technology. They'd shot the Elvis shows with a team of 16 mm cameras that allowed them to capture all angles and elements of the concert experience, and wanted to present the images they'd collected across a triple split screen. As early sequences were cut together, it looked like the results were going to be exciting and involving. But the filmmakers were after something more. They hadn't come to the project as dedicated Elvis fans, but had been completely charmed and won over by the "man" rather than the "star." They'd come to realize something that Elvis himself had put into words at a press conference before the wildly triumphant Madison Square Garden shows: "The image is one thing, the human being another." And, frankly, I think they were surprised by his natural intelligence—his ability to read a person or a situation quickly and deeply.

They decided that what the movie needed was Elvis's story in his own words, and they wanted him to sit for an audio-only interview to be used against images in the film. They hoped Elvis might open up and, in discussing his life and career, show the thoughtful, reflective side that they sensed was there but had never been showcased in any past interviews. The Colonel, predictably, was completely against it. Allowing Elvis to talk freely and openly to a running tape machine went against all his showman's instincts. But he didn't tell the filmmakers that he wouldn't allow it, only that he would do nothing to facilitate it. I'm sure he figured that without him setting things up, the interview would never happen. He was wrong.

Over a period of weeks, when I had the chance, I talked to Elvis about the film and told him about what I was seeing in the editing room: This wasn't just concert performances on film, it was turning into something important. This documentary felt like it would be a great piece of legacy, and Elvis could be proud to put as much of himself into it as possible. Again, he got it. And, more importantly, he trusted me. The interview was on.

One day in late July, he sat in a dressing room on the MGM lot, with Abel and Adidge, myself, Joe, and Charlie. The room was nothing fancy, but it had a pedigree—it was one of the few dressing rooms reserved for the biggest stars—all others got a trailer out on the lot. This had been Clark Gable's room, and it had been Elvis's when he made his MGM films. Elvis was at a table, facing the filmmakers, and I sat in a director's chair behind them, making eye contact with Elvis over Abel's shoulder. I could see right away that Elvis was a little uncomfortable being on the spot this way, knowing that every word was on the record. So I decided to try to break the ice a bit.

"Hey, E," I said. "Why don't you tell them about what your daddy said about you being a guitar player."

He laughed a little. "My daddy said, 'I never saw a guitar player that was worth a damn.'"

Everybody laughed, and the atmosphere in the room loosened up. The filmmakers began handing Elvis some old photographs, asking him to reminisce about some of the images, and he began to relax into a friendly, storytelling mood. He discussed his childhood, and his early days as a performer, even the inspiration for his sideburns (Memphis truck drivers). When asked about the screaming reaction of his early fans, he said that the first time it happened, it scared him to death. He didn't know what he'd done to elicit that response and went backstage to ask the manager, "What'd I do? What'd I do?" Elvis said the manager responded, "Whatever it was, go out and do it again."

When asked about his current fans, his respect for his audience was obvious. But he also said something that hinted at a more frustrating side of his career. "If I do something good, [the fans] let me know. If I don't, they let me know that. For a while there was the theory that anything I did would sell. I knew that was not true. It's according to the material. You've got to have good material—whether it's a song or a script or whatever. It's got to be good."

The interview stayed easy and conversational, though at times Elvis did not seem interested in delivering the kind of quotable self-examination the filmmakers were after. When they asked how he would describe his early sound, he simply said, "It was good." But when the talk turned to a discussion of Elvis's movies, he was not only forthcoming, he was shockingly honest about the disappointment and frustration he'd felt in Hollywood. When asked how deeply he cared about the quality of his films, he answered, "I cared so much until I became physically ill. I would become violently ill . . . At a certain stage I had no say-so in it. I didn't have final approval of the script, which means I couldn't say, 'This is not good for me' . . . I don't think anyone was consciously trying to harm me, it was just Hollywood's image of me was wrong, and I knew it, and I couldn't say anything about it. I couldn't do anything about it.

"The pictures got very similar. If something was successful, they'd try to re-create it the next time around. So I'd read the first four or five pages of it, and I knew that it was just a different name with twelve new songs—the songs were mediocre in most cases. That's what might have made it seem like indifference. But I was never indifferent. I was so concerned until that's all I talked about. It worried me sick."

I could tell that Elvis wanted to voice some of these heavier thoughts—things I'd always felt to be true but had never heard him put into words before. I'd been with him on days when the stress of starting another film had made him physically ill, and I'd been there on days when studio representatives rushed to his home to insist that he stay on the work schedule he'd been contracted to. Abel tried to steer the interview toward some of the artistic successes in the movies, like the memorable dance sequence in *Jailhouse Rock*, but Elvis didn't go for it. He was more interested in speaking to a troubling truth of his movie career: Right from the start, he'd been made false promises. That again and again, from *Love Me Tender* on, he'd been told that he'd get a chance to do some real acting, only to be handed underwritten nice-guy roles and songs that existed simply to move along story lines.

"I didn't know what to do. I just felt that I was obligated a lot of times to things that I didn't fully believe in. And it was very difficult ... I had thought they'd give me a chance to show some kind of acting ability or do a very interesting story," he said. "But it did not change. It did not change. And so I became very discouraged. They couldn't have paid me no amount of money in the world to make me feel any self-satisfaction inside."

Adidge seemed a little taken aback at the idea of Elvis feeling so conflicted about his work. "But you still did them—you must have forced yourself ..."

"I had to. I had to," said Elvis.

There was an almost eerie hush in the room for a moment. This was not the punchy, upbeat interview the filmmakers had been after, and they weren't sure what to make of it. Elvis, sensing that he'd moved into some disturbing territory, backtracked a bit, pointing out that he was the only one to blame for the course of his career (it was impossible not to sense the Colonel's name hanging in the air, but Elvis wouldn't say a word about him, even when asked directly for "a Colonel story"). And he pointed out that not all the films were so bad, and that some of them worked as pure, escapist entertainment. There was a bit more back-and-forth, and then after about forty-five minutes, the interview was over.

Elvis had been quite candid with Abel and Adidge, but I think they left that dressing room at MGM feeling he was more of a mystery than ever. They'd gotten Elvis in his own words, but those words didn't quite fit the film that had been shot. They were putting together a celebration of his music and talent, but he'd been most open with them expressing regret about his career. I thought the interview was powerful enough to be the basis of the film, and would work brilliantly against current footage of Elvis on stage. But only a few lines would make it to the final cut of the film, most notably Vernon's quote about the worthlessness of guitar players.

My role in both the montage and interview situations improved my status in Abel and Adidge's editing room, and pretty soon I'd moved up from grunt work to some real assistant editing. Working near Scorsese was like taking a master class in the art of filmmaking. He worked frantically—to the point that sometimes you thought he might just explode—but in addition to his amazing eye for striking images, he was brilliant at cutting to music, creating rhythms in the picture that moved with the music to create a powerful whole. I admired his skills, but I didn't get to know the man very well—he was so buried in his work that there wasn't much time for conversation. And when he got up from his editing bay, it was usually to dart straight out the door for one of his therapy sessions.

One night, after a long day of editing, we were sitting around on the floor, getting ready to shut the office down, when he surprised me with a direct question.

"Jerry, you know what I got?"

"No, Marty. What?" I was sure he was going to tell me about some strange medical diagnosis he'd just received.

"I got 'That's All Right Mama,' " he said. "On Sun. A seventy-eight."

Elvis went on to another monthlong Las Vegas engagement while I continued to work on the film. We were pushing for a November opening, and everything was coming together well. With most of the film cut, the final challenge was coming up with a strong end title sequence—something that would both sum up the film and give some added entertainment to an audience that stuck around for the very end of the credit crawl. Abel and Adidge were having a hard time coming up with the right song to use. They struggled with whether to end with an old song or a new one, a ballad or a rocker, but mostly they wanted something that had the right feel—something that could sum up the hour and a half that moviegoers had just spent with Elvis. Pierre Adidge asked me to come up with three or four songs I thought might work.

I thought about it for just a moment, and the choice seemed obvious to me: "Memories," a ballad Elvis had introduced in the '68 TV special, which was all about taking a bittersweet look at the past. I played it for Bob and Pierre, and they agreed it was perfect. Pierre was excited enough about the song to say, "Jerry, I'm going to put a diamond in your TCB." And better than that, he made me an offer. If I wanted to come into the office over the weekend and try out my own cut for the end sequence, I was welcome to. I told him I'd be there.

I felt like a slightly overwhelmed kid in a candy shop facing the editing equipment by myself that weekend. I had the same buzzing mix of excitement and nervousness that I'd felt during my first solo plane flight in Memphis. I didn't think crosswinds could affect a film splice, but I kept the windows closed anyway.

I sweated it out at first, getting the feel of the process and slowly matching image to music. After a while, the mechanics of what I was doing started to feel natural, and I felt free to get creative. In the back of my mind, I wanted to impress the hell out of Bob and Pierre, and I wanted to do right by Elvis. But mainly I wanted to create something that I was proud of. There were thousands of feet of film to pull from, but I concentrated on building something that would work as a coda to the film, and tell a little story on its own. Here were the moments that tour memories were made of: the moments of laughter backstage, the time spent between band and fans, the moments of anticipation at rehearsals before the show, and the moments of calm on the rolling Greyhound bus afterward. I worked with the flow and rhythm of the music, and found some nice places to let the lyrics match up literally with the images: over the a line about "quiet nights," I laid in an image of the band slumbering away on their plane.

My sequence ended with what Abel would later say was the most powerful and poignant image the filmmakers had captured: Elvis peering out the window of a limo with a thousand-mile stare. An image that almost perfectly duplicated the famous image of him peering out a train window back in 1956. It was striking that whatever young Elvis had been looking ahead for out that window back then, he was still looking for now.

The following Monday, for the first time in my life, I got to experience the elation of a good review. Pierre and Bob took a look at the end sequence and pronounced it to be perfect. The diamond Pierre had promised never actually turned up, but when the film was released, not a single frame had been changed on my editing to "Memories."

I stayed on with Abel and Adidge for a couple more projects, including the feature I'd offered my services for, *Let the Good Times Roll*. Working on that film was almost as satisfying as working on the Elvis film, because it combined great archival "birth of rock and roll" footage from the fifties with contemporary concert performances by Chuck Berry, Bo Diddley, Fats Domino, Little Richard, and others. In some ways, this project felt like the perfect companion piece to *Elvis On Tour*. The Elvis film showed where my friend and I had gotten to, but *Let the Good Times Roll* said everything about where we'd come from. When Bo Diddley said in an interview sequence that he still cooked chicken in his hotel rooms—a habit he'd developed after being turned away from segregated restaurants—I thought about how he might have been treated at Uncle John's Little Kitchen.

As I was cutting film, Elvis was out on the road again, making concert stops that included a weekend of sellout shows in Hawaii (maybe that's how Elvis punished me—it seemed every time I stepped away he rubbed it in by heading back to the islands). After spending the holidays in Memphis, he returned to Hawaii to begin 1973 with his biggest show ever, reaching a global television audience with the live satellite broadcast of his *Aloha* concert.

At the end of January, *Elvis On Tour* surprised all of us by winning the Golden Globe Award for Best Documentary of 1972. With *Let the Good Times Roll* completed and no immediate follow-up work lined up with Abel and/or Adidge, I felt that award was a good way to end my second stint at an editing career. I'd keep an eye out for more film opportunities, but a couple of weeks later, I was back with Elvis as he worked through another Vegas engagement at the Hilton.

By most measures, Elvis was as big a success as he'd ever been. He had an award-winning film out, had just played to the largest television audience ever assembled, was continuing to sell out concert appearances, and had a song on the pop charts ("Separate Ways" made the Top 20). And on a personal level, Elvis seemed to have found great happiness with a new romantic interest: Linda Thompson. Linda was a lively, beautiful Memphis girl—a Miss Tennessee—who had made appearances on George Klein's local TV shows and had met Elvis on one of his nights at the Memphian. Linda was an extrovert with a fine sense of humor, and was great at bringing out the fun-loving side of Elvis. She fit into the Elvis world very comfortably, and was easy to talk to and kid around with. And it was nice to have her around—Linda was in some ways a conservative Southern girl, but she wasn't afraid to wear the sexiest outfits imaginable (I can still hear Lamar Fike saying, "Oh Lord—where's the rest of that dress?").

But despite the career successes and the new romance, Elvis's work was starting to take a heavy physical toll on him. He'd put on weight again, and was often in pain from a variety of ailments. The guy with what had seemed for so long to be a superhuman constitution now turned out to be vulnerable flesh and blood, and during this February engagement he had to cancel several shows due to illness.

There was no question that his pain and ailments were real, but some of us began to worry about the treatments he was getting. Dr. Nick tried to keep Elvis's intake of prescription drugs balanced, but Elvis had a way of getting to other doctors to get other prescriptions he thought would help him and it seemed there wasn't any doctor who would say no to Elvis Presley. I really don't think Elvis wanted to be "high"—he just wanted to function. He didn't want to step away from his music and tune out—he wanted to keep at what he'd been doing for years, giving his all doing two shows a night, and then bouncing back to do it again the next night. As his body aged and tired, he wanted to find some way to coax more music and more performances out of it, and if that could be done with prescription medication, he wanted it. But now, what had started as a way of managing his problems was turning into a problem itself.

My own career seemed to be right where I wanted it. But my personal life was falling apart. Being on the road with Elvis had pulled me apart from Sandy, and in the spring of 1973, I realized that I'd become infatuated with someone else. My new love interest was an L.A. girl who'd been a part of many of the weekends in Palm Springs, and while I didn't know if this had any chance of being a long-term relationship, I knew that my relationship with Sandy couldn't be the same anymore.

The more I thought about my situation, the more I hated thinking about myself as just another lousy, unfaithful husband. I knew that, at the very least, I had to be honest with Sandy. So one night, at that little Culver City apartment, I decided to tell her everything: that I'd been untrue, that I thought I loved someone else, that I didn't see any way for us to stay together. It wasn't easy to get the words out—I felt flushed, my heart was pounding, my mouth was dry. And looking into my beautiful wife's eyes—so full of worry, concern, and, still, love—I became physically overwhelmed. I'd barely started speaking when my knees went weak and I suddenly found myself on the floor—taken down by some kind of anxiety-triggered fainting spell. The pain in my bumped head was rivaled only by the guilt I felt over the fact that the woman whose heart I was breaking was now doing everything she could to comfort me.

On April 4, 1973, I sat with Elvis, Linda, and some of the guys at the Monovale house to watch the American network broadcast of the *Aloha* special. In contrast to the state of mind Elvis had been in when I watched the rough cut of the '68 special with him, he was in a great, fun mood. I think the big difference was that in watching *Aloha*, he knew that the concert itself had already been a success—he'd already heard the applause of a live crowd, and he was hearing it again on TV. Knowing that he'd already pleased his fans, he could relax and enjoy the show himself.

The good mood lasted a few days, and it had him feeling energetic enough that he decided to accept an invitation to check out a karate tournament that Ed Parker had organized in San Francisco. Parker had some phenomenal karate abilities and a powerful personality to match, and he and Elvis had connected with a real friendship. I liked and admired Parker, too, and briefly also studied karate with him. I'd felt honored that, at no charge, I was receiving instruction from such a master, but I moved on when I began to feel that we were spending more time talking about Elvis than working on our karate forms. Elvis wanted a close group of friends to travel with him to attend Parker's tournament: Linda, Joe, Charlie Hodge, Patsy and Gee Gee Gambill, Master Rhee, and myself. All our spirits lifted as we made all the required preparations, chartering a plane, lining up limos, reserving hotel rooms. The spirits stayed high on the flight to San Francisco. But in the limo on the way to the hotel, we passed the venue where the tournament was going to be held, and I saw something that I knew was going to shatter the mood.

Across the auditorium marquee, in great big letters, it said, ELVIS PRESLEY—IN PERSON. This was a legal problem—the contract for an upcoming Lake Tahoe appearance stipulated that Elvis was not supposed to be promoted within a 500-mile radius in the weeks before the event. But more to the point, this was a violation of the loyalty that was so important to Elvis. Elvis thought he had accepted an informal invitation to his friend's tournament, and he was happy to support Parker in that way. But he had no interest being part of the event's promotion.

Once Elvis got to the hotel, I headed back to the venue and insisted that Parker's associate Dave Hebler get up on a ladder and take Elvis's name off the marquee. This violated all local labor-union regulations, but it got done. By the time I got back to the hotel, Joe had already chartered a flight back to Los Angeles. This incident in a small way illustrates how Elvis's fame could wear down his spirit. He wanted to have a fun, getaway weekend, and wanted to pursue his passionate interest in karate. But instead of being able to attend as simply a friend or a guest, he saw himself used as a name that would sell tickets.

Elvis was having some trouble keeping himself healthy and in shape, and I was still terribly conflicted about my extramarital romance. But despite our personal problems, I hadn't ever felt that there was a problem between us. Over the course of some of our Palm Springs weekends, however, I detected a strain in our friendship that I couldn't explain. When a group of us sat and talked, Elvis seemed to go out of his way not to make any eye contact with me. He'd laugh with the other guys, but when we talked, it felt perfunctory—a basic exchange of information. At first I tried not to think too much about it, but after a while it was impossible not to be aware of the chill between us.

A week after the San Francisco trip, we were out in Palm Springs again, and, for the first time in a while, just he and I sat together in the living room. Conversation was a little awkward, and it seemed that something was really bothering him. Finally, he said, "Jerry, there's something I've got to tell you." What he told me was that he'd slept with my girlfriend.

It was a one-night fling between them, on a Palm Springs night when I'd fallen asleep early. Something that had just happened. I didn't care about the details—I was furious. And stunned. As tangled together as our lives had become, this was a horrible crossing of boundaries. It hurt like hell that the guy who had done so much for me could do something so awful to me.

It was extremely rare for Elvis to apologize about anything, but he stood there fumbling for an explanation, telling me, "It never happened before and it'll never happen again."

As angry as I was, I couldn't help thinking of what I would have done if I had heard about this some other way. I looked him in the eye and said, "Thank God I heard it from you and not from anybody else." I could tell he was embarrassed, and I was furious, but the truth was that he'd had a fling with a woman I was having an affair with—there wasn't any high moral ground for anyone to take. And it didn't sound like he'd had to work too hard at a seduction—the fling had happened between two willing parties.

Within a couple of days, all my anger had turned into a feeling of emptiness. I'd related to Elvis songs on a personal level before, but now I had the awful feeling I was stuck in some lines from one of his heaviest ballads from the fifties: "When you find your sweetheart in the arms of your best friend, brother, that's when your heartaches begin." I didn't think the incident had to mark the end of my affair with the girlfriend (though in fact it did). But I knew for certain that this romantic mess was just unacceptable, even in the midst of the crazy lives we were living. This wasn't any kind of fun—it just felt sick and depressing.

By the end of May, I was standing in a Glendale apartment, helping Sandy pack up for her flight back to Hawaii. She'd been accepting of my unfaithfulness, was willing to try to work things out, and had thought that maybe a move would help us start with a clean slate. An editor from Paramount I'd gotten close with was leaving his apartment to buy a house, so we moved in. But it didn't help. We tried to set up a new life in the new rooms, but I couldn't shake the old guilt and confusion.

Sandy's middle name was Lilinoe, a Polynesian name meaning "goddess of the mist of the mountains," and I had always thought that perfectly captured her natural beauty and purity. But I'd let that mist drift away, for no good reason. I'd broken a good woman's heart. And watching her pack her simple belongings into a few cardboard boxes, it broke my heart to think just how little she'd gotten out of our time together.

Elvis and I were standing in the Meditation Garden at Graceland, drinking iced tea to fight off the heat of a June evening. The Palm Springs incident had brought us up to the edge of what was acceptable within our friendship, but once the hurt and anger had burned out for me, the episode was over. Nobody in that situation came out looking good, and I had no desire to be bitter toward a friend who was sincerely sorry. Now we had a few weeks off between strings of concert dates, and were back to spending days at Graceland and nights at the Memphian.

"Colonel got me a deal," Elvis said. "A whole lot of money and I don't have to do a damn thing."

In all the years I knew him, Elvis hardly ever talked about specifics of the business side of his career, but he seemed excited to do so this day. The deal was a big one—the Colonel had brokered a lump-sum, $5.4 million buyout of Elvis's rights to artist royalty payments for all the recordings he had made up to that point. At the time, his excitement was at least partially justified. The payment figure was huge, and in the days before golden oldies and classic rock were hot radio formats, it was hard to imagine how Elvis's back catalogue would ever generate that much money in royalties. Elvis's recordings had already been repackaged and resold so many times already, it didn't seem likely that there was much more profit to be wrung from them.

Standing in the garden, I tried to be happy for Elvis, too. But there was something sad and final about cashing in all that great music. Sure it was a lot of money for Elvis, but I didn't feel like I could possibly put one big price tag on Dewey Phillips playing "That's All Right," and "Hound Dog" at Ellis Auditorium, and "I Was the One" at the Stand, and watching the performance of "How Great Thou Art," and feeling the goose bumps during "If I Can Dream." His music was a soundtrack to my life, and to lives all over the world. It didn't feel right to total it up in any lump sum, even $5.4 million.

My mist of the mountains was gone, and Elvis's music was gone. There was no way we could think of ourselves as a couple of North Memphis kids anymore. We were grown men, living lives that were wonderful in so many regards, but lives that were not immune to frustration, disappointment, and pain. In a couple of weeks, we'd be back on the road, hitting city after city again. But beyond the tour schedule, I couldn't tell what the future was supposed to look like.

12

. . .

BLACK-BELT BLUES

In all my years with Elvis, I never witnessed him go through any elaborate vocal warm-ups before he sang. He'd keep his voice irrigated by washing out his throat with hot salt water, but before a performance you never heard him singing scales or bellowing "mi mi mi"s—he would have been as bored with that kind of exercise as he was with sit-ups. He was a natural talent who simply drew upon his natural gifts whenever he hit the stage. The amazing thing was that even with all the stress and strain of the road, and with all the trouble he was having staying physically healthy, the voice only got stronger. The more he worked in Vegas and out on the road, the more that instrument of his became both more powerful and more nuanced, and he continued to challenge himself by taking on vocally demanding material such as "Bridge Over Troubled Water," "An American Trilogy," and "My Way."

On a good performance night, when Elvis was on and the band was cooking, you could still get goose bumps hearing him hit the high notes, or hearing him put his heart into one of the ballads. But not every night could be a good night, and it was becoming evident that there was something wrong in Elvis's world.

He still liked to see himself as the hero of the comic books—the Superman or Captain Marvel who could take care of all problems and keep everybody happy. And, generally, he was always able to be exactly that—a rock-solid presence that we could all depend on. Even when he stumbled, all of us around him understood that we were leading extraordinary lives because of one man's talents and generosity. His moods could shift and his timing could drive you crazy, but you always believed that Elvis would be there for you. If anyone could pull off playing Captain Marvel, it was him. But even a comic book hero has to have new adventures to keep his powers at their peak, and as time went on, and Elvis settled into the routine of Las Vegas engagements and concert tours, his world became as squared off and contained as the panels of a comic page. Hotel suite, showroom, plane, limo, stage. Repeat. There were weeks and months in which that was all any of us saw of the world around us. For a guy who had once jumped off roller coasters for a laugh, and who had once been able to karate kick a pack of cigarettes out of an opponent's shirt pocket, the confinement of the "good life" Elvis was leading started to feel like a burden. And for a guy who had put together a huge private library of works that explored spirituality, consciousness, and the meaning of life, the routine of his days must have started to feel empty. The strain on him was obvious.

At a Las Vegas show in early 1973, a guy from a table in the front of the showroom climbed up on stage to get to Elvis. Elvis was facing the band, and when the guy came up behind him, Elvis quickly took him down with a hard reverse kick to the midsection—an understandable reaction for an exposed public figure who had received more than one serious death threat. When a second guy from the first one's table started to get up on stage, I automatically reacted as a bodyguard, rushing from the wings to pick him up and hurl him back down on his table. Red and some of the players from the band got ahold of two others who had come up, and pretty soon hotel security had whisked the four stage-rushers out of the showroom. The chaos and confusion were over in a minute or two, and Elvis got back to his performance.

From the reports we got after the show, none of these men had criminal records and it seemed likely that they hadn't meant any real harm to Elvis—the first guy had done something stupid and the others had probably thought they were coming to their friend's defense. Whether they were fans or not didn't matter to us. Elvis had been hurt in the past by overenthusiastic fans, and this time we'd all done the most basic part of our job: protecting Elvis. But after the show, up in his suite, Elvis worked himself into an increasingly agitated state. He wouldn't accept that these guys were just dumb, or rowdy, or both. Not only did he insist that they had been out to do him serious harm, he came to the conclusion that they had been sent by Mike Stone, a karate instructor Priscilla had become romantically involved with. Joe, Lamar, Red, Sonny, Linda, and I were all there, and the idea didn't seem very believable to any of us. But we were more taken aback by the ferocity of Elvis's anger as he ranted and raged about Stone. We'd seen him angry before, but this time, Elvis seemed truly out of control. Nobody was sure if he knew exactly how wild he sounded to us.

I think all of us were aware that Elvis needed a way to vent his emotions, and Stone was the perfect target for all the anger and guilt Elvis felt over his failed marriage. Also, if Priscilla's new romance might have been an affront to his sense of manhood, it probably hurt even more that Stone was a top-ranked karate master in peak physical condition. As much as karate was still a passionate hobby for Elvis, he had slipped out of practice, and there wasn't much question that in any kind of match of karate skills, Stone would easily defeat him. All of Elvis's bottled-up frustrations and disappointments were now focused on Stone, and while his theory sounded irrational and his rage was overblown, it seemed like maybe this was just what he needed to work the turmoil out of his system. He didn't have a therapist to talk things out with. He wasn't going to cry on my shoulder, and certainly not on Red's. If he needed to rage around the room, so be it. Also, you could never discount the fact that Elvis was a performer. And while his anger and hurt were real, on some level he was giving us a masterful rendition of the heartbroken husband.

All of that we could handle, but as Elvis raged on, the relief never came. He pushed further and further, until he came to a decision that scared the hell out of all of us. He decided that he wanted Mike Stone dead.

It was a losing battle to try to change Elvis's mind about anything while he was in this kind of state. And we'd all been in situations where Elvis had talked big about something that he knew, and you knew, he wasn't going to follow through on. The next day, however, when all of us gathered back in Elvis's suite for a five P.M. breakfast, he was still going on about his desire to have a contract taken out on Mike Stone. Nobody could quite get a read on Elvis—maybe he was still the actor playing the part; maybe he wanted to know just how far he could push our loyalty; maybe he really was in such a state of despair that he wasn't thinking clearly. It was a very uncomfortable breakfast table to be sitting at. I felt bad for Linda, who wanted to give Elvis her love and support, but who was starting to get worn down by his unpredictability. All of us had always felt we'd do anything to protect Elvis from any and all outside forces, but now I had the sick feeling that maybe we needed to protect him from himself.

The more Elvis talked about Stone, the more Red looked like he was going to explode. Finally Red got up and left the table, heading off into the kitchen to make a phone call. He returned a few minutes later, went straight to where Elvis was sitting, and whispered something in his ear. We knew then that Red had made "the call." I'd learn later that Red, very much against his will, had already made a contact for Elvis, and had found out that $10,000 would get the dirty job done. When he whispered to Elvis at the table, it was the moment of truth—if Elvis gave the OK, the hit would be carried out.

At the words from Red, Elvis immediately went pale. Suddenly we saw not the raging actor but the Elvis we all knew who, in so many situations, chose to be the nice guy rather than the tough guy. He did know how crazy he'd been talking, and he knew that his words had taken us right up to the edge of a terrifying cliff. He wasn't going to take us over it.

"That's a little heavy," he told Red. "Let's just leave it alone for a while."

Elvis had conquered Las Vegas, but it was impossible to be the conquering hero at every single show. To fight off the boredom of being on that same stage every night, Elvis began to talk to the audience a great deal—cracking jokes, telling stories, and generally speaking freely about whatever was on his mind. It was a jolt to the guys—we'd heard him talk that way around our dinner tables or down in the TV room at Graceland, but never up on stage. Priscilla, who still attended some of the shows, would later say that she was shocked at how open he'd become on stage about his private thoughts.

There were many nights when the audience loved seeing a looser, talkative Elvis having fun on stage. But there were nights when the talk and the jokes made the music suffer, and some audiences left the shows obviously disappointed. On one night of the fall 1973 engagement at the Hilton, he had a table of people up front at the early show who responded enthusiastically to his running commentary between songs. As the show progressed, Elvis directed more and more of his performance to that one particular table until he was almost fully engaged in private conversation with that group and hardly singing at all. By the middle of the show, audience members in the back of the showroom who felt they weren't getting what they'd paid for began leaving.

Elvis had used those natural talents of his to entertain millions of fans by this point, and it was an awful shock to see him lose an audience's interest. It was even more shocking to see a sight I never thought I'd see: people walking out on an Elvis Presley show. Joe looked as upset as I felt, and we agreed that the situation had to be addressed. Our job was not to tell Elvis he was great no matter what he did—as his friends, we felt we had to be honest with him. And we wouldn't be worth much as employees or friends if we backed away from telling him a difficult truth. When Red and Sonny joined us backstage, it was clear that they were just as bothered by what they'd seen. And the especially dark scowl on Lamar's face let us know the way he felt. We decided that when Elvis went downstairs to his dressing room, we'd have a sit-down meeting with him.

It wasn't unusual for Elvis to sit at the dressing-room table with us for a few minutes after the show, before he began to change out of his wardrobe. He'd ask us how the show went, and usually we'd relay to him what we thought were the highlights of the night, and we'd give him a rundown on any technical problems or unusual occurrences. He sat with us again this time, and looked to be in a great mood. The stage lights may have blinded him to the back of the showroom, so as far as he knew, he'd done a great job of connecting with his fans.

"How was the show?" he asked.

Lamar, who never shied away from putting things in the bluntest of terms, spoke up first.

"You know, Elvis," Lamar said. "About three hundred people walked out tonight."

Elvis tried to laugh it off, as if Lamar didn't know what he was talking about. But what came out of him was a forced, hollow laugh. "The people up in front enjoyed it," he said.

I tried coming at it from a less confrontational approach. "Of course they did, E. They had the star of the show paying attention to them all night. But what about everybody else?"

Elvis's eyes went cold, and his smile disappeared. I think he knew that if we felt strongly enough about his performance to become critics, there had to be a problem. But he wasn't going to hash it out with us. His expression got tighter, and he got very quiet. After a moment, he said, "Get the Colonel."

Whatever went on between them, the shows were better for a while. Of course, Elvis wasn't going to put on better shows because the Colonel told him to—he was going to put on better shows because that's what felt right to him. But on the last night of the engagement he again began to indulge in some onstage jokes and pranks, even singing "What Now My Love" as he kicked around on a bed that had been rolled out on stage. The audience was completely with him this night, and enjoyed the fun. But Elvis also had a point to make that he felt was serious. He told the audience that the Hilton was about to fire his favorite waiter, who had prepared so many great meals up in his suite, and he didn't understand how the hotel could do such a disservice to such a good, hardworking person. He talked disapprovingly of the hotel management, and his remarks started to carry the emotion of a social crusader standing up for the oppressed little guy. His critique didn't stop when the music started—he got a few further digs in by twisting some lyrics to include off-color anti-Hilton lines.

The Colonel thought he had gotten things under control, but was now outraged. He prided himself on his business relationships, and now, publicly, Elvis had embarrassed him with one of his most important business associates. Not only did he think Elvis's comments were unprofessional—he had reason to take them personally. The Colonel had come to consider the hotel's owner, Barron Hilton, as a personal friend, and he felt that Hilton had gone out of his way to accommodate every request made on Elvis's behalf. For the first time in their partnership, the Colonel was in the position of being humiliated by Elvis.

The Colonel was down in the dressing room almost immediately, and he and Elvis went alone into a small private area behind a closed door. All we heard were loud, angry voices. When they emerged, neither looked happy. And nothing seemed settled. But the Colonel went up to his room, and Elvis and the rest of us went up to the suite.

Usually we'd all get together for a relaxed celebration after a final show, but this night Elvis seemed distracted. He'd sung well and left his audiences satisfied that night, but it seemed that he was working over whatever had gone on between him and the Colonel. Things stayed quiet in the suite, and, after a while, Elvis said the words again: "Get the Colonel."

The Colonel hadn't calmed down from the earlier encounter, and he was also unhappy about being called out of bed at that late hour. He charged into the room like an angry bull elephant. Right away the two faced off. This was another scene that none of us thought we'd ever see. For so long, the relationship between the Colonel and Elvis had been a strange, complicated dance in which they rarely dealt with each other directly. You never heard them discussing business and you rarely witnessed them expressing raw emotion toward each other. But here they were, going right at each other, not seeming to care at all that there was a room full of witnesses. Elvis was angry with the way the Colonel had talked to him after the show, and he was angry that the Colonel seemed to think it was more important to defend the Hilton than to side with him. But mainly he was angry over the Colonel's lack of interest in getting an overseas tour together. We'd seen a raging Elvis, but now he was focused and intent, laying out his points forcefully. The Colonel responded angrily in the same loud, gruff voice that had terrified so many of his own staff. But Elvis stayed strong—he wasn't going to be talked out of his demands by the Colonel's bluster.

The Colonel talked about all that the Hilton had done for Elvis—how Elvis was being ungrateful. Elvis responded that he did appreciate the way he'd been treated in the Hilton showroom. But that wasn't the point. The bigger question was: When was he going to get out of that showroom? Why hadn't the Colonel done a damn thing to make an international engagement happen?

Apparently, Elvis had already spoken about his ideas for a karate film with the Colonel, because that became a part of the escalating argument, too. Elvis felt the Colonel had brushed off the film idea without any thought toward making it happen. Elvis didn't put it in so many words, but his complaint was clear: He wanted to make some kind of artistic stretch, but the Colonel couldn't see past bottom line and business-as-usual.

The Colonel's tone indicated that he had no confidence in Elvis's abilities to handle the business of filmmaking. And I think he may have undercut Elvis out of self-interest. What Elvis saw as professional growth, the Colonel saw as a threat. I still had some sympathy for the position the Colonel was in—to his way of thinking, he'd made tremendous things happen for Elvis. The strength and smarts in all the deals he'd made for Elvis couldn't be disputed. But he didn't ever seem to fully understand that Elvis wasn't going to measure himself in profits made—he had creative desires that needed to be nurtured and fulfilled. The language of creativity was a foreign one to the Colonel, though, and this showdown had been a long time coming.

The two went back to the issue of overseas touring, and the argument finally came to its climax. The Colonel shouted, "If you want to go over there, you'll do it without me."

Without hesitating, Elvis shot back, "That's just what I was thinking. You're fired."

There was a stunned silence in the room as the Colonel stormed to the door, pausing only to shout out a final point: "If you're going to fire me, you're going to have to pay me what you owe me."

I didn't think the night could get any stranger, but when I finally got back to my room I got a call from the Colonel requesting me to come to his room down on the fourth floor. There I saw a sight that would have been comic under any other circumstances: The Colonel was in his pajamas and robe, with his reading glasses down at the end of his nose, furiously pecking away on a typewriter that seemed old-fashioned even then. He looked like a character out of a Dickens novel—the embittered, vengeful schoolmaster.

He'd been at work drawing up a to-the-penny accounting of everything he felt Elvis owed him and would owe him as contracts that the Colonel had negotiated were paid off. The Colonel had sheets and sheets of figures worked out, all of which tallied up what Elvis was required to pay him if he wanted to walk away from their partnership. Whatever anger or hurt the Colonel felt was simply being channeled into hard, cold business. It just seemed sad to me that he was playing the kind of hardball with Elvis that he normally played on Elvis's behalf.

When the Colonel had his papers in order, he handed them to me to deliver to Elvis. This was one of the most unpleasant tasks I carried out in all my years with Elvis, mainly because of the mixed emotions it brought up. I'd always wanted to see Elvis's creativity and artistic ambitions fully encouraged and supported. I wanted him to tour overseas, and I wanted him to make his karate film. But I also knew how hard the Colonel had worked for Elvis, and I'd often wondered if anyone less than the Colonel could have handled this powerful, unique talent.

Over several days, the tempers of that night settled into an uncomfortable silence. Vernon began to worry about the consequences of the split, wondering how they would ever pay off the Colonel, and whether they really could get along without him. Elvis had meant every word he said, but he wasn't happy about dealing with the continuing fallout. The Colonel took a Snowman's approach to the situation—he made a play for sympathy, sending messages through the room-service waiters that he was ill and looking quite sickly.

The Colonel had a few reasons not to feel so well. By now, all of us were aware that he was a flamboyant and reckless gambler. Although he would squeeze every possible dollar out of business deals, he thought nothing of dropping thousands of dollars in one night at the casino. A kind of fever gripped him when he gambled. I once saw his good friend and associate George Parkhill crumple over right beside the Colonel at a roulette table, the victim of a stroke. As casino security put Parkhill in a wheelchair and sped him away for medical assistance, the Colonel's eyes never left the game—it was a losing night and nothing was going to break his concentration. It was hard to tell exactly how much money the Colonel was throwing around night after night—he always played with unmarked chips. But the way he played, there was no way he was coming out ahead.

Elvis turned to karate to work off the frustration over the standoff, flying in Khang Rhee from Memphis. I can still picture Master Rhee hopping up and down on the couch as he and Elvis used the suite's living room as a dojo. And when they kicked and punched through all the wooden demonstration boards Master Rhee had brought with him, they began breaking up the furniture.

The situation would eventually resolve itself more quietly than it had begun, but not before Elvis made a real effort at working without the Colonel. He had Lamar Fike contact Tom Hulett about booking some road dates, but Tom had been brought into the Elvis world by the Colonel and wouldn't work against him. Elvis felt the one thing he could do for himself was go out and tour, and tried to follow through, but no one he contacted wanted to step into a manager's role. I think Tom and whoever else Elvis spoke to must have realized that there was really only one person strong enough to successfully manage Elvis Presley—the Colonel.

In the end, no legal action was taken to sever the partnership between Elvis and the Colonel, and within a couple of weeks Elvis had moved on to Palm Springs and the Colonel was overseeing negotiations over the completion of Elvis's next RCA album. But Joe and I wouldn't be around for any of that. Elvis had promised to send Joe and me on a European vacation, a trip that he thought would help us clear our heads after having gone through divorces. Days after the blowout with the Colonel, we told Elvis that considering what was happening, we were canceling the trip to stay with him. He wouldn't hear of it.

"We've been through a rough engagement," he told us, "and you guys deserve it even more. You're going to go."

I got excited about the trip, and was looking forward to a mix of high culture and carefree fun—I was ready for both after some of the heavy times over the last year. But I could sense that Joe wasn't quite ready for this kind of escape. The wounds of his divorce were too fresh, and his split with Joanie weighed heavily on him. That said, Joe was a solid traveling companion, and proved to be an expert driver on European roads. Over three weeks, we made our way through Greece, Italy, Belgium, France, and England. We got to see the Vatican, the Louvre, and the statue of David in Florence. We discovered the pleasures of French wine and Belgian ale. On nights when Joe was not up for exploring a city, I went out by myself. In Innsbruck, Austria, I found myself alone in an elevator with Mick Jagger. I said hello, thinking I'd tell him how much Elvis had dug the Stones' early covers of American blues tunes. But he ignored me, and for the twenty or thirty seconds in which we stood just inches away from each other, made no acknowledgment at all that there was another human being in his vicinity. Didn't spoil my night. I just stepped out of the elevator thinking, *Screw you, Mick.*

Joe and I ended up in London, spending time with James Darren ("Moondoggie" of the *Gidget* films) and his wife, Evie, who were friends of Joe's. I took the opportunity to upgrade my wardrobe with several shopping trips to King's Row and Carnaby Street. The whole trip was just what Elvis had wanted for us—a great escape. I hadn't realized quite how claustrophobic our lives had become until I got over to Europe—I almost felt as if I'd been holding my breath for months and was now finally breathing again. Even Joe was loosening up a little by the end of the trip. We were refocused and reenergized. And we were going to need that energy, because back in the U.S., things were only getting heavier.

After Sandy and I had split up, Elvis had offered me a room in the Monovale house, which I gladly accepted. I was at that house on October 9, 1973, when Elvis and Vernon headed to a courthouse in Santa Monica so that he and Priscilla could finalize the arrangements of their divorce. There's a well-known photograph of Elvis and Priscilla leaving the courthouse that day, in which they are walking arm in arm. That shot says a lot about the relationship between the two. Even after going through a divorce, there was still a love there that they both felt.

It was obviously a hard time emotionally for Elvis, and all of us around him wanted to be as supportive and understanding as we could. But less than a week after the divorce proceedings, back in Memphis, something we'd all feared finally happened: Elvis suffered a physical collapse. He'd been having breathing troubles at Graceland that Linda Thompson felt were serious enough to warrant calling in Dr. Nick. After a couple of days of monitoring Elvis at the house, the doctor felt his situation was critical enough to check him into Baptist Hospital.

As much as Elvis trusted his personal doctors, he hated the idea of hospitals. To make him more comfortable there, Sonny, Al Strada, and I took on the odd task of preparing a room in an isolated wing of the hospital as though it were the bedroom in the suite at the top of the Las Vegas Hilton. The windows were blacked out with aluminum foil, phone lines were set up, special arrangements were made for the food that Elvis would want, and an extra bed was brought in so that Linda could stay in the room with him. A room directly across from Elvis's was reserved so that Sonny and I could take turns spending the night at the hospital.

There was something awful and scary about watching a guy who had once been such a perfect physical specimen just fall apart. Elvis was undeniably overweight now, and had respiratory problems, intestinal ailments, liver dysfunction, and early-stage glaucoma, all of which had been induced or exacerbated by his work schedule and his overuse of prescription medications. I had to admit that, getting him checked into the hospital, I also felt a sense of relief. Maybe a hospital stay was what it was going to take to wake him up and get him strong again.

The doctors at the hospital were puzzled by some strange bruises on Elvis's body, which he said were from acupuncture treatments he received in Los Angeles. Months before, my back had gotten extremely sore—a lingering condition from my football injuries and motorcycle accident. Elvis had insisted that his acupuncturist could take care of the pain, and promptly took me not to the doctor's office, but to his home in Beverly Hills. I didn't know anything about acupuncture—Elvis was again ahead of his time in embracing this form of treatment—but I was willing to give anything a try to be able to stand up straight. Obviously I couldn't see exactly what the doctor did to my lower back, but after a half-hour session I walked out of there feeling great. The doctors at Baptist couldn't figure out how acupuncture needles could leave such bruises, and Dr. Nick tracked down the acupuncturist to make some inquiries about his procedure. It turned out that this doctor was helping the acupuncture process along by administering shots of Demerol, a powerful painkiller. Suddenly I understood how my back pain had disappeared. The doctors at the hospital realized that in addition to having his other ailments treated, Elvis was going to have to be carefully weaned off a doctor-created opiate addiction.

We knew that it wasn't going to be enough simply to treat Elvis's physical troubles. His psychological dependency on his medications had to be treated, too, if he was truly going to get well. But this was a touchy area. Elvis needed to maintain his dignity, and no one was sure how he would react to any attempt to get inside his head. One of the team of doctors treating Elvis was Dr. David Knott, a drug-addiction specialist. Joe, Vernon, and I talked with Dr. Nick, who consulted with the doctor. It was decided that Dr. Knott would give Elvis all the treatment he felt was necessary, but he would be presented to Elvis as a liver specialist. Even in his diminished state, though, Elvis was a sharp guy. I was in his room one day when Dr. Knott came by, talked to Elvis a bit, checked some charts, and then left.

"You know," Elvis said calmly, "Dr. Knott's a psychiatrist."

Elvis did get well. He got off the medicines that weren't doing him any good; he lost weight; he started sleeping better; and he even started eating better (though it was hard for the cooks at Graceland not to want to spoil their "patient" by serving him his favorite dishes). After a couple months of rest and recuperation, he looked good and had better energy than any of us had seen in a while.

He was back for a two-week engagement at the Hilton in January of 1974, and this time the shows were strong and exciting. The gatherings in Elvis's suite after the show were upbeat, too, and he was the host to some remarkable mixes of people. I remember one night up in the suite, Elvis decided to give Liza Minelli a complete beginner's guide to karate. A small group of us moved to Elvis's private bedroom, where I became Liza's practice partner while Elvis provided the instruction. Liza was game, and handling her kicks and punches was a lot of fun. But what made the night even more memorable was that the small group watching the lesson included Chubby Checker, famous for dancing "The Twist," and Linda Lovelace, famous for doing what she did in *Deep Throat*. Linda was there with her boyfriend, David Winters, who had worked as a film choreographer for Elvis. Much later that night, Linda and David were arrested at the Dunes Hotel on drug possession charges. It seemed clear that the couple had been set up and were being harassed because of Linda's notoriety, at a time when Vegas had become interested in cleaning up its image. They didn't know who to turn to, so they called Elvis. He offered to post bond for them, but the charges were dropped before that was necessary.

By March, we were out on the road for the first of four national tours that year. When Elvis was in good form, it was easy for good feelings to trickle down to the rest of us, and as we all went back out on the road, I realized that I was falling in love again.

The Sweet Inspirations, Elvis's trio of female backup singers, were comprised of Myrna Smith, Sylvia Shemwell, and Estelle Brown (Cissy Houston, Whitney's mother, was part of the group at Elvis's 1969 Las Vegas engagement). Any of the Sweets could have been remarkable lead singers on their own, but I thought Myrna had a phenomenal talent. I also thought she was gorgeous, and I loved watching her on stage. For a long time I didn't know what to say to Myrna, but any chance I could I engaged in some low-key flirting. We were both shy enough, though, that I don't think we would have ever gotten past the flirting stage if it weren't for Sylvia Shemwell. I was spending more and more time around the Sweets on the road, and I guess Sylvia could tell how much of a crush I had on Myrna. One night I was talking to the singers in their dressing room when Sylvia said, "Hey, Jerry, if you're not going to ask me out, why don't you take Myrna out?"

That was all the icebreaking I needed. I'll never forget the look of surprise on Elvis's face when I told him I was going to date Myrna. He didn't make any attempt to sugarcoat his reaction. "She won't go out with you." The way he said it, it sounded like there was a part he was leaving unsaid: "She wouldn't go out with me."

Elvis had an extremely special relationship with the Sweet Inspirations. He was with them in their dressing room after almost every show, and I think he opened up to them in ways that he didn't with anybody else. I know Elvis was also attracted to Myrna, but he valued her much more as a friend than as a potential romantic partner. He may have also been a little intimidated by her—Myrna would tell me later that the one time she and Elvis danced together at a party, she could feel him trembling.

In the summer of '73 we'd had some interesting transportation on tour—Elvis chartered Hugh Hefner's *Playboy* jet—the DC-9 *Big Bunny*—as his tour plane. With my marriage over, I'd actually had some romantic liaisons with a Bunny attendant. But given a chance to live a life of debauchery, I always preferred to go with my romantic streak. Falling in love always had more appeal than just falling into bed. And as

Myrna and I began to spend more time together, my crush quickly blossomed into Sweet love. Myrna and I began really dating, going out for dinners and going to see shows together on nights we weren't working with Elvis. Vernon's marriage to Dee Stanley was over, and he had just begun a romance with a nurse from Denver named Sandy Miller. Myrna and I double-dated with the couple the very first time they went out together—we all went to a Diana Ross show. It was rare for Elvis to allow little Lisa to go out without him, but he allowed Myrna and me to take her out on another of our dates. We attended a Jackson 5 concert at the Sahara in Lake Tahoe a day after Elvis had ended his engagement there, and after the show I introduced five-year-old Lisa to a teenage Michael Jackson.

Myrna and I got serious very quickly. When she wasn't working with Elvis she spent a lot of time at her home in Newark, New Jersey. I decided that when she did come out to Los Angeles, I wanted her to be able to stay with me. I remembered how concerned the Colonel had been about living arrangements when Sandy and I lived with Elvis and Priscilla as unmarried couples. It seemed to me that to be with Myrna, the best thing to do was to move out of Elvis's house and get my own place. But when I told Elvis that I was going to start searching for an apartment, he almost looked hurt.

"You got a place at my house. What's wrong with that?"

"Myrna's going to be staying with me out here," I said. "I just didn't want to make any trouble for you with the fans."

"What are you talking about?"

I'd fallen in love with Myrna because she was beautiful and wonderful. But it had occurred to me that at the Monovale house, we'd be driving past a group of fans at the gate every day. The fact that an unmarried white guy and black woman were living with Elvis might create complications for him.

"E, there are some fans that might have a problem with Myrna and me being together."

"Myrna's my friend," he said. "And I don't have a problem with it."

He insisted I forget about apartment shopping. When Myrna came to L.A., she stayed at the Monovale house. There was never a problem.

. . .

Elvis had been way ahead of the pop culture wave when it came to karate, but now karate was everywhere. *Billy Jack* had been a sleeper hit in 1971, and in 1973, Bruce Lee's *Enter the Dragon* had kicked off massive mainstream interest in the martial arts. *Kung Fu* was a huge hit on television, and by the end of 1974, "Kung Fu Fighting" would be at the top of the pop charts.

As a film buff and a karate devotee, Elvis had become almost obsessed with seeing the martial arts films that came out of Tokyo and Hong Kong, along with the American exploitation and "blaxploitation" films that were picking up on the martial arts trend. When we were in L.A., we'd often head out to a little theater in Santa Monica that screened these films. Some of them were brilliantly surreal, a lot of them were just plain awful, but Elvis always found something in them worth studying. And despite the lack of support he'd gotten from the Colonel on the subject, he was still very interested in putting together his own karate film.

He and I had many conversations about what this film might be, and he got most excited about the idea of producing and starring in a film that would mix serious drama and action with a hip sense of humor, similar to Dean Martin's *Matt Helm* or James Coburn's *Flint* movies. At the same time, he was talking to Ed Parker about putting together an all-star martial arts team to compete in international tournaments and possibly serve as the subject of a karate documentary. The more we talked, the more Elvis sounded like he really wanted to make something happen. And so he was very receptive when I pointed out that we had an old fraternity contact that might help get a production started: Rick Husky. My Arkansas State fraternity brother—and Elvis's honorary brother—had gone on to become a very successful television writer and producer, with credits that included *The Mod Squad*, *The Rookies*, and *The Streets of San Francisco*. Rick and I had gotten close again in L.A., often going out to nightclubs together. And Rick had never stopped being an Elvis fan—he'd been to several shows in Las Vegas.

I made the arrangements, and Rick came up to Elvis's house to have a meeting with him and Ed Parker. But right away, we ran into a problem of creative differences. Rick liked Elvis's original idea of a *Matt Helm*- or *Flint*-style film, and felt that with the right story we could come up with a movie that might do for Elvis what *From Here to Eter-*

nity had done for Frank Sinatra. But Ed Parker had been selling Elvis hard on the idea of the documentary, and now that's what Elvis seemed to be leaning toward. Looking back, I think that even though the dramatic film had the chance to be everything Elvis had always wanted in his films, he also knew his limitations at the time. He knew he was out of shape, and he knew what would be demanded of him as the star of the film. The documentary, in which he would serve as a guide, instructor, and narrator, must have started to look like an easier option.

At the house, Rick kept trying to proceed as if this were the same kind of story meeting he'd been at for all his other projects. He'd built a successful career taking the ideas discussed at meetings like this and steering them toward becoming finished projects. But Elvis wasn't much of a meeting guy. He dismissed the *From Here to Eternity* comparison and let Parker do most of the pitching of the documentary idea. Unfortunately, Parker's idea of pitching was mainly to demonstrate karate moves. At the end of the meeting, I could tell that Rick was frustrated. I went out with Rick that night, and by then he was down and depressed—he saw a great opportunity for Elvis in a dramatic karate film, but didn't think he'd been given a chance to make his case.

He didn't give up, though. Shortly after the meeting, he put together a thirty-page treatment for the film he had in mind. Elvis would be an ex-CIA agent running a karate school who sets out on a mission to avenge the death of a close friend done in by drug dealers. Rick got it to me, and I carefully placed the treatment on Elvis's bed at the Monovale house, where I was sure he'd pick it up and read it. But Rick and I never heard a word about it from Elvis. He'd made up his mind. He wanted to put together that all-star team and move forward with the documentary.

I may have felt bad that our involvement with Rick hadn't worked out, and that Elvis had decided against making the kind of film that I thought would be better for him professionally and commercially. But those kinds of feelings were quickly erased by another decision Elvis made. He was going to executive-produce the documentary—a position that would give him final say on all aspects of the production. And he wanted me to be the film's hands-on, day-to-day co-executive producer. We were going to make the movie together.

When I worked on *Elvis On Tour*, I was happy to have the chance to edit a film about Elvis. Now I was actually going to produce a film with him. Being a creative partner with him on something this big really was incredibly exciting. And it meant a lot that, after all the difficulties he was going through, he obviously had a respect for the work I'd done away from him, and, more importantly, a real faith in our friendship.

Rick Husky and I had been spending a lot of nights out at the Candy Store, a private nightclub in Beverly Hills. There he introduced me to Ron Smith, a successful young entrepreneur who was running a modeling agency at the time. Ron invited me to a big party he was throwing for the agency, and at the party, I found myself standing next to a large, unmistakably athletic guest—Wilt Chamberlain. Wilt had no reason to talk to me, and I couldn't think of much to say to him—I was aware of his reputation in the press as a gruff, unfriendly personality. But we both sat down at a little table set away from the center of the party. We'd been there a minute or two when a couple of short, extremely nonathletic guys came over and told us that we were sitting at their table, and they wanted it back.

The request seemed both rude and absurd. Maybe they didn't know about the Golden Gloves in my past, but who asks a muscular seven-footer to get out of his seat? I looked at Wilt, he looked at me, and we both started laughing. We gave the guys their table, and as we stepped back toward the party, we bumped into Ron, who officially introduced us. We talked for a while, and then Wilt asked me if I felt like getting out of there. I did. And about a half hour later Wilt and I were sitting at Theodore's coffee shop on Santa Monica Boulevard, eating hamburgers, drinking milk shakes, and laughing it up like a couple of old buddies. At the end of the night, he said he wanted to have me up to his place sometime for dinner. He gave me his phone number and I gave him my answering-service number.

The next night, I was out with Priscilla, Lisa, and Joanie Esposito for a belated celebration of Lisa's sixth birthday at one of her favorite restaurants, the Luau. I felt privileged to be a part of the family celebration, and I was a little surprised when Joe Stellini, the maître d', came to the table and told me that I had a phone call. It was Wilt. This was the night he wanted to have me up to his place. He had his private chef at work on a special dinner for us and wanted to know how soon I could be there. I told Wilt that I was already having dinner, and I told him who I was having dinner with—it wasn't something I could dash away from. Wilt's advice: "Don't eat too much, and come on up to my place for a late dinner." That was easy enough to say yes to.

Wilt had done the designing and engineering of his home, which had been featured in all kinds of designer magazines—it was sort of a modern marvel, with a retractable roof that opened up to allow stargazing from the master bedroom, and TVs that would rise out of the floor at the touch of a button. Wilt gave me a tour of the place and showed off all the furnishings, which that night included a couple of beautiful young women. Wilt hadn't invited me to be part of some larger get-together—we were it: Wilt, me, the girls, and the chef. I wasn't all that interested in the girls—I was, after all, crazy about Myrna. But it was a heck of a dinner party to be a part of. Before I left that night, I told Wilt that Elvis had an engagement at the Sahara in Lake Tahoe coming up and that I wanted to have Wilt there as my guest.

Early in the run at the Sahara, I got the call—Wilt was on his way up to Tahoe. I made all the arrangements with the hotel so that he'd be well taken care of. Just before the show, I let Elvis know Wilt was going to be out there, and that he'd had me over to his home. I asked if I could bring him backstage to say hello after the show. Elvis seemed indifferent to meeting with Wilt.

The show was a strong one. Elvis was in great voice and delivered the music with great energy. About halfway through the show, Elvis stopped the band to speak to the crowd. "Ladies and gentlemen," he said. "There's a man in the audience tonight who many a Saturday I've spent watching on TV. I've seen him wearing a rubber band around his wrist, and he wears a headband up around his hair. But what you notice most about this man when you watch him is that he is a true champion. Ladies and gentlemen—Mr. Basketball, Wilt Chamberlain."

Wilt stood up and got his own ovation from the crowd. It was an unusual moment because while Elvis might introduce a celebrity or a notable from the stage, he rarely did it with that kind of feeling and detail. I had no idea how Elvis knew about the rubber band Wilt always wore when he played. After the show, I thanked Elvis. I told him it was a great introduction, and that I was surprised to learn he was such a basketball fan.

"I'm a fan of anyone who's the best at what they do," he said.

Not only did Elvis welcome Wilt backstage, he asked him to come up to his suite. There, while the rest of us had our usual after-show gathering, Elvis and Wilt sat on a couch together in deep discussion, going one-on-one until about five in the morning.

The karate documentary began to move forward. We were going to film the travels of the all-star team that Elvis and Ed Parker assembled, which featured a number of national champions and renowned martial-arts specialists. Parker began setting up tournaments for the team in the U.S. and Europe, while I worked out the filmmaking details with staff we'd brought on board: producer George Waite and director Bob Hammer. In between some of the tournament footage would be some more interesting work—Elvis would be on-screen himself, demonstrating moves and explaining the history, principles, and spiritual elements of karate. We'd film him watching some of the tournament scenes and he'd point out what you were seeing, serving as a fight commentator.

In some of the extra demonstration scenes he wanted to include another collection of karate notables, including Khang Rhee, and national champions Jim Kelly, Joe Lewis, and Bill Wallace. Elvis himself wrote up a scene for the end of the film, in which he'd stand on a windblown hilltop, in tight close-up, performing "The Lord's Prayer" in Native American sign language—a gesture he thought would emphasize the spirit of inclusiveness in the martial arts. As the camera panned back by way of a helicopter shot, we'd see that Elvis was not alone on the hill—he was surrounded by all kinds of masters of the arts. The large group would be spread across the hillside, filling the frame, and from our distant perspective we would see them begin to go through some precision karate forms led by Elvis. The words "The Beginning" would mark the end of the film.

The filming of the team began without a problem, but I found that it was hard to get the all-important Elvis scenes. He worked Las Vegas in August and toured in October, and when he had time off I tried to set up the shoots with him. But the period of good health he'd had after his hospitalization was slipping away, and he was often in a state of exhaustion again. He always wanted to put the shoot off a week so that he could lose five or ten pounds, though I could see he really needed to lose maybe ten or fifteen pounds. It was hard for him to step away from his draining performance schedule and give the film the attention he wanted to. Finally, on the spur of the moment one night, he arranged to have some footage of himself shot at a karate school in Memphis. The effort was well-intentioned, but the results weren't very good as either quality filmmaking or serious karate. I began to worry that if we didn't maintain some discipline and direction through the production process, the film might spin out of control. I also began to worry that too many pressures were again going to take their toll on Elvis.

Elvis was worried, too. During his hospitalization, he'd gotten off all his medications and had tried to get his body to function without the sleeping pills he'd relied on for so long. Doctors hoped that without the medications, he'd get physically tired enough to reset his body clock. It didn't happen. In the hospital, Elvis had wanted to get well. He didn't complain. He didn't ask for any pain relief or sleep medication. But he couldn't sleep. The most vivid image I have of him during that hospital stay is of him sitting on the edge of his bed, rocking back and forth, waiting and waiting for his body to let itself rest. After seventy-two hours of uncomfortable wakefulness, his body was under such stress that the doctors gave him a sedative. Since then, he'd been using medication under the watch of Dr. Nick. But both Nick and Elvis realized that in trying to keep up with the unbending demands of travel days and performances, his reliance on medications was getting out of control again.

In November, Elvis decided to try to get thin and rested using a new therapy he'd heard about—a "sleep diet" that could reset his metabolism and his sleep cycles through a three-week regimen of liquid nourishment and carefully monitored sedatives. This therapy had been created by Dr. Elias Ghanem, a Las Vegas "doctor to the stars" who had previously treated Elvis during some of his Hilton engagements. In mid-November, Elvis moved into the upstairs bedroom of Ghanem's home.

Linda Thompson and Elvis still had a strong relationship, but Linda had been smart enough to realize that she was going to need some breaks from the Elvis lifestyle. She was also very aware of the fact that when she wasn't around, Elvis might be with someone else. When Elvis came to Dr. Ghanem's house, he was accompanied by Sheila Ryan. Sheila was a shy, pretty young girl with a deceptive independent streak, and she and Elvis had become involved during his August Las Vegas run. For additional moral support, Elvis also had Charlie Hodge staying nearby at the Hilton.

I went to Dr. Ghanem's in mid-November to give Elvis what I thought was a very encouraging report on the documentary. I sat with him in his bedroom and laid out papers and checkbooks and told him what had been shot and how the production was doing. I told him we now had enough footage that it was time to take the next step—we needed a post-production facility. I'd found a space on Hollywood and Vine that would work as a business office and editing studio, and I told him what we needed to do to get in there and get working. I'd already secured the services of Bert Lovitt, a top editor who'd done some great work on *Elvis On Tour*. The movie was really happening, and contrary to all the Colonel's dismissive comments about Elvis's ability to handle business, we were sticking to our budget. Elvis was right on top of everything I was telling him, asking all the questions a sharp executive producer would and seeming satisfied with the progress that had been made on the film.

It was after midnight when we finished talking, and I told Elvis I was going to head back to the Hilton, where I was staying. But Elvis casually asked me to stick around downstairs at Dr. Ghanem's house for a while. I killed some time down there, and about a half hour later Charlie Hodge came down and told me that Elvis wanted to talk to me again.

I went into his bedroom and walked over to the side of the bed, where he was sitting up. He looked very serious and was focusing on me hard, like he was really taking note of me. Without saying anything, he handed me a piece of paper.

It was a check, for an enormous sum, made out to me. It didn't match up with any of the film budget items we'd talked about, and I thought he must have misunderstood something I told him.

"Elvis, what's this?"

"Jerry, you've been working hard for me. I'm buying you that house you've been talking about."

As comfortable as I'd been at Monovale, I'd still felt like I wanted to get my own place. And I knew I wouldn't be able to stay at Monovale much longer anyway—Elvis had let us know he intended to sell it. Rick Husky was getting ready to sell his home—a great, hillside house off Sunset Boulevard, and I'd been doing everything I could to scrape together a down payment. But banks were taking a dim view of my unusual, entertainment-industry employment record, and it didn't look like I was going to be able to make the deal. The check Elvis handed me wasn't for a down payment. It was to buy Rick's house outright. While I'd been downstairs, Elvis had called Rick—waking him up—and negotiated the deal. Elvis was buying me a house.

My hands started shaking so badly that I dropped the check.

"Elvis—this—this is too much."

He leaned forward with a smile, picked up the check, and put it back in my hands.

How many friends buy you a house? I felt more connected to Elvis than I ever had. But back at the hotel, a thought crossed my mind. The Colonel was not particularly sympathetic to matters of the heart, and it was possible he'd find a way to quash this deal and cancel out Elvis's gift, just the way he'd rendered my "Personal Public Relations" business cards useless. This gift meant enough to me, and to Elvis, that I decided to take action to prevent any possibility of the Colonel's interference. I got a security guard from the Hilton to accompany me to a bank, where I cashed the check. I then flew back to Los Angeles with a suitcase full of money. I can say from experience that when you travel with a carry-on full of cash, you don't sleep on the plane.

The deal with Rick happened quickly. He told me that in his conversation with Elvis, Elvis had asked if Rick wanted him to send some guys over to help him move out. Rick had asked, only half-jokingly, if he could finish his night's sleep there before worrying about moving. Rick did let me move in while all the paperwork was being handled, and I'd been in the house a couple of days when a housewarming party showed up. Elvis arrived with Joe Esposito, Dean Nichopoulos and Linda Thompson (he was going to spend Thanksgiving with Linda in Palm Springs).

Elvis loved the place as much as I did. Set high up on the side of a canyon, the house had a spectacular view of Hollywood and the city beyond, which Elvis said reminded him of his Hillcrest house. I enjoyed the warm conversation with everybody, and it occurred to me that for the first time in my life, I was the host and Elvis was the guest. When he and I had a moment alone out on the home's beautiful balcony, I thanked him again.

And, as he stared out at the spectacular view of the twinkling city below us, looking absolutely at home here at my new place, I thought again about something he'd told me a few days before at his house. He'd said, "You know, I drove the other guys crazy when I bought that for you. But Jerry, your mother died when you were a year old. You never had a home. I wanted to be the one to give it to you."

13

. . .

BECKET

None of us were sure whether or not Dr. Ghanem's therapy accomplished anything, but the time Elvis spent at his house gave him a chance for deep rest that he found hard to get anywhere else. In December, he checked back in with Ghanem for a second round of the sleep diet. This time it was Linda Thompson (and Charlie Hodge) who accompanied him. I flew back out in the middle of the month to give Elvis another report. But before I made that trip, I got my first unscheduled visitor at my new home. The doorbell rang, I went to answer it, and I found myself facing a mountain of muscle.

"Rick? Rick Husky?" the mountain asked.

"No. I'm a friend of his. He used to live here. It's my place now."

"Oh, sorry to bother you," the mountain said. "Just tell him Jim Brown came by."

Jim Brown, the record-setting former running back with the NFL's Cleveland Browns, had been Elvis's favorite football player. Elvis admired Brown's hard-charging running style, but what he really loved was the way Brown would get up and walk back to a huddle after he'd been tackled. Brown never ran back to a huddle—he walked like he owned the field. And no matter how hard he was taken down, he got up and walked back to his team with the same confident, unhurried strides. It was a walk I'd seen Elvis emulate time and time again in our football games. Brown had moved on from football to pursue a film career, and apparently wanted to meet with Rick Husky to discuss some kind of film or television project.

It was another one of those moments where all I could do was shake my head: I'm standing in a house Elvis Presley bought me, turning Jim

Brown from my front door. And as Brown walked away, I got to see up close and in-person that same nonchalant swagger that Elvis loved so much.

I'd been going to our film production office at Hollywood and Vine every day to work with the editors, and I was feeling confident that the karate documentary was progressing smoothly. The team that Ed Parker had put together performed incredibly well, and footage shot at tournaments in England and France looked great. I felt that the film had every chance of becoming an exciting feature documentary. What was taking shape in the office matched up very well with Elvis's vision for the project.

The Colonel had put his objections to the project in writing, pointing out that if a business plan he had designed was not strictly adhered to, he wanted to be completely absolved from any involvement with the film. So much for a manager's vote of confidence. The Colonel continued to insinuate that Elvis had no idea what he was doing getting involved in film production. But Elvis was a bright guy who had already made thirty-three films—he had picked up a thing or two about moviemaking along the way.

I flew out to Las Vegas, checked into the Hilton again, and headed over to Ghanem's house to meet with Elvis. I gave him a report on all the finances, and told him things were going well—it was another positive meeting. Elvis didn't look like he had lost any weight, but he had good color and looked healthy.

This time, after we talked, I did head straight back to the hotel and went to sleep pretty quickly. A couple hours later, I was woken up by the phone.

"Jerry." The voice sounded so weak I almost didn't recognize it.

"Elvis?"

"Can you help me?"

"What's wrong, E?"

"I can't move."

"Who's there?"

"Nobody."

I got over to Ghanem's house as fast as I could. Up in the bedroom,

Elvis was lying facedown on the floor. Linda was there, but hadn't been able to lift him up.

"Jerry, my legs won't work."

Elvis had gotten up to go to the bathroom, had fallen, and then found that he didn't have the strength or coordination to get himself back up. I picked him up and got him into bed and as comfortable as possible. His breathing was all right, and he wasn't in any pain—he just felt he couldn't control his legs. We didn't talk about calling an ambulance—we were already at a doctor's house. But we needed to get ahold of the doctor. Ghanem was out somewhere and wasn't reachable when Linda tried to call through to him.

When we were sure that Elvis wasn't in any further distress, I went downstairs to wait for Ghanem. I liked the doctor personally, but I was furious that whatever he was doing to Elvis had reduced him to this state. And when Ghanem finally showed up, after a night on the town, I tore into him, questioning him harshly about the therapy. Ghanem insisted he was treating Elvis with placebos, but I didn't believe that placebos could knock him to the floor. I yelled at the doctor until it was pretty obvious that he wasn't going to debate his idea of therapy with me. I left the doctor with these words, "This is a proud man, and I better not see him like this again or I'll go all the way."

The next morning I went back over to the house with Charlie, and I was happy to see that Elvis was feeling well enough to be up on an exercise bicycle in his room. He was also feeling well enough to be angry. He'd called out to me when he needed help, but he also hated to be found in that undignified situation. And he did not appreciate my criticism of Dr. Ghanem. He pedaled a little harder, looked over at Charlie, and said, "Goddamn it, when you guys get your medical degrees you can tell my doctors what to do." He went on and on about how unqualified we were to judge his condition, but it was always directed toward poor Charlie. Elvis was obviously aware that I had a temper, too, and he didn't want to get into a face-to-face confrontation.

A couple of hours later, when he'd calmed down, I felt I could talk to him. But I was still very conscious of how vulnerable Elvis was at this moment, and I didn't want to say anything that would embarrass him. I simply tried to put across my viewpoint as tactfully as possible: After a month's worth of treatment with Ghanem, Elvis wasn't in the shape he wanted to be in. When he'd been under Dr. Nick's care, in the hospital, he'd come out feeling strong and healthy. I suggested that he get back with Dr. Nick again.

Elvis, a guy who never had a problem spending money, shot back, "He's too damned expensive."

But a few hours later, we were out of Ghanem's house and on a plane to Memphis.

Elvis got comfortable at Graceland, where, this year, the holiday season was going to be very quiet. I wasn't sure how well my words at Dr. Ghanem's had sunk in, but I knew better than to push the matter. Elvis had grown up vulnerable—poor and unaccepted. As an artist, he was willing to make himself vulnerable on stage. Offstage, he wanted to be the guy who took care of everybody else's problem. It was almost impossible for him to admit that he had a problem. I always wanted to speak the truth to him, but I was usually careful to speak it in a way that he would actually hear, and just possibly accept. I'd said all I could say at Ghanem's. So as Elvis settled in for quiet holidays with Linda and family, I headed off to New Jersey to spend them with Myrna and her family.

Myrna lived in a poor neighborhood in Newark (members of the Elvis circle teased me that I was probably the only white guy who headed to the ghetto for a vacation). She lived in an old, three-story wood-frame house in the city with her grandmother, mother, and brother, all of whom helped her raise her son from a previous marriage (Elvis was particularly fond of her son and made him the only recipient of a specially designed kids' TCB). Myrna had an apartment up in the attic of the house—a cool, bright, comfortable place that she'd fixed up beautifully—it would have been a wonderful creative oasis in any town. And as we spent time together up there, we took advantage of the chance to open up a little further with each other, and I really got a sense of just what a creative talent Myrna was. Her vocal abilities were obvious, but she was also a fine songwriter, lyricist, and poet. She'd even written a play that had been performed in town. I'd fallen in love with a beautiful singer—now I was finding out there was a lot more to love about her.

Myrna's family was very accepting of me, and I found myself having some great conversations with her brother, John T.—a smart, talented athlete who was working as a schoolteacher and a karate instructor. I think maybe the only thing close to an awkward moment during the trip came when he and I went out for a drive around town.

I'd made it out of North Memphis, I'd survived showing up in New York City without a dollar in my pocket, I'd been at ease both in the Oval Office and the humble Hawaiian fishing village where I'd courted Sandy. So as out of place as I was, I can say that it didn't even dawn on me to feel scared of the surroundings in Newark. Parts of town were run-down, the neighborhood around Myrna's place was obviously pretty rough, and I didn't see any other white faces around. But I guess I just didn't know enough about what went on to feel threatened.

John T. and I went out for a drive, and decided we were going to pick up some White Castle hamburgers—the famously small burgers very similar to the Krystalburgers that Elvis and I enjoyed in Memphis. We parked the car, and I started to get out to head into the busy White Castle. John T. looked stricken. I suppose I should point out that at the time, I was wearing my winter coat—a white rabbit-fur jacket (not something I'd ever put on again, but it seemed pretty cool at the time).

"You can't go in there."

"What do you mean?" I asked. "I thought we were getting burgers."

He just shook his head, and probably got ready to put some of his karate to use. We went into the White Castle—I think we had to step over a few drunk guys to get in—and though we turned a few heads, nothing happened. We got our bag of burgers. If anybody in there was looking for trouble, I guess they figured a white guy in white rabbit fur buying burgers in that part of town was just too crazy to be worth messing with.

At the end of January 1975, Elvis took the step I'd been hoping for and checked himself back into Baptist Memorial Hospital. There was some fallout from this decision—for one, an engagement at the Hilton had to be postponed. Also, work on the karate film was halted and the production office was shut down. We had a great rough cut put together, but without the Colonel's support, and with Elvis's health now a primary concern, the film couldn't move forward. It was sad to see the project lose momentum, but it was more important for Elvis to get well.

Tests were done on his liver once more, and his chronic intestinal problems were monitored. Once more we treated the floor of the hospital like a Vegas suite, setting up Elvis's room the way he wanted it, which again included a bed for Linda. And once again Sonny and I took turns sleeping in a room across the hall. After the first few days Elvis was doing great, and was no longer confined to bed. It wasn't unusual to have him stroll into my hospital room as if I were the patient and he were the visitor.

The threats to Elvis's health were serious, but we shared one good laugh early in his stay when I noted the names of a couple of the staff that would be taking care of him: Nurse Marian Cocke and Nurse Kathy Seamon.

"Cocke and Seamon?" I remarked. "Elvis, what kind of hospital is this?"

As Elvis laughed, Nurse Cocke herself walked very calmly across the room, got a pitcher of ice water, and poured it down my shirt. Elvis laughed even harder. That was the beginning of a friendship between him and Marian Cocke—she'd later become his personal nurse at Graceland.

After a few days some of the new guys moved into the extra hospital room and Sonny and I left to stay at Graceland. Elvis wanted to get off his medications, but he wasn't happy about eating hospital food, so each day one of the guys—usually Al Strada—would bring a meal the Graceland cooks had put together—typically meat loaf, corn bread, and greens. Clean pajamas, favorite books, and anything else Elvis wanted in his hospital room would also be delivered. One day, Aunt Delta told me that Elvis's food was ready, but that Sonny, who had offered to make the delivery that day, was still sleeping. I said I didn't have any trouble making the run, since I was going over to the hospital anyway. In the kitchen, I picked up the big brown bag that held food containers and some pajamas. On top of all that was a small box that had come through the mail for Elvis. It had no return address, but was postmarked "Las Vegas."

"What's this?" I asked Delta.

"I don't know. I just thought Elvis might want it," she answered.

Sonny was just getting up, and I showed him the box and asked if he knew what it was. He didn't. He and I figured the best thing to do was open it up—Elvis's standing order was to open any suspicious packages. I opened it, and found, at the center of a lot of packing, one large vial of pills. This was an upsetting discovery, and I had the awful feeling of being in the middle of a no-win situation. But I didn't want to just turn this stuff over to Elvis if it was part of the problem. Instead of heading straight to the hospital, I took the pills over to Dr. Nick's office in Midtown and told him how I'd found them.

Dr. Nick said that maybe we should give whoever had sent them the benefit of the doubt—maybe a doctor was helping treat Elvis with some kind of placebo. He sent his head nurse, Tish Hensley, out to have the pills tested.

I waited in Dr. Nick's office for a while as he saw some patients. Elvis's meat loaf was getting cold, but this was a more important concern. After a while, the nurse came back with the results. The pills were not a placebo of any kind—they were a powerful narcotic. Anger and frustration flashed across Dr. Nick's face.

"Elvis is doing fine right now," he said. "But I can't get help from any of these other doctors."

I wasn't sure what to do next, but Dr. Nick had an idea how to handle the situation.

"Look, Jerry, Elvis is in a good place emotionally. Take the package to him just like it is. He may handle this well."

I got over to the hospital, and made it up to the room. Vernon and a couple of the guys were there talking with Elvis, who was in bed. I made the food delivery and showed Elvis the small, opened package.

"E, I didn't know what might be in here, so I opened it up . . ."

He knew exactly what I was showing him, and quickly spoke to his father and the others, "Would everybody excuse Jerry and me for a moment?"

I got nervous—thinking maybe he was going to explode at me. But when the others were gone, he stayed perfectly calm and smiled. "It's OK, Jerry. I just didn't want to embarrass my daddy. He has a prostate problem and that's just some medicine I got for him. Go ahead and put it in the medicine cabinet in the bathroom."

From what Nick had said, this was obviously not any kind of prostate medicine. I was worried about leaving the pills there, and checked back with the doctor as soon as I could. Dr. Nick pointed out that he was in the room at least twice a day and he knew where the pills were and how many were in the vial. If he suspected Elvis had used any, he would confront him. But days went by and the pills remained untouched. Finally, at one checkup, Dr. Nick pulled the vial from the cabinet and asked Elvis where this medicine had come from.

"I don't know," said Elvis. "Whoever was here before me must have left it there."

"Maybe I should just flush them," said Dr. Nick.

"Yeah, good idea," said Elvis. The pills were disposed of.

The incident points to what Elvis was up against. Even while he was in the hospital trying to overcome the problem, he was being sent opiates as a kind of twisted token of esteem (we never did figure out who sent the pills—Elvis had dealt with many doctors during his stays in Las Vegas). A lot of us close to Elvis wanted to do everything we could to get him well. But there were too many doctors happy to write prescriptions just so they could have some connection to Elvis Presley.

He did get healthier during the second hospital stay, and was days away from being discharged when another Presley had to be checked in. Elvis called me one afternoon from the hospital. "Jerry, I'm worried about my daddy. He's not feeling good. Would you go by and pick him up—get him over to the hospital?"

I headed over to the house behind Graceland, where Vernon now lived with Sandy Miller. Sandy, a former nurse, had called Elvis at the hospital to let him know that Vernon needed medical attention. When I walked in, Vernon was white as a ghost and obviously in tremendous pain. Sandy hadn't wanted to alarm him, but she told me how serious she thought the situation was. I spoke to Vernon.

"Mr. Presley, I don't think we should wait for an ambulance."

"I don't think so either, Jerry," he whispered.

I found myself making the same speedy drive to the hospital that I had when Priscilla went into labor with Lisa Marie. But now there was an expressway to use, and on that road, we caught a break—just as I got on the highway I was able to get behind an ambulance with its lights on and siren blaring. I stayed behind the ambulance all the way to the hospital, where the doctors told us that Vernon had suffered a major heart attack. We'd gotten him there just in time.

Once he was out of intensive care, Vernon was checked into the room next to Elvis. And I think Vernon's situation may have helped Elvis—it gave Elvis a chance to be a strong, steady caregiver, rather than just a patient. And it made clear to him, and to all of us, just how quickly the things we counted on in life might be taken away.

Out of the hospital, Elvis's spirit and energy improved a great deal. In Los Angeles, he got ready for some recording sessions and prepared for his rescheduled Vegas gig. There was one particular night that proved to me his crazy sense of humor was still intact. Through Tom Hulett, I'd become friendly with Richard Cole, who'd begun his career working with the Who and the Yardbirds and had gone on to become the tour manager for Led Zeppelin. Richard was a brash character who also happened to be brilliant at what he did. Elvis had met some of the members of Zeppelin—Jimmy Page, Robert Plant, and John Bonham—before a show at the Los Angeles Forum in 1974. But the group's bassist, John Paul Jones, had never met Elvis personally and wanted to try to set up a meeting while the group was coming through Southern California on tour.

Richard got in touch with me and made the request. Richard had been treating me very well—I'd attended a number of Zeppelin shows with him, riding in his limo and sticking around for the champagne and partying afterward. I felt I owed him something, so I said I'd check with Elvis. Elvis said it would be all right for them to come by the Monovale house.

I was there on the night of the planned meeting, and was a little surprised to see that Elvis was in pajamas and robe—he and Sheila Ryan were getting ready to go upstairs. I reminded him that Richard and John were coming by, and that all he had to do was stick around to say say hello. "If they're waiting on me they're backing up," he grumbled. He didn't look happy about the prospect of visitors, but he stayed downstairs.

Richard and John showed up a little later, and things did not get off to a good start. The band had played a show in San Diego that night, and Richard, who was actually more eccentric than any of the band members, was pumped up with post-show energy. From the moment he stepped into the house, he was loud and profane—packing an amazing number of f-words into everything he said.

"You know," Elvis said to him. "I'd appreciate it if you'd watch your language in front of my lady."

Things got very quiet. Everybody sat down. And it stayed quiet. Then Elvis decided to break the ice, and asked if he could see the fancy watch that Richard was wearing. Richard handed the watch over, and when Elvis put it on, Richard quickly said that if Elvis wanted the watch, he could keep it.

"Does it have any special meaning to you?" Elvis asked.

"Well, a bit. Atlantic Records gave them to the group," said Richard.

"OK, thanks," said Elvis.

I don't know if Richard expected to lose his watch that easily, but about twenty minutes later Elvis went upstairs and came back down with another watch, a real piece of jewelry, covered in diamonds—a wristwatch you could trade in for a car. Maybe a couple of cars. "Here," he said to Richard. "Take this one." A very stunned Richard accepted.

From then on the night was nothing but fun, with a lot of laughs and a lot of quoting *Monty Python* routines (Elvis was the first *Monty Python* fanatic I ever knew). Elvis and Richard obviously shared a sense of humor. And I could tell Elvis also liked the much quieter John. At one point, Elvis excused himself, went back upstairs, and returned with an equally impressive watch for the bassist.

Before the evening was over, Elvis said he wanted to make another exchange. He was out of watches, but had another bit of fashion in mind. So he stood, eyed John, and said, "Let's swap pants," while simultaneously, in expert Python fashion, letting his pajama bottoms drop beneath his robe. The loud Richard was shocked into silence, while quiet Sheila and John burst out laughing. Nobody accepted Elvis's offer, but it was a great note to end the night on.

At the end of a previous Hilton engagement, a group of us had gone with Elvis to see a Barbra Streisand concert at one of the other hotels. We went backstage after the show, and I was standing with Elvis when Barbra asked him what he thought of what he'd seen. He told her that it was a great show, and a great performance, but that she did too much with her hands—her gestures sometimes covered her face and distracted from her voice. Maybe it was meant as some helpful performer-to-performer advice, but I assumed that was the last time we'd ever see Barbra Streisand.

It wasn't. On the next-to-last night of the March '75 Hilton run, during the midnight show, the maître d' informed us that Barbra was in the audience and wanted to come backstage after the show to see Elvis. She was with her boyfriend, Jon Peters, who had previously been her hairstylist, and the two indicated that they had something serious to discuss with Elvis. People were coming and going from Elvis's dressing room, so for some privacy, Elvis, Joe, Barbra, Jon, and I all moved into the room's walk-in closet and sat on the floor there. Barbra began to pitch Elvis.

Streisand had become a film star with roles in movies such as *Funny Girl*, *Hello Dolly!*, and *What's Up, Doc?* and she'd become a true Hollywood power after the success of *The Way We Were* in 1973. Now she was looking to executive-produce her own film, in which she'd also star, and she had a project in mind: She wanted to redo the dramatic Hollywood tale *A Star Is Born*. The film had been originally made in 1937, starring Janet Gaynor, and again in 1954, starring Judy Garland. The film's female lead character climbs the slippery ladder of Hollywood success while her husband, a former star, sees his career head in the other direction and proceeds to drink himself into oblivion. In the original, the husband's character, Norman Maine, had been played by Frederic March, and in the Garland version it was played by James Mason. For Streisand's version, the story would be set in the world of rock and roll rather than in Hollywood. And when Streisand stepped into the lead role, she wanted Elvis as her Norman Maine.

When we all first sat and Barbra started talking, Elvis was simply attentive and courteous, willing to hear out whatever she had to say. But as he got ahold of what she was offering him, he got very excited. So many years earlier, when Elvis was making all those films for producer Hal Wallis at Paramount, he screened a movie at the Memphian one night that he fell in love with—*Becket* starring Richard Burton. That film was also produced by Hal Wallis, in between Wallis's work on the

Elvis films *Fun in Acapulco* and *Roustabout*. Elvis realized that the profits of all his "little," "unimportant" films were what allowed Wallis and the studio to make an artistic picture like the Burton film. So the next time Elvis was on a set, he approached the producer and asked, "Mr. Wallis, when do I get my *Becket*?" He never got an answer.

But here was his shot. A top star and proven film talent understood what Elvis was capable of as an actor, and she was offering him the role of a lifetime. He and Streisand talked about the old films, how things would change in the new film, other ideas for casting, ideas for particular scenes. Elvis was thrilled with the character of Norman—for once he would not have to play the attractive nice guy. He'd be playing a textured tragic character. Food was ordered and brought into the closet so that the talk could continue uninterrupted. And I almost choked with surprise on whatever I was eating when I heard Elvis make the comparison he had dismissed just months before: "You know," he said, "this could be like *From Here to Eternity* for me."

The only catch was Streisand's choice of producer. She wanted Peters, a completely unproven talent, to handle the role. She assured Elvis that Peters had the vision and skills for the job, and said she now had enough weight with the studios to insist on his participation. Elvis had never been much of a meeting guy, but sitting in that closet, he had one of the most focused, constructive meetings of his life. By the time we were saying good-bye to Streisand and Peters, Elvis's eyes were just about blazing with the excitement of this new opportunity.

Once they'd gone, Elvis, Joe, and I hung out in the dressing room, where Sonny and Red were still on security duty. Elvis let them know what he'd been offered and how good it sounded to him. I was truly thrilled for him. But I'd just seen another dream—our karate film—fall apart largely because the Colonel had been allowed to undermine the project at a time when Elvis wasn't well enough to fight for it. In all their years together, the Colonel never directly told Elvis he couldn't do something, and whenever Elvis really stood up to the Colonel, Elvis won. But the Colonel could win a slow war, making a simple demand look so complicated that eventually Elvis didn't see any upside in the fight. It had happened with the karate film. It had happened with the overseas touring. I didn't want it to happen this time. If Elvis thought this Streisand film was worth fighting for, I wanted him to be ready for the fight.

"You know, Elvis, the problem with this is that this guy Peters hasn't produced anything before."

"Well that's not a problem. Barbra and I are gonna do what we're gonna do anyway."

"Well, that's what I'm afraid of," I heard myself saying. That line changed the mood of the night.

Elvis got very angry. He was angry at me, but I think he was also angry because he, too, knew what kind of battle was coming. In that little closet, anything seemed possible. But once Elvis left the dressing room and brought this opportunity out into the light of day, he was going to run into the same old resistance from the Colonel. Elvis knew it better than I did. My comments just made that reality set in a little faster.

And when I think back to that night, it's the one time I wish I could take back something I said to Elvis and do it over. I wanted to support him—in my heart I did support him. This was a fight I wanted him to win. But it didn't happen.

The Colonel was predictably outraged that deal-making had been done behind his back, in a dressing-room closet of all places. He was not happy about people getting to Elvis without going through him. As a manager, this was an understandable concern that came not only from self-interest, but also from his responsibility to protect his client. But this was a case of a top talent approaching another top talent. They didn't need to be protected from each other—they wanted to do something powerful and creative together. The Colonel's old-school sensibility didn't give much weight to the creative, though. Aside from Elvis, talent was talent, a deal was a deal, and there was a right way for business to be done.

Over the following weeks, the Colonel played some of the toughest hardball of his career. He insisted that Elvis could not participate in the film unless he was billed over Streisand, and demanded double what was being offered as Elvis's fee, plus half of all the film's back-end profits and all kinds of creative approval. Streisand's people tried to negotiate in good faith, but eventually had no choice but to give up.

When the film came out the following year, it won an Oscar for Best Original Song and picked up three other Oscar nominations. Kris Kristofferson won a Best Actor Golden Globe for his portrayal of Norman Maine.

This was the last time Elvis let himself fill with hope about a chance to stretch artistically. When that hope curdled, Elvis knew: He was never going to get his *Becket*. And after this incident, one of the saddest truths of Elvis's career was crystal clear to me: The pills he took were only Band-Aids. What was sucking the life out of Elvis Presley was creative disappointment.

14

. . .

GOOD LUCK EMERALD

"Who the hell's limousine is that?"

"I think it's probably Eric's, E."

"Who's Eric?"

"Eric Clapton. You said he could come by to say hello, remember?"

"Yeah. That's OK. Just don't need the damn limousine parked in front of the theater."

Elvis didn't normally have anything against limousines, but at the moment he was at the wheel of a pickup truck, wearing boots and cowboy hat, and feeling a little more down home than usual. After a spring and summer of heavy touring, Elvis was back in Memphis for a while, and Myrna and I were back there with him. We'd gone for a ride down across the Mississippi state line so that Elvis could show Myrna some of the old Circle G Ranch land, and we headed back up to the General Cinema to screen a movie at midnight (*Jaws*, *Godfather II*, and especially *Monty Python and the Holy Grail* were Elvis favorites at the time).

About a week before, I was at Graceland when I received another call from Richard Cole. This time he was on tour with Clapton, who'd become a huge American concert draw with his number-one hit "I Shot the Sheriff." Eric had a big show scheduled at the Liberty Bowl in Memphis, and was going to come to town a day early if he could meet Elvis. There had been less and less entertaining at the house over the last few years, and I knew Elvis would not want to have somebody visit him there. We'd been going to the movies a lot, though, and I thought maybe Eric could say hello to Elvis at the theater. But the theater was also a place where Elvis wanted some privacy, and he didn't like the look of that great big limo in front of the place. I worried for a moment that the sight of the car might darken Elvis's mood and sour the meeting with the guitarist. But when I introduced the two inside, Clapton was the perfect British gentleman, and it was clear from the start how much respect he had for Elvis. Elvis became a relaxed and charming host, and he and Clapton fell right into a friendly conversation. The more they talked, the more Clapton looked like he was having a life's dream come true. And it struck me again how much Elvis meant, not just to his audience, but to fellow musicians. For some time, it hadn't been unusual for Elvis's records and concerts to be treated harshly by the press. His own ambitions and desires for his career were being left unfulfilled. But here was Clapton—a superstar still on the rise—wanting nothing more than a chance to talk with Elvis.

The two got along well enough that Elvis asked Eric and his girlfriend Patti (George Harrison's ex-wife) to stay and watch that night's movie. The couple gladly accepted the invitation. As everybody took their seats, Elvis asked me to come with him to the bathroom.

"You know, Jerry," he said to me when we were alone, "that Eric is all right."

The next morning, I heard from Richard Cole again. Eric wanted Myrna and me to be his guests at the concert, and would come by in his limo to pick us up before the show. Most times, if you introduced someone to Elvis, they sort of forgot about whoever it was that made the connection for them, which was to be expected. But Eric was gracious and thoughtful enough to want to return the favor I'd done for him.

He came by early in the afternoon, and we had a chance to get to know him a little better on the ride to the stadium. Once we got to the Liberty Bowl's backstage area, Myrna and I received all our passes and credentials, and when Eric went off to get ready for the show, Myrna and I decided to go out into the stadium itself just to soak up the atmosphere. Elvis played some big arenas, but they were always indoor shows. I was fascinated by the different feel of a daylight, outdoor concert setup, and took some mental notes about how the whole event was put together. When it seemed like it was about time for the show to start, we started to head backstage again.

And ran into trouble. A huge Memphis policeman manning the

backstage access said we couldn't come through. I showed him our VIP passes, but that didn't seem to make a difference. He just told us again he wouldn't let us through. I told him we'd come to the show in Eric Clapton's limousine, but he still wouldn't let us through. Then I realized what the problem was. It was obvious that Myrna and I were a couple. A white man and a black woman. That was the problem.

For a moment, I was completely at a loss. Myrna and I had been together in cities all over the country and hadn't had any trouble. We'd been in Memphis many times before and hadn't had any trouble. But this time, back in my own hometown, I could feel it: This big policeman hated us on sight. I could tell by the way he looked at us. I'd grown up seeing that look, but I'd never been on the receiving end of that look before.

"Hey, Jerry, how's it going?" Behind us was a Memphis police captain I'd gotten friendly with when he helped set up security details for Elvis. The captain understood exactly what was going on. Our laminates may not have meant anything to the big policeman in front of us, but he wasn't going to hassle us if his superior officer knew me well enough to say hello. He stepped aside, and we walked through.

The show was great, and we heard some of the finest guitar playing we'd ever witnessed. We didn't let the isolated ugly encounter at the gate ruin our day. But it did strike me as a little ironic that because I had an in with the police captain, I got to listen to Eric Clapton sing "I Shot the Sheriff."

I never got the opportunity to co-executive-produce the karate film to completion, but by the middle of 1975 another career opportunity had presented itself to me. The Sweet Inspirations were spending most of their time working with Elvis, but they also had a career of their own. Before joining Elvis, they were one of the most in-demand studio vocal groups in the business, working with everyone from Wilson Pickett to Van Morrison, and in 1968 they'd had a Top 20 single of their own titled "Sweet Inspiration." Now, they performed under their own billing as an opening act at Elvis shows, and sometimes made their own appearances. They also recorded and performed with Aretha Franklin, and were just finishing their own David Porter–produced album for the

Stax label. They had tremendous past credits, and a very promising future. What they didn't have was a manager.

I'd never managed, but being so close to Elvis and the Colonel for so many years was really a kind of master class in the do's and don'ts of the manager/artist relationship. I'd been spending nights listening to Elvis pour his heart out about his creative frustrations, and during the day I was watching the Colonel take care of the business end of things. From those two experiences I'd already developed a management philosophy: Business concerns could not trump creativity, and creativity couldn't completely disregard business concerns. The two had to overlap at least a little bit to move an artist's career forward, but if the management side and the creative side couldn't communicate, a career could be destroyed.

Myrna had been handling business for the group, and doing a good job of it. But Sylvia and Estelle suggested bringing me on as manager, and Myrna agreed that it was a good idea. I liked the idea of doing work that would keep me close to Elvis as a friend, but would give me some satisfaction of having my own career. What I suggested to the group was this—since they'd already worked out all their deals with Elvis, I wouldn't have anything to do with that side of their business, and obviously wouldn't take the usual manager's cut of whatever money they made through those deals. I'd earn money only on deals made as we moved forward. I was still an Elvis guy, but the Sweet Inspirations became the first act signed to a brand-new company: Jerry Schilling Management.

There were nights on the road when Elvis was still every bit the master entertainer. But there were other times when you could sense just how tired he'd become of night after night of one-night stands, and when you could see what a toll it had taken on him. His stage jumpsuits had originally been designed to accommodate his intensely physical performances—the way he moved on stage he'd rip regular clothing to shreds. But now his jumpsuits were designed to mask his heavier frame. As he got bigger, so did the cut of the suits and the size of the belts he wore. We guys had once jokingly had an "Over 200" Club—membership was based on our ability to work up a belly when we were back in Memphis between films. Now there wasn't anything funny about Elvis's battle to keep himself in shape.

Though his big hopes for his movie career had been crushed with the fizzling of *A Star Is Born*, in the fall of 1975 he made a move that showed he still wanted to change the routine: He bought a plane. To be exact, he bought an out-of-service Convair 880 jet that had previously belonged to Delta Airlines. But this wasn't just an impulse purchase of some sort of ultimate flying Cadillac. Elvis thought that if he had his own plane with his own crew, he had a better chance of making that overseas tour happen. I know that's what he was thinking, because before that Convair was purchased, Vernon and I had made a trip to New Jersey to look at an available Boeing 707. The plane was in great mechanical shape, and had already been customized to include personal quarters, a meeting area, and even a dance floor. But the previous owner had been Robert Vesco, the fugitive financier who had fled to South America after allegedly embezzling hundreds of millions of dollars from international investment firms. Buying his plane would involve some complicated wrangling with the IRS. And Elvis was warned about another complication: If the plane ever landed in any of the countries Vesco was establishing a base in, there was every reason to believe that he might try to seize it. On the other hand, the Convair had a clean record and would have no problem flying to any country around the globe. So that's the plane Elvis purchased. He immediately rechristened it the *Lisa Marie*.

The plane was in a hangar at Meacham Field in Fort Worth, and for months Elvis took great pleasure in flying friends—including Priscilla—out to Texas to check on progress as the interior of the plane was refurbished to his very specific design requirements (he bought another plane to make those trips—a smaller Lockheed JetStar). Elvis wanted a seating area, a conference room, and a private bedroom on the plane (with space for an in-flight reading library). He picked fabrics, decided on color schemes, chose the onboard audio-visual system, and even OK'd the gold fixtures in the bathrooms (he counted heavily on some aesthetic input from Priscilla, too). He was especially excited about the fact that the same design team working on the *Lisa Marie* had previously customized *Air Force One*. Every trip out, he'd proudly walk a group of us through the plane, and he'd take Polaroid pictures so he could check the progress of the renovation. The craft slowly came together as an airworthy mix of modern function and Graceland elegance. When the final paint job was applied to the exterior, there was a prominent "TCB" logo on the tail.

The Christmas season in 1975 was not the usual family event at Graceland. Priscilla and Lisa Marie were in Los Angeles. Myrna had gone back to Newark. On Christmas Eve, Elvis and I were sitting alone up in his bedroom, while a mix of friends and visitors waited down in the living room. I could see that he just didn't have any excitement for the occasion.

"You know, I really don't want to go down there this year."

"Then don't, E. You don't have to."

It would be the first time Elvis didn't make an appearance downstairs to at least go through the routine of a gift exchange with the guys. He was simply not feeling in much of a Christmas mood, and didn't want to deal with a holiday party. So we just sat and talked for a while. Around ten o'clock he said, "You know, I want to get something for Grandma. Why don't you call Harry Levitch and see if he can come up."

Harry, Elvis's longtime Memphis jeweler, was used to being on call for Elvis's holiday purchases, and he arrived at the house shortly with a wide selection of items. Elvis picked out something for his grandma, then decided he'd get something for Vernon, too, picking out a ring for his father. I made out the check for Harry, and then Elvis had a private moment with the jeweler to thank him. After Levitch left, Elvis and I were alone again.

Elvis sat down on the edge of his bed and said, "I want to read you something, Jerry." He picked up his well-worn copy of *Cheiro's Book of Numbers*. Over the last couple of years, he'd returned to his interest in all forms of spirituality. He was reading *The Impersonal Life* and *Autobiography of a Yogi* again. He'd been in touch with Daya Mata at the Self-Realization Fellowship. He had even, much to the Colonel's dismay, resumed a friendship with Larry Geller, who was now often on the road with us.

With a favorite work like the *Book of Numbers*, Elvis didn't just read it once or twice and move on. If the work grabbed his imagination, he went back to it again and again, scribbling notes to himself on the pages and marking off significant passages. Now he flipped open the book to a page he'd marked. "You're a number six, Jerry. You know what that means?"

"No, E."

He began reading. " 'They are very determined in carrying out their plans, and may, in fact, be deemed obstinate and unyielding, except when they themselves become deeply attached: in such a case, they become devoted to those they love. When roused by anger they will brook no opposition and will fight to the death for whatever person or cause they espouse. But the Number 6 people have got the power of making more friends than almost any other class, and they lean to the romantic and ideal in all matters of affection.' That sound like you, Jerry?"

"That's dead-on," I laughed.

"There's one more thing. It says a number six should always have an emerald close to his skin for good luck." He closed the book, laid it on the bed, and reached into his pocket. He produced a beautifully detailed ring with a carved emerald set in it. He reached out, took my hand, and slid the ring on.

"I want you to have plenty of good luck, Jerry."

I thanked him, but it hardly seemed enough. Even when I was so worried about him, he was still giving so much to me.

"What does it say about your number, E?"

He picked the book back up and flipped it open. He began reading. " 'Number 8's have deep and very intense natures, great strength of individuality; they generally play some important role on life's stage, but usually one which is fatalistic, or as the instrument of Fate for others . . . They often appear cold and undemonstrative, though in reality they have warm hearts towards the oppressed of all classes; but they hide their feelings and allow people to think just what they please.

" 'All persons who have the Number 8 clearly associated with their lives feel that they are distinct and different from their fellows. At heart they are lonely; they are misunderstood, and they seldom reap the reward for the good they may do while they are living. After their death they are often extolled, their works praised, and lasting tributes offered to their memory.' "

He put the book back down. We sat quietly for a moment. He smiled a bit. "Merry Christmas, Six."

"Merry Christmas, Eight," I answered.

Elvis had always taken a break from performing during the weeks between Christmas and his birthday, but this year the Colonel squeezed in a New Year's Eve show at the huge Silverdome in Pontiac, Michigan. The show drew a huge crowd and was a financial success, but it was not a good experience for Elvis. The freezing weather had everyone shivering through the night, and the situation was made worse by a two-tiered stage setup that had Elvis separated from the band. At showtime, Joe, Dick Grob, and I walked Elvis to the upper platform of the stage, and I could tell right away that he was very uncomfortable—the spontaneity of his shows depended on direct contact with the band, and up here that would be impossible. He met the challenge and put out a great effort that night, but the sound system in the domed stadium functioned so poorly that, at midnight, many of the 60,000 fans turned their attention from the stage and treated the event as their own large-scale New Year's Eve party.

Elvis was extremely agitated about the show afterward and thought it was a lousy way to start the year. But in Memphis, a couple of days later, he came up with an idea that he thought would get the year started right: a big, group vacation ski trip to Vail, Colorado.

The impulse was wonderful, but the vacation was far from relaxing. After a two-week December run at the Hilton, the not-so-festive Christmas, the New Year's in Michigan, and a quick flight back to Memphis, the group around Elvis was feeling a little ragged. Whipping together a ski vacation on the spur of the moment felt more like work than time off—especially since our group of Memphis boys didn't have a single skier in it. And there were some tensions and differences emerging between the older guys and the newer guys—differences that mainly centered on whether you considered Elvis a friend who was also your employer, or whether you simply considered him an unpredictable boss. The Memphis Mafia had once prided itself on our "us against the world" spirit, but now the differences in lifestyle and attitude among us made it increasingly harder to pull together as a group.

We flew out of Memphis—Elvis and Linda Thompson, Myrna and myself, Joe and girlfriend Shirley Dieu, Billy Smith, Sonny and Red, Lamar, Dean Nichopoulos, Al Strada, and several others. As it was already the height of the holiday season, we all holed up in a Denver hotel while Joe Esposito took on the almost impossible task of lining up accommodations—we needed a house for Elvis, and condos for everybody else. Not so surprisingly, Joe got the job done.

In Vail, Elvis settled in to a large house right by one of the ski lifts. After three days in a hotel, he wanted to get out on the slopes that night and have some fun, and we all joined him. But it looked to me that the work of getting the arrangements together had exhausted Joe—the last thing he was interested in was night skiing. He stayed in to catch up on sleep.

One of the first full days in Vail was January 8, Elvis's forty-first birthday, but Elvis let it be known he didn't want to celebrate it at all. That seemed to be fine by everyone else—we all split up and settled into our own separate condos. But that night, Linda called over to my place—Elvis was feeling down. Did Myrna and I want to come over?

We joined Elvis and Linda, and before long it felt like we were all having the kind of vacation fun Elvis had been after. He seemed really pleased to have Myrna and me with him, and we just stayed in and had a simple, friendly celebration. Linda even made a little cake for Elvis. But the evening had, literally, a dramatic ending. We began to talk about favorite movies, and Elvis asked Myrna if she'd ever seen one of his recently rediscovered favorites, *Across 110th Street*, a gritty New York City Mafia flick starring Anthony Quinn, Yaphet Kotto, and Tony Franciosa. Myrna hadn't seen it. And so Elvis acted it out for her. I don't mean he told her the story and quoted a few lines of dialogue. He began to act out the whole movie, setting up each scene and then presenting just about every line of dialogue in the script. He brought each character to life with walks, vocal mannerisms, and the subtlest of gestures.

It was a bravura performance, and Elvis drew upon that photographic memory of his, the talent for voices that had always made his *Dr. Strangelove* and *Monty Python* reenactments so funny, and the intense physical movements of his stage performances. Elvis loved *110th St.*'s story of mob betrayal and revenge, but he was also taken with smaller elements of the film—the kind of perfect details he was so good at focusing on. Tony Franciosa had a way of stroking his chin in a subtly menacing fashion—Elvis had the move down cold. And Yaphet Kotto barely raised his rumble of a voice above a whisper in the film, which Elvis perfectly mimicked.

It was great to see him up and excited, and a thrill to be his private audience. Linda, Myrna, and I would have been happy to just sit and talk with Elvis, the way the evening had started. But Elvis didn't stop until he got to the final scene of the film, which took us into the very early hours of the morning. I'd seen the film with him two or three times in Memphis, but I had to admit—this was the version I enjoyed the most.

Everybody started to have a good time over the next week. Guys, wives, and girlfriends did get out on the slopes, and though Elvis never put skis on, he insisted that everybody else take lessons. At the end of the day, when the slopes were closed to the public, Elvis would appear, bundled up in his snow gear, and we'd go snowmobiling or ride inner tubes down the bottom of the runs. There were times when the fun seemed a little forced and there were times when the fun got dangerous— riding inner tubes down dark sections of the slopes was an easy way to get hurt, and one night we had to take Dean Nichopoulos to the emergency room with a broken foot. We took some forbidden nighttime snowmobile runs across the slopes, and one night Lamar, taking an uncharted path through the woods, rode his snowmobile over the deep, soft snow that had piled over a building foundation. He sunk down well over his head, and probably would have been there until the spring thaw if Elvis hadn't found him and pulled him out.

Off the slopes, Elvis spent a lot of time with Ron Pietrafeso and Jerry Kennedy, Denver policemen he'd met on past trips to the city. They had always been supportive of Elvis, even welcoming him into their own inner circle of police officers, and during this trip, Elvis bought them Cadillacs as thank-you gifts.

After two weeks in Vail, we were all thoroughly exhausted—I think everybody needed a vacation from our vacation, and, probably more importantly, needed some private time before our next tour began in March. Lack of sleep had become a terrible problem for Elvis. As much as his body needed rest, he just couldn't get it, and he was often in a state of almost manic energy. Trying to keep up with him put a lot of pressure on an already fractured group. The physical activity of the ski trip hadn't seemed to do anything to diminish Elvis's restlessness. And the fact that his vacation idea had actually worked out pretty well didn't seem to give him any satisfaction. If two weeks in Vail was good, wouldn't a few more days be better? Elvis wanted arrangements made so that we could all continue to stay on the slopes. The rentals that Joe had worked out were up, and Joe himself had already headed back to California with Shirley. Myrna had also left, flying back home to Newark. Elvis wanted me to take on the job of finding a whole new round of condos for the group.

Now I was the one who had to stay up for a day and a half, doing everything I could to get some available condos to materialize, and figuring out who would go where and how everybody would be moved around. Somehow, I got it done, and the arrangements were made. I'd found a house for Elvis and had extended the rental period on one of the nicer condos that he had also been using (he and Linda had been switching between the house by the lift and this condo). The place I'd been staying at with Myrna was gone, so I moved my stuff to Elvis's condo and went to sleep in the master suite.

The phone rang at three in the morning. It was Billy Smith. He told me that Elvis was coming over. Elvis wanted to move from his house to his condo. And he wanted me to move out of the condo to the house. I couldn't imagine why we had to make this switch at three in the morning. And I was tired enough that I didn't really feel like moving anywhere. The condo had the master suite and two smaller bedrooms, one of which wasn't much more than a closet. I moved my stuff into that smallest bedroom, figuring I'd be well out of the way if Elvis wanted to take over the master bedroom.

I fell asleep again, but was woken up once more by Elvis's voice: "I thought you were asked to move back to the house."

I was tired enough to be in a rotten mood. Instead of being shown any appreciation for making the moves happen, I was getting moved around some more.

"You've got the suite, Elvis."

"Yeah, but I need Red and Billy to stay here."

There was an ugly edge in his voice, a dismissive tone—like I was just another one of his problems. He was talking to me as if I were one of the new guys in the group. One of the guys who called him "Boss."

"Damn it, Elvis, I've been up two days working all this out. I need to sleep."

He didn't answer. He stormed off into the master bedroom, and I heard him yelling with Red. Then he came back to the room I was in, said loudly, "All right," then mumbled, "You can stay."

Something ripped inside me. "You know what, E—I don't want to stay here," I shouted. "In fact, I'm leaving."

"I said you could stay, damn it."

I looked at him. He'd been acting like someone I didn't know. But I could also tell he knew he had pushed me too far. I was so tired. Maybe he was tired, too. Everybody around us was worn down. It was time to go.

"No, E. I'm going to leave. I'm going home."

I moved over to the house, where Dean Nichopoulos had been staying with Elvis, and spent the night there. In the morning, I heard the phone ring. Dean came by my room to let me know that Elvis was on the line for me.

"Hello?"

"Jerry, how's it coming with those condos?"

He wasn't being sarcastic, or pretending that nothing had happened. He didn't know anything had happened. The night before was a complete blank to him.

"Elvis, I've always said our friendship is more important to me than this job."

"What are you talking about?"

I didn't want to get into it again, but I told him I was going back to L.A. "Look, Elvis, I just need a change. No hard feelings."

He seemed a little surprised, but accepted it. "Well, I guess you have to do what you have to do," he said.

Maybe it would have been just as easy for me to pretend that the night before hadn't happened. But it had, and even in the cold light of the morning after, it felt right to follow through on my decision. I didn't see any way to balance our friendship with the way things were working around him now. If I stayed, I felt I'd end up with no choice but to become either a complete yes-man or a pain in the ass. I didn't want to be either one to him. If Elvis and I had any chance of remaining true friends, I had to get out of there.

I'd enjoyed the managing I'd been doing for the Sweet Inspirations, and thought maybe I could pursue that work further. I got in touch with Tom Hulett and asked if he had any contacts that might help me learn more about the management side of the concert business. Tom was still promoting Elvis's shows, and he told me that before he set anything up for me he'd have to check with Elvis. At the time, all I knew was that Elvis told Tom he didn't have a problem with Tom helping me. Years later, Tom would reveal that Elvis told him he was willing to pay half my salary if it would help me get a better position.

Tom set up a meeting for me with Caribou Management, a firm founded by musician Jimmy Guercio (no relation to Joe) that was having success with acts such as Chicago and the Beach Boys. I got a meeting with some Caribou executives, Howard Kaufman and Larry Fitzgerald, over at the firm's Melrose offices. They had somebody else they wanted me to meet—a young, smart woman from New York. She sounded very savvy about the music business, and began asking me what sounded like job interview questions in a kind of roundabout way. I suddenly figured out what she was getting at.

"Are you asking me if I'd have any trouble working for a woman?"

She smiled. "Yes, that's exactly what I'm asking you."

"I don't have any problem with that."

"All right, then. You're working for me. We're flying to Colorado tonight."

I'd just been hired by Elizabeth Joel to be a tour manager for her husband, Billy. Billy Joel had already found some radio success with "Piano Man" and "Captain Jack," but his career had hit a lull. He decided that the best way to move forward was to build from the ground up again, touring small venues with his own kick-ass band. Billy and his musicians had based themselves at Jim Guercio's Caribou Ranch, a live-in, state-of-the-art recording facility set in some beautiful foothills of the Rocky Mountains, where they were just finishing up work on the *Turnstiles* album.

My first night at the ranch, the most important job I was trusted with was to shuck the oysters the musicians would have for dinner. But I hit it off with the guys, and got along with Billy right away, though our respective North Memphis and Long Island figures of speech sometimes confused the heck out of each other. He played up the tough-guy side of his personality, but you knew right away you were dealing with not only an exceptional musical talent but a very smart guy. After the ranch, we headed to New York City, where Billy began to put his touring show together. I got some precious office space—half a table in the back room of Billy and Elizabeth's apartment—and became very involved in the process of finalizing an East Coast tour. I spent many nights getting to know Billy better down at JP's Tavern, and I have to give the piano man credit for turning me on to a pleasure I hadn't sampled in all my years with Elvis: I never had a martini until Billy Joel ordered one for me.

I was able to see Myrna before she went on the road again with Elvis. But he and I hadn't spoken yet. I was worried about him, but I was also extremely busy with my new work, which seemed to present a hundred new details and difficulties every day. We launched Billy's tour in the spring, piling Billy, the band, and all the gear into one big temperamental bus and heading out for college towns and a number of important showcase clubs (such as the Bottom Line in NYC, the Cellar Door in Washington, D.C., and the Ritz in Memphis). It should have been a rough transition for me, after all those years of chartered planes, penthouse suites, and unlimited room service. Now we were sleeping on couches and hoping we had enough money to get fries with our burgers. I loved every minute of it.

By the time I'd signed on with Elvis, he was already an established star. Touring with Billy, I could feel the buzz and excitement building show by show—maybe something close to what Elvis felt in those earliest days with Scotty Moore and Bill Black. At soundcheck, our touring soundman, Brian Ruggles, would get the band's sound dialed in just right, and Billy's lighting designer, Steve Cohen, would work out some way to get the most theatrical impact out of a venue's system. At showtime, I'd watch Billy and the band win over a crowd song by song, working up the emotions with some of the gentler ballads, and then providing some rock-and-roll release on the tunes powered by Liberty DeVito's rock-steady drumbeats and Richie Cannata's wailing sax. In a way the applause at the end of the night felt like it was for Billy, the band, and the rest of us, too. We were all part of the same hardworking team.

Billy enjoyed just about every show he played, but there were certain kinds of gigs that he came to hate—the shows where he was an opening act for a bigger group. One night, he opened for the Beach Boys, another Caribou act, at the open-air Pine Knob Theater in Detroit. I watched from the side of the stage as Billy tried to get into the first few songs, but he got upset as he realized he basically had no crowd to play to—the people were still finding their seats or lining up at the concession stands. He tried to keep it interesting, making faces, singing in different voices, playing all sorts of crazy runs on the piano. None of it mattered much, though. Nobody was listening. I felt bad for Billy— I'd quickly become a fan as well as an employee, and I knew how much his songs depended on an emotional connection with the audience. Much later that night, he came to my hotel room looking very distraught, and swore that he would never be an opening act again.

The show hadn't been without its benefits for me, though. I enjoyed having the chance to watch how the tour organization of the bigger group worked. The Beach Boys hadn't ever made much of an impression on me. Compared to the R & B stuff I grew up listening to, their music seemed light and easily dismissed. "Help Me, Rhonda" was no "Roll with Me, Henry," and I much preferred "Don't Be Cruel" to "Be True to Your School." But there was no denying the connection they had with their fans, and I was greatly impressed with the smooth way the band's support staff managed the show. I met their tour manager, Rick Nelson (not the singer), and talked with him a bit after the show, when we had to settle up payment for Billy. We said we might get in touch again when we were both in L.A. at the same time.

The last show of Billy's tour at the Cellar in D.C. was one of the great ones, with Billy headlining and playing encore after encore for an enthusiastic house. But I had another reason for considering our stop there an important one: Elvis was in town. He had a show at the Capital Centre Arena in Landover, Maryland, a day after our show, and I called Joe Esposito and asked if I could come see Elvis. Joe made the arrangements.

I was waiting in the backstage area of the arena when the bus bringing Elvis to the show pulled in, uncharacteristically running late. As I waited for those bus doors to open, I realized just how eager I was to see him, but how nervous I was, too; it had been six months since I'd walked away—was he seeing me just as a courtesy, or, like me, did he really miss an old friend? The worries melted away as soon as he stepped off the bus steps and looked my way. Before we could even get hellos out, we were in a big hug, and that's all it took to sweep Vail away. As we talked on the way to his dressing area, he seemed up and sharp and strong. We had only a few minutes before showtime, but he didn't try to rush things between us. In fact, when somebody stuck their head in the room and told Elvis that a top-name rocker was still waiting to see him, Elvis made it clear that the rocker would have to wait. Elvis would say hello to Elton John when he was done talking to Jerry Schilling.

The show itself was a good one. It was exciting to see the band working away and Elvis knocking out another audience. There were still a few of the old faces around Elvis—Joe, Red, Sonny, Rick, and David Stanley—but there were newer ones, too: Dave Hebler, the karate instructor Elvis had met through Ed Parker, and Linda Thompson's brother, Sam, an ex-deputy sheriff from Memphis, were also working steadily for Elvis now.

I went back with Elvis to his hotel suite later, and at one point played a tape of a Billy Joel song for him that I thought would give him a good idea of Billy's talents as a songwriter. The song was "You're My Home," from Billy's first album. I'd thought the song was strong, but now, as Elvis and I listened together, I felt like it was putting into words things that I could have never said to my friend.

> *Well I never had a place to call my very own . . .*
> *That's all right . . . 'cause you're my home.*

I could see that Elvis liked it very much. When the song was over, he was quiet a moment. Then he said, "Can I hold on to this? I'd like to record it."

"Sure, E."

* * *

Billy's *Turnstiles* album had been picking up a larger global audience than Billy was aware of, and Walter Yetnikoff at CBS Records decided that what had begun as a national tour ought to go international. Shortly after D.C., we headed to Australia for a string of dates. I was extremely happy for Billy, and very excited to be tour-managing the overseas dates. I also thought about the fact that after all that had gone on between Elvis and the Colonel on this issue, it turned out that it wasn't that hard at all to put an international tour together if an artist's support team wanted it to happen.

I was home in L.A. for a few days before heading out with Billy again, and I got a call from Rick Nelson. He invited me to be his guest at a Beach Boys concert at Anaheim Stadium, and I accepted. It was a big show for the band, celebrating the release of their new album, *15 Big Ones*, and was an emotional one for the band's fans, because it marked a return to the stage of the band's brilliant, troubled songwriter, Brian Wilson. A huge BRIAN IS BACK banner hung across the stage, and whenever Brian chipped in a harmony or played a bit on his piano, the crowd went wild.

I'd had an interesting encounter with Brian just the year before. I was with Elvis at the RCA Studios in L.A. as he rehearsed his band for a March Hilton engagement. Things were moving along quite well, when suddenly the studio doors flew open and in walked a huge, bearded, sloppily dressed guy. There was always plenty of security around the studio on Elvis nights, so it startled everybody that such a big, strange guy could have gotten into the place. Before anybody had a chance to react, the big guy walked right up to Elvis and said, "Hi. I'm Brian." Elvis said hello, not having any idea who "Brian" was. And I could tell that Elvis was angry at us—he did not like anybody interrupting his recording or rehearsal sessions. None of us knew who "Brian" was, either. Elvis was angry that someone had gotten through security, but he was also curious. This guy was big and burly, but gentle and childlike, too, and I know Elvis sensed something special about him. Just about anybody else that walked into Elvis's studio like that would have been promptly thrown out. But Elvis let Brian stay. He didn't know what to make of him, but he gave him his full attention.

"Elvis, I'm recording next door," said Brian. "Would you come over and listen?"

"Yeah," said Elvis. I could tell he was wondering what this guy might possibly play for him. As Brian left the studio, Elvis and a few of us followed. We got to the recording studio down the hall, where Brian had been working on some solo demo recordings with producer Terry Melcher (who also happened to be Doris Day's son). Terry and Brian cued something up and played it. Brian eyed Elvis intently. "Elvis, do you think we got something?"

Elvis waited just a beat, then gave his answer. "No."

That was the end of the personal interaction. For the rest of the night, two of the most brilliant talents in rock and roll worked side by side in separate studios.

Watching Brian and the Beach Boys perform in Anaheim, I started to understand that their sunny music had a depth and power I hadn't picked up on before. While the banner was for Brian, and it was singer Mike Love who led the group on stage, I could tell that it was Brian's brother Carl who was in control of the music—and the level of the band's musicianship was unbelievable. When the bandmembers put their voices together for their complicated five-part harmonies, the beauty of the sound could give you goose bumps. And there was that connection between band and audience that, though quite different, was as heartfelt as what Elvis had with his fans. The whole scene was pretty wild, and despite the harmony onstage, there were some backstage dramas between factions of the band that obviously weren't getting along too well. I couldn't imagine being the guy who had to pull a show like this together. At one point I leaned over to Rick Nelson and said, "I'm glad I don't have your job."

Elizabeth Joel was with us for the first few dates Down Under, including some triumphant debut shows at the Sydney Opera House (Billy was the very first pop act to play there). She oversaw all the press Billy did to kick the tour off, then flew back to the U.S. and gave me strict instructions not to let Billy do any more press. Those first shows were great, but Billy quickly became frustrated that he wasn't getting more radio support and didn't seem to be selling many records. He came to my room one night looking depressed. I'd picked up some news from an Australian CBS executive that I thought might help him out.

"Billy, what I'm hearing is that if you do some radio press before the last few shows, you'll have a certified gold record over here. Elizabeth doesn't want you doing more press, but why don't you talk to her about it?"

He thought a moment.

"You're my tour manager, Jerry?"

"Yeah."

"And am I on tour right now?"

"Yeah, Billy."

"Then you're my manager. Set up the press."

I went to work over the next week setting up the radio interviews, and by the time Billy's Australian tour ended he had his first international gold record. Billy was thrilled, but I don't think Elizabeth was too happy with my insubordination. When Billy got ready for his next tour, I wasn't asked back.

But I wouldn't be out of work for long. Rick Nelson was looking for an assistant tour manager for a fall Beach Boys tour, and felt I was the right guy for the job. He gave me the call. I didn't like the idea of stepping down from tour manager to assistant tour manager, but I made a deal with Rick—if he'd let me sit in on the box office settling-up with promoters and venue owners after each show, I'd be his assistant. Rick said that would be all right. I was working for the Beach Boys.

I'd also heard about some huge changes in the Elvis world. Just a couple weeks after I'd seen Elvis at the show in Maryland, Red West, Sonny West, and Dave Hebler had been fired. I didn't know much about Dave's situation, but it seemed to me that Elvis, Sonny, and Red had been growing apart for some time. For all the years they'd been together, the old camaraderie just wasn't there anymore, and I think Sonny and Red were both frustrated with Elvis and irritated by the atmosphere that had developed around him. I'd stepped away in order to maintain a friendship with Elvis. It seemed that maybe Red and Sonny had stayed long enough to let things turn ugly.

I went out with the Beach Boys to do some dates in Canada before the U.S. tour began. We flew from Canada to Florida, and I was at the Miami airport doing my best to watch over the huge amount of gear and luggage coming through customs, when a rough voice barked out at me.

"Where's Rick Nelson?" It was Dennis Wilson, Brian and Carl's brother—the strikingly handsome wild-man drummer of the group.

"He's already at the hotel, Dennis. Making all the room arrangements."

"Well, come on. Let's get out of here."

"I've got to watch all this stuff."

"Let the roadies watch it. You come with me."

I made a quick call to Rick, to see if it was OK to leave my post. Having dealt with Dennis himself, he was very understanding. "He's your boss," Rick told me. "Go with him."

Dennis and I threw our own bags in a limo and headed to our hotel. Dennis instructed me to get cleaned up and meet him in the lobby. I made myself presentable, and when I went back downstairs I almost didn't recognize Dennis. He'd transformed himself from a good-looking surfer dude to an incredibly sharp leading man. And he now let me know that he and I were going to paint the town together. We got back in the limo and headed to the Forge, the city's most upscale nightspot. My first night with Billy Joel, I was shucking oysters for the band. My first week with the Beach Boys, I was eating caviar and drinking thousand-dollar bottles of wine with the drummer.

There weren't any other nights like that one—helping to manage a big act like the Beach Boys on the road was a huge job, and I was usually so busy that I didn't even have time to listen to the performances. I continued to appreciate the shows the band put on, but most of the time I was probably the only guy in the venue who couldn't tell you what song the guys were playing. I did start to know the band, though. Brian Wilson had been struggling against some pretty frightening personal demons and was not a guy you could sit and have any kind of regular conversation with—it seemed like what he really had to say came out in his music. But for all he'd been through, there was something touchingly open and incredibly honest about Brian—something Elvis had recognized. I enjoyed any chance I had to spend time with him. The lead singer, Mike Love, a cousin to the Wilsons, was a curious mix of frontman, spiritual-seeker, and bottom-line businessman. He had become very involved in transcendental meditation, but he was also the guy most concerned with selling records and selling tickets to shows. He could be charming when he wanted to be and could have a great sense of humor, and I saw that his drive was a key part of the band's commercial success. Rhythm guitarist and vocalist Al Jardine was a great singer and a steadying presence in the group, although he could occasionally drive an assistant tour manager crazy with long lists of requests and suggestions before each performance. Carl Wilson, Brian and Dennis's youngest brother, was the quietest of the band members. But I could see that, in many ways, he was the strongest. Brian was the songwriter, and Mike was the showman, but Carl was truly the heart of the group, and any decisions about music had to go through him. I didn't know all the group's songs yet, but the ones Carl sang always grabbed at me. Early in Elvis's career, he had been accused of making "devil music." People often said Carl had the "voice of an angel." I was glad I could work on both sides of the fence.

After a run of Beach Boys dates in the fall of 1976, I was back in L.A. and decided to treat myself to some spa time at a fitness club in Century City. In the sauna, I ran into John Irwin, an attorney I knew as a former partner of Elvis's lawyer, Ed Hookstratten. Irwin had become involved in overseeing a deal for a book that Red, Sonny, and Dave Hebler were writing. He told me that he'd just closed the deal and that the book was going to happen.

I'd first heard about the book a few weeks before, when I got a call from Sonny. He'd told me that he and Red and Dave were writing something on their experiences with Elvis. I could tell from the conversation that they were interested in making me a part of it, too, though I was never directly asked. It wasn't something I wanted to get involved in. But it was happening, Irwin told me. Sonny, Red, and Dave had teamed up with a writer named Steve Dunleavy, who worked for the tabloid *The Star*. The deal for the book was signed. I felt it was something Elvis should know about as quickly as possible.

Elvis didn't have a Los Angeles home anymore—the Monovale house had been sold. But he'd gotten an L.A. apartment for Linda Thompson, and sometimes stayed there. I'd heard from Joe that Elvis was going to be in town. I hurried over to the apartment.

Elvis was in a good mood, and remarked how much he liked the Beach Boys tour jacket I was wearing. He asked if I could get tour jackets like that made up for his tours, and I told him I would. Then I let Elvis know I had some information for him—information he wasn't going to like. I told him everything I knew—that Sonny had called me, that I'd run into Irwin, that the book was being worked on, and that a deal with a publisher was done. Elvis took it all in and became very upset. Rumors of the book had been out there, but he, and a lot of us, had assumed that it wouldn't really happen, that Sonny and Red wouldn't follow through. Elvis didn't want to believe that the rumor had become a reality.

I went out for some more dates with the Beach Boys in early October, and when I was back in L.A., I got a call. Elvis wanted me to come back over to Linda's place. This time just he and Linda were there. It was nice to be with them, and at first it felt like a regular social visit. But after a while, Elvis got very serious.

"Jerry, I just want to tell you. I want to thank you for not getting involved in this book thing."

It didn't seem to me that not getting involved in a book I didn't want to be part of required much of a thank-you.

"Elvis, it wasn't a big deal."

"It was to me, Jerry. It meant a lot to me."

Our visit was interrupted by the arrival of John O'Grady, the private detective who'd worked for Elvis a few times over the years. O'Grady seemed to go out of his way to present himself as the tough-talking, no-nonsense gumshoe, and always seemed to assume that his involvement with Elvis was the most important thing in Elvis's life. The very first time I'd met him, years before in Las Vegas, he'd come up to Elvis's suite and started telling stories about some of the celebrity clients and cases he'd worked on. Elvis, like any great storyteller, enjoyed hearing a good story, and he enjoyed O'Grady's lurid tales. But I had an uneasy feeling about the detective. After O'Grady left the suite, I asked Elvis, "If that guy's telling us everything about all those people, what's he going to tell people about you?" But my opinion of the detective hadn't stopped Elvis from hiring him over the years.

"I need to speak privately with Elvis," O'Grady now announced.

The room was quiet for just a moment, then Elvis spoke. "Anything you have to say to me, you can say in front of Jerry. I want him here."

O'Grady wasn't happy about that, but he went ahead and gave Elvis the news he'd brought. Red, Sonny, and Dave had turned down Elvis's offer of substantial sums of money to walk away from their book deal. They'd been willing to meet with O'Grady, but had already accepted an advance and had no choice but to complete the book. It would be published the following summer.

Elvis had felt bad about the way things had ended with Red and Sonny, and realized they probably did deserve some decent severance pay for all their years of service. But he was still very concerned about what they were going to put in their book. Elvis was used to being a public figure, and had been praised and panned throughout his career. He'd still managed to maintain a degree of privacy in his private life, though, and now he was enraged that insiders were going to expose the most personal details about him, his family, his girlfriends, and even his doctors.

"Every goddamn thing's already been written about me, but they're going to hurt people around me," he said. "What went on is between me and them. But my family's going to get hurt, and my eight-year-old daughter's going to get hurt, friends are going to get hurt, and professional people around me are going to get hurt. Damn it, that just isn't right. It isn't right."

There wasn't anything I could say to him to make the situation any better. O'Grady left. Linda, Elvis, and I talked some more, but I could tell he was still distracted and unhappy. At the end of the night, I told him that I was going back out on the road again with the Beach Boys.

"Thanks for being here, Jerry," he said.

Linda and I met again not too long after that, this time professionally. I'd finished my fall tour with the Beach Boys, the Sweets were on the road with Elvis, and I had time to make a brief return to my acting career, lining up some parts through Rick Husky and my old assistant director friend, Chris Morgan. Rick called me in for a part on a police drama he was producing and writing for, *The Rookies*, and when I showed up on set I was pleasantly surprised to find that Linda was part of the cast as well. I was to be one of the bad guys that week—an evil Hollywood-player type—and Linda was the well-meaning young actress who'd gotten romantically involved with me. We were both a little surprised to discover that in one scene the script called for us to kiss.

We were sitting together before the first take of our romantic moment when she whispered, "What's Elvis going to think about this?" We laughed about it—but we were a little worried, too. As a guy who's worked at everything from manning a cotton gin to loading trucks to hauling film reels, I can say that kissing Linda Thompson is very easy work. And as it turned out, we didn't have too much to worry about—to our relief, Elvis never saw the episode.

In the spring of 1977, I was managing the Sweet Inspirations and taking the occasional acting job (I also had the pleasure of being a bad guy on *Charlie's Angels*). One day I got a call from Carl Wilson. I hadn't dealt much directly with Carl before, but being on the road with the band, I had started to feel a connection with him. I could see that, in the Beach Boys' world, he was the kind of levelheaded peacemaker that I'd often tried to be in the Elvis world. He was nothing like any of the Memphis guys I'd spent so many years with, but for some reason I found him very easy to talk to.

This wasn't just a friendly call, though. Carl wanted to know if I'd come back to work with the band as their tour manager. It was a great offer. But I didn't like the idea that I was going to take the job from Rick Nelson—the guy who had brought me into the Beach Boys organization in the first place. I told Carl I didn't want to take Rick's job from him. But Carl told me Rick wasn't with the band anymore. Carl had suggested me to the band as a replacement, and the members had agreed I was the right one for the job. That made it easy to say yes to the offer. In addition to managing the Sweets, I'd now be working for the Beach Boys full-time.

On paper, the Beach Boys were still one of the biggest rock-and-roll bands in the world. They played huge concerts to sellout crowds, and their records still charted (they'd just had a Top 5 hit with a cover of Chuck Berry's "Rock 'n' Roll Music"). In March of 1977, they signed a huge, $8 million contract with CBS Records. On a personal level, though, the band was in turmoil. After years as a near recluse, Brian Wilson was functioning and capable of appearing on stage with the band, but there were doubts about whether he could return to greatness as the band's producer and primary songwriter. Dennis was the sex symbol of the group, and brought a fierce energy to the stage that fans loved, but his wild lifestyle made him an unpredictable and sometimes undependable bandmember. Mike and Al, the meditation enthusiasts, had embraced a clean-living philosophy, and were scornful of Dennis's and Brian's indulgences. Carl tried to put the music ahead of all the personal clashes, but he was having a rough time handling the pressure of the situation.

It was amazing to me that a band known for such sweet, musical harmony could have so much tension and disagreement behind the scenes, and more amazing still that when the band got out on stage, the music did rise above whatever had been going on backstage. I started watching what the group did on stage, and I became a fan, too. I began to think that if you could roll together Brian's musical brilliance, Dennis's sex appeal, and Carl's gentle spirit and intelligence, you might have an Elvis.

In addition to troubles between band members, there was trouble with the group's management. Steve Love, Mike's brother, had been managing the band for a while, and from what I could see had done a very good job for the group. But there were disagreements over some money issues, and Steve was fired. With the CBS deal signed, the band was about to embark on a major European tour that would include a concert at a major CBS Records convention in London, but they no longer had a steady management organization to make a tour like that run smoothly.

Elvis was out on a series of short, eight- or nine-date tours that spring and summer, and I was checking in with Myrna to see how things were going. A couple of the concerts were going to be filmed for a CBS television special, and I called Myrna after those dates to see how the shows had gone. She said that Elvis was looking good for the special—that he'd lost some weight and given strong performances. I also heard that my brother had been in touch with Elvis. When Sheriff Roy Nixon was elected mayor of Shelby County in 1976, my brother was bumped up from number-two man to number-one man in the Sheriff's Department. He hadn't been on the job long before Elvis came to see him. Elvis showed Billy Ray the deputy sheriff's badge he'd gotten back in 1970, and said he felt he was ready for a promotion. Billy Ray told Elvis that the only higher badge available was the one he was wearing. Elvis repeated that he wanted the promotion, and said, "Billy Ray, you don't want me to run against you, do you?"

Billy Ray handled the situation perfectly. He gave Elvis his badge (he eventually found an identical backup that he could carry). And Elvis thought it was only fair that if he was being promoted, he should turn in his old badge—which, in the six years he'd had it, he'd customized with diamonds and gems. At Elvis's insistence, Billy Ray received the jeweled badge, and the next day put it in a safe-deposit box, thinking he'd give it back to Elvis at some future date.

I tried to get ahold of Elvis at Graceland at one point when I was on the road. Billy Smith answered the phone, and after we talked for a while, I told him I wanted to speak with Elvis if he was available. Billy went to check, and then got back on the line.

"Hang on, Jerry—Elvis says he wants to talk to you."

I waited for Elvis to pick up. And waited some more. After about twenty minutes of silence, I gave up and hung up the phone. It seemed a little strange, but I just figured something must have come up to pull his attention away from the phone call. I would just call back later.

The Beach Boys' summer European tour was set to be my first chance to show what I was capable of as a tour manager. But the tour never happened. Without proper management, none of the extensive paperwork that needed to be in place for an overseas tour had been properly executed. It all fell through, before there was anything for me to manage. The only gig that was booked was the appearance at the CBS convention on July 30. That event looked like it could be a really positive one for the band, a way for them to rally back together as bandmates and show their enthusiasm for their new record company. After sets from other CBS talents such as Boz Scaggs and James Taylor, the Beach Boys would be presented as the headliners—the newest addition to the CBS roster. And they'd be performing primarily for a roomful of CBS executives—people who had believed in the band enough to sign them, and who wanted nothing more than to believe that their $8 million had been well spent.

The band got a phenomenal welcome when they took the stage,

and again, despite all the personal tensions that still lingered among the members, the group pulled together and began delivering fantastic versions of hit after hit. Label executives usually make for a pretty jaded crowd, but this time, the roomful of people were up on their feet, singing along. Brian was on stage with the band, but wasn't counted on to do much—the setlist had been designed so that he contributed a few spotlight vocal lines, but was really more a presence than a performer. At one point during the concert, he sat at his grand piano looking like he had tuned out of the show entirely. That sight enraged Mike. He ran across the stage and gave the piano a hard shove, startling Brian and nearly rolling the piano into the audience. The room went dead. And a lot of executives must have worried that they'd just spent a lot of money on some very bad vibrations.

After trying to tour-manage a tour that didn't happen, and trying to keep things calm among the splintering Beach Boys, I needed a break. Instead of flying back to the U.S. with the band, I headed for Monte Carlo, where a week of sunshine and Bordeaux put me in a much better mood.

Back in L.A., I was working out of the Beach Boys' production offices in Santa Monica. I was beginning to consider Carl Wilson a good friend as well as an employer, and we had some long talks about the band. I was impressed with his insight, and his ambitions for his career. He could see the group's problems as clearly as anyone could, but he still felt the band was capable of better records, better tours, and better music. Brian had been described for years as the "genius" of the band, but I came to believe that there wouldn't be a band at all without Carl. Carl and I were both excited about the band's next tour, which would give everybody a chance to put the European fiasco behind us. The tour would include some very high-profile East Coast gigs, including a huge free concert in New York City's Central Park. The tour was set to begin on August 17.

On August 16, I was out on the balcony of the hillside house that Elvis had given me. The phone had been ringing all day as I worked through all the last-minute preparations for the Beach Boys tour. I'd managed to pull things together and had set up what looked to be a solid, productive time on the road. All arrangements had been taken care of. All we had to do now was get on the first plane, and I'd begin my first proper tour as the tour manager of a major rock-and-roll band.

I looked down at the parched hillside below my home. Southern California had been suffering through a drought the last few years, and I wondered how long the cactus and eucalyptus and scrub brush could survive in the dry heat. The phone rang again. I was tempted to ignore it. It felt good just to enjoy the house and the view for a moment. But I went in and answered. I barely recognized the distressed voice on the other end. But I made out that it was Pat Parry, the woman who'd been a friend of Elvis and us guys over the years.

"Elvis is dead," she said.

I hung up the phone. I started to cry. I went back out on the balcony. It started to rain.

15

. . .

BELLS

He was only forty-two. And now he was gone. I didn't doubt that this was true, but it didn't feel real to me, either.

The *Lisa Marie* had been ready to take Elvis out on his next tour, also scheduled to start August 17. Now, Vernon was sending the big plane to Los Angeles, so that Priscilla, her mother and father, her sister Michelle, Joanie Esposito, Joe's girlfriend Shirley Dieu, and I could fly back to Memphis for Elvis's funeral.

Rick Husky picked me up to give me a ride to the airport. There wasn't much for Rick and me to talk about. He put on the car radio softly to fill the silence. The station was playing Elvis. A ballad. At the end of the song, the DJ said, "One of the great ones, by the late Elvis Presley." The late Elvis Presley. That hit me hard.

It was real. He was gone.

When I got to the airport, the *Lisa Marie* was there waiting. But the crew wasn't on the plane. And Priscilla and the others hadn't arrived yet. The stairs were down, and the doors were open, so I went aboard.

I thought about the first times I'd been on the plane, when it was just a gutted shell. Trip after trip to Meacham Field, I'd been aboard to watch Elvis excitedly take his Polaroids as the interior was slowly transformed into what he wanted. Now, every detail of the plane's cabin was an extension of Elvis, from the leather chairs he'd picked, to the intercom system he'd requested, to the bar he'd kept stocked with soda and Mountain Valley Spring Water. With so much of the man around me, it was hard not to think that he'd be stepping onto the plane any minute.

I walked to the back of the plane, to the bedroom. Laid out neatly on the bed were a pair of his pajamas—still ready for him to wear on the flight to his first concert tour city. A few of his favorite books were on a little night table, some opened to the page where he'd stopped reading.

I knew the funeral and the days ahead were going to be especially hard on Vernon, Grandma, Priscilla, and Lisa, and I wanted to be as strong as I could for them. There were going to be a lot of details and logistics to handle, and I wanted to do whatever I could to help. As much as I hurt, I didn't feel I could give myself over to grief. It wasn't the time for me to become sentimental. But alone in that bedroom, looking at my friend's empty pajamas, I found myself wanting to touch something of his. I sat on his bed and grabbed his pajama top, holding it close. I sat like that for just a moment, then went back to the conference room, sat in one of the leather chairs, and waited for the others to arrive.

The loss became even more real for me when I saw the pain in Priscilla's eyes after she stepped on the plane. We embraced for a moment, but could hardly put into words what we were feeling. In fact, there wasn't much talk among any of us on the flight to Memphis. I realize now that all of us were in shock, sunk into a sadness so deep there wasn't much energy for anything else. I do remember that about an hour into the flight, we detected the unmistakable smell of something burning, and soon saw that smoke was coming from somewhere inside the plane. And we were in such a state that we barely reacted to the possibility of a fire onboard. A crew member went to the cabinets in the conference room and discovered that a blanket had been up against an exposed wire and had begun to burn. The blanket was extinguished. The flight made its way to Memphis.

I know Vernon wanted to be strong for his family, but he was absolutely devastated by the loss of his son. And seeing those who had loved and been loved by Elvis only sharpened the pain. He was sitting in a back room at Graceland when our group from Los Angeles arrived at the house, and, at the sight of Priscilla, he broke down into uncontrollable sobs. I went over and put my hand on his shoulder, hoping I could provide some small comfort to him.

I hadn't been at Graceland for a while, and I don't think my name came up at first when the list of pallbearers was being decided on. But when George Klein mentioned me to Vernon, Vernon had insisted I be one of the guys to carry his son's coffin. I was one of nine, along with Joe Esposito, George Klein, Charlie Hodge, Lamar Fike, Billy and Gene Smith, Felton Jarvis, and Dr. Nick.

A public viewing of Elvis's body was held at Graceland. Several people had tried to talk Vernon out of this, but he felt very strongly that Elvis himself would want this last opportunity for his fans to say good-bye. I don't remember much at all about the days around the funeral, but I do remember the incredible sight of so many people wanting to pay their respects to Elvis. That Elvis was loved by his fans was no surprise—you could always feel it coming back at him from the audiences at his shows, and you could feel it in the excitement he created everywhere he went. But now all that love had a new physical presence. It was there in the tens of thousands of people, lined up from the Graceland front door down the driveway, through the gates, and out along Elvis Presley Boulevard—all of them waiting patiently in the Memphis summer heat to say their own personal farewell to Elvis.

Vernon extended the hours of the public viewing to accommodate as many of those fans as possible, and later, in the Graceland living room, there was time for a private viewing for the family and those closest to Elvis. Memories of the time are a blur to me, but I do remember one awful detail—the whole time we friends and family members were paying our respects, there was a single sound that cut through the room: Vernon howling in anguish.

And I do remember that after that private service, I went to Grandma Presley's room to check on her. She was very old by then, and looked so small and fragile. She and Elvis had shared a home almost since the day he was born, and Elvis had cared for her so much. On the small night table near her bed, she still had two framed photos: one of Elvis, Gladys, and Vernon, and one of Priscilla. Now she took my hand, and in a trembling voice asked, "Do you think you could come back and live at the house, son?"

There was a moment when I found myself alone in the living room with Elvis, and I thought about a day long ago when I'd been just steps away from the very same spot—looking through the living room to the music room, where Elvis sat by himself playing the piano. The powerful, beautiful music had drawn me up from my room in the basement, but as I got closer, I thought maybe I was intruding on something personal. Elvis was lost in his singing and playing, and I didn't want to interrupt his private moment. But I couldn't walk away from his music, either. I was trying to figure out which way to go, when he happened to look up and see me. He didn't stop playing. And, with just the hint of a smile on his face, he gave me the faintest of nods to let me know it was OK to stay and listen. He turned his attention back to his hands over the keyboard and continued singing the song that had drawn me, a song that had long been one of his favorites, "You'll Never Walk Alone."

The funeral procession from the house to Forest Hill Cemetery was slow and stately. It may have taken over an hour to travel the short distance down Elvis Presley Boulevard. Riding in one of sixteen white limousines behind Elvis, I kept thinking about a song he had played for me several times in the TV room at Graceland—a song that was on one of the records he kept in his special drawer down there. It was "The Bells" by the Dominoes—an almost operatic pop song about a man witnessing the funeral of his true love. Elvis loved listening to the way the lead singer, Clyde McPhatter, actually broke down and cried his way through the verses. Now, I couldn't stop thinking of Elvis singing along with the record:

> *Well, I know why they're ringing*
> *They're ringing out for me . . .*

As we slowly made our way down the boulevard, I witnessed a sight that was powerful and heartwrenching—thousands and thousands of people lined both sides of the street, standing in solemn, respectful silence as the procession passed by. I saw children crying, grandparents crying, cops standing at attention with their hats over their hearts, and the toughest-looking bikers with tears in their eyes. White folks stood side by side with black folks.

A huge part of Elvis's legacy became clear to me on that slow ride to the cemetery. Before Elvis and his music, there was nothing that could have brought all these different people, from all these different walks of life, together. His music had pulled together gospel, blues, country, and

R & B into one sound. Now here were all the faces and lives behind each strand of that sound, standing as one. All those faces, all those people, had become one living tribute to Elvis, feeling his loss as one, and expressing their sorrow as one. In death, Elvis had done what he'd always sought to do in life—he'd brought us together.

I stayed busy enough in the days around the funeral that emotions never had a chance to take over. All the guys worked together—the same way we had in our football games, on the movie sets, at the ranch, on show nights—knowing that this was the last time we'd ever be together this way, doing what we could for Elvis.

I was still in a daze when I traveled from Memphis to New York to catch up with the Beach Boys before their big Central Park show. My old friend Tom Hulett was promoting the tour, and before I left L.A. he'd let me know his staff would get the tour started smoothly (Tom had also been at the funeral, attending with the Colonel). I was running on autopilot as I made the rounds to let the band and road crew know I was back. Everyone certainly knew what had happened and knew where I'd been, but nobody seemed to want to talk to me about it. They didn't know what to say, and I suppose I didn't look very approachable.

Most of the band members were staying at the Plaza, but Carl and his wife, Annie, were staying at the Sherry Netherland. He called me from there and said that he was in his room with his wife—a beautiful, gentle spirit just like Carl. The two of them wanted to know if I would come over just to sit and talk for a while. He said they could only imagine what an awful time I was going through, and that they wanted to be there for me. I didn't think I really wanted to talk about anything, but I went over to meet with them. I'd always thought of myself as a strong guy, but there was a strength and a centeredness in Carl that I respected. I'd felt comfortable talking to him as long as I'd known him, and I felt I'd be comfortable with him now.

"Jerry, how are you doing?" Carl asked.

"Are you OK?" asked Annie.

I had thought I was all right. But I wasn't. As I began to answer them, it hit me like a punch in the stomach: I was never going to see Elvis again.

Then it all came pouring out of me, everything I'd held back for a week: anger, rage, pain, loss, grief. My best friend was dead. We didn't have to lose him like this.

I hit the room's stone mantel so hard I broke my hand. Carl and Annie grabbed hold of me and held me as long as it took to calm me down. And they sat with me until my hurt and my anger had left me exhausted.

We'd been sitting quietly for a while in Carl's room when the phone rang. I wasn't surprised to hear that the call was for me, but I was surprised to hear who was on the line—Billy Joel. He and Elizabeth knew the Beach Boys were in town, and decided to track me down. They wanted to offer some comfort, too, and asked if I'd come see them. I went over to the Joels' apartment and right away could sense the deep concern for me that Billy and Elizabeth shared—the same kind of concern I'd felt from Carl and Annie. We sat and talked for a while, but Billy had something he thought would communicate his feelings a little better—he had some music he wanted to play for me, if I was up to it.

"When I heard the news, I didn't know what else to do," he said. "I figured Elvis would just want us to rock."

Billy had been down at JP's Tavern when he heard about Elvis. He'd gotten up on the tiny stage there, sat at the piano, and played an impromptu forty-five-minute set of Elvis songs to an almost empty room. Somebody in the club had the sense to roll tape. I really wasn't sure if I was ready to listen to the performance, but I asked Billy to play the tape. And as I sat there listening, all I could think of was what a beautiful tribute he had created on the spot. The hurt was still fresh and I was already missing Elvis like I was missing a part of myself. But that night I began to think about how much Elvis had left behind for me, and for all of us.

The next day the Beach Boys were scheduled to take a flight out of New York City. I had calmed down enough to worry about brother Brian, and how Elvis's death might have affected his sometimes fragile state of mind. I asked Carl if Brian had said anything about it, and Carl told me that Brian wouldn't talk about it. When we got on the plane I sat with Carl. As the plane took off, Brian, who at that point had still never initiated a conversation with me, came up and sat facing Carl and me. He looked very nervous. And for the first time, he spoke directly to me. In a trembling voice he said, "Jerry, what happened? What happened? I'm scared. . . ."

"It's OK, Brian. We can talk about it."

I tried to comfort Brian as best I could on the plane that day, but frankly, I was scared, too.

Elvis had been there for me every day of my adult life. Now I was going to have to walk alone.

EPILOGUE

. . .

I still live in the house Elvis gave me. I always wear the emerald ring he gave me. And it doesn't take more than a few bars of any of his songs to send me right back to the Rainbow skating rink, or the pool room at Graceland, or the Paramount lot, or backstage at the Las Vegas Hilton. In the years since he's been gone, my life has been rich, eventful, and rewarding. And I don't ever forget that I've had a chance to live that kind of life because of the time I spent with Elvis.

The Beach Boys became a very big part of my life. By the end of 1977, I was working as Carl Wilson's personal manager, and in 1978, at Mike Love's recommendation, the Beach Boys voted to make me their manager. I was proud to be trusted with the career of one of America's greatest rock-and-roll bands, and in 1980, I was able to follow through on an idea of Mike's and organize the first of a series of shows that marked one of my most satisfying accomplishments as a manager: the Fourth of July concerts on the Mall in Washington, D.C. I worked with the Beach Boys for more than a decade, years that included some hard times, but some great times and great music, as well.

After losing Elvis, I was especially sensitive toward Brian Wilson's situation. I took the initiative to bring therapist Eugene Landy back to work a second round of intensive treatment with Brian, a decision that was supported by Carl, the band, Brian's attorney John Branca, and promoter Tom Hulett. Landy's approach was controversial, but we kept Brian alive. With the help of a lot of other friends, family, and musical colleagues, Brian became an active, creative artist once again. And, on a November night in 2004, I was privileged to be at Disney Hall in Los

Angeles when Brian triumphantly led his own band through a beautiful performance of his long-anticipated masterpiece, "Smile."

Myrna and I were married in 1980, with Carl Wilson serving as best man. We had a very small service in Hawaii for just a few friends and family members, but we were surprised by one unexpected guest: Dennis Wilson. We put him up in our bridal suite. I also continued to work with the Sweet Inspirations, and reached a high point with them when they were signed to Robert Stigwood's RSO Records and were also chosen to be the opening act on the Bee Gees' worldwide "Spirits" tour. Myrna and Carl also developed a great creative relationship, working closely together on a pair of solo albums that Carl recorded for CBS, and cowriting a national number-one hit, "Heaven."

At the end of 1980, I had a chance to bring together my Memphis and California roots on one stage: When the Beach Boys celebrated their twentieth anniversary with a big show at the Forum in Los Angeles, the band was introduced by Priscilla Presley. It was one of the last great nights the original band was together on stage. In December 1983, while I was having dinner with my father and Colonel Parker, I received the call from the L.A. County Coroner's Office: Dennis Wilson had drowned in the waters off Marina del Rey, California, gone at the age of thirty-nine.

In October of 1977, I had watched when CBS first aired *Elvis in Concert*, the TV special that had been shot weeks before his death, and I'd been shocked and saddened at what I saw: Elvis looked pitiful. I'd never seen him looking so unwell. And though the special contained a few moments of heartbreakingly beautiful singing, Elvis was clearly in a state of physical distress. I was furious, and got in touch with the Colonel right away, asking him how he could have possibly let Elvis continue to work—in front of the cameras, no less—when Elvis was in such terrible shape. The Colonel didn't try to defend himself, but he gave me his explanation, one he thought would make sense to me as a fellow manager. He'd asked CBS for a ridiculous amount of money to do the special, assuming that they would say no. But they'd said yes. He felt obligated to report the offer to Elvis, assuming that Elvis still might not want to do the show. But Elvis did want to do the show, and the Colonel didn't feel he could stand in Elvis's way.

My disagreements with the Colonel didn't stop us from becoming friends. In the years after Elvis, we spoke almost every day, and I know I was one of the very few people he had that kind of friendship with. He was a smart, tough, complicated man, and also, quite often, a heck of a lot of fun to be around. Our differences were honest ones, and I maintained a great deal of respect for him. Those who think of the Colonel as an evil puppet-master forget that such a role makes Elvis a puppet. That was not the case. The Colonel eventually paid me the highest professional compliment he could. When he was considering making deals on a book of his life story, and granting rights to his story for a 20th Century Fox production of *Last Train to Memphis*, he had me handle the negotiations. Our friendship lasted right up until his death in 1997. I truly miss him.

Over the course of thirty years, I had the pleasure of becoming a friend of Sun Records founder Sam Phillips, and discovered that, in addition to being a man of courage and talent, he was an incredibly smart and principled man. As esteemed as he had become, he remained a champion of the underdog. One of the deepest honors of my professional career came when I was asked to accept, at Sam's request, his Lifetime Achievement Award from the Blues Foundation (I saw it as a formidable task to speak on behalf of one of the most charismatic speakers I'd ever met). I remained close with Sam up until his death in 2003. He was a personal hero, who became a cherished personal friend.

In 1985, after five years of marriage and ten years together, Myrna and I realized that we had grown apart. We divorced, but have been able to stay close friends in the years since.

In 1987, I moved on from the Beach Boys to work for Elvis once again—I was appointed the creative affairs director for Elvis Presley Enterprises. Part of the job felt very familiar to me—I had to protect Elvis, although now it was his name and likeness that I was watching over. But the more satisfying part of the job was in finding new ways for Elvis's legacy to be extended and strengthened. First, and most importantly, I was able to play an instrumental role in untangling what had been a very litigious relationship between EPE and RCA records. Once Elvis's name and his music could work easily together, the way was cleared for all sorts of film and television projects. I got to play a strong consultant role on a number of those. I was also able to facilitate a film shoot at Graceland for U2's *Rattle and Hum* documentary, in the process beginning a great friendship with fellow Elvis fan Bono.

I've also had the pleasure of working directly with another Sun Records legend, Jerry Lee Lewis. I became his manager in 1987, and one of the first challenges was to take care of some terrible troubles with the IRS and make it possible for Jerry Lee to become an active performer again. My first memory of being on the road with him is that we were sitting in the back of a Learjet, on the way to a show at Tipitina's in New Orleans. Jerry Lee often speaks in great quotes, and this was the first time I got to hear one. He was in a three-piece suit, looking lost in deep thought as he scratched his chin and pulled on his pipe of tobacco, when he turned to me and said, "Jerry, if God created anything more lovely than a woman, he kept it to himself."

I worked hard to get Jerry Lee the royalties and publishing rights that he deserved, and I got him actively involved in the soundtrack of the biopic based on his life, *Great Balls of Fire*. At the premiere for that film, he asked me to be the one to walk down the red carpet with him. He's still a great talent, and a good friend.

Through the nineties, my dream of a film career became a very busy reality. I worked as a producer on such projects as *Elvis: The Great Performances*, *Elvis in Hollywood*, and coproduced the ABC TV series *Elvis: The Early Years* with Priscilla and Rick Husky. In 1995, I was the executive in charge of talent for the ten-hour documentary *The History of Rock 'n' Roll*, coproduced by Quincy Jones and my dear friend Andrew Solt. In that position I oversaw interviews with legends and superstars ranging from Sam Phillips to Sex Pistol Steve Jones, Little Richard to Robert Plant, B. B. King to Bono.

As the new millennium began, I was back where I started, in Memphis, serving a term as the president and CEO of the Memphis and Shelby County Music Commission, during which my proudest achievement was starting a Memphis musicians' health-care plan. During my time back in Memphis, I also received the amazing honor of becoming the first white member appointed to the board of the International Black Broadcasters Association, which I still serve on.

I found my soul mate—a bright, beautiful, vivacious woman named Cindy Bennett, who I couldn't help falling in love with. Through the years she has been an incredible source of strength, support, friendship, and love, and in 2000, after thirteen years together, I finally got smart enough to officially make her Cindy Schilling. For our wedding, we traveled to India, where we were the guests of Ambassador Richard Celeste and his wife, Jacqueline Lundquist. Cindy and I were married in a traditional Hindu ceremony that was wonderful in every way possible. I know that Elvis would have appreciated the ceremony's beauty and spirituality. And, as Cindy was brought to the ceremony in a horse-drawn carriage, I made my groom's approach on top of an elephant, which I know the Colonel would have approved of.

In the years after Elvis's death, Carl Wilson became my closest friend. Cindy and I spent a lot of time with Carl and his second wife, Gina Martin (Dean's daughter). Carl's calming presence and quiet wisdom were always an inspiration to me. Sadly, he was also taken away too soon. He and Gina spent their last holiday together up at my house, on New Year's Eve 1997, along with Carl's sons, Jonah and Justin, and their girlfriends, Rona and Britta. Carl was very ill at the time, but it was a beautiful evening of celebration and togetherness. Carl died just a few weeks later on February 6, my birthday.

A few months after Elvis's funeral, Priscilla and I got together in Los Angeles and went out to dinner. We decided we'd treat ourselves right, and went to one of the more upscale spots in town, Le Dome. Both of us had been under a good deal of stress figuring out what our personal lives would be like without Elvis, and Priscilla was under a particularly harsh media spotlight. It was great to be together because we each had a deep understanding of what the other was going through. But it was still a little hard to talk about everything.

The talking got a little easier when a bottle of champagne was sent over by another patron (and part owner)—Elton John. We finished that bottle, then, uncharacteristically, ordered another. Suddenly, Priscilla and I were opening up to each other in ways we never had before—talking about Elvis, growing up at Graceland, and all our times together. We recounted a lot of very happy memories, and shared a lot of laughter. It was a wonderful healing night—the first night like that for either of us. We finally walked out to get our cars, and became aware that there was a large group of paparazzi waiting for some kind of Priscilla picture.

"Prim and proper" Priscilla turned to me and said, "Let's give them something to talk about." We shared a good-night kiss, which we followed with an extra-long hug—cracking up as the cameras went into a frenzy of clicking and flashing. In the years since that night, Priscilla has become one of my dearest friends in the world, and someone I can always count on. She's a strong woman, and an incredibly generous soul. She's a sharp businesswoman, but she's also got a great sense of humor. I'm honored to consider her my friend.

It's hard to come up with words for the relationship I have with Lisa (or, as I've nicknamed her, "Memphis"). We started early—I drove her parents to the hospital the day she was born. After she lost her dad, she was often with me on Christmas Eve—when in addition to celebrating the holiday, we'd spend a lot of time talking about her father. As a teenager, Lisa's first job was working for me as my personal assistant in the office at Jerry Schilling Management, a job she took seriously and executed well. There, we learned that not only did we have a unique way of communicating with each other, but we could match each other temper for temper. In her early twenties, when Lisa began her career as an artist, I was her first manager, and even in that earliest phase of her career I recognized the beauty of her writing and depth of her talent. There's no question that she's her own person, but there are many times that I'm wonderfully aware that there's a lot of her father's spirit within her.

In the fall of 2004, in New York City on a business trip, I was in the back of a cab when I noticed something terribly wrong—the emerald had fallen from the ring Elvis gave me. It wasn't anywhere in the cab, and couldn't be found in my hotel room. My token of good fortune was gone. I can only assume that some New York pedestrian got very lucky that week. I continued to wear the ring anyway, and at Priscilla's birthday party the next spring, Lisa noticed the missing stone. She asked if she could have the ring, to try and have it reset. Months later, on Christmas Eve, thirty years to the day her father had first given me the extraordinary gift, Lisa, with the same casually overwhelming generosity of her father, gave me back the ring—now set with the most brilliant, exquisitely cut emerald I'd ever seen. Coming from Elvis, the ring had great personal meaning to me. Now, as a gift from father and daughter, it is a personal treasure.

In January 2006, I traveled to Kyoto, Japan, on a trip that had some of the feel of a top secret mission: it was there that Lisa—in the presence of her children, Benjamin and Riley, her mother, and a tight-knit group of family and friends—married her fiancé, Michael Lockwood (a great guy). And I was very honored to be the one Lisa and Michael asked to conduct the marriage ceremony (I became a credentialed clergyman in the Church of Spiritual Humanism for the occasion). As that beautiful wedding day came to a close, it occurred to me that I was in my fifty-second year as a member of the extended Presley family. The fact that Elvis and his loved ones have welcomed me into their lives is the single greatest blessing of my life.

Elvis was my friend, and I received more from him than from any other person I've known. I can only hope that I gave something of substance back to him. Losing him was the greatest loss I've ever suffered. But it also has occurred to me that those words I once heard Elvis sing in the Graceland music room have turned out to be absolutely true.

With everything he gave me, and with all the love, friends, memories, and music in my life—I don't ever walk alone.

ACKNOWLEDGMENTS

. . .

A very special thanks to Peter Guralnick, for believing in me, and for guiding me through this process with insight, honesty, and friendship. I could not have done this without you.

Special thanks to Chuck Crisafulli, who lived my story with me and captured my life and my voice in a way I could not have done on my own. You're now an honorary member of the Memphis Mafia, and I consider myself lucky to have found not just a writer, but a friend. A heartfelt thank-you also to Kyra Thompson, for her generosity and unwavering support of this project.

I'd like to offer my sincere gratitude to many other people who helped make this book a reality.

At Gotham Books: Special thanks to Bill Shinker, who got what I wanted to do at our first meeting, and offered my story a classy home. Thanks to editor Brendan Cahill, who made the book more than the "10 percent better" he promised, and who always supported my decisions on how this story should be told. Thanks to Patrick Mulligan, who was always there to answer my questions, and whose attention to detail was greatly appreciated. Thanks also to Lisa Johnson, Annsley Rosner, Robert Kempe, Ashwini Ramaswamy, and Melanie Koch.

At Fish & Richardson: Thank you to John Taylor "Ike" Williams and Hope Denekamp, who provided encouragement and enthusiasm throughout the process.

At Elvis Presley Enterprises: Thank you to Jack Soden for his gracious support of this endeavor. Special thanks to Todd Morgan, who knew I should write a book before I did, and who was extremely generous with his time and knowledge—You helped keep this book honest and true. Thank you to Scott Williams, Kevin Kern, and Susan Sherwood for all their efforts on my behalf. Thanks to all my friends at Graceland who have been so tremendously helpful through the years. Thanks also to the David Beckwith Company.

Thanks to Kevin Kane for his support and friendship.

Thank you to Andrew Solt, for generously providing a loving environment in which to write this book.

Thank you to Ernst Jorgenson, who improved the accuracy of this work by sharing his vast historical knowledge of the subject with me.

Thank you to Erin Hosier, an early believer in this book who gave me all the right information before I could comprehend it. Thanks most of all for finding Chuck for me.

Some very personal thank-you's go out to the following:

To Mamaw and Papaw Gilkey—I would not have survived without you. To Bill Schilling, for being a loving father. To Billy Ray Schilling, for sticking up for me when I needed it. And to Aunt Jinky, who gave me so much new insight about my mother.

To Myrna Smith, who shared so much of this story with me. To Sandy Kawelo, a truly pure and wonderful spirit.

To George Klein, for being my lifelong North Memphis friend, and for sharing his great memory of our Memphis Mafia days. To Joe Esposito, for all his years of friendship. To Linda Thompson, for always being the caring, positive person that she is. To all my brothers in the Memphis Mafia.

To Gary Hovey for his personal and professional insight, and to Michelle Hovey for her support and for sharing her family stories with me. To Col. and Anne Beaulieu, whose reminiscences helped me relive some of the great times we shared.

For guidance, support, and friendship throughout the years, thanks to Emily Kuroda, Steve Einczig, Ross Schwartz, Dennis Arfa, Glen Brunman, and Tom Hulett. Thanks to Randy Poe for sharing his expertise and making me feel comfortable as an author. Thanks to Scotty Moore, a great musician and a great friend. Thanks to D. J. Fontana for steady beats and steady friendship. Thanks to George Brooks and Bud Tedesco for refreshing my memory of my film-editing days.

I'd also like to take this opportunity to thank all the fans around the world who have always been so kind to me.

Special thanks to the Sam Phillips family for their friendship.

Special thanks to the Carl Wilson family for their love and support.

Special thanks to my loving wife, Cindy Schilling, who was always there for me every step of the way through this process. Her contributions were invaluable. I wouldn't have wanted to share my 3:00 A.M. notes with anyone else.

Thank you to Priscilla, for growing up with me at Graceland, and for understanding and appreciating the love that went into this work.

Thank you to Lisa, the reader I most wanted to share my story with.

E—Thanks for everything.

INDEX

. . .

PHOTO CREDITS

. . .

First Photo Insert

Page One
Courtesy of the CBS archives

Page Two
Courtesy of the author

Page Three
Courtesy of the author

Page Four
Top: Courtesy of the author

Right: Courtesy of
  Elvis Presley Enterprises

Bottom: Courtesy of
  Elvis Presley Enterprises

Page Five
Top: Courtesy of the author

Bottom left: Courtesy of
  Elvis Presley Enterprises

Bottom right: Courtesy of
  The King's Ransom

Page Six
Courtesy of Elvis Presley
  Enterprises

Page Seven
Left: Courtesy of
  Elvis Presley Enterprises

Right: Courtesy of the author

Page Eight
Top: Courtesy of
  Elvis Presley Enterprises

Right: Courtesy of the author

Bottom: Courtesy of the author

Second Photo Insert

Page One
Top: Courtesy of the author

Bottom: Courtesy of
  Elvis Presley Enterprises

Page Two
Courtesy of
  Elvis Presley Enterprises

Page Three
Courtesy of
  Elvis Presley Enterprises

Page Four
Courtesy of the author

Page Five
Courtesy of the author

Page Six
Courtesy of the author

Page Seven
Top: Courtesy of
  Elvis Presley Enterprises

Left: Courtesy of the author

Bottom: Courtesy of the author

Page Eight
Courtesy of the author